INFLUENCE AND RESISTANCE IN
NINETEENTH-CENTURY ENGLISH POETRY

Also by G. Kim Blank and published by St. Martin's

THE NEW SHELLEY
Later Twentieth-Century Views (*editor*)

WORDSWORTH'S INFLUENCE ON SHELLEY
A Study of Poetic Authority

Also by Margot K. Louis

SWINBURNE AND HIS GODS
The Roots and Growth of an Agnostic Poetry

Influence and Resistance in Nineteenth-Century English Poetry

Edited by

G. Kim Blank
Department of English
University of Victoria, Canada

and

Margot K. Louis
Department of English
University of Victoria, Canada

St. Martin's Press — New York

First published in the United States of America in 1993

Printed in Great Britain

ISBN 0–312–10211–9

Library of Congress Cataloging-in-Publication Data
Influence and resistance in nineteenth-century English poetry / edited
by G. Kim Blank and Margot K. Louis.
p.   cm.
Includes bibliographical references (p.   ) and index.
ISBN 0–312–10211–9
1. English poetry—19th century—History and criticism.
2. Influence (Literary, artistic, etc.)   3. Romanticism—Great
Britain.   I. Blank, G. Kim, 1952–   .   II. Louis, Margot Kathleen,
1954–   .
PR581.I54   1993
821'.809—dc20   93–25254
                                                                      CIP

Contents

Preface

This volume was conceived, quite innocently, during a conversation that took place in a corridor in a university building. Two colleagues whose offices more or less face each other are leaning in their doorways after a hard day of negotiating memos, talking with students, marking papers, and carrying on with the load of other non-trivial pursuits that constitute work in the academic profession. One teaches and works predominantly in Victorian poetry; the other, Romantic poetry. Says one: 'So how's Robert Browning? Still trying to cope with Shelley's vaporous trail of influence?' Says the other: 'No. Not really. Actually, at the moment I'm more concerned with Barrett Browning's ambivalent engagement with Byron.' Well, one thing led to another, and the rest, as they don't quite say, is literary history. It remains our somewhat immodest hope that this volume will promote the continued questioning of the historical, aesthetic, psychological and cultural transmission of poetry through informed acts of criticism.

We would like to thank the following for their assistance in various aspects of this project: Miranda Burgess, Sandra Graff, Claire McCutcheon, Robin Cryderman and Jane Sellwood. We are grateful to Teresa Carlson, Colleen Donnelly, Diana Rutherford and Ruth Widdicombe for typing out parts of this collection. Finally, we thank the contributors for their shared expertise and considerable patience.

G. Kim Blank and Margot Louis
University of Victoria

vii

Notes on the Contributors

Roland A. Duerksen, Professor in the Department of English at Miami University in Ohio, is the author of *Shelleyan Ideas in Victorian Literature* and *Shelley's Poetry of Involvement*. His periodical articles have dealt primarily with the Romantics (both British and American) and the Victorians.

Mary E. Finn is an Assistant Professor at the University of Alabama, Tuscaloosa. She is the author of *Writing the Incommensurable: Kierkegaard, Rossetti and Hopkins* in the Penn State Press *Literature and Philosophy* series.

Barbara Charlesworth Gelpi is a Professor in the English Department at Stanford and was the editor of *Signs: Journal of Women in Culture and Society* from 1980 to 1985. The author of *Dark Passages: The Decadent Consciousness in Victorian Literature*, she recently published *Shelley's Goddess: Maternity, Language, Subjectivity*. She is also working on a book-length study of Christina Rossetti's poetry and prose.

Keith Hanley is a Senior Lecturer in English and Director of the Wordsworth Centre at Lancaster University. He has published critical editions of Meredith and Landor, has co-edited collections of critical essays, *Politics and Rhetoric: Revolution and English Romanticism* and *Romantic Revisions*, and has published scholarly papers on Wordsworth, Ruskin and Romantic discourse.

Antony H. Harrison is Professor of English at North Carolina State University. Editor of *The Collected Letters of Christina Rossetti*, he has recently published *Victorian Poets and Romantic Poems: Intertextuality and Ideology*, *Christina Rossetti in Context*, and *Swinburne's Medievalism: A Study in Victorian Love Poetry*. He has co-edited *Gender and Discourse in Victorian Literature and Art* and is author of a new book entitled *Victorian Poetry and the Politics of Culture*.

Theresa M. Kelley has published numerous essays on Romanticism and eighteenth-century British aesthetics and philosophy. She is author of *Wordsworth's Revisionary Aesthetics* and is completing a book-length study of allegory in Romantic and post-Romantic culture and criticism. She is Associate Professor at the University of Texas, Austin.

U. C. Knoepflmacher is Paton Foundation Professor of Ancient and Modern Literature at Princeton University. The author of four books on nineteenth-century literature and co-editor of three others, he is completing a study extending his previous work on Wordsworth's relation to writers such as Coleridge, DeQuincey, Arnold, George Eliot, Emily Brontë, Pater, Lewis Carroll, and others.

Kerry McSweeney is Molson Professor of English at McGill University in Montreal. His publications include *Tennyson and Swinburne as Romantic Naturalists*, *'Middlemarch'* (Unwin Critical Library), *Moby-Dick: Ishmael's Mighty Book*, *George Eliot (Marian Evans): A Literary Life*, an edition of Carlyle's *Sartor Resartus*, and an edition of Elizabeth Barrett Browning's *Aurora Leigh*.

Joanna E. Rapf is an Associate Professor of English and Film at the University of Oklahoma. In addition to publishing on the Romantic poets, she is author of a bio-bibliography of Buster Keaton. Other projects include an edited volume on Woody Allen and a book on her grandfather, producer Harry Rapf.

John R. Reed is Distinguished Professor of English at Wayne State University in Detroit, Michigan. He has published widely on nineteenth- and twentieth-century English Literature. His books include *Victorian Conventions*, *The Natural History of H. G. Wells*, *Decadent Style*, and *Victorian Will*.

Anne Marie Ross has published essays on Arnold, Trollope, and Disraeli, and she is currently researching perspective and landscape in Emily Brontë's poetry. She teaches at California State University, Los Angeles.

W. David Shaw, author of *The Dialectical Temper*, *Tennyson's Style*, *The Lucid Veil* and *Victorians and Mystery*, is Professor of English at Victoria College, University of Toronto.

Herbert F. Tucker, Professor of English at the University of Virginia, is the author of *Browning's Beginnings: The Art of Disclosure* and *Tennyson and the Doom of Romanticism*. He is at work on a study of epic in the nineteenth century.

Introduction

VICTORIAN POETS AND ROMANTIC PRESENCES

In 1816, when *Alastor* appeared and Keats published his first poem, Elizabeth Barrett was 10 years old: already 'my poetry was entirely formed by the style of written authors,' she recalled a few years later, 'and I read that I might write' (Barrett 1974, p. 124). Within six years she had read Wordsworth, Shelley, Byron and Keats; 'her idea of a beautiful poem was Shelley's *Adonais*' (Forster 1988, p. 28), and she had had dreams of 'dressing up like a boy and running away to be Lord Byron's page' (E. B. Browning 1897, p. 115). Three years later, the 15-year-old Tennyson was scratching 'Byron is dead' on a rock; and as late as 1836 the schoolboy Matthew Arnold could win an elocution prize by declaiming Byron's verses. Through the 1820s and early 1830s, the first generation of Victorian poets grew up into a world imaginatively dominated by the Romantic poets, among whom Byron appeared to be the most vividly representative, the most dramatically popular.

The second edition of Coleridge's *Poetical Works* was released in the same year as Alfred Tennyson's *Timbuctoo* won the Chancellor's Medal for English verse at Cambridge (1829); *The Sonnets of William Wordsworth* appeared simultaneously with E. B. B.'s *The Seraphim and Other Poems* (1838). Between these years, according to Matthew Arnold, Wordsworth's poetry had become 'established in possession of the minds of all who profess to care for poetry' (Arnold 1960–77, IX, p. 36); when Wordsworth accepted the Laureateship in 1843, some who had 'learned his great language, caught his clear accents, / Made him [their] pattern,' lamented their disillusionment (R. Browning 1981, I, p. 410). In the year that Wordsworth became Poet Laureate and Coleridge's *The Ancient Mariner and Other Poems* appeared among the Pocket English Classics (1843), Robert Browning published the fourth and fifth volumes of *Bells and Pomegranates*, and the second edition of Tennyson's *Poems* was announced; the careers of the great High Victorians were already well underway when the works of the great first-generation Romantics achieved – at last – a magisterial popularity.

Fifteen years later, the second generation of Victorian poets was beginning to publish – at a time when interest in Shelley and his circle was booming: William Morris's *Defence of Guenevere and Other*

1

Poems, and Algernon Charles Swinburne's first published verses in *Undergraduate Papers*, coincided appropriately with Hogg's *Life of Percy Bysshe Shelley*, Trelawny's *Recollections of the Last Days of Shelley*, and Peacock's *Memoirs of Shelley* (1858). Through the 1860s and early 1870s, the Pre-Raphaelite circle struggled to bring the long-neglected William Blake into the public eye; Dante Gabriel Rossetti completed Alexander Gilchrist's *Life* of Blake in 1863, Swinburne published his groundbreaking commentary on Blake's poetry late in 1867, and William Michael Rossetti in 1874 produced the Aldine Edition of Blake's poems. Meanwhile, the other Romantics were not neglected; in 1870 D. G. Rossetti's long-awaited *Poems* coincided not only with another volume of *Poems* by his brother, but also with W. M. Rossetti's editions of Shelley and Wordsworth; in the same year a new edition of Coleridge's poems was published, and so was Swinburne's *Ode on the Proclamation of the French Republic*, written in the very accent of radical Romantic prophecy. By the 1880s, the political and moral tensions between leading Victorian poets could express themselves in an argument as to which were the greatest poets of the early nineteenth century: Wordsworth and Byron, Arnold claimed (1881); Shelley and Coleridge, retorted Swinburne (1884). Disturbed by Dowden's 1886 *Life of Percy Bysshe Shelley*, which told him far more about Shelley than he could bear to know, Arnold reaffirmed his denigration of that particular high-flying Romantic in 1888; but beneath this debate lay fundamental disagreements (*within* the late Victorian literary community) about moral behaviour, the appropriate style of agnostic rhetoric, and the possibility of political commitment. From the early eighties up to 1914, it was common to view Swinburne, Morris and the Rossettis as 'the Pre-Raphaelite heirs of Keats, Coleridge, and Shelley' (Sambrook 1974, p. 15); in attacking Shelley, Arnold differentiated his own moderate, cosmopolitan liberal agnosticism from the sensually 'French', sometimes anti-clerical and revolutionary fervour of a more radical school. When the debate became more explicitly personal, the Romantics were invoked by way of vituperation: Arnold described Swinburne as a 'pseudo-Shelley', and Swinburne in turn called Arnold a 'pseudo-Wordsworth' (Arnold 1896, I, p. 227; Swinburne 1925, XIV, p. 85). Insults like these implicitly acknowledge the power and huge stature of the Romantics, while underlining the way in which their fame was exploited near the close of the century.[1]

As this discussion has briefly suggested, nineteenth-century poetry shows significant continuity, and – in terms of the production of Romantic and Victorian texts – significant overlapping. The 'Chronology of Nineteenth-Century English Poetry' included in this volume (pp. 269–82) fully confirms the point, and makes it clear that, while the Victorians were writing, Romantic poetry was being circulated widely, and was the subject of impassioned critical debate. Indeed, it could be argued that this very debate marks the beginning of modern literary criticism. For many, Romantic poetry became the rule against which Victorian poetry was to be measured. Leon Gottfried's vivid metaphor still applies:

> [T]he Romantic movement tended to divorce the Victorian writer from the past in a special way. It stood like the Chinese Wall separating the nineteenth century from the dominant literary tradition of the eighteenth century represented by such key figures as Dryden, Pope, and Johnson, and from the antecedent tradition of wit going back to Donne....Indeed, it is scarcely exaggerating to say that the general effect of Romanticism on the Victorian landscape of the literary past was virtually to destroy the fruitful availability of two centuries of work. (Gottfried 1963, p. 3)

Or, to change the metaphor, first-generation Victorians found them-selves like second-generation immigrants born in a new land with no grandparents available – only Romantic parents, whose very present version of the past could not well be checked or corrected. So Elizabeth Barrett, who knew of several women of letters before her own century, could not discern a poet among them earlier than Joanna Baillie; only a Romantic could strike her as a 'poetess in the true sense' (E. B. Browning 1897, pp. 229–30), and consequently she lamented, 'I look everywhere for grandmothers and see none' (qu. Leighton 1986, p. 11). However, all this neither confirms nor disaf-firms the proposition that the quality, style, or ideas of Romantic parents and Victorian offspring are continuous and consistent; more subtle investigation of a critical kind is needed here, and hence this volume.

While it is clear that Romantic poetry was being read widely, we have to determine how it was being read by those who were working in the same business. In the correspondence and the diaries of the Victorian poets we have a kind of context – personal, casual, honest – that reveals how these poets referred to their precursor-contemporaries; and in contemporary reviews we can sense how all of the leading nineteenth-century poets were placed and related by their readers. We might begin with Tennyson on Wordsworth, as these two delineate a significant historical boundary: the passing of the Laureateship, exactly halfway through the century. In 1841, Tennyson finds himself in 'the classic neighbourhood of Bolton Abbey',

> led by some half-remembrance of a note to one of Wordsworth's poems [*The White Doe of Rylstone*], which told me (to speak the truth) more than the poem itself: Wordsworth having stated [...] that everything which the eyes of man could desire in a landscape was to be found at the Abbey aforesaid. I coming with an imagination inflamed, and working upon this passage, was at first disappointed, but yesterday I took a walk of some seven or eight or, by our Lady, nine miles, [...] and you may conjecture that no ordinary charms of nature could get nine miles walk out of legs (*at present*) more familiar with armchair and settle than rock and greensward, so that I suppose there is something in what Wordsworth asserts, and that something will probably keep me here some time.... (Tennyson 1990, I, p. 193)

Tennyson's memory has very slightly betrayed him, since in fact it is not Wordsworth himself who so belauds the Bolton landscape; the passage which Tennyson echoes appears within Wordsworth's long quotation from another author.[2] Still, it is striking that Tennyson is willing to be led by, to test, and finally to confirm what he takes to be Wordsworth's judgement. Like thousands of his contemporaries (not to mention many generations of later tourists), Tennyson makes a point of enjoying 'the charms of nature' in Wordsworth's manner. The sense of Wordsworth as a magisterial presence is underlined ten years later, when Tennyson is contemplating the uselessness of an elaborate epitaph for Wordsworth: 'Is Wordsworth a great poet? Well then don't let us talk of him as if he were half known:

> To the Memory
> of
> William Wordsworth
> The Great Poet.'
>
> (Tennyson 1990, II, p. 10)

And in 1882, in explaining and giving examples of how he would take a rough verbal description of a scene and then transform it into poetry, he says about one example that it is 'quite as *true* as Wordsworth's simile and more in detail' (Tennyson 1990, III, p. 239). Wordsworth is both the model and the competition. Meanwhile, contemporary reviews inevitably compared Tennyson not only with Wordsworth, but with Byron, Keats, Shelley and Browning – and one reviewer even went so far as to claim that Tennyson had plagiarised Shelley (Jump 1967, p. 302).

The Brownings too are placed among the Romantics, both by themselves and by their contemporaries. In reviewing Robert Browning's *Paracelsus* in 1836, a critic suggests that 'Without the slightest hesitation we name Mr. Robert Browning at once with Shelley, Coleridge, Wordsworth...'. On the other hand, E. B. B.'s *The Seraphim* is reviewed as being modelled on 'the very worst portion of Keats and Tennyson', while some of her other poetry is 'marked with Byronic energy' (Kelley and Hudson 1984, III, p. 172; IV, pp. 408, 394). We also know from first-hand accounts that when Robert Browning wanted some 'real poetry', he would 'take out some Shelley or Keats, Coleridge or Tennyson' – though Byron was 'the singer of his first enthusiasm' (Meredith 1985, pp. 148, 142). Browning's passionate engagement with the work of Shelley, in particular, is so well known as to need no discussion here. Meanwhile the adult E. B. B. had lost none of her ardent veneration for the Romantics, although her worship now was more critical, discriminating and specific; each of the great Romantics calls forth a vivid response in her letters. In 1837, she is not ashamed of her 'creed' of 'susceptibility' to nature because it was Wordsworth's 'creed' as well, and she records being told that she has 'left the classicalists, & joined the Romanticists – but I always maintain that the true classicalists *are* the romanticists' (Kelley 1984, III, pp. 277–8). In a thoughtful discussion of mystical poetry in 1841, she expresses some ambivalence toward Shelley, 'who froze in cold glory between Heaven & earth, neither dealing with man's heart, beneath, nor aspiring to communion with supernal Humanity', thus producing a chill and glittering poetry which shows only 'by momentary stirrings' the 'power of sweet human love & deep pathos' which she believes existed in Shelley the man (E. B. Browning 1983, I, p. 229). Of Keats she remarked that 'Jove is recognized by his thunder'; in Blake, she found 'wild glances of the poetical faculty thro' the chasms of the singer's shattered intellect' – which is perhaps as far as appreciation could go in 1842 (E. B. Browning 1983, I, pp. 297,

391). She speaks scornfully in the same year of 'the present fashion of decrying Byron as a poet', and describes him as 'a great and wonderful poet – passionate – eloquent – witty – with all powers of swift allusion and sarcasm and satire – full and rapid in the mechanical resources of his art, and capable of a sufficient and brilliant conveyance of philosophic thought and argument'. Yet she adds that Wordsworth is 'the profounder thinker,...more full and consistent in his own poetic individuality, – and more influential for good upon the literature of his country and age' – while Coleridge is 'more intensely poetical (in the appreciation of mind) than either' (Barrett 1955, pp. 254–55). This mood of discriminating veneration was to reappear in the Pre-Raphaelite circle (who were also admirers of E. B. B.).

Barrett had personal contact only with Wordsworth among the leading poets of the early nineteenth century, and she lamented that 'Byron, Coleridge...how many more?...were contemporaries of mine without my having approached them near enough to look reverently in their faces, or to kiss the hem of their garment' (E. B. Browning 1983, II, p. 300). But Barrett's reverential acquaintance with Wordsworth can hardly be compared to Matthew Arnold's long family intimacy with the Laureate: Arnold's 'boyhood had been spent in the Lake Country and under Wordsworth's affectionate eye' (Trilling 1949, p. 18), and this early exposure was to be momentous, both for Arnold's career as poet and critic and for Wordsworth's later reputation. Arnold's selection of Wordsworth's poetry (1879) attained not only popularity but also authority as a school text; yet Arnold followed literary fashion as much as he led it. In 1848, when Byron was out of favour, Arnold wrote in his letters of 'that furiously flaring bethiefed rushlight, the vulgar Byron' (Arnold 1932, p. 92); when Byron's reputation revived again in the 1860s and 1870s, Arnold climaxed the revival by repeatedly quoting Swinburne on Byron's 'splendid and imperishable excellence [...] of sincerity and strength', in his famous introduction to his selection of Byron's verse (1881; Arnold 1960–77, IX, pp. 232, 234, 236). But since this volume includes an essay which deals fully with Arnold's way of reading the Romantics (especially Shelley), it would be superfluous to discuss his reactions at length here.

And the same applies to Christina Rossetti. It is necessary to make only one point about her in this place: if, as Antony H. Harrison suggests below, Rossetti strongly resists and criticises the secular vision of the Romantics, she is also resisting and criticising a very powerful impulse in her brothers' work (as is not unlikely). For both of her male siblings were ardent romanticists. The Rossettis had, of course, a family connection with Byron's doctor, John Polidori; but they did not confine their interest to Byron. In 1844, Dante Gabriel Rossetti 'bought a small pirated Shelley, and surged through its pages like a flame' (W. Rossetti 1895, I, p. 100); when Milnes's *Life, Letters, and Literary Remains of John Keats* came out in 1848, Gabriel read it that summer, pronounced it 'exceedingly interesting', and was delighted to find in Keats a comment which valued Raphael's predecessors above Raphael himself (D. G. Rossetti 1965–67, I, p. 40). Within a month the Pre-Raphaelite Brotherhood was formed. Later Hall Caine was to write of Dante Gabriel: '"The three greatest English imaginations," he would sometimes add, "are Shakespear [sic], Coleridge, and Shelley." I have heard him give a fourth name, Blake. He thought Wordsworth was too much the high-priest of Nature to be her lover' (qu. W. Rossetti 1895, I, p. 415).

Gabriel Rossetti spent his last years re-reading the Romantics in order to help Mrs Gilchrist with her revision of Blake's life, and H. Buxton Forman with his edition of Keats's letters. But his activities in this direction pale beside his brother's. William Michael Rossetti edited a cheap edition of Keats's poems; he put together an annotated list of Blake's paintings and drawings; he produced the *Poetical Works of Blake, with a Memoir* (1863, 1880, 1874). He also edited Wordsworth (1870). But his passion was for Shelley; as one of his most recent editors has said, William Rossetti was 'the best informed Shelleyite of his day' (Peattie 1990, p. xviii). He was one of the founding members of the Shelley Society; moreover, he owned a sofa which once belonged to Shelley that his children 'rather knocked about' (Peattie, p. 546), and he also had a fragment of Shelley's charred skull. In 1867, when invited to put together an edition of Shelley's poetry along with a 'biographic note', he celebrated the fact in his diary: 'Of all the literary work,' he wrote, 'this is the very one I would have chosen for myself' (W. Rossetti 1970, p. 307). It was this very edition which, appearing in 1869, 'stimulated Swinburne to a fresh examination of radical Romanticism' (Louis 1990, p. 191).

Swinburne had always read the Romantics with deep attention – his early poetry was evidently modelled on texts by Keats especially (Swinburne 1927, passim) – but up to the late 1860s he had distrusted the ideological and 'doctrinaire' philanthropy which he

perceived in Shelley and other highly politicised Romantic vision-
aries (Swinburne 1959–62, I, p. 115). After his long review of
Rossetti's edition of Shelley (*Notes on the Text of Shelley*, 1869), all
Swinburne's public and private writings testify to his enormous
knowledge of, and enthusiastic reverence for, the radical
Romantics. He can hardly refer to a vaccination without quoting
Blake, or to flat-hunting without an allusion to Shelley:

> I must find a temporary shelter for my roofless head (which is
> now, as Shelley says, 'like Cain's or Christ's,' so far as lodging
> goes).... (Swinburne 1959–62, II, p. 147)

> I have just been vaccinated and it is taking sufficiently to confirm
> me in my views...concerning the true character and tempera-
> ment of One whose Name shall never pollute this page, but
> whose 'joys are tears, his labour vain to form Man to his image.'
> I will merely say that pox in all its branches of cow, chicken, and
> man is an Emanation worthy of the 'mistaken demon of heaven,'
> at whose vegetating and spectrous birth the Eternal Female
> groaned. (Swinburne 1959–62, II, p. 148)

This staggering and casually-worn erudition (Swinburne has
managed to quote from *Visions of the Daughters of Albion, Jerusalem,*
and *The Marriage of Heaven and Hell* in one fell swoop) is entirely
typical. His letters show continual reverence for Blake, and for 'the
Divine' Shelley; yet they also show that he was careful not to tread
'too much on ground preoccupied by Shelley' – a phrase which suggests respect for Shelley's achievement, and a sense of the shared
labour of radicals through the century (Swinburne 1959–62, II,
pp. 12, 120). But Swinburne did not read the radical Romantics
exclusively. His allusions to Wordsworth were confident if irrever-
ent; in an unpublishable French play, Swinburne made Queen
Victoria describe how Wordsworth seduced her by reading *The
Excursion* aloud – 'et je suis tombée' (Henderson 1974, p. 49). In
1886, when Swinburne sent his list of the 'hundred best authors' to
the *Pall Mall Gazette* upon request, it included all of the 'major'
Romantics, and more: Shelley, Landor, Lamb, Coleridge, Scott,
Blake, Wordsworth, Keats, Burns, Byron, Hunt, Campbell and
Crabbe all appeared, in that order (Swinburne 1959–62, V, pp. 133–5).
   Hardy, who, by the turn of the century, was beginning to see
some space between his times and the age of Wordsworth,

Coleridge, Landor, Scott, Keats, Shelley and Byron,[3] and also to get some perspective on it, nonetheless thought that Byron was 'the greatest natural force, the greatest elementary power, I cannot but think, which has appeared in our literature since Shakespeare' – yet Byron, Hardy also thought, lacked the definitive modern spirit (Björk 1985, I, pp. 106–7). But then again he believed that Coleridge 'rose above the genius of any other poet on record' in terms of 'creative imagination and coequal expression of the thing conceived' – and next to Coleridge, Shelley. By 1907, he saw the renewal in English literature in the nineteenth century as three consecutive waves, each gathering strength: 'Byron, Scott, Shelley, Keats, Coleridge, and Wordsworth, followed by Tennyson, Browning, Newman, Dickens, Carlyle, and they in turn by Rossetti, William Morris, Swinburne, Ruskin, Hardy, and Meredith' (Björk II, pp. 188, 349). In other words, Hardy feels himself to be part of a swelling tide which has been flooding in since 1792.

These random examples represent just a few of the hundreds of more informal references which the Victorian poets made to their poetic precursors. Overall, the more complete record indicates, first, that the major Victorian poets were extraordinarily familiar with the Romantics and their work; secondly, that, for the most part, they shared a very high regard for the poetry of the Romantics, and were deeply concerned with the kind of lives which the Romantic poets led; and thirdly, that there was a desire to continue to write, if not always with the same sensibility as the Romantics, then at least with the same artistry and authority. The first two of these propositions are evident in the record. But the last item, the kind of gesture that appears in the poetry, raises more subtle and more complex issues.

INTERTEXTUALITIES: QUESTIONS AND PROSPECTS

To what extent (if at all) is the distinction between 'Romantic' and 'Victorian' valuable or just? Is the Romantic / Victorian demarcation merely a convenience for the sake of the curriculum? How is the quarrel among different strains of Romanticism continued and developed in the Victorian period? How is the present 'canon' of Victorian literature conditioned by twentieth-century reactions to certain Romantics? Do theories of intertextuality undermine the historical considerations which have hitherto rationalised traditional differences between the Romantic and Victorian periods? Alternatively, how do these historical considerations structure our perception of intertextuality in this context? How do Victorian texts interact with, echo, or resist Romantic texts? Finally, in what ways did the Romantic poets establish the terms within which, or against which, Victorian poets were debating?

These are the questions we were asking as we set out to put this book together. In the nature of things, not all of them could be so briskly answered; in the nature of things academic, several of these queries have received three or more very persuasive answers, all mutually contradictory. However, there seems to be a feeling among most (not all) of our contributors that the distinction between 'Romantic' and 'Victorian' is valuable – though perhaps not always just; opinion on this point ranges from strong reaffirmation of this distinction, in, for instance, the essays of Antony Harrison and Ann Marie Ross, to the complex celebrations of nineteenth-century continuity in the essays of Barbara Gelpi or Kerry McSweeney. If theological perspectives, views on historical contingency, perceptions of landscape, dominant images, faith in performative language and even the degree of politico-poetical energy all seem to shift from one period to the next, our contributors have also found that nineteenth-century poetic practice is held together by a common debt to the tradition of sentimentality (in the technical sense), by a common fascination with allegorical figuration and aurality, by debates (on poetics, for example) continued throughout the century – in short, by a shared framework, philosophical, passional and linguistic. Certainly this volume demonstrates how well the Romantics wrought, and with what ferocious diligence the Victorians engaged with, denied, affirmed, reworked the Romantic vision.

The Shelley revival, not surprisingly, has marked this book. Indeed Wordsworth sometimes seems here to be the Romantic villain or 'bad father' of the piece, Shelley the 'good father' or enabling archetypal guide of the earnest Victorian quester. (For Shelley, of course, Wordsworth was both a good *and* a bad father.) This startling reversal of Matthew Arnold's evaluations may have much to do with current critical fashion, but certainly reveals that the quarrel among different strains of Romanticism does perpetuate itself, formidably, through the Victorian period; Arnold may not be the reliable guide to his own period – or the dominant shaper of thought within it – for which he is sometimes taken.

If this trend of thought in Victorian studies continues, it is reasonable to suppose that the more Shelleyan Victorians (Swinburne and D. G. Rossetti, for instance) will benefit in future, although this volume does not explicitly disturb the present canon of Victorian literature. Meanwhile, the rise of the new historicism may create a more complex sense of the differences between one period and another, as, for instance, when Keith Hanley shows how popular simplifications of Wordsworth in Ruskin's day provoke Ruskin's own increasingly sophisticated critique of Wordsworth's inadequacy. (Shelley and the Victorians have in common an ambivalence about Wordsworth's self-consciously triumphal presence.)

But the questions to which all of the contributors in this book chiefly address themselves are the last two: How do Victorian texts interact with, echo, or resist Romantic texts? And in what ways did the Romantic poets establish the terms within which, or against which, Victorian poets were debating? Here we turn the debate over to our contributors.

John Reed traces the flow of water-imagery throughout the nineteenth century, but finds that generally such poets as Wordsworth, Shelley, Coleridge and Byron have some 'sense of identification with and participation in' the power represented by the watercourse – whereas for Victorian authors like Carlyle, Tennyson, Arnold and even Swinburne, 'the visionary current no longer drives through and buoys the spirit, but now engulfs it' (p. 27). 'Everywhere among the Victorians a great sense of potential and energy is matched by a feeling of entrapment and weariness....The Romantics concentrated upon the sources of power and its transmission – on mountain heights and strong coursing waters. The Victorians looked instead chiefly to the ends of power – the lower slopes, the slowing stream that winds to the sea' (p. 37).

Like Reed, Shaw and Duerksen, Ann Marie Ross finds the Romantic and Victorian periods distinguished by a basic difference in mood and temperament – by a slide, from confident if questioning energy, to weary doubt. In her view, the shift from a metaphysical to an epistemological emphasis creates a self-conscious and sceptical subjectivism which radically differentiates the Victorian 'landscape emblem' from its Romantic model, and produces a widespread generic mutation as well. The polyvocal medleys of Clough, Arnold and Tennyson investigate the process of knowing and feeling, and thereby evoke a 'land of shadows' apprehended unsteadily. (Ross also finds a parallel blurring of outline or ambivalence of impulse in poems by Emily Brontë and Hardy.) The special value which Victorian poets place on 'the partial, the fragmentary, the contingent' (p. 253) is emphasised if we contrast passages in Wordsworth or Shelley in which ruins or shadows adumbrate a sacred whole. Yet, more than Reed and especially Duerksen, Ross is inclined to celebrate the effects of the Victorians' wearier and more sceptical mood – 'the subtlety of visual effect and the richness of polyvocal texture which result from the suffusion of landscape with ... [a] melancholy scepticism' (p. 268).

W. David Shaw also perceives the two periods as distinguished – and in different ways enriched – by energetic confidence on one side, and scepticism on the other. His close reading of Shelley's *Adonais* and Arnold's *Thyrsis* stresses 'the deep discontinuity between Romantic faith in words of power and Victorian distrust of performative language' (p. 39); the wording, pacing, metre and aural complexities of the poetry all testify to the profound difference of attitude between the Romantic voyager who boldly transgresses boundaries and the uncertain Victorian rambler who appreciates horizons. Similarly, Joanna E. Rapf finds in Tennyson's scepticism a significant divagation, if not from Coleridge, at least from Wordsworth, whose best work is about 'the evolution towards faith, towards finding stability for the "wavering" mind...in...the world outside himself' (p. 73). Yet, for Rapf, Tennyson's doubt is consistent with the 'condition of doubt' established (according to L. J. Swingle and Susan Wolfson) by the interrogative mode of Romantic discourse; one may be tempted to conclude that Wordsworth could be seen as the first Victorian, and Tennyson as a later but truer Romantic (pp. 60,74). In any case, Tennyson's work is connected to the Romantic tradition by its aurality, its extreme valorisation of the ear over the eye as the enabler of poetic 'vision'.

If several critics perceive scepticism as the quality which, more than any other, defines Victorian poetry as essentially different from Romantic poetry, Antony H. Harrison's study of Christina Rossetti and the Romantics reveals the opposite dynamic: Rossetti reinscribes Blake and Coleridge within her own religious vision, while severely criticising 'the secular ideologies propagated in the poetry of Wordsworth and Keats' (p. 132). Harrison focuses on 'revisionist reworkings' of specific Romantic lyrics (p. 148), such as Blake's *The Lamb*, Wordsworth's *Intimations Ode*, Coleridge's *Ancient Mariner* and *Dejection*, and Keats's *To Autumn*; for instance, the tragic alienation with which Wordsworth and Coleridge struggle in their great odes, in Rossetti becomes the valuable pre-liminary to a true *contemptus mundi*. Yet Barbara Charlesworth Gelpi exposes a profound debt to Shelley, of all people, in *Goblin Market*, and deftly shows how the much-debated eroticism of the 'sucking scenes' in that poem can be viewed as 'sentimental' in the technical sense of the word. Like Shelley, Rossetti uses sucking as 'a metaphor for breast-feeding which in turn is the paradigm for, first, the fusion of mind, heart, and body as "soul", and then the exchange or interchange of that totality' (p. 161). This essay challenges us to reexamine the entire corpus of English nineteenth-century poetry with reference to the tradition of sentimentalism – arguably the basis of both Romantic and Victorian literature.

Theresa M. Kelley finds a continuity between Romantic uses of allegory and Robert Browning's grotesque fantasies of allegorical figuration. If Wordsworth, Keats, Shelley and (as a critic) Coleridge are all fascinated by allegorical figures whose shifting, all but protean shapes move to transgress the boundaries of realism, Browning 'works to offend readers' sense of realism by offering exaggerations that imply a typological or mythological order of meaning. By such means, he makes the material edge of nineteenth-century realism a *figure* whose implied ground is elsewhere, abstract and general more than concrete and individual' (p. 171). And yet, the 'realist details' within the poems of the 1860s and 1870s press 'material vehicles so close to figural tenors that they risk being absorbed or debased by the material grotesque' (p. 172), so that the Shelleyan impulse toward the heavenly abstract is reversed; the deconstructive impulse remains, but now draws us back toward the tactile, particular world.

Mary E. Finn comes to a similar conclusion about Browning and Shelley, from a very different ground. In her study of Shelley's *The Cenci* and Browning's *Cenciaja* and *The Ring and the Book*, she shows how the historical facts supplied by Shelley's source are distorted, in *The Cenci*, to highlight the poet's vision of Beatrice as the 'heroic individual' who can distinguish criminality (in the legal sense) from wrong (p. 198). But where Shelley strips history of its complexities to show the essential pattern of tyranny and martyrdom which he sees beneath the veil of detail, Browning restores these complexities, with carefully-researched particularity, to undermine the legitimacy of petty tyrannies. So *Cenciaja* accurately restores the contingencies omitted in *The Cenci*, and The *Ring and the Book* undercuts Guido's defence *honoris causa* by showing that 'Franceschinihood' is not so essential to Roman society as Guido likes to think. Historical contingency, which is Shelley's enemy, is Browning's friend; it is the instrument of that providence by which God permits an unjust system to collapse like a house of cards.

From a new-historicist perspective, Keith Hanley examines Ruskin's historicism as a radical shift from Wordsworthian Romantic naturalism, and one which allows Ruskin to explode Wordsworth's bland assumption that his own discourse constitutes the normative national discourse. In Arnold's anti-Romantic reading of the Romantics, on the other hand, Roland A. Duerksen perceives a lapse of nerve. Arnold's inadequacy to the challenge which the Romantics represent is hinted in his trivialising response to Wordsworth (poetry becomes a handy mild tranquilliser) and vividly demonstrated in his repudiation of Shelley. 'With the excuse of always first needing to "know enough," Arnold lets slip the Shelleyan urgency to "apply the modern spirit"', and this failure of political will shows 'how strongly influence can manifest itself as resistance and how subtly resistance can take the form of the faint praise that damns' (p. 245).

Are models of resistance and influence sufficient in dealing with the vast range of nineteenth-century intertextuality? For Herbert F. Tucker, Swinburne's *Tristram of Lyonesse* shows how one Victorian poet can dispel 'Victorian anxieties of influence by ... assimilating the Romantic rhetoric of lyrical autonomy' (p. 86). 'Swinburne proves a curiously noncombative author' in that he responds and alludes more to texts than to poets. The materials provided by Dante, Milton, Shelley and Wordsworth are impersonally accepted and deployed, without much wallowing in the agonies of rivalry (Oedipal or otherwise); in this respect Swinburne sets himself apart from both the Romantic and the Victorian traditions, with their anxious originalities. Paradoxically, here Swinburne's own originality is striking: instead of 'troping difference *as* independence' (p. 85, italics Tucker's), Swinburne's allusions assimilate the past and at the same time neutralise its ethical and theological imperatives. (It would be interesting to know if Swinburne's detached manipulation of allusions assimilates the practice of that great classicist of the Romantic and early Victorian eras, Walter Savage Landor, whom Swinburne so deeply admired.)

Kerry McSweeney, like Tucker, focuses on the reactions of a late Victorian to his Romantic and Victorian predecessors; more explicitly than Tucker, McSweeney suggests that the Bloomian model of influence is inadequate. Hardy, at least, is deeply engaged with several predecessors, rather than with one Laius (or Shelley); and that engagement frequently involves 'assimilation and adaptation as well as resistance' (p. 110). For McSweeney, however, assimilation at a deep level is the fruit of tension and 'resistance overcome' (p. 92); Hardy's easy affinity with Shelley and Swinburne produced less vigorous poetic issue than did his difficult rapprochements with Wordsworth, Tennyson and Browning.

U. C. Knoepflmacher also provides – not one, but two – unusual perspectives on intertextual relations. His reading of Hardy's lyric, *Shelley's Skylark*, resists McSweeney's and places the poem in a long ornithological debate about poetics, from Wordsworth and Shelley's skylarks through Keats's nightingales; Hardy's dead skylark testifies to Hardy's own 'inability to follow a precedent he genuinely admires' (p. 121). This is the melancholy failure of influence. On the other hand, in *The Darkling Thrush* Hardy reanimates a hope of 'cyclical continuity' with the hopes of Romantics at the beginning of the century; and in his later poems commemorating Keats, the Victorian poet finds in the Romantic 'another self' (pp. 125,129).

At the end of the day we are left with texts and the problem of what to do with them. This is doubly difficult in that texts do not always do what they intend to do. In the later poetry of the century, are we reading homage, repetition, pastiche, reaction, integrations, ambivalence, competition, the kinds of revisionary ratios promoted by Harold Bloom in his theory of influence? Are these kinds of integrations necessitated by and understandable in terms of historical, psychological, social, aesthetic and stylistic considerations? Are we talking about intricate attitudinal changes or just textual differences? And more importantly, for this volume at least, do these changes validate the Romantic / Victorian demarcation which apparently defines the content of university courses, the subject boundaries for a number of academic journals, and the general characterisation of nineteenth-century culture – including, of course, poetry?

'Romantic' is certainly one of the two murkiest terms in twentieth-century criticism (the other is 'deconstruction', itself a rather Romantic concept). But one thing we do know is that, at least at this moment in literary history, the terms 'Romantic' and 'Victorian' will not go away. Like many of our contributors, we have found the terms irresistible. We can at least say that to examine Victorian poets in relation to their immediate predecessors is a strategy endlessly fruitful, and that fact in itself suggests how thoroughly, and at how deep a level, the Victorians were engaging with the Romantics, in love or battle – or both. (Contrast the relatively simplistic strategies of wholesale repudiation with which some modernists located themselves in opposition to the Victorians, or Renaissance writers in opposition to the Middle Ages; the nearest parallel to the Victorian–Romantic relation, indeed, may be the relationship between modern and contemporary literature in our own century.) At what point does a discontinuity become a continuity? How can the differences between the 'Romantic' and 'Victorian' periods be articulated without appeal to a common frame of reference? For instance, if some Romantics are confident as to the power of performative language, and some Victorians dubious, is it not still true that both parties are deeply concerned with the power of such language; that it is, throughout the century, a living issue? Again, is it not true that the conditions of academic discourse favour the production of differences, of distinctions? How often nowadays is the phenomenon of simple echoing seriously examined *per se*?

We institutionalise the demarcations between 'Romantic' and 'Victorian' whenever we step into a classroom for a course using either term. Yet anyone who has tried to teach Victorian literature to students who have not enjoyed (or endured) the former must have experienced a sense of exasperated frustration, when some students could not appreciate the originality – or even the central purpose – of an author whose sense of reader-expectation was formed by immersion in Romantic literature. (The struggle is as maddening as teaching the second generation of Romantics to students who have not studied the first generation.) Still, it is clear from the bulk of the essays in this book that the high Victorians at least do resist Romanticism in a self-conscious and significant way; it is predominantly the group of critics concerned with late Victorian writers – Swinburne, Hardy, Rossetti – who have tended to upset the applecart of the traditional periodisation. Did the late Victorians, in their own resistance to their immediate High Victorian precursors, tend to look back to their grandparents for support, example or inspiration?

And, finally, if the interrogative mode is the crucial feature of Romantic discourse, is not this Introduction in itself a testimony to the continued power of that vision, that discourse, that way of being which we call Romanticism?

The order in which these essays have been discussed is not the order in which they appear. We have thought it best to frame the case-studies here within two essays of wider scope – both, significantly, focusing on visions of landscape within the century, and thus drawing attention, not only to the major variations in this respect from one period to another, but also to the continuous presence of natural objects as topic or figure within nineteenth-century English poetry. In a somewhat Victorian spirit of particularism, we have then foregrounded some very particular case studies which lead us gradually into the variety of intertextualities outlined above. The second half of the volume is primarily concerned with forms of historicism and historical contextualisation.

Notes

1. With regard to the shifting popularity of the major Romantics, it is of some interest to compare the number of references to each in the letters of Tennyson and Swinburne respectively. Omitting allusions which appear only in the editorial notes, we find in the three volumes of Tennyson's correspondence, as edited by Lang and Shannon, 18 references to Wordsworth; 5 to Keats; 4 each to Coleridge, Byron and Shelley; and none to Blake. In the six volumes of Swinburne's correspondence as edited by Lang we find 225 allusions to Shelley; 115 to Blake; 114 to Byron; 53 to Wordsworth; and 46 each to Coleridge and Keats.
2. 'Whatever the most fastidious taste could require to constitute a perfect landscape, is not only found here, but in its proper place' (quoted from Whitaker's *History and Antiquities of the Deanery of Craven*). Wordsworth follows up at the end of his notes by simply recommending the area to 'all lovers of beautiful scenery' (Wordsworth 1936, pp. 718–21).
3. See Hardy in the *TLS*, 19 May 1905, pp. 157–8.

1

Romantic to Victorian Iconography of Nature

JOHN R. REED*

The most notable feature of the Romantic affection for nature is less the humble admiration of earthly marvels than its ability to discover in nature intimations of spiritual realities that transcend picturesque or sublime dispositions of rocks, and grass and trees. By denaturalising nature, the Romantic poets managed to revivify it. By making *décor* nature less significant, diminishing its picturesque and ornamental role, and by emphasising a signature nature that stressed its inherent recuperative powers, they lent greater imaginative force and emotional meaning to both. In doing so, they also established a pattern of response that continues to the present day, though I shall argue that Victorian poets (and, for that matter, modern poets) substantially altered the nature of that pattern. Michel Serres has argued that each era is isomorphic, and Michel Foucault has interpreted changing patterns of thought in terms of the *episteme* (see Descombes 1982, pp. 90ff and Foucault 1973). What these scholars suggest in an elaborate and intense form is that a given cultural locus exhibits a tendency to employ similar patterns of thought and even similar modes of expression. I believe that certain basic patterns of references and images are surprisingly consistent in Romantic poetry, that they persist in an altered form to the present day, and that these references and images condense a fundamental but evolving outlook on nature.

With the boldness of a poet, W. H. Auden offered in *The Enchafèd Flood* a few prominent symbols that he argued typified the Romantic enterprise. Auden's assemblage of symbols is, as E. M. Forster observed, 'chancy in its effects', for it offers a generalised landscape in which sea and desert represent fruitful and barren versions of wilderness through which the Romantic spirit journeys toward the

* I wish to express my appreciation to my colleague Michael Scrivener for his generous assistance.

Happy Island or the Oasis (Forster 1972, p. 261). Auden sees the Romantic progress as a traceable quest with appropriate adventures in appropriate settings. Desire must traverse chaos and waste to reach the frontier of its gratification. Although Auden does not argue this point, as often as not the chaos or waste to be mastered begins as a potentially threatening and encircling power which the poet conquers largely by a process of assimilation. An early version of the diagram preceding this localisation into landscape might be Blake's declaration in *The Marriage of Heaven and Hell* that 'Energy is the only life, and is from the Body and Reason is the bound or outward circumference of Energy,' and also that 'Energy is Eternal Delight' (Blake 1965, p. 34). Energy, the upwelling creative force, is traversive – what, in Auden's terms, engages the chaos of sea and the void of desert. Reason, the calculating ability, is the spoor left by the movements of energy across these topographies. Genius is the directive power which cunning restrains. To Shelley, for example, creative imagination is a progressive force, whereas reason, which can only assemble, is the resistance against which creativity moves (Shelley 1977, pp. 480–1). However, genius, or creativity, or energy may be seriously circumscribed. Reason may exist not only as the trace of energy's movement, but as its prison-house. Blake again in *The Marriage of Heaven and Hell* states:

> The Giants who formed this world into its sensual existence and now seem to live in it in chains, are in truth, the causes of its life and the sources of all activity, but the chains are, the cunning of weak and tame minds, which have power to resist energy, according to the proverb, the weak in courage is strong in cunning. (Blake 1965, p. 39)

The nay-saying, rule-minding calculators have won and the heroic adventurers have been enchained.

The Romantic journey may follow different routes to avoid being overtaken by the clerks, but two fundamental avenues frequently recur. Although influenced by Auden's scheme, I offer a different programme of images. Thus I shall trace one avenue through a variety of watercourses leading to a recognition of boundaries (but boundaries that now participate in the genius's pure command), and another through wastelands toward a promontory epitomising the dilemma of self-reflection.[1] The poet of Shelley's *Alastor* and Coleridge's *Ancient Mariner* have taken versions of the first route; Byron's Manfred and Shelley's Prometheus have followed the second.

Many Romantic poems deal with heights and waterways in a descriptive manner. Coleridge's sonnet *To the River Otter* is a record of the comforting memories of his childhood experiences on its banks. And in *Reflections on Having Left a Place of Retirement*, Coleridge gazes out from the hills above Tintern Abbey simply to appreciate the delightful view, though that view calls to mind the pious thought that the earth is God's temple. Passing over poems of this kind, I would like to begin with the poet mounted to Pisgah surveying the natural world that is his promised land. Thus, gazing at the scenery around Tintern Abbey, Wordsworth recalls the animal pleasure he once enjoyed there when, he says, the 'sounding cataract / Haunted me like a passion' and other forms of nature 'were then to me / An appetite' that required no intellectual embellishment or penetration. But those excursions through nature were, strangely, 'more like a man / Flying from something that he dreads, than one / Who sought the thing he loved'. For Wordsworth, the journey through nature is ultimately benign, only hinting at the dangerous emotions suggested by 'haunting', 'appetite' and 'dread', but leading finally to the high ground from which he can now more philosophically observe that he has internalised that natural scene and become acquainted with a 'presence that disturbs me with the joy / Of elevated thoughts...' (Wordsworth 1965, pp. 109–10). The prophet has been able to infiltrate his promised land and harvest its fruits even if he cannot dwell there permanently. As Northrop Frye puts it, the enterprise of the Romantic 'redemption myth' was to revive the 'numinous power of nature' and replace a sense of separation from nature with a sense of identity with it' (Frye 1968, pp. 16–18).

This may not be Auden's Happy Island or Oasis, but it is that isolated domain that is the destination of the Romantic quest. Of course the destination is ultimately internal; the sacred place has been created by the poet, not merely discovered, and so Wordsworth says more directly in his 'Prospectus' to *The Recluse*. He has described the manner in which Beauty has always been his companion on his journey.

> Paradise, and groves
> Elysian, Fortunate Fields – like those of old
> Sought in the Atlantic Main – why should they be
> A history only of departed things,
> Or a mere fiction of what never was?

For the discerning intellect of Man,
When wedded to this goodly universe
In love and holy passion, shall find these
A simple produce of the common day.

(Wordsworth 1965, p. 46)

His project has been to show how exquisitely the Mind and the external World are fitted to one another and how they cooperate in creating the beauties the poet then discovers in the natural world. Put differently, Reason becomes the congenial and conniving *enceintement* or confinement to energetic emotion that yearns toward enchantment and renewal. In a tiny rendition of the Romantic quest by water, Wordsworth records the famous episode when, drifting in a borrowed boat on Ullswater, he is awed and frightened by the apparent animation of a 'huge peak', an experience that unsettles him and introduces in his brain 'a dim and undetermined sense / Of unknown modes of being', a sense that matures into an appreciation of the modelling power for the mind of 'high objects' and 'enduring things', 'purifying thus / The elements of feeling and of thought, / And sanctifying, by such discipline, / Both pain and fear, until we recognise / A grandeur in the beating of the heart' (Wordsworth 1971, p. 58). The great Presences of Nature, Wordsworth explains, haunted him; they

> Impressed upon all forms the characters
> Of danger or desire; and thus did make
> The surface of the universal earth
> With triumph and delight, and hope and fear,
> Work like a sea.

(Wordsworth 1971, pp. 60ff.)

The sea is just a simile, though the lake was real. The passage over water is threatening, but ultimately life-enriching. The young boy who drifts in the boat and looks up awed at the peak and the young man who bounds among caves, trees, woods and hills will come to be the adult man who stands upon the high ground surveying the valley of the Wye, having taken possession of the scene and its significance within himself. Oceanic nature provides the grove Elysian or Fortunate Field within the poet's soul once he has conquered the Atlantic main through the efforts of his poetic imagination.

For Wordsworth, water is the medium bearing the self toward the goal of its quest. The wise individual learns to consider nature a partner in a spiritual endeavour. The natural world is not merely organic and inorganic substances to be analysed and manipulated by the intellect and its extensions. In Wordsworth, this pattern of cooperation is generally successful. His microcosmic pleasure in natural locations and his concern that their integrity be preserved manifest themselves in a simple poem like *Nutting*, where, having found a pleasant nook to idle in, the poet feels guilty for having spoiled it by picking hazelnuts. The poem ends with his caution to his companion to 'move along these shades / In gentleness of heart; with gentle hand / Touch – for there is a spirit in the woods' (Wordsworth 1965, p. 112). At the macroscopic level, the local domain with its preserving spirit toward which his whole career is moving is Grasmere, both as a real place and as the symbol of poetic maturity and purpose. M. H. Abrams has argued that *The Prelude*, reinforced by allusions to *Paradise Lost*, is an account of the recovery of a sense of nature's worth at an intellectually and morally elevated level, a spiralling route that Abrams considers a typically Romantic pattern (Abrams 1971, pp. 113–14). This journey may be more complicated than it seems, however, since it begins before conception. Wordsworth's *Ode: Intimations of Immortality* suggests that the soul leaves a previous existence to begin its pilgrimage in this one, where youth must travel away from the east until its splendour fades 'into the light of common day' (Wordsworth 1965, p. 188). Nature as Earth does all she can with her natural pleasures to make man forget the glories he has known. In this stage of human awareness, Nature is a nurse or comforter. But another stage is required, a stage at which the mind discovers the spirit transcending material nature. Oddly, this occurs not so much through the delight in physical nature, as in *Nutting*, but in the perception that all such physical manifestations of nature pass away. The poet is grateful not for the delights of nature but 'for those obstinate questionings / Of sense and outward things, / Fallings from us, vanishings…' (Wordsworth 1965, p. 189). These sensations lead to an awareness of much greater truths about all of life that never again depart. Thus even though the soul may find its domain, it will always recall the watery course it traversed to get there:

> Hence in a season of calm weather
> Though inland far we be,
> Our Souls have sight of that immortal sea
> Which brought us hither,
> Can in a moment travel thither,
> And see the Children sport upon the shore,
> And hear the mighty waters rolling evermore.

> (Wordsworth 1965, p. 190)[2]

In an intriguing reversal of the *Tintern Abbey* pattern, it is now the infant, still 'trailing clouds of glory', that stands 'yet glorious in the might / Of heaven born freedom on [its] being's height' surveying the natural world it has yet to enter (Wordsworth 1965, pp. 187–9). It thus appears that the adult poet looking down at the beloved valley of the Wye has *reascended* the visionary height. He has been welcome in the cordial Inn of nature but now hears the washings of the great ocean upon which he and the natural world are merely transitory phenomena. At first this pattern seems to prefigure Tennyson's 'From the great deep to the great deep', a journey out of eternity into time and then back again. But, as we shall see, the concepts of nature's role in this circular track have different implications for Romantic and Victorian poets.

The high place, whether above Tintern Abbey, on Snowdon or in the Alps, is the suitable vantage point for the Romantic imagination to reassess itself. The promontory is an extremity between two abysses – the vault of heaven and the gulf below. On Snowdon, Wordsworth perceives the mountain as the type of the creative mind. Unlike the domain, however, where the creative mind may come to sheltered rest, the promontory requires a return or it becomes an emblem of extinction. Shelley's *Alastor* describes the Poet's false movement through experience. The image of the spirit borne along a watercourse in some sort of vessel is a consistent one in Shelley's poetry, but in *Alastor* the poet's spirit is misguided, committed to an idealism that has no root or operation in the material world. The stream that bears the Poet along in this poem may be seen as the flow of existence or as the individual poet's life. In either case, it brings him to certain familiar symbols of introversion. That this is decidedly a metaphorical and symbolic stream is evident in that it *ascends* a mountain and brings the poet to 'a pool of treacherous and tremendous calm' (Shelley 1977, p. 79),

a wood, and then a fountain, and lastly to a location characterised
by a precipice, a pine tree, a torrent and the nook or cave where the
Poet expires.

As the Poet himself realises, the stream is an image of his own
life with its stillnesses, 'loud and hollow gulphs', and unknown
source (Shelley 1977, p. 82). Everything in the poem is emblematic
rather than suggestive of a real landscape. And when the Poet is
dead, worms, beasts, and men live on and 'mighty Earth / From sea
and mountain, city and wilderness', still lifts its solemn voice
(Shelley 1977, p. 86). Even this brief summary of what survives the
Poet suggests that the emblematic earth is more significant than the
material one, for the contrasts are precisely those that inform
the poem and provide its locations of repulsion and attraction. The
sea is the mystery surrounding existence and present in the stream
that carries the poet to his mountain precipice of self-discovery and
despair. The city as the embodiment of the commonplaces of the
civitas repels the poetic spirit, which seeks its ideal in the wilderness. But, as Wordsworth knew, and Shelley argued, a poet must
come down from the mountain bearing his written tablet for the
use and improvement of those who have not reached his *O altitudo*.
A poet must realise that the stream is not merely an image of his
life, it is a part of his life and he is a part of the life of nature. The
creative force represented by images of water flows through the
poet as much as it transports him.

Torrent and pinnacle are more fortunately joined in *Mont Blanc*,
where there is also a clear recognition by the poet – now the voice
of the poem, not merely its subject – of the harmonious labour of
human mind and the abiding power in nature:

> The everlasting universe of things
> Flows through the mind, and rolls its rapid waves,
> Now dark – now glittering – now reflecting gloom –
> Now lending splendour, where from secret springs
> The source of human thought its tribute brings
> Of waters, – with a sound but half its own.

> (Shelley, 1977, p. 89)

The Poet of *Alastor* similarly viewed the stream as an image of his
soul, but he did not bring his tributary stream into conjunction with
the infinite power of nature. He did not realise that to exploit the

stream one must contribute to the current. The poet of *Alastor* could not steer his craft. The poet of *Mont Blanc* is ever conscious of the need for channelling.

Man has the capacity to participate in the direction of his life. In *Prometheus Unbound*, Shelley describes man's Will 'as a tempest-winged ship, whose helm / Love rules, through waves which dare not overwhelm, / Forcing Life's wildest shores to own its sovereign sway' (Shelley 1977, p. 205). Asia, in the same poem, describes her soul as 'an enchanted Boat' floating on the music of the Spirit of the Hour's song. And at the end of *Adonais*, Shelley writes that his 'spirit's bark is driven, / Far from the shore, far from the trembling throng / Whose sails were never to the tempest given', attracted by the shining star of Adonais' transformed soul (Shelley 1977, p. 406). For the Romantic poets, images of sea and promontory are generally positive and 'spiritual', signifying danger if one's motive or understanding is faulty, but signifying potential triumph if they are pure. The Ancient Mariner must live out his error again and again for the sake of others. His is a stagnant sea that does not bear him to a spiritual destination. He never ascends the mountain that would give him insight, but is swept aloft by spirits from whom he only *overhears* his condition. Manfred may climb his mountain and encounter a real spirit there, but his self-recognition gives him no peace, only a desire to control his own death. He is at war with his own nature and hence with the natural world that seems to insult his imperious nature. Always it is what these natural figures stand for that is important to most Romantic poets. Even at the level of immediate revelation of pleasure – the discovery of a new range of poetic interest – these images leap forward, and so Keats likens his discovery of the beauty of Chapman's Homer to that of an explorer staring at an ocean, 'Silent, upon a peak in Darien' (Keats 1982, p. 34).

My point so far is that although the Romantic poets openly revered the lineaments of the natural world, ultimately the real pleasure that they found in nature was in rising, as Wordsworth described in *Tintern Abbey*, to an intellectual or spiritual appreciation of the natural world through a species of interbreeding with it, a discovering that the boundaries of the self and of nature were alike illusory.[3] I shall now try to show that, although much of this attitude remains with the Victorian poets, there are some significant and characteristic changes.

A passage from *Prometheus Unbound* provides an illustration of how Shelley viewed the alienating power of oceanic energy in nature. Panthea and Ione become aware of 'the deep music of the rolling world', and Panthea offers a set-piece describing 'two runnels of a rivulet' that make a 'path of melody' that separate and turn 'their dear disunion to an isle / Of lovely grief, a wood of sweet sad thoughts', but which are connected more intensely and more keenly 'Under the ground and through the windless air' (Shelley 1977, p. 200). There is only one rivulet, but it has divided temporarily, forming by this benevolently 'dear disunion' an island of 'lovely grief', because the island only emphasises by its temporary separation of the two runnels their actual unity in the ocean of that power which moves all nature. Put another way, the apparent alienation of humans in a world of material nature is an illusion. Once discover our unity with the power represented by the flowing stream and we accept our identification with and participation in that power. Shelley knew the pains of human existence; he had fallen upon the thorns of life and bled. But he and other Romantics also felt the sustaining power of nature.

How different from Shelley's image is Carlyle's characteristic picture of human existence! The underlying assumptions are the same, but the tone and viewpoint are altered: 'We, the whole species of Mankind, and our whole existence and history, are but a floating speck in the illimitable ocean of the All; yet *in* that ocean; indissoluble portion thereof; partaking of its infinite tendencies: borne this way and that by its deep-swelling tides, and grand ocean currents; – of which what faintest chance is there that we should ever exhaust the significance, ascertain the goings and comings' (Carlyle 1896–9, 28: pp. 25–6)?[4] Similarly, in *Sartor Resartus*, Carlyle writes: 'Such a minnow is man; his Creek this Planet Earth; his Ocean the immeasurable All; his Monsoons and periodic Currents the mysterious Course of Providence through Aeons of Aeons' (Carlyle 1896–9, 1: p. 205). For Carlyle, man is still a part of nature and is still carried by its tidal force, but he is no longer capable of controlling that force or even mapping out a journey across it. He can but paddle as earnestly as he can in the immediacy of his being and hope that the great Course of Providence will bring him to some shore at last. Man is confined in the bell-jar of mechanism and consciousness, but it is within his power to escape (Carlyle 1896–9, 27: p. 81). Carlyle's solution sounds something like that of his Romantic contemporaries, but it puts its faith in an invisible, even unknowable, process. The invisible can be known only through symbols. Hence scepticism, the compulsion to analyse through reason, may burn itself out and the principle of life 'may then withdraw into its inner sanctuaries, its abysses of mystery and miracle; withdraw deeper than ever into that domain of the Unconscious, by nature infinite and inexhaustible; and creatively work there. From that mystic region, and from that alone, all wonders, all Poesies, and Religions, and Social systems have proceeded: the like wonders, and greater and higher, lie slumbering there; and, brooded on by the spirit of the waters, will evolve themselves, and rise like exhalations from the Deep' (Carlyle 1896–9, 28: p. 40). The visionary current no longer drives through and buoys the spirit, but now engulfs it. There is no progress, no quest, no self-confrontation on the revelatory peak, but a healthy forgetting and submergence, a circling down in the comforting whirlpool with faith in a later healthy 'exhalation from the Deep'. The Romantics also recognised the importance of tapping what Carlyle here calls the Unconscious. Woodring notes that for Wordsworth and other romantics 'Nature' is found not in external spectacle, but 'by internal, spiritual descent' (Woodring 1989, p. 14). This spiritual 'descent', however, manifests itself in poetry as physical ascent to promontories of illumination. For Carlyle and many who came after there is no comparable ascent.

Carlyle's altered point of view introduces an outlook that is largely characteristic of the Victorian poets. The onward flow of the Romantic stream suggests power and forward movement, but it also suggests the overflow of spirit and an osmosis through boundaries. The basic water images as they relate to the human spirit or imagination are positive and constructive, though not without their ominous qualities. There is dread in the face of this power, as Wordsworth noted, and the poet might fail to command his inspiration, as Shelley indicated in *Alastor*. But the general character of the Romantic flood is positive and energetic. With the Victorians, the stream is slowed and more menacing, becoming more closely identified with nature as a limiting and controlling rather than a liberating force for man. In many cases it becomes almost synonymous with death. Merlin's song about Arthur in Tennyson's *Idylls of the King* ends with a line that summarises one tendency of Victorian thoughts about the sea as a symbol: 'From the great deep to the great deep he goes' (Tennyson 1987, Vol. 3, p. 560). Arthur comes magically from the ocean waves and, stricken and near death, is borne away across the calm sea to Avilion, his career symbolically figuring that of all mankind. *Crossing the Bar* is Tennyson's personal recognition of this view that the sea surrounds us like eternity in which we are, as Carlyle says, but 'floating specks'. When Merlin, representative of the power of the human imagination, loses faith and falls into a melancholic depression, he finds a little boat and sails away. But unlike the poet of *Alastor*, who is swept to a promontory hinting at the great prospect and power he is incapable of realising, and who dies in his humble cave, Merlin's water journey is simply to another shore and a dark wood, where he is enchanted by Vivien and uselessly incarcerated in an oak tree, reminiscent of the lone pine tree by Shelley's poet's remote cave. The Romantic drive may end up being destructive, but it still has a tendency to ascend. The Victorian impulse slackens toward lowlands and levels.

An early and dramatic example of this pattern is The *Lady of Shalott*. We first encounter the Lady in her tower – significantly the product of human artifice, not a natural outcropping – and she is engaged in an intricate art of her own that turns her away from the world beyond her tower. Her craving for that natural world eventually overcomes her and her art is lost. All that she can do is name herself and drift in her boat down to Camelot where people may wonder at and pity her. The same pattern is repeated with Elaine, who, knowing that she cannot have Lancelot, leaves the tower where she has worked her craft and dreamt about the owner of the fine shield she has treasured and drifts in a 'barge...clothed in black' down to Camelot (Tennyson 1987, Vol. 3, p. 453). Most deeply significant to Tennyson was the ship carrying the body of his beloved Arthur Henry Hallam across the sea to his grave. This pattern is the reverse of the Romantic vessel that bears the spirit toward life, or at least upward toward available vision. In *In Memoriam*, Hallam journeys across the sea already dead to have his death sealed by interment and in *Crossing the Bar* Tennyson envisions himself taking ship for eternity.[5] Even that great quester, Ulysses, 'yearning in desire / To follow knowledge like a sinking star, / Beyond the utmost bound of human thought', can see his action only as a staving-off of death by setting forth into death, into the sunset and the baths of the western stars until possibly the gulfs will wash Ulysses and his mariners down, or 'It may be we shall touch the Happy Isles, / And see the great Achilles, whom we knew' (Tennyson 1987, Vol. 1, p. 619).

Wordsworth had seen the Happy Isles or Fortunate Fields as a metaphor for the poet's capacity to find a home in nature. For Tennyson's Ulysses they are located outside himself in the domain of death. If the Romantics inclined to blend their spirits with nature, the Victorians, perhaps with advances of science in mind, seemed more inclined to imagine a union of molecules. Tennyson in *Lucretius* and Arnold in *Empedocles on Etna* offer two of many instances in Victorian poetry where figures expect themselves to be atomically redistributed in nature. The natural world is not the home of spiritual presences, but the reservoir of matter. Only beyond nature, if at all, is the spirit to find companionship. *Ulysses* balances the two terminal conditions available as the lines I have quoted show. Carl Woodring suggests that this changing attitude may be attributable to an increasing respect for realism during the nineteenth century. 'Romantics', he says, 'had rashly delved for power; Victorians would settle for truth' (Woodring 1989, p. 117). This contrast is epitomised in Robert Bernard Martin's account of Wordsworth's response to Tennyson, where the opposition between nature viewed as spectacle and nature as signature of the ideal is dramatic.

For all their shared devotion to nature, they were very different in their perceptions, a point illustrated by Tennyson's saying that in the future balloons would be fixed at the bottom of high mountains so as to take people to the top for the views. At the time Wordsworth merely grunted in disagreement, but the remark evidently still rankled in his memory when he wrote that Tennyson was 'not much in sympathy with what I should myself most value in my attempts, viz. the spirituality with which I have endeavoured to invest the material Universe' (Martin 1980, p. 291).

So fundamental is the sea as a region of death to Tennyson, that he often employs it as the last stage of a downward spiritual course. Thus the couple in *Despair*, who have lost their positive faith and can find no comfort in the bleaker creed of their dissenting minister, decide to commit suicide by drowning. The wife succeeds but the husband is saved. However, still seeing the world as a ghastly place, he remarks to the minister who has saved him, 'Hence! she is gone! can I stay?' (Tennyson 1987, Vol. 3, p. 91) This seems quite clearly to indicate that he'll try once more to join his wife in death. And the speaker in *The Wreck* describes the sea-voyage with her adulterous lover that was ended by shipwreck in a storm on the very day that her abandoned child died and on which her lover also dies.[6]

Tennyson had not always insisted on this movement down to death. In his youthful *Armageddon*, later greatly revised as *Timbuctoo*, the speaker of the poem ascends a mountain where an angel – later the spirit of Fable – addresses him. This is the Romantic ascent to the promontory of poetic vision:

> I felt my soul grow godlike, and my spirit
> With supernatural excitation bound
> Within me, and my mental eye grew large
> With such a vast circumference of thought,
> That, in my vanity, I seemed to stand
> Upon the outward verge and bound alone
> Of God's omniscience.

> (Tennyson 1987, Vol. 1, p. 81)

This grand vision fades to something darker and more threatening as the poem proceeds. In the revised version called *Timbuctoo*, the speaker stands on a Mountain overlooking the narrow seas that part 'Afric from green Europe', thinking of legendary marvellous domains of the past such as Atlantis and Eldorado. He thinks of Timbuctoo, wondering if it is also legendary, and suddenly the spirit of Fable appears to him and enhances his vision. But the poem ends with Fable's acknowledgement that Discovery, usually taken to signify science, will soon invade her world of mystery. The disappearance of Fable is figured in the form of a river 'whose translucent wave, / Forth issuing from the darkness, windeth through / The argent streets o' the city' reflecting its many beauties, but now 'it passeth by, / And gulphs himself in sands, as not enduring / To carry through the world those waves, which bore / The reflex of my City in their depths' (Tennyson 1987, Vol. 1, p. 198). Thus for Tennyson, even in his youth, the Romantic flood is endangered.[7] 'Come Down, O Maid,' from *The Princess* could be seen as Tennyson's acknowledgement that, practically, we must live in the lowlands of the ordinary and social, not in the mountains and high grounds of idealism, whatever form that idealism takes (Martin 1980, p. 307; Tucker 1988, p. 371).

Tennyson did not altogether abandon the Romantic hope. It resurfaced late in his life as part of a revised landscape of creation and religious faith in *The Ancient Sage*. The sage of this poem leads a young man to a cavern 'whence an affluent fountain poured /

From darkness into daylight', almost like the Spirit of Fable's stream reappearing not as a river but as a fountain, a pattern reminiscent of Arethusa who dove into the Ionian sea to elude the river god Alpheus only to have him surface with her in Syracuse where she was transformed into a fountain. The sage tells his young companion that the waters might seem to issue from the cave, but 'the source is higher...'. He himself intends to seek that higher source (Tennyson 1987, Vol. 3, p. 139). It is Faith that finds the fountain where others wail 'Mirage'. Faith can dive into the abyss of self and discover there the Nameless who has the power of mind. The sage ends by advising his companion to 'curb the beast' and leave 'the hot swamp of voluptuousness' which is a cloud between him and the Nameless.

> And lay thine uphill shoulder to the wheel,
> And climb the Mount of Blessing, whence, if thou
> Look higher, then – perchance – thou mayest – beyond
> A hundred ever-rising mountain lines,
> And past the range of Night and Shadow – see
> The high-heaven dawn of more than mortal day
> Strike on the Mount of Vision!

                              (Tennyson 1987, Vol. 3, p. 146)

But this is a religious, not an aesthetic vision. This is an ascent to spiritual enlightenment, not the power in nature that moves man to creation. It converts nature into emblem in the manner of Carlyle and the Victorians, but with a difference. The sage sets out for the hills because they are antipodal to the 'hot swamps' of the lowlands, not because he wishes to trace the source of the life-giving cascade and muse upon its power. The sage now passively entrusts himself to the Nameless. The poem is, fittingly, also a movement toward death, for it is the culmination of the sage's life and its conclusion. Nonetheless, this survival of the promontory-and-water motif recalls similar ones in Wordsworth and Shelley, though the very resemblance clarifies the difference that that motif had for the Romantics and the Victorians. Nature is often allegorical in Romantic poetry, too, as in Shelley's *Euganean Hills* and *The Triumph of Life*, but the tone is substantially changed in Tennyson. Only through a moral purgation, a labouring effort, and an acquiescence in death can Tennyson accept the pattern of ascent. Christina

Rossetti's *Uphill* comes to mind as another symbolic ascent that offers after long effort only the consolation of rest in death all in the parable of a journey up a steep road to a final Inn. There is no water in Rossetti's poem.

Matthew Arnold brought other famous mountain-tops into poetry. The only vision that the high slopes of the alps provides for him is his sense, among the Carthusians at the Grande Chartreuse, with its 'icy fountains' and 'humid corridors', that he is 'Wandering between two worlds, one dead, / The other powerless to be born...' (Arnold 1965, p. 288). He considers himself more like the monks than like the ordinary people of his day because he feels the same isolation from the modern world. The best are silent now, he says, because though they feel the same grief as those gone by, they see no reason to wail like the Romantic poets, who changed nothing. They watered with their tears 'this sea of time whereon we sail' but nothing has changed; 'Still the same ocean round us raves, / But we stand mute, and watch the waves' (Arnold 1965, p. 290). Water and promontory are joined here, but in hopelessness and futility, not in energy and creation. The images call up the very Romantics who so valued energy and creation, but reveal them to have been misled, even contributing with their false aspirations to the increased bitterness of the 'salt estranging sea' with their salt tears.

Empedocles climbs Etna not for a vision of poetic creation, though Callicles struggles to provide him with antidotal melodies for his despair. He climbs to where a 'sea of cloud' rises 'To moat this isle of ashes from the world', ironically converting the visionary mountain into an island solitude. In this solitude the philosopher ponders his alienation from the world and his inability to find a source of hope. He flies to solitude because he is tired of being 'miserably bandied to and fro / Like a sea-wave, betwixt the world' and Apollo, god of poetry. Like the Romantics, Empedocles sees that man and nature are of one stuff spun, 'That we who rail are still, / With what we rail at, one; / One with the o'erlaboured Power' of nature (Arnold 1965, pp. 188, 185, 168). But while this inspirited the Romantics, it wearies Empedocles. His solution is dissolution by leaping into Etna and resuming his elemental molecular identification with nature.

If the promontory offers primarily a despairing vision and disillusionment for Arnold, water is no better. We are all familiar with Arnold's famous countering of Donne's hopeful view of mankind from *To Marguerite – Continued*:

Yes! in the sea of life enisled,
With echoing straits between us thrown,
Dotting the shoreless watery wild,
We mortal millions live *alone*.

(Arnold, 1965, p. 124)

But just as this poem ends with a God declaring severance as the human condition, so other poems emphasise the inability of human beings to penetrate the barriers separating them. Frequently this separation is indicated by water images. If Ulysses could sail off to the west and sink into the ocean courageously, Arnold sees us all as confined to islands in an alienating ocean. We are not going anywhere. There is no quest. In fact, there is a reverse quest for poets, as *The New Sirens* indicates. These new sirens are spiritual muses calling to a group of poets who cannot believe in the sirens' spiritual aims and whose disbelief proves correct by the end of the poem. The new sirens cannot provide the poets with the vigour to create poetry, yet the poets have abandoned the inspiration that they once enjoyed, in what one might easily take as a conscious reversal of Tennyson's pattern in *The Ancient Sage* if Arnold's poem hadn't come first.

From the dragon-wardered fountains
Where the springs of knowledge are,
From the watchers on the mountains,
And the bright and morning star;
We are exiles, we are falling,
We have lost them at your call –
O ye false ones, at your calling
Seeking ceiléd chambers and a palace-hall!

(Arnold 1965, p. 36)

Water and promontory are alienating forces for Arnold. The image that concludes *The Scholar-Gipsy* of the Tyrian trader sailing to the Atlantic to carry on his trade away from the rude and worldly Greek intruders is just another metaphor for the manner in which ocean sunders man from man. In this case the poet suggests that isolation is a good choice; at other times, as in *To Marguerite – Continued*, it is simply the sad way things are. In *A Summer Night* Arnold asks if there isn't some alternative between the madman's or the slave's response to the hardness of life. His image for the madman is reminiscent of the eager Romantic sea-voyager or perhaps an inept or unfortunate Ulysses. He has set out on the ocean of life where trade-winds 'cross it from eternity' but now what his quest has brought him to is 'Only a driving wreck' manned by a 'pale master... Still bent to make some port he knows not where, / Still standing for some false, impossible shore' until 'the roar / of sea and wind' and the 'deepening gloom' hide him in oblivion (Arnold 1965, p. 270). The poem ends on a hopeful supposition that the stars may offer a better metaphor of what the human spirit can aspire to. *The Buried Life*, written about the same time, also provides a modest hope for human self-understanding. We cannot truly communicate with one another, not even with those we love, the poet says, but then we cannot even understand ourselves. Our buried self is kept obscure so that we will not pervert its laws. Only on rare occasions will the presence of a loved one offer us an inkling of what that buried life is. 'A man becomes aware of his life's flow, / And hears its winding murmur; and he sees / The meadows where it glides, the sun, the breeze.' And this brief moment offers relief from the hot race of life. 'And then he thinks he knows / The hills where his life rose, / And the sea where it goes' (Arnold 1965, p. 275).

But if that momentary vision brings transient peace, we should not overlook the fact that it describes the downward movement of the river of life toward the sea of death. A. Dwight Culler (1966) has amply explored the way in which the symbolic landscape of Arnold's poetry figures the human condition and the progress of the individual through time. The famous ending of *Sohrab and Rustum* offers an especially strong instance of the pattern, where the Oxus river flows strongly at first until it reaches the lowlands where 'sands begin / To hem his watery march, and dam his streams, / And split his currents' much as life divides the life of man and fragments his powers. The Oxus now forgets 'the bright speed he had / In his high mountain-cradle in Pamere, / A foiled circuitous wanderer' and flows out into the sea (Arnold 1965, p. 331). If the river of life must inevitably flow into the sea of death, the heights of vision may prove inaccessible or false.

This general pattern of viewing the natural world as helpful but potentially hostile is so pervasive in the Victorian period that even one of the most 'Romantic' of its poets, Algernon Charles Swinburne, nonetheless exhibits clear Victorian traits. Though he was a Shelleyan spokesman for political and personal freedom and an aggressive atheist, he still manifested, if not a Victorian

Hebraism, a classical stoicism that pictured the natural world as inevitably defeating the purposes of man. And the reasons are much the same as for Tennyson and Arnold – that death ends all of the material aspirations of man. Tennyson could wish for something more beyond this world, Arnold could hope for some elevation of the spirit within this world, but Swinburne more grimly harked back to a simple *carpe diem* view with the one difference that he valued not only the blossoms of life but also its thorns, upon which poor Shelley had fallen and bled. Thus, although the ocean is often a representative and symbol of the pleasures of the natural world, it is at the same time an image of death. In *Thalassius* Swinburne describes himself as a sea-born poet who is endorsed by his procreator, the Apollonian sun-god in these words:

> 'Child of my sunlight and the sea, from birth
> A fostering and fugitive on earth;
> Sleepless of soul as wind or wave or fire,
> A manchild with an ungrown God's desire;
> Because thou hast loved nought mortal more than me,
> Thy father, and thy mother-hearted sea...
> Have therefore in thine heart and in thy mouth
> The sound of song that mingles north and south,
> The song of all the winds that sing of me,
> And in thy soul the sense of all the sea.'

(Swinburne 1905, Vol.3, p. 310)

This seems a very positive result of Swinburne's relationship with the sea, but even here it is apparent that his skill as a poet is bought at the price of sacrificing a little of life's reward. The ambiguous nature of the sea as a Swinburnian figure is more evident in *The Triumph of Time*, which rises out of the poet's acceptance that he cannot have the woman he loves. The sea, he says, will be his consolation, 'the great sweet mother, / Mother and lover of men...'. In an apostrophe to the sea he asks: 'Set free my soul as thy soul is free' (Swinburne 1905, Vol.1, p. 42). Man is a part of the ocean, a part of nature, just as Carlyle indicated. More in Shelley's view, however, Swinburne sees man as a sentient part of a living being, not a fragment in chaos. But that sentient being is amoral and purposeless. The poet admits that the sea may be 'subtle and cruel of heart' and that she is full of the dead and cold like them. But death is the worst that comes of her. 'Thou art fed with our dead, O mother, O sea, / But when hast thou fed on our

hearts? or when, / Having given us love, hast thou taken away?'
All else will vanish while the sea endures.

> But thou, thou art sure, thou art older than earth;
> Thou art strong for death and fruitful of birth;
> Thy depths conceal and thy gulfs discover;
> From the first thou wert; in the end thou art.

(Swinburne 1905, Vol.1, p.44)

No wonders will rise like exhalations from this deep. Submergence
into this gulf of the unconscious is the simple molecular reunion
with the source of being. The great mother is metaphorical but not
emblematic.

The association of love, ocean, and peace is developed
elaborately in *Tristram of Lyonesse*, where the turmoil of passionate
life is appeased finally by the comforting sea of death. There are, to
my recollection, no notable promontories in Swinburne's poetry.
The only famous hill is the Venusburg, and Tannhäuser lives *inside*
that. Most of Swinburne's landscape inclines to the level as it
approaches the ocean, a landscape beautifully typified by one of his
most famous stanzas from *The Garden of Proserpine*.

> From too much love of living,
>   From hope and fear set free,
> We thank with brief thanksgiving
>   Whatever gods may be
> That no life lives for ever;
> That dead men rise up never;
> That even the weariest river
>   Winds somewhere safe to sea.

(Swinburne 1905, Vol.1, p. 171)

It may not be Tennyson crossing the bar or Arnold's Oxus finding
its way to the sea, but it is Swinburne's own version of the trope.

The Romantics wrote in a period of uncertainty and new possibilities. Political revolution and reform promised new opportunities
for mankind. Aesthetic revolution was everywhere successful as a

powerful spirit of intellectual and creative opportunity spread over Europe. The poetry of the Romantics reflects that traversing and transcending spirit. In general, they feel capable of escaping earlier limitations on the self; they pioneer into the otherness around them that is being redefined even as they explore. And they believe that they can themselves shape by the illuminating power of their own imagination the manner in which the world around them will be perceived. This latter sense survives in the Victorians, but a distrust of rapid reform and a caution about new theories of existence create distinctive tints. Carlyle wants to retailor the universe with new symbols for a new faith, but he knows that any such faith is provisional and that behind it resides a mystery that demands of mankind hard, slow work, not a leap to triumph and joy. Tennyson has a geological sense of man's task – the slow accumulation of virtues, the plodding up the stairs of a questionable social progress toward a remote condition of improvement. His way is marked for him and he must make that way very much on his own strength and against odds. For Arnold even the way has disappeared. The path itself must be created and the energy with which to create it is much diminished. Everywhere among the Victorians a great sense of potential and energy is matched by a feeling of entrapment and weariness. In Swinburne, one of the least characteristic Victorians, the energy and weariness paradoxically blend together. The Romantics concentrated upon the sources of power and its transmission – on mountain heights and strong, coursing waters. The Victorians looked instead chiefly to the ends of power – the lower slopes, the slowing stream that winds to the sea.

Of course, there is a great variety of water and promontory imagery in the poetry of the nineteenth century, much of which is merely ornamental, much of which does not move in the directions I have indicated. But so much of this axis of images does indicate a characteristic difference between the early poets known as the Romantics and later poets known as Victorians that I believe the patterns may be taken as tributary evidence to a swelling concourse of other streams of evidence to provide a broad distinction between the two periods.

Notes

1. My essay is indebted to Marjorie Hope Nicolson's pioneering *Mountain Gloom and Mountain Glory: The Development of the Aesthetics*

of the Infinite (Ithaca: Cornell University Press, 1959) that traced the intellectual significance of the evolution of mountain landscapes in English literature.

2.   This association of the sound of waters with a condition of pleasure and joy is familiar in Wordsworth. See *Resolution and Independence*, for example: 'And all the air is filled with pleasant noise of waters' (Wordsworth 1965, p. 165). This image is very likely derived from Biblical sources, such as the highly positive occurrence in Revelations 14: 2: 'And I heard a voice from heaven, as the voice of many waters....'

3.   Carl Woodring reminds us that, much as they valued 'imagination and vision, the Romantics never abandoned particularity' (Woodring 1989, p. 62). Nonetheless they placed imagination over sense; 'imagination was made noumenous,' the one certain organizing power for experience (Woodring 1989, p. 61).

4.   In *Characteristics*, Carlyle describes Nature as a kind mother, a 'bottomless boundless Deep, whereon all human things fearfully and wonderfully swim...' (Carlyle 28: 3).

5.   There is an eerie repetition of this anticipation of death being delivered by water in Tennyson's awaiting the arrival of the boat bearing his son Lionel's body. The body, however, was buried at sea. In his poem on this subject *To the Marquis of Dufferin and Ava*, Tennyson used the *In Memoriam* stanza.

6.   The image of shipwreck was a standard device for indicating moral, financial, or other forms of overthrow and disaster (Landow 1972).

7.   Herbert Tucker discusses *Timbuctoo* as Tennyson's confrontation with the poetic tradition, especially with Romantic poetry (Tucker 1988, pp. 54ff).

2

Shelley's *Adonais* and Arnold's *Thyrsis*: Words of Power in Pastoral Elegy

W. DAVID SHAW

Few poems better reflect the deep discontinuity between Romantic faith in words of power and Victorian distrust of performative language than Shelley's *Adonais* and Arnold's *Thyrsis*. As pastoral elegies, both poems try to emulate Milton's *Lycidas* by recreating quasi-imperative words capable of expressing through verbal magic, as Orpheus expressed through music, an energy common to art and nature. In Shelley, as in Milton, such an energy or force is best expressed as a metaphoric identity of subject and object. Lycidas is the risen sun; Adonais is the beaconing star; and Arnold would like to say that Thyrsis is the 'single elm-tree,' 'Bare on its lonely ridge' (lines 26, 160). Unfortunately, Arnold, like many Victorians, is a sceptic: he does not believe in the seer's metaphoric identities. He cannot substitute a tree or even a landscape for the presence of his friend, nor does he share Shelley's faith in the almost physical energy released by words and their power to tame a hostile or indifferent world.

To realise the illusion of abiding life is to abolish its future and turn it into a living presence, like the starlike soul of Adonais. But the elusive elm that might make Clough's future a present reality for Arnold is difficult to track. When Arnold, crossing a field, glimpses the elm only from a distance, then fails to pursue it farther, the transitive verbs of a pilgrimage turn into the intransitive verbs of a failed pilgrimage – a mere ramble or excursion. Phrases like 'Roam on' or 'wandered till I died' (*Thyrsis*, lines 237–8) lack the teleologically directed future of a pilgrimage, whose traditionally transitive verbs carry a believer like Dr Arnold from the rocks of the wilderness to the City of God in *Rugby Chapel*. Lacking Shelley's faith in the power of a godlike mind to cross boundaries, Arnold believes intransitively. He is faced with the challenge of manifesting the light's existence, not merely gazing at it from afar. Whereas Keats's creative energy has already made the illusion of immortal life a reality for Shelley, Arnold, like many Victorians, must make Romantic illusion real through his own creative energy. Unlike Shelley's trumpeting proclamations, Arnold's discoveries can be communicated only in silence, in the caesural pauses and breaks between lines. With Arnold's help, Clough's whisper may restore everything the mourner has lost, but only at the last moment, and only after it seems to have disappeared forever.

PERFORMATIVE LANGUAGE: ROMANTIC POWER AND VICTORIAN RESISTANCE

The ritualised language of all pastoral elegy retains strong traces of verbal magic. As a species of liturgy that releases emotion even while controlling it, the ancient language and traditional symbols promote the form of utterance J. L. Austin calls 'performative' (1962, p. 25). To say something is to perform an act, if you will – the act of saying something. It is important to distinguish, however, between a mere act of saying that Lycidas is dead and the elegist's performance of an act of ritual naming, a kind of baptism, in which Lycidas is pronounced 'the genius of the shore' (line 183). By functioning as an imperative in disguise, exhorting Lycidas to live up to his new name, to 'be good' in his 'large recompense.../ To all that wander in that perilous flood' (lines 184–5), such a baptism, if felicitous, may even release quasi-physical power. Moreover, as both a summons to activity and the outward sign of self-communing, the mourner's resolution to return 'Tomorrow to fresh woods and pastures new' (line 193) is a self-commissioning or 'doing-by-saying,' as Geoffrey Hill calls it (1984, p. 119). Without such 'doing-by-saying,' an elegy may remain a self-isolating meditation, not a socially responsible or fully human act.

Milton assumes that creation by verbal fiat is God's prerogative : prophets and poets exercise verbal power only as God or the Holy Spirit inspires them. For Shelley, however, man makes his own world, and at the centre of that creation is the 'doing-by-saying' of the poet. Instead of enslaving himself, like Frankenstein, to what he creates, Shelley's elegist must celebrate, in Northrop Frye's words, 'the recovery by the imagination of what it has projected' (1971,

p. 96). The opening stanzas of *Adonais*, for example, are both descriptive and performative, and they tend to look two ways at once. At the beginning, Adonais seems swallowed up in the first line's dash and late-breaking seventh-syllable caesura: 'I weep for Adonais – he is dead!' But the next line initiates a sudden and striking shift: 'I weep' becomes the deceptively similar but potently different 'O, weep'. A mere 'saying' becomes a 'doing-by-saying', a resolve by the poet to mourn properly by commemorating Keats in an elegy.

By framing a word of power, a decree, inside a second decree, the first stanza makes its performative language self-embedding and reflexive:

> I weep for Adonais – he is dead!
> O, weep for Adonais! though our tears
> Thaw not the frost which binds so dear a head!
> And thou, sad Hour, selected from all years
> To mourn our loss, rouse thy obscure compeers,
> And teach them thine own sorrow, say: 'With me
> Died Adonais; till the Future dares
> Forget the Past, his fate and fame shall be
> An echo and a light unto eternity!'

(Adonais, lines 1–9)

The echoing that the 'sad Hour' decrees is itself an echo of the elegist's threefold decree to the hour: 'Rouse thy obscure compeers', he exhorts, 'And teach them', then 'say'. One might think that such pervasive echoing would attenuate the force of the decrees. But in the acoustic chamber of the long, concluding alexandrine, the echoing of the poet's undying fame, sounding 'unto eternity', amplifies rather than attenuates the performative force of Shelley's words. Trembling on the brink of each indefinite caesura, like the mourner's mind, the stanza advances by coiling back on itself in self-impeding loops. As if replicating Coleridge's picture of the mind's innate resilience and energy, the interlocking quatrains, which keep doubling back on the same rhyme word, move like a serpent, 'which the Egyptians made the emblem of intellectual power'. At each step the poet of power 'pauses and half recedes, and from the retrogressive movement' of his Spenserian stanza 'collects the force which again carries him onward' (Coleridge, 1906, p. 173).

Whenever Arnold tries to emulate Shelley by making the landscape before his eye match the landscape in his mind, he finds he has lost the Romantic poet's adventurous confidence in the power of words to make something happen. Before baptising Oxford as the loveliest of cities, Arnold uses language that is already half-performative, capable of invoking absent seasons such as spring and the heightened beauty of Oxford in June as mid-winter blessings. But there is still a sense that such consecration has to be achieved, that it is a triumph of making believe rather than being descriptive. The boundary between stanzas 2 and 3, visible to the eye but inaudible to the ear when the lines are read aloud, fortifies the challenge of having to cross the divide between descriptive and performative speech:

> Humid the air! leafless, yet soft as spring,
>   The tender purple spray on copse and briers!
>   And that sweet city with her dreaming spires,
> She needs not June for beauty's heightening,
>
> Lovely all times she lies, lovely to-night! –
>   Only, methinks, some loss of habit's power
>   Befalls me wandering through this upland dim.

> (*Thyrsis*, lines 17–23)

The white space of the break also stands for the silent powers of change, for the ravages of time which the elegist must try to exorcise through a magic, ritualised use of words. That magic power is clearly latent in Arnold's benedictory phrase, 'Humid the air!', which recalls Keats's 'tender is the night' from *Ode to a Nightingale*. Though leafless on this warm winter evening, the tender purple spray on copse and brier is also 'soft as spring', partly because the poet provides the felicitous simile. But the pause we expect at the end of stanza 2, after 'beauty's heightening', is less emphatic than the pause that occurs at the end of the next line, after which the aspiring celebrant, the would-be user of ritual words, laments 'some loss of habit's power'. In the triply enforced break after the phrase 'lovely to-night', which is created by the exclamation point, the dash and the ending of the line, the celebrant's consecration and elation subside into sudden disenchantment and fear. In the loss of a rooted expectation, Arnold seems to experience once again the loss of his friend Clough, which is like the loss of a habit or a skill.

Though at first surprised, a reader is also half-prepared for what takes place after the dash in line 21. Is there not, after all, something sinister about Oxford's 'lovely' lying? Is she not trying to seduce Arnold into a delusive picture of her, as Peele Castle seduces Wordsworth? As the fond haven of an unreal paradise, Oxford may lie in the sense of 'deceive', and she may also lie or repose in the attitude of one who wants to seduce Arnold. The sinister possibilities resurface three lines later in his admission that he once passed here 'blindfold'. That could mean either that he knew every cranny of Oxford intimately, or that he was blind to the delusiveness of her charm. The second, more disturbing possibility seems confirmed a moment later when the words that complete the ritual, making the landscape in the mind match the landscape before the eye, are used to concede defeat: 'I miss it! is it gone?' (line 27). All words of power are now consigned to the past: while the elm '*stood*,' 'we *said*, / Our friend, the Gipsy-Scholar, *was* not dead' (lines, 28–9; emphasis added). The shift to a past-tense sequence in Arnold's allusion to the culminating words of power in *The Scholar-Gipsy* – 'No, no, thou hast not felt the lapse of hours!' (line 141) – places any triumph of 'doing-by-saying' over descriptive matching in a world that now seems as remote from Arnold's Oxford as Moschus's *Lament for Bion*, Virgil's seventh Eclogue, or (more to the present purpose, perhaps) the Romantic poet's almost Pelagian faith in the natural goodness of a godlike soul like Keats.

SOURCES OF POWER: SHELLEY'S BREATHING AND ARNOLD'S RUN-ONS

Whereas Arnold in *Thyrsis* cautiously associates poetic power with his use of run-ons to cross the breaks between stanzas and lines, Shelley more confidently identifies this power with a spirit animating nature and breathing through the poet's words. Many stanzas in *Adonais* are exercises in controlled breathing: occasionally they even use the word 'breath.' Stanza 50, for example, makes the last exhaling of breath in an ideal reading coincide with the phrase 'scarce extinguished breath' (line 450): the stanza and the breath expire together. In stanzas 38 and 43 the breath that labours to meet and surmount obstacles seems to compact pain in the reader's lungs with strain 'in the pure spirit' (line 338) and an almost physical sensation of its 'plastic stress' (line 381). 'Spirit' means 'breath', and Keats's own 'poignant sense of breathing and the heart', as Christopher Ricks finely calls it (1987, p. 64), informs the great concluding stanzas of Shelley's elegy.

The extraordinary immediacy that Shelley keeps imparting to 'breath' makes it easy for him to develop the word into a performative decree, or word of power. In stanza 25, as readers appropriately pause for breath after a polysyllabic Latin noun, 'annihilation', which seems to level everything in its vicinity by taking up five syllables in the line, Keats's own lips are miraculously stirred to life by his reviving breath:

> In the death-chamber for a moment Death,
> Shamed by the presence of that living Might,
> Blushed to annihilation, and the breath
> Revisited those lips, and Life's pale light
> Flashed through those limbs, so late her dear delight.

> (*Adonais*, lines 217–21)

The announcement that 'breath /Revisited those lips' is an astonishing decree. It is fortified as a performative utterance, or a miraculous 'doing-by-saying', by the strongly transitive verb, 'Revisited', at the head of line 220, and by the caesural pause after 'lips'. That break literally gives breath time to 'revisit' the lips of each reader, as if the statement were also a decree, a command no sooner spoken than obeyed.

In stanza 43, both the reader's breath and 'the one Spirit's plastic stress' (line 381) are checked by a perilous thickening of alliterative sounds and stresses. The harshly compacted triad, 'dull dense world' (line 382), is spoken as laboriously as Hamlet's words: 'And in this harsh world draw thy breath in pain /To tell my story' (*Hamlet*, v. 2. 359–60). The breath is drawn in pain becaue it has to voice three successive stresses. Momentarily thwarted by harsh accentual stresses, the final release of the spirit depends on replacing two transitive participles – 'compelling' and 'Torturing' (lines 382, 384) – with a participle, 'bursting' (line 386), that is defiantly intransitive, liberated at last from any need to shape or inform matter:

> He is a portion of the loveliness
> Which once he made more lovely: he doth bear
> His part, while the one spirit's plastic stress

Sweeps through the dull dense world, compelling there,
All new successions to the forms they wear;
Torturing th' unwilling dross that checks its flight
To its own likeness, as each mass may bear;
And bursting in its beauty and its might
From trees and beasts and men into the Heaven's light.

(*Adonais*, lines 379–87)

In *Lycidas*, even when the felt pressure of despair and pain is at its most intense, Milton manages to exclude us from any immediate experience of it. The reverberating wail of the Muse's grief for Orpheus seems to touch off all chords of lament in a mighty diapason, appropriate to the death of her own 'enchanting son'. But we are too enchanted by the intoning of sounds and the tremor of open vowels to melt with grief for Orpheus. In *Adonais*, by contrast, the constriction of pain and the intimacies of loss are as immediate as the reader's own laboured breathing. At the end of stanza 43, after clearing the triple hurdle of Aristotle's vegetable, animal and rational souls – 'trees and beasts and men' (line 387) – which are spaced out by polysyndeton and made more obstructive by the coincidence of harsh stresses and long quantities, the lungs of each reader seem as ready to 'burst' as the Spirit. Only in the lighter stresses of the stanza's concluding adverbial phrase, 'into the Heaven's light', is the reader's own breathing made lighter. Having used up their breath to experience the triumph of spirit over nature, readers may now feel content to fade out like the air they breathe. A perfect finish, as Yeats understood, makes it easier to accept death as a consummation, as an expenditure of life without remainder.

Like Urania's descent into the inspired elegist in the last stanza, the descent of breath into a reader's lungs allows the voice to drive the lines forward, even as the spirit's bark is driven:

The breath whose might I have invoked in song
Descends on me; my spirit's bark is driven,
Far from the shore, far from the trembling throng
Whose sails were never to the tempest given;
The massy earth and spherèd skies are riven!
I am borne darkly, fearfully, afar;
Whilst, burning through the inmost veil of Heaven,

The soul of Adonais, like a star,
Beacons from the abode where the Eternal are.
                              (*Adonais*, lines 487–95)

The bare final copula has a blankness on the page which only a reader's voice can quicken into life. But no reading aloud of the last hemistich can hope to achieve what the written words achieve. For we can imagine several contradictory ways of reading them. If we read the last six syllables as two dactyls, we ponder the mystery of existing eternally. If we read them as a trochee followed by two iambs, we subordinate the mysteries of eternal existence to the mystery of bare being. To speak the final copula inconclusively may even imply that the elegy remains unfinished: 'where the Eternal are [what?]' Inhabitors of the ancient earth, perhaps? 'Inheritors of unfulfilled renown' (line 397)? Like the late-breaking caesuras after 'fearfully' and 'Adonais' (lines 492–4), which create a rhythm that hovers sorrowfully over death even as it exults in the adventure of moving on, the sublime blankness of the copula verb, its withholding of any indication of what 'white radiance' (line 463) might be like, induces numbness as well as awe. A driving forward that is also a slow descent into death exactly describes the reader's experience of inhaling breath, which is gradually expended in the performative act of propelling the poem forward to its last fearful word, the most withholding word of all, which opens on the unknown.

Shelley's simultaneous mention and use of the word 'breath' displays an adventurous confidence in the power of language to convince the nerves and make something happen. It is important to note that Arnold's far more modest confidence, typical of the agnosticism and self-doubt of the Victorians, expresses itself in his initially cautious but gradually bolder crossing of the boundary spaces between stanzas. The space between stanzas 11 and 12, for example, stands for an unseen undertow more potent than any current in an Oxfordshire tributary of the Thames. Using anaphora to straddle both sides of the boundary – 'I know the wood', 'I know the... tree', 'I know these slopes' (lines 105–6, 111) – the elegist must make his steady advance across the slow effacements of time, the abyss in things. Though the anaphora builds up rhetorical momentum, so that in the absence of any period at the end of stanza 11 there is no obstacle to prevent Arnold's crossing the boundary between stanzas, he also makes us subliminally aware of that other brook, that 'unseen cataract of death', as Frost calls it, 'That spends to nothingness' (*West-Running Brook*, lines 56–7). More has gone 'Down each green bank' than 'the ploughboy's team' (line 118). By the end of stanza 12 the elegist's resurgent hopes and confidence have also subsided.

The crossing of the boundary between stanzas 11 and 12 proves to be no permanent crossing, then, but a quick reversion to old fears and doubts. By contrast, the crossing of the breaks between stanzas 17, 18 and 19 is grammatical as well as typographical: it marks a sustained transition from descriptive to performative speech. In stanza 16 a prayerful optative and injunction usher in the climactic vision: 'But hush! the upland hath a sudden loss / Of quiet!' (lines 151–2). The imperative force of 'hush' prepares for the hortatory verbs 'let me fly, and cross' (line 156), and for the final prayerful injunction, 'see', whose direct object, 'the Tree! the Tree!', is suspensefully delayed for three lines. To 'cross / Into yon farther field' (lines 156–7) is also to cross a line and to break through a boundary created by the enclosure of lines 151–6 by the widely-separated rhyming of 'loss' and 'cross'. The imperative Hear's that follow – 'Hear it from thy broad lucent Arno-vale', 'Hear it, O Thyrsis, still our tree is there!' (lines 167, 171) – can be heard calling across the boundary that divides one stanza from another. No longer an idle apostrophe to a tree (line 167), the self-referring 'Hear' of line 171, which invites us to hear other uses of 'hear', is now a poetic happening, a way of doing something unexpected with words.

No sooner, however, has Arnold crossed the space between stanzas 17 and 18 than he wakes up on the far side in a state of disintoxication and despair: 'Ah, vain!' (line 172), he concedes. When he sees the tree, he turns to share his transport of joy with his old comrade Clough, but his words to Clough are dismissed as doubly 'vain'. Buried in the Protestant cemetery at Florence, Clough is no longer in England: more to the point, he is no longer alive. Is Arnold, unlike his Romantic counterpart, too despairing? Or is he just trying to recognise, like his fellow Victorian, Clough, that ambivalence and uncertainty are central rather than peripheral features of a fully-examined life?

In stanzas 18 and 19 Arnold slowly recovers his confidence by making his utterance once again performative, a 'doing-by-saying'.

> Hear it, O Thyrsis, still our tree is there!...
>   And now in happier air,

> Wandering with the great Mother's train divine
>   (And purer or more subtle soul than thee,
>   I trow, the mighty Mother doth not see)
> Within a folding of the Apennine,
>
> Thou hearest the immortal chants of old!

> *(Thyrsis,* lines 171–81)

As Arnold momentarily strays within the folding of a parenthesis, so Clough is said to wander within a folding of the Apennine. But not even the grammatical 'wandering,' the straying of the participle 'Wandering' (line 177) from the pronoun 'Thou' it modifies, can impede the march across lines, brackets and stanzaic boundaries of the reiterated performative use of the verb 'Hear': 'Hear it, O Thyrsis,' 'And now.../Thou hearest' (lines 171–2, 181). Unlike the previous stanzaic boundary, the space between stanzas 18 and 19 acts, not as an absence, but as the divide between art and life, where the imaginary can be felt trembling for a moment on the brink of the real. As we enter stanza 19, we find ourselves in a cornfield that, though mythical, is as immediate to the senses as Arnold's Oxford landscapes. The heavenward ascent of Daphnis is made more miraculous, not this time by a run-on, but by an odd backing-away motion of the word 'brink' from the brink of a poetic line:

> And heavenward from the fountain-brink he sprang,
> And all the marvel of the golden skies.

> *(Thyrsis,* lines 189–90)

Instead of falling off the brink of the line, we find ourselves on the edge of heaven and 'all the marvel of the golden skies'.

More characteristic, however, than this strongly end-stopped line bound by punctuation, is Arnold's performative use of the run-on at the end of line 156, which allows him to cross the last remaining boundary between himself and the tree:

> Quick! let me fly, and cross
> Into yon farther field! – 'Tis done; and see,...
> Bare on its lonely ridge, the Tree, the Tree!

> *(Thyrsis,* lines 156–60)

Merely to say that he crosses into the farther field lacks a dimension of enactment, of 'doing-by-saying', that operates in the placement of the verb 'cross' at the very place where the eye must pass across the space between lines. "Tis done', Arnold says, partly because his rite of crossing boundaries has actually crossed the line break and partly because his seeing ahead is literally a peering forth across the dash and the grammatical space separating the rhyme word 'see' from its completion three lines later in the long deferred 'Tree'. Unlike Shelley's triumphal apotheosis of Adonais, Arnold's performative rites usually involve an unobtrusive use of enjambment to cross the breaks between lines and stanzas. Clough comes to life, not in response to a Shelleyan trumpet-call, but in the hyphens and dashes of 'the great town's harsh, heart-wearying roar' (line 234). Only in the poetry that lies between the lines, in the strange half-silences, fraught with suspense, may Clough finally be heard addressing Arnold, in a barely audible whisper.

TRANSFORMATIONS OF POWER: A GENRE IN TRANSITION

What inferences are we to draw? Is Victorian pastoral elegy merely a foreseeable development of its Romantic counterpart? Or are its transformations so radical that the genre itself seems under siege? Answers may depend on how 'Romantic' and 'Victorian' are defined. If a Romantic, like a Marxist, is a latter-day Pelagian, an optimist who does not believe in the Fall of man, then Shelley's Romantic gesture of bringing the 'one Spirit's plastic stress' down to earth, allowing it to sweep freely 'through the dull dense world', is clearly at odds with Arnold's Victorian attempt to revive, even in the legend of the scholar-gipsy, a traditional centre of moral or spiritual authority. Being 'driven / Far from shore' in response to a beaconing star may be all very well for visionary geniuses like Shelley or Galahad. But salvation for most Victorians will depend on work in their allotted field and service to humanity. At the heart of Arnold's attempt to revive traditional centres of authority, however, lies a negative agnostic moment of self-questioning and doubt, corresponding to the rise of Victorian agnostic theology. As doctrines of utility and self-making encourage Victorians to conduct experiments in living that allow them to evolve their idea of the world from their experience of the world, rather than the other way round, Victorian culture enters a third and final phase. Allied to the moral theology of the evangelicals and the legacy of the post-Kantian idealists, the teaching that we forge an identity for ourselves through moral vocation and work is reflected in Arnold's resolve in *Thyrsis* to become the architect, like Clough, of his own humanity and values. In substituting performative for descriptive speech, Arnold might simply seem to be reviving the Viconian, Romantic doctrine that each individual self is, by birth and by nature, an artist and creator, a lesser god, capable of fashioning new and better worlds. But the ease with which Adonais ascends to his star, collapsing the distinction between nature and grace by bestowing a kiss upon the universe, suggests that in Romantic elegy nature is still largely responsive to human control. In Victorian elegy, by contrast, the external pageant of *mens* in nature, which God alone can understand because he is its author, often seems about to end in terrifying absurdity, as in section 123 of Tennyson's *In Memoriam*. The more faithful a Victorian elegist like Arnold or Tennyson is to Vico's revolutionary idea that literature and history provide the privileged form of knowing (*verum /factum*), the greater the gulf he creates between *mens* in nature and *mens* in human affairs.

This brief comparison of *Adonais* and *Thyrsis* discloses five more specific differences between Romantic and Victorian elegy. Whereas Shelley's more consistent Platonism unifies his sensibility, conflicting philosophical impulses pull Arnold in opposite directions. Shelley, moreover, never doubts the intrinsic worth of Keats's 'godlike mind' (*Adonais*, line 258) or his own ability to celebrate it. Arnold, by contrast, is deeply critical of Clough: tortured at the centre of his faith, he spends most of his elegy preparing for the kind of ritual exercise of verbal power that Shelley blithely takes for granted. A third difference is the Romantic elegist's preference for the view from inside: he draws us into his elegy, making our breath conspire with the spirit's 'plastic stress' and the breathings of Urania. Arnold, on the other hand, excludes us from intimacy: he marks the limits of sympathetic trespass. A marginal figure and observer, looking on from outside, Arnold seldom allows his empathy with Thyrsis to deepen into sympathy. This last contrast brings us to a fourth difference. Though the stanzaic form of both elegists tries to adjudicate the rival claims of parts and wholes, Shelley is a monist, consistently subordinating the many to the One, whereas Arnold, like Tennyson, dreads absorption of the individual soul in a general soul. However threatened Arnold may feel by the 'world's multitudinousness', he is compelled to honour pluralism. Finally, as a descriptive poet, Arnold finds himself entombed in a grave of dead words, the legacy of a correspondence theory of truth. Though responsive to 'the immortal chants of old' (*Thyrsis*, line 181), the Victorian elegist is a sceptic who fears that pastoral convention may also shackle him to a mummified mythology. Shelley, by contrast, believes that forces can be released by the pastoral elegist's words of power. He forges metaphorical identities that retain strong traces of a magical view of language.

Both Arnold's wavering allegiance to the values of Cambridge Platonism and Shelley's more consistent Platonism can be studied in their verse forms. In Shelley's hands, the Spenserian stanza becomes a war zone in which the Platonic One wages battle against the constraints of matter and celebrates in the concluding alexandrine its anticipated victory. The final release of the *c* rhyme (*ababbcbcc*) is celebrated in the hypermetric alexandrine, where it seems to boast of its victory over the *a* and *b* rhymes, just as 'the white radiance of Eternity' boasts of its victory over the shattered 'many-coloured glass' (*Adonais*, lines 462–3). In stanza 52, the One at first occupies a mere four-syllable unit, and six syllables are allotted to the changing many. But in the contest between Heaven and Earth, Heaven has begun to crowd out its adversary: seven syllables – or six if we take 'Heaven's' as monosyllabic – are devoted to the One's domain, while the remaining shadows of earth are given a mere four syllables:

> The One remains, the many change and pass;
> Heaven's light forever shines, Earth's shadows fly;

> (*Adonais*, lines 460–1)

As spirit wages its Platonic war against matter, and the One combats the many, victory is predictable but never final. Because of Shelley's metrical dexterity, the sense of fulfilled expectation also seems the opposite of obvious.

Unlike the Romantic elegist, whose Platonic allegiances are seldom in doubt, Arnold veers in *Thyrsis* between the realism of a Cambridge Platonist like Joseph Glanvill, the scholar-gipsy's seventeenth-century chronicler, and the nominalism of Vico and Herder. Even Arnold's verse form becomes a playing field on which the ambitions of the Cambridge Platonist, in quest of some authoritative ground, the equivalent of a Platonic Idea or universal, is continually being challenged by the scepticism of a Viconian nominalist, who would locate the truth nearer home. In Arnold's stanza the hallmark of the Petrarchan sonnet – the quatrains' *abba* rhyme scheme – does not appear until the last four lines, where only half the octave is given. Arnold not only reverses the order of octave and sestet in a Petrarchan sonnet. He also reverses the pattern Keats uses in *Ode to a Nightingale*. In Keats the Petrarchan sestet comes second, and the quatrain – in Keats's case Shakespearian rather than Petrarchan – comes first. Arnold recalls Romantic convention, but self-consciously inverts it. In seeming to stabilise the wayward, oracular impulse that is sanctioned in Keats by the irregularity of the Pindaric ode, Arnold's elegy accommodates two conflicting impulses. He shares the oracular poet's desire for some authoritative ground, and to that end he uses ancient pastoral conventions and the ode's irregular line-lengths to revive the mysteries of Cambridge Platonism. At the same time, he believes that to be accessible, Victorian values must be fashioned through some version of Clough's religion of work: it is not enough to lose oneself, like Tennyson's Galahad, in pursuit of some elusive grail or Unknowable God. To this second end Arnold transplants the mysteries: creating an authentic English form of pastoral out of homely, but possibly more enduring materials, he writes of Platonism on very familiar Oxford soil. Though Glanvill is a Cambridge – not an Oxford – Platonist, whose scholar-gipsy will act only after he has something to teach, Arnold, like Clough, is committed to the Viconian doctrine that he will know only after he acts. Truth becomes a property of what the elegist himself can create out of common words and familiar themes.

A second difference between the Romantic and the Victorian elegist is the reluctance of the latter to use ritualised words of praise. In *Adonais* Shelley does all he can to distance his own adverse view of Keats's early poetry from the criticism of the hostile reviewer who hastened Keats's death. Like the dream looking at the tear awakened in Keats by the dream itself (*Adonais*, lines 85–7), Keats is both a dead fellow-poet and an introjected power, a region of Shelley's mind. Though Clough was Arnold's closest friend, no comparable appropriation of the dead man takes place in *Thyrsis*. It is true that Arnold's refusal to force his praise of Clough early in the elegy makes his tribute at the end all the more moving. The power of his tribute to a 'fugitive and gracious light' not to be 'bought and sold' on the markets of this world (lines 201, 205) comes in no small part from Arnold's recognising elsewhere the limits of an imperfect sympathy. But Arnold is far more diffident than Shelley. He is sceptical about his capacity to address his dead friend, and far more critical of Clough than Shelley is of Keats. The Victorian elegist spends most of his poem preparing for what his Romantic predecessor confidently assumes at the start: the mourner's power to praise the dead poet and address him as a living presence.

Implicit in the distinction I have just drawn is a third difference: Shelley gives the interior view, and Arnold the view from outside. As an alienated Victorian, Arnold gives an unforgettable sense of what it is to be an outsider, on the boundaries or margin. Whereas Arnold wants to exclude us from intimacies of feeling he once shared with Clough, Shelley can experience events from the perspective of even a Judas or Cain. Even in loading vituperation upon Keats's destroyer, for example, Shelley finds it hard not to empathise. Sundered syntax conveys, not just the mourner's anguish, but also the desperate swoop and rush of the murderer's own feelings, as words are shredded to pieces in an agony of frustration:

> It felt, yet could escape, the magic tone
> Whose prelude held all envy, hate, and wrong,
> But what was howling in one breast alone,
> Silent with expectation of the song,
> Whose master's hand is cold, whose silver lyre unstrung.

> (*Adonais*, lines 320–4)

Until the grammatical sense is completed, it sounds as if Keats's music contains, rather than subdues, 'all envy, hate, and wrong', and that, as an exception to that disorder, only the 'howling' in the murderer's 'breast' is able to express the accents of genuine grief. Because 'Silent' is sundered by an intervening line and a half from 'held', the word whose sense it reaches back to complete, the grammar, like the viper, is made to sound for a moment quite as 'unstrung' as the dead poet's lyre. Arnold has little of Shelley's 'negative capability', except perhaps for domestic animals and pets. The Victorian elegist hopes that posterity will remember him as the owner of a pathetic, soul-fed little creature, with long, 'liquid, melancholy' eyes (*Geist's Grave*, line 13), who walked on all fours and who lived only four short years, one for each leg. Arnold is a poet who can love animals if not people. Even when he allows us to empathise with Clough's premature migrations, he refuses to soften toward Clough's impetuosities. Any sliding from empathy into sympathy is gently resisted. Dogs have one advantage over people: they will not argue back, the way Clough did with Arnold. And so the Victorian elegist can be closer in some ways to Geist and Kaiser than he can be to Clough or Wordsworth, or even to his own father in *Rugby Chapel*. Perhaps this is why the elegies on dogs are far warmer poems than the austere *Rugby Chapel* or even the reflectively solemn *Thyrsis*, which are seldom so full of solicitude or good temper.

A fourth difference between Romantic and Victorian elegy concerns the way in which each elegist tries to honour what is individual without allowing the whole to fall apart into fragmentation and separateness. Like his beloved Geist, Arnold is a Shelley on all fours, more in danger of being overwhelmed by the world's multitudinousness. More eager than Arnold to bring the parts of his elegy into ampler connection with the 'One,' Shelley allows no run-overs between stanzas. The One controls the many, and the boundaries proclaiming the One's authority are strictly observed. *Thyrsis*, by contrast, uses a longer ten-line stanza, whose boundaries Arnold feels free to cross, even while respecting the limits imposed by his ingenious adaptation of ode and sonnet forms.

It is not easy for a monist like Shelley to adjust the claims of the many and the One: there is always a danger that the Romantic elegist will retreat into a Platonic mist that God himself would think twice before penetrating. 'The burning fountain' in *Adonais*, for example (line 339), is a kind of nuclear furnace or volcano. If this furnace does not truly absorb the spirit, then the spirit changes but is not truly a portion of the eternal. If, on the other hand, the spirit is truly absorbed by the fountain, it becomes 'unquenchably the same' (line 341). But then in annihilating all sustaining difference it also annihilates Keats. Though logic cannot quite resolve the dilemma, Shelley provides at least a formal demonstration of how the parts and the whole might harmoniously relate. He grants each Spenserian stanza its own autonomy, but without allowing it to devour its parts too greedily by collapsing a chain of intricately linked sounds and rhymes.

In *Thyrsis*, by contrast, Arnold sometimes dawdles with the painted shell of the universe, lingering fondly over the 'blond meadow-sweet,' the 'darting swallows' and 'light water-gnats' (lines 124–5), even while deploying them in his *ubi sunt* formula. Unlike Shelley, he is even prepared to honour a wayward sound or half-forgotten impression, which he is likely to restore just when it seems to have dropped from view. In stanza 13, for example, 'shore' echoes 'door', but at a distance of six lines. Like a dying echo of 'door,' 'shore' falls off into silence at the end of its short, three-stress line (line 126). Because Arnold's stanzas read like Petrarchan sonnets from which he has removed the octave, we have the uneasy feeling that the rhymes and thoughts we hear should echo something that has gone before, something much more fleeting or subliminal than anything we hear in Shelley. The Romantic elegist is a self-confident visionary. His Victorian counterpart gives us a more tentative experience of *déja vu*, of vision which eludes the memory and defies precise recall.

A final difference between Arnold and Shelley is the former's sense that classical elegy is not just a genre in transition: it is a genre under siege, whose very survival is at stake. How can its traditional language and ancient symbols hope to live again if the biblical beliefs and classical legends that nourished them have now become mere superannuated myths? Traditionally, a pastoral elegy expresses corporate grief, like a liturgy. But because Oxford has changed and Clough died abroad, there is really only one mourner in *Thyrsis*, the solitary elegist himself. Mourners like Byron and Moore, who attend Keats's funeral in *Adonais*, are displaced by an inventory of absent people who might, under different circumstances, have mourned Clough. Where is Sibylla, late keeper of the local inn (line 4)? Where is the girl who unmoored their skiff (line 121)? Where are the mowers (line 127)? Pastoral conventions survive in Arnold, but often in disguised form. He replaces the traditional floral tributes in *Lycidas* with native English flowers, with the bounty of musk carnations, 'gold-dusted snapdragon' and 'Sweet-William with his homely cottage-smell' (lines 63–5). And these flowers in no sense adorn the dead friend's hearse, since Clough has died in Florence and been buried abroad.

Shelley's agnostic essay *On a Future State* and Arnold's sceptical essays on religion identify an area of overlap between them. For Shelley, God is beyond being and language, as Plato says, and 'the deep truth is imageless' (*Prometheus Unbound*, II, iv, 118). Arnold's agnosticism may have originated in the doctrine of learned ignorance advocated by his seventeenth-century hero, Joseph

Glanvill. But Arnold is agnostic in a further sense than Shelley. In one of the reading-lists found in his early diaries, Arnold makes mention of Victor Cousin's lectures on modern philosophy. As I have argued elsewhere, Victorian agnosticism can be said to begin with Sir William Hamilton's seminal review essay on Cousin's course of philosophy, published in the *Edinburgh Review* in October 1829 (Shaw, 1987, pp. 142–3). The sublime transcendence of the Hindu God apparently appealed to Arnold, who was already familiar with the grandeur of that concept from his study of Victor Cousin, from his knowledge of the theology of the *Bhagavad Gita*, and from an awareness of the striking affinities between the Vedic apology for art and his own critical idea of disinterested objectivity. But the 'incognisable' God of Kantian, agnostic thinkers such as William Hamilton and Henry Longueville Mansel is also criticised by Arnold for being too Asiatic, too indistinguishable from the Brahma of Indian theology. Arnold tries to retain the venerable emotive meaning of mystery words like 'God' and 'immortality' while giving them a new descriptive meaning with some specific content in sense experience. In his prose writings Arnold keeps proclaiming the futility of metaphysics, and concludes that all transcendent religious speculation, as opposed to concrete moral and cultural inquiry, is meaningless.

In Romantic elegy essence precedes existence: in Victorian elegy the reverse is true. The change of models from Shelley to Arnold involves a change from a devolutionary to an evolutionary scheme. Theories of evolution and self-making prompt Victorian elegists as diverse as Arnold, Tennyson and Swinburne to conduct experiments in living that allow them to evolve their idea of the world from their experience of the world. By contrast, Shelley's cosmos in *Adonais* is as hierarchical as Milton's. Despite its yearning for a developing world, in harmony with the Romantic poet's revolutionary temper, *Adonais* has a strangely medieval feel. The soul's Platonic essence, 'the white radiance' of its 'Eternity' (*Adonais*, line 463), *precedes* existence. Like Shelley's 'dome of many-coloured glass' (line 462), life on earth 'stains' the mind's transcendent consciousness, restricting it to Kant's two forms of space and time. According to William James, *Adonais* illustrates a 'transmission' or 'filtration' theory of immortality (see Gardner, 1983, pp. 323–4). Because Keats's brain keeps transmitting his experiences to a 'godlike mind' that exists before he is born and presumably outlasts his earthly life, there is no need for God to recreate Keats when he dies. His earthly conciousness is an interval of darkness between two eternities of light.

In striking contrast, Arnold is convinced that Clough creates his own immortality. If Clough possesses life after death, it is because of the inexhaustible energy of the new life he originates on this side of the grave. The key to Arnold's theory of immortality is the remarkable passage in *Culture and Anarchy* where he attacks Puritanism's merely mechanical use of the word 'resurrection'. 'In nine cases out of ten where St Paul thinks and speaks of resurrection', Arnold claims, he is referring 'to a new life before the physical death of the body, and not after it' (5: 183). Since we are all architects of our humanity and values, nobody's immortality can be guaranteed in advance. Moreover, the dead Clough is powerless to speak to Arnold until Arnold, in his search for Clough, has come, 'within the limits of his present life, to a new life' himself. In emulating Clough's own self-making, Arnold substitutes for essentialist theology's 'mechanical and remote conception of a resurrection hereafter' (5: 183) St Paul's own notion that life in the resurrection is already here, waiting to be recognised.

Like Nietzsche's God, Arnold's Thyrsis is not really dead: he is merely buried in a dead language. Until Arnold can substitute a new model, a new 'taste in universes', as C. S. Lewis calls it (1964, p. 222), Clough is merely the casualty of the Puritan use of the word 'resurrection' in a single mechanical sense that seems wholly to miss or change the 'grand Pauline idea' of a 'living and near conception of a resurrection now' (5: 183). Shelley's Romantic cosmology assumes, in Lewis's phrase, 'that all perfect things precede all imperfect things'. In Arnold's new Viconian world, however, 'it is axiomatic that "the starting point (*Entwicklungsgrund*) is always lower than what is developed"' (Lewis, 1964, p. 222). Readers may have to play Orpheus to Eurydice: from a grave of dead words, they may be asked to raise up spirits, as the voice itself resurrects from marks on the printed page the ghosts of departed sounds. Even in *Adonais*, for example, the conservative Platonic model of Keats's frightened 'angel soul' (line 153), the mere 'earthly guest' of its body, introduces a Gnostic split that is quite at odds with the radical incarnational model of a Neoplatonic world-soul sweeping through nature. Just as Shelley, in the strangest, most beautiful stanzas of *Adonais*, has to turn Keats from a noun into a verb, into an energy streaming through the verses like a comet's hair, so Arnold discovers that Clough, like the Dorian shepherds and vanished ploughboys, can be reclaimed from the grave of a discarded classical mythology only by the elegist's own ritual exercise of power. For a moment, in stanza 12, after the poetry of the classical myths has become 'the reality,' as Arnold says in his Preface to Wordsworth, and sceptical 'philosophy the illusion', the revival of a lost glory carries the elegist across the divide between sestet and quatrain. The strong run-ons extend to the penultimate line, where 'gleam' and its rhyme word 'team' seem to come from different planets. Though a ploughshare may gleam, this is Wordsworth's visionary gleam. And 'team' reaches out to rhyme with a different part of speech, a verb, which is still awaiting grammatical completion in a direct object, the 'orphans of the flowery prime' (line 120). Though such feats of resurrection could be performed only by Arnold, we seem to hear behind them the voice of classical elegy itself. This we feel, even in an age of growing scepticism and doubt like the Victorian, is the kind of faith in the magical properties of words, and in an energy common to man and nature, that pastoral poetry exists to commemorate and preserve.

Such created realities as Clough's hortatory whisper, which is physically absent but spiritually present, preserve an openness of attitude that is foreign to the strong sense of closure in Shelley's elegy. When the 'plastic stress' in *Adonais* empties into the world, in a Neoplatonic version of Paul's conception of *kenosis*, what dies for Shelley is the antithesis between a human subject and divine object. But so remote has God become for the agnostic Arnold, that when he starts to search for an abstract formula that will give peace to his soul without insulting his intelligence, he finds God has become as fugitive and elusive as the notorious elm tree. Even the final whisper amid the heart-wearying roar is not a sound Arnold actually hears. Because the whisper is an illusion made real by a fiat of the poet's inner ear, his culminating hope must be inscribed in a tentative optative mood: 'Let in thy voice a whisper often come', he prays diffidently (*Thyrsis*, line 135). Both Shelley and Arnold seem to understand God as a verb. But when the godlike soul of Adonais ascends with ease to its star, Shelley is using God as 'a verb of simple asserted existence', whereas Arnold understands God as a 'verb implying a process accomplishing itself' (Frye, 1982, p. 17). Instead of closing anything off dogmatically, Arnold, like many post-Romantic poets, is ready to believe and quest intransitively. Like Clough and the scholar-gipsy, the Victorian elegist 'travels yet the loved hill-side' (*Thyrsis*, line 240), not in pursuit of something objective like Adonais' star, the elm tree, or even God conceived as a noun, but in an act of disinterested searching as such. Unlike a boundary, a horizon is not a finite line: it is always relative to the elegist's changing point of view, like the untravelled world glimpsed through the arch by Tennyson's Ulysses, whose margin fades for ever and for ever as he moves. Because Arnold wants to find a vision that promises still more vision, he prefers to wander in the wilderness like the children of Israel rather than arrive at the Promised Land itself. To live with horizons rather than boundaries Arnold is content to be homeless.

3

Aurality and Re-vision: The Case of Wordsworth and Tennyson[1]

JOANNA E. RAPF

The 'romantic' temperament has been defined in many ways since Schlegel talked about it as 'the expression of a secret longing for the chaos which is perpetually striving for new and marvellous births, which lies hidden in the very womb of orderly creation' (Thorlby 1966, p. 2). Early in our own century, although A. O. Lovejoy elegantly insisted that there was no 'romanticism', only 'romanticisms', Morse Peckham was able to encompass the term under the umbrella classification of a worldview based on *becoming* as opposed to a neo-classical emphasis on *being*. More recently, L. J. Swingle (1987) and Susan Wolfson (1986) have pointed to the interrogative mode as a defining element of 'romantic discourse', a rhetorical device that situates the poetry in the condition of doubt. But regardless of the source and manifestation of its temperament, there is something about 'Romantic' poetry that ideally aspires to silence, beyond the noisy chaos of aspiring births. In the *Intimations Ode*, Wordsworth writes:

> But for those first affections,
> Those shadowy recollections,
> Which, be they what they may,
> Are yet the fountain-light of all our day,
> Are yet a master-light of all our seeing;
> Uphold us, cherish, and have power to make
> Our noisy years seem moments in the being
> Of the eternal Silence.... (152–9)[2]

These 'noisy years' also reverberate throughout Tennyson's poetry and stand in sharp contrast to the silence that is achieved at

60

the end of human endeavour, at death. At the end of *In Memoriam* VII, after stating with characteristic bluntness, 'He is not here', Hallam is no more, Tennyson writes: 'The noise of life begins again,/ And ghastly through the drizzling rain,/ On the bald street breaks the blank day'.[3]

It has long been commonplace to stress 'vision', and its concomitant concept, 'visionary', but, paradoxically, 'Romantic vision' is often achieved not through the sense of sight, but through hearing, listening to the point where sound finally dissolves into what Wordsworth ideally calls 'eternal Silence'. Herbert F. Tucker has written extensively about Tennyson's use of the same two words in *Ulysses* which he sees as a conscious rejection of Wordsworthian immanence and an assertion of Tennysonian alienation (1988, pp. 223–8). Significantly, Tennyson juxtaposes his use of 'eternal silence' with the phrases 'something more,/ A bringer of new things', and he stresses the desire of Ulysses,

> To follow knowledge like a sinking star,
> Beyond the utmost bound of human thought.

> (lines 31–2)

The same yearning for transcendence is here, as in Wordsworth, the same desire for that 'immortal sea' (*Intimations Ode*, line 167). It is just that the younger poet is unable to accept blindly an idealism not founded in culturally-accepted dogma. And so his Ulysses sets off on a mortal sea, 'To strive, to seek, to find', but with no assurance of a distant shore.

Margaret Lourie has described Tennyson as a 'Romantic Revisionist', although she stresses his acknowledged links to Keats and builds from there to argue for 'an equal debt to Shelley' (1979, p. 5). But, in many ways, Tennyson is closer to the feelings of doubt and loss that permeate the best writing of that first generation of Romantics: the torment of a loveless Coleridge adrift in an existentially meaningless universe or the passion of a Wordsworth, straddling the past and present, struggling with doubt and finding faith in the truth of feeling as opposed to the truth of reason. Certainly it is the emphasis on the truth of feeling that is one of the characteristics of so-called 'Romantic art', although by the time of Tennyson it has become increasingly difficult even to have faith in feeling as a means of transcending our 'noisy years'. Yet what Wordsworth said in his revolutionary *Preface* to the *Lyrical Ballads* in distinguishing between his poems and 'the popular Poetry of the day' became the foundation for almost all poetry that followed: 'the feeling therein developed gives importance to the action and situation, and not the action and situation to the feeling' (Wordsworth 1965, p. 248). What is rarely noted, however, in discussing this commonplace of 'romantic art', is how often the source of feeling is something heard. To look at only two of the more famous poems from the *Lyrical Ballads, The Idiot Boy* is built around hearing the phrase, 'The cocks did crow to-whoo, to-whoo,/And the sun did shine so cold', and we are drawn into *Tintern Abbey* initially through the sound of water, and only secondarily through the sight of the landscape:

> Five years have past; five summers, with the length
> Of five long winters! and again *I hear*
> These waters rolling from their mountain-springs
> With a soft inland murmur.

> (lines 1–4, italics mine)

In the 'Conclusion' of *The Prelude*, as another example, the reification of the unifying power of the Imagination is achieved when darkness has shrouded the visible world and the dominant sense is of sound:

> The Moon hung naked in a firmament
> Of azure without cloud, and at my feet
> Rested a *silent* sea of hoary mist.
> A hundred hills their dusky backs upheaved
> All over this *still* ocean; and beyond...
> ... the clear presence of the full-orbed Moon,
> Who, from her sovereign elevation, gazed
> Upon the billowy ocean as it lay
> All meek and *silent*, save that through a rift –
> Not distant from the shore whereon we stood,
> A fixed, abysmal, gloomy breathing-place –
> Mounted the *roar* of waters, torrents, streams
> Innumerable, *roaring with one voice* !
> Heard over earth and sea, and, in that hour,
> For so it seemed, *felt* by the starry heavens.

> (lines 40–4, 53–62, italics mine)[4]

Feeling is achieved through the experience of sound, the 'roaring with one voice', that links heaven and earth and sea.

Tucker has argued that, as with Wordsworth, 'the most memorable and characteristic moments in Tennyson's poetry occur as sight is swallowed up in darkness and the visual is overwhelmed by an ascending power of sound that moans round with many voices, voices that themselves merge...into the roar or pulse of an inevitable, unutterable power' (1983, p. 12). In *Ulysses*, as the leader prepares to depart, Tennyson writes that 'The long day wanes: the slow moon climbs: the deep/ *Moans round with many voices*' (lines 55–6, italics mine). At moments of intense feeling such as these, sight is dimmed by darkness and the ears take in the prelinguistic, primordial sounds of essential being, like the hollow sound of the sea heard in a conch, or the 'sound as of the sea' at the end of *Mariana in the South*, heard as night deepens 'through the silent spheres' telling her of a time when she shall cease to be alone, forgotten, and forlorn.

It makes sense that sound should predominate over sight within the context of Romanticism because of its unique relationship to interiority. 'The human sense of sight', Walter Ong has argued, 'is adapted best to light diffusely reflected from surfaces.... The eye does not perceive an interior strictly as an interior'. Sound, on the other hand, 'can register interiority without violating it' (1982, p. 71).[5] Since human consciousness is totally interiorised, sound offers the best possibility of receiving its truth or essence without distortion or 'violation'. Wordsworth says this quite clearly in Book II of *The Prelude*:

> ...for I would walk alone
> Under the *quiet* stars, and at that time
> Have *felt whate'er there is of power in sound*
> *To breathe an elevated mood, by form*
> *Or image unprofaned*; and I would stand,
> If the night blackened with a coming storm,
> Beneath some rock, *listening to notes that are*
> *The ghostly language of the ancient earth,*
> Or make their dim abode in distant winds.
> Thence did I drink the visionary power...

(lines 302–11, italics mine)

Images, what we see with our eyes, can be 'profaned'. The poet, therefore, drinks 'the visionary power' through his ears, hearing 'the ghostly language of the ancient earth' which was spoken before there were men and women to distort experience through 'naming'. Ong has perfectly articulated this essential aspect of sound when he writes that it 'incorporates' as opposed to sight, which 'isolates'. 'Whereas sight situates the observer outside what he views, at a distance, sound pours into the hearer.... You can immerse yourself in hearing, in sound; there is no way to immerse yourself similarly in sight' (1982, p. 72).

There are, consequently, far fewer examples of *mis-hearing* in the literature of the nineteenth century than of *mis-perceiving*. Wordsworth, who called the eye 'the most despotic of our senses' (*XII*, 129), writes often of terrifying misperception: in the boat-stealing episode in Book I of *The Prelude*, the poet's guilt and fear make it seem as if a huge black mountain peak, 'with a purpose of its own / And measured motion like a living thing', strode after him (lines 383–4). Sight fails the seer completely during the Simplon Pass section of Book VI as Wordsworth and his companions choose the wrong path, 'the only track now visible' (line 570), and have their 'hopes that pointed to the clouds' dashed as they learn there was no epiphany, no experience of an apex, for without knowing it, they '*had crossed the Alps*' (line 591) – an anti-apocalypse, a kind of poetic apocope, where the loss of the one moment necessary for visionary completion deflates the 'Romantic' endeavour to transcend the limitations of mortality.

In his later years Wordsworth even wrote what is unfortunately a rather tedious poem entitled *On the Power of Sound*. Like so many of the poet's later works, when an almost stern faith had replaced the daring explorations of the darkness of doubt that characterise his early years, it lacks the *feeling* that imbues his more famous poetry with the intensity of greatness, but it does contain some lines that reveal how important aurality had always been for him. The opening three lines – 'Thy functions are ethereal / As if within thee dwelt a glancing mind, / Organ of vision!' – explicitly locate the ear as the source from which to receive 'visionary power'. The concluding stanza of the poem quite rightly emphasises that in Genesis 1:3 it was sound, the *voice* of God, that gave birth to light: a 'Voice to Light gave Being' (line 209). As in the *Intimations Ode*, and with clear echoes from that poem, Wordsworth suggests that the final quest is to return to that 'eternal Silence' from which we all began: 'O Silence! are Man's noisy years / No more than moments of thy life?' (lines 217–18).

Tennyson's most completely aural poem may be *Maud*, which opens with the sound of an echo which speaks '"Death"', and the expression of a longing for 'calm' (line 76). Section after section of this poem begins with the hearing of sound – 'A voice by the cedar tree' (line 162), 'Did I hear it half in a doze / Long since, I know not where?' (lines 285–6), 'I wish I could hear again / The chivalrous battle-song' (lines 381–2), 'Birds in the high Hall-garden... They were crying and calling' (lines 412–15), 'Is that enchanted moan only the swell / Of the long waves that roll in yonder bay?' (lines 660–1), 'All night have the roses heard / The flute, violin, bassoon' (lines 862–3), culminating in the powerful beginning of section V in Part II where we again hear the sounds of death, but this time evoked by the rhythm and sense of the language itself:

> And the hoofs of the horses beat, beat,
> The hoofs of the horses beat,
> Beat into my scalp and my brain,
> With never an end to the stream of passing feet,
> Driving, hurrying, marrying, burying,
> Clamour and rumble, and ringing and clatter,
> And here beneath it is all as bad,
> For I thought the dead had peace, but it is not so;
> To have no peace in the grave, is that not sad?
> But up and down and to and fro,
> Ever about me the dead men go;
> And then to hear a dead man chatter
> Is enough to drive one mad.
>
> (lines 246–58)

Noteworthy through all these brief excerpts from *Maud* that highlight its auditory structure is that familiar 'romantic' mode of the question growing out of the condition of doubt: darkness leads to hearing which leads to questioning, even rhetorical questioning about how sad it is not to have peace in death. One of the most interesting sections of *Maud* in terms of the use of the relationship between darkness, sound and death and Tennyson's affinity with Wordsworth is in I.xiv where the narrator talks of standing by Maud's garden gate in the greyness of the waning night:

I heard no sound where I stood
But the rivulet on from the lawn
Running down to my own dark wood;
Or the voice of the long sea-wave as it swelled
Now and then in the dim-grey dawn;
But I looked, and round, all round the house I beheld
The death-white curtain drawn;
Felt a horror over me creep,
Prickle my skin and catch my breath,
Knew that the death-white curtain meant but sleep,
Yet I shuddered and thought like a fool of the sleep of death.

(lines 516–26)

The parallel here with Wordsworth's *Strange fits of passion* is quite striking. In both a lover approaches or stands near the house of his loved one and in semi-darkness (the 'dim-grey dawn' of Tennyson or the night lit by the 'evening moon' in Wordsworth) hears a sound that suggests the relentless process of time, rhythmic and unending, in contrast to the human heart, that will stop beating. The speaker in Tennyson's poem hears water, a 'rivulet' or 'the voice of the long sea-wave', while in Wordsworth's poem the sound is that which comes at the end of *Maud*, the horse's hoofs: '...hoof after hoof / He raised, and never stopped' (lines 21–2). The result in both is the evocation of death, the horror of that eternal sleep that leaves the living so empty. Although the thought is chastised as 'foolish' in Tennyson and 'wayward' in Wordsworth, these one-line admonitions hardly assuage the consuming passions – what Wordsworth rightly calls 'Strange fits of passion' – that link madness to love and death.

The use of Wordsworthian language in *The Two Voices* again invites a reading that sees in Tennyson a re-visioning of 'Romantic' idealism. Begun before the death of Hallam, it was finished in the full swell of grief after hearing the devastating news. Tennyson was reading a good deal of Wordsworth at this time, and the voices of this poem aurally present two sides of an argument that is, in somewhat different terms, set out in Wordsworth's *Intimations Ode* between youthful idealism and the 'inevitable yoke' of despairing adult experience. There is a pragmatic acceptance of the inevitability of process in both Wordsworth and Tennyson, but unlike Wordsworth, Tennyson does not embellish it with philosophic grandeur. Rather, he writes simply in a poem such as *Ulysses*, 'that which we are, we are' (line 67), or more negatively in the words of the 'silent voice':

> 'A life of nothings, nothing-worth,
> From that first nothing ere his birth
> To that last nothing under earth!'

> (lines 331–3)

But to the question of loss, the interrogation of which might lead to what Coleridge, in *Limbo* called 'the blank-naught-at-all' –'Whither is fled the visionary gleam?/Where is it now, the glory and the dream?' – Wordsworth characteristically evokes an answer: 'In the faith that looks through death,/In years that bring the philosophic mind' (lines 186–7). The positive voice in *The Two Voices*, searching for a rebuttal to the vision of a 'life of nothings', similarly echoes Wordsworth:

> Moreover, something is or seems,
> That touches me with *mystic gleams*,
> Like glimpses of forgotten dreams –
>
> Of something felt, like something here;
> Of something done, I know not where;
> Such as no language may declare.

> (lines 379–84, italics mine)

This also sounds a little like *Tintern Abbey* – 'a sense sublime/Of something far more deeply interfused' – but the 'dull, one-sided voice' (line 202) in Tennyson does not allow the comfort of Wordsworthian peripeteia. 'Thy pain is a reality' (line 387), it insists and, as the dialogue closes, neither speaker has been more convincing than the other.

Tennyson does not share the inner strength that the mature Wordsworth came to find in the memory of the past for the nourishment of the present and the shaping of the 'philosophic mind'. The difference between the two here is overtly manifested by the different forms they chose: Wordsworth an introspective lyrical ode and Tennyson the externalised form of a dramatic dialogue.[6] Like *The Ancient Sage* some fifty years later, with its contrast between the devout words of the Seer and the words of cruel fact on the 'scroll of verse' carried by the one who follows him out of his ancient city, idealism and painful reality play a see-saw game in Tennyson. Where Wordsworth finds a spiritual *locus* in the natural world, in his memories of a sense of place, Tennyson is on shakier ground, so to speak. *The Two Voices* initially gives the reader no context. It is not until line 400 that we discover that the dialogue we overhear has taken place in a room at dawn. The poet rises and opens a window so that both literally and symbolically light comes in. From the window he watches a family walking to church. The unity of man, woman and child, the sense of one generation passing both life and faith to another which was earlier belied in the passage about a 'life of nothings', melts the frozen heart of the poet and it begins 'to beat, / Remembering its ancient heat' (lines 422–3).

Whether or not the use of the word 'ancient' here is supposed to summon thoughts of Coleridge's *The Rime of the Ancient Mariner* is purely speculative, yet what follows can certainly be compared to that moment of unself-conscious identification with the water snakes that releases the Mariner from his spiritual stasis: 'And I blessed them unaware'. Tennyson's speaker says, 'I blest them', and at that moment 'The dull and bitter voice was gone', replaced by a second voice that mysteriously says, 'I see the end, and know the good' (lines 424, 426, 432). This is enough to transform the gloomy, self-absorbed speaker into an apparent 'romantic' optimist, even ending his poem with the same word with which Coleridge concludes his rescue from despair in *Dejection: An Ode* : 'Rejoice'.

But unlike Wordsworth, who, as he grew older, seems to have forced himself into a comfortable faith, Coleridge and Tennyson remained tormented by doubt. If the Mariner thinks his blessing of the water snakes set him free, there is, in fact, no firm or factual evidence for this except the testimony of the Mariner himself who may well be deranged from his ordeal at sea. 'He prayeth well, who loveth well/ Both Man and bird and beast' is a moral tag that has been criticised as inadequate for Coleridge's poem just as the Sabbath morn conversion has been criticised for Tennyson's (Ricks 1977, p. 175). However, it may well be that both poets have the same ironic intention here, and that in echoing Coleridge, Tennyson, like his predecessor, is evoking the desperate human need to explain the inexplicable, to create myths, even to invent gods. Coleridge, who in his most honest works had too penetrating a mind to deceive himself into faith, is probably closer to Tennyson in this respect than Wordsworth who was always seeking 'resolutions'.

In some ways, this determination to force resolutions, to replace questions with answers, makes Wordsworth an uncharacteristic 'Romantic', or perhaps a better description is 'reluctant Romantic'. This is because his best poetry, up through about 1810, although it may have longed for the comfort of believing that everything has its reasons in this 'best of all possible worlds', still refused to yield to easy solutions. In his inner struggle to fix what he called in Book I of *The Prelude* 'the wavering balance' (line 622) of his mind, to resolve that uneasy tension between the terror of madness and the drab solidity of certainty, came the intensity of his art. But unlike the later Romantics, unlike his friend Coleridge, he was not intellectually, philosophically or emotionally suited to the condition of doubt.

In an ability to accept the anguish of doubt, Tennyson is closer to Coleridge, Shelley, Keats and even the iconoclast, Byron. But the best of his poetry is like Wordsworth's in that it has its origins in loss, in moments of spiritual and creative crisis, and it attempts to trace a path of recovery. But where Wordsworth found his imagination, and thereby meaning and comfort, through the contemplation of loss, Tennyson found little peace. As Jerome J. McGann (1983) has suggested, the 'Romantic' reponse in finding solace in the imagination may in fact be a culturally determined one. By the mid-nineteenth century, such a simple faith was seen to be illusory and those poets of faith were seen as 'ineffectual angels' – to quote Arnold on Shelley – mere dreamers of another existence removed from the economic and political realities of Victorian England.

Often cited in this respect is the comparison between Margaret in Wordsworth's *Ruined Cottage* who, until her death, holds out the hope of her husband's return, and Tennyson's Mariana who admits simply, 'He will not come' (line 82). Both poems are structured around images of desolation which are symbolic of the inner lives of the abandoned women. Wordsworth writes of Margaret's garden:

>   ... carnations, once
> Prized for surpassing beauty, and no less
> For the peculiar pains they had required,
> Declined their languid heads, wanting support.
> The cumbrous bind-weed, with its wreaths and bells,
> Had twined about her two small rows of peas,
> And dragged them to the earth.

>   (lines 724–30)

Tennyson describes Mariana's landscape similarly, as a mirror of his heroine's inner life:

> The rusted nails fell from the knots
>   That held the pear to the gable-wall.
> The broken sheds looked sad and strange:
>   Unlifted was the clinking latch;
>   Weeded and worn the ancient thatch
> Upon the lonely moated grange.

(lines 3–8)

But Mariana's desolation remains unrelieved; no faith in the human spirit is renewed by her tale. Tennyson's is a poem of bleak isolation and despair, heightened not by the visual scene of ruin, but by the sounds of the external world which Mariana hears, sounds which suggest fullness and the orderly passing of time in 'confounding' contrast to her emptiness and sense of entrapment in a meaningless existence:

> The sparrow's chirrup on the roof,
>   The slow clock ticking, and the sound
> Which to the wooing wind aloof
>   The poplar made, did all confound
> Her sense...

(lines 73–7)

In Wordsworth, on the other hand, the story of Margaret's tortured hope and ultimate death becomes a story of 'Faith' and the 'secret spirit of humanity',

> Which, 'mid the calm oblivious tendencies
> Of nature, 'mid her plants, and weeds, and flowers,
> And silent overgrowings, still survived.

(lines 928–30)

The repetition of "'mid' is important, stressing the equilibrium of 'the wavering balance' of his mind. Also important is the achievement of 'calm', an idyllic blend of external and internal worlds that is rarely found in Tennyson. *Mariana* ends with a painful juxta-position of these two worlds, but the story of Margaret ends with an epiphanal vision of silence:

> I well remember that those very plumes,
> Those weeds, and the high spear-grass on that wall,
> By mist and silent rain-drops silvered o'er,
> As once I passed, into my heart conveyed
> *So still an image of tranquility,*
> *So calm and still,* and looked so beautiful....

(lines 942–7, italics mine)

The inability in Tennyson to achieve the peace necessary to hold 'communion with the dead', is explicitly set out in XCIV of *In Memoriam* where he writes that the spirits 'haunt the silence of the breast,/ Imaginations calm and fair,/ The memory like a cloudless air,/ The conscience as a sea at rest'. But when the poet cannot achieve this Wordsworthian moment of 'eternal silence', he finds himself forever excluded, left outside the gates of a world where his spirit can find peace. XCIV concludes:

> But when the heart is full of din,
> And doubt beside the portal waits,
> They can but listen at the gates,
> And hear the household jar within.

The following section of *In Memoriam*, XCV, has sometimes been compared to a Wordsworthian lyric 'in that the thought develops out of and as a counterpart to the natural setting' (Langbaum 1970, p. 66). But what has not been stressed is how the 'natural setting' is more aural than visual. Both *Tintern Abbey* and XCV are prime examples of what M. H. Abrams calls 'the greater romantic lyric', where, in the course of meditation, the speaker comes to grips with a tragic loss and emerges with heightened understanding (1965, pp. 527–8). However, once again Tennyson, as opposed to Wordsworth, fails to achieve any assurance that the moment when 'We see into the life of things' is more than a 'vain belief'.

The meditation begins at twilight, when darkness envelops sight, forcing the ears to become the dominant sense, as a congenial group sings 'old songs'. This warmth and togetherness will stand in sharp contrast to the solitude that comes when the poet's friends leave – as Coleridge's do in another Romantic lyric, *This Lime-Tree Bower My Prison* – and night firmly establishes itself as 'light after light' goes out in the house, and the poet is left alone. Like Shelley, but unlike Wordsworth, Tennyson's imaginative strength does not come from the self in solitude, but from the emotional intensity of relationship. Consequently, much of his poetry is about the paralysis of a mind left alone with itself, a mind like Enoch Arden's which becomes 'the loneliest in a lonely sea' and which, without a sense of God, would have 'died of solitude' (lines 549, 617). For Wordsworth, however, thoughts of 'deep seclusion' lead to a moment in which 'we are laid asleep/ In Body, and become a living soul', resulting in an imaginative union of the transient and the permanent, a connection of 'The landscape with the quiet of the sky'. Recalling his childhood, he remembers how the 'sounding cataract' haunted him 'like a passion' (lines 76–7), and how the colours and forms of the landscape were an unmediated 'appetite' that needed no mental embellishment to instil powerful emotions. Now, as a grown man, the immediacy of childhood feeling is gone, but in its place, Wordsworth writes of *'hearing* often times/ The still, sad music of humanity' (lines 90–1, italics mine), and of discovering,

> In nature and the language of the sense
> The *anchor* of my purest thoughts, the nurse,
> The guide, the guardian of my heart, and soul
> Of all my moral being.

> (lines 108–11, italics mine)

Tennyson has no 'anchor'. Alone in the house, he writes a 'hunger seized my heart', a feeling akin to what Wordsworth describes as 'appetite' in *Tintern Abbey*. But where Wordsworth's appetite is inspired and satisfied by nature, Tennyson's comes, in this case, from the 'noble letters of the dead'. He reads Hallam's letters, 'And strangely on the silence broke/ The silent-speaking words'. Like Wordsworth, he hears through silence, and it is through aurality that an epiphanal moment is reached and 'The living soul was flashed on mine'. In this union with Hallam, like Wordsworth's with nature, the poet feels the 'deep pulsations of the world' and hears

Æonian music measuring out
The steps of Time – the shocks of Chance –
The blows of Death. At length my trance
Was cancelled, stricken through with doubt.

(lines 41–4)

Both poets, in silence, hear what Wordsworth describes as the 'still, sad music of humanity', but Tennyson abruptly stops the orchestra, breaks the record, cancels the sound: aurality is 'stricken through with doubt'.

T. S. Eliot once commented that *In Memoriam* is 'not religious because of the quality of its faith, but because of the quality of its doubt' (1950, p. 294). Although Wordsworth's best poetry is permeated with doubt, it is ultimately about the evolution towards faith, towards finding stability for the 'wavering' mind in the experiences, and in particular in the memory of the experiences the poet has of the world outside himself. The old leech-gatherer in *Resolution and Independence*, for example, teaches him the importance of perseverance, and out of the grief of his brother's death expressed in *Peele Castle* comes 'fortitude, and patient cheer'. In both the past and present Wordsworth manages to find 'life and food' (to continue the metaphor of 'appetite' and 'hunger') 'For future years' (*Tintern Abbey*, lines 64–5), and in this solace, Wordsworth is 'unromantic', at least to the degree that we understand this term to contain a profound recognition that the human condition is ultimately inexplicable. Paradoxically, then, in some respects Tennyson may be *more* 'Romantic' than Wordsworth.

Another essential distinction between Wordsworth and Tennyson lies in their contemplation of the past, loss and death. Tennyson finds the present largely empty except in so far as it resonates with memories of the past. Of 'Tears, idle tears' he remarked to James Knowles: 'It is what I have always felt even from a boy, and what as a boy I called the "passion of the past". And it is so always with me now; it is the distance that charms me in the landscape, the picture and the past, and not the immediate to-day in which I move' (Ricks 1969, p. 785). Much of his poetry represents a struggle between that distant time and the now, but unlike Wordsworth, he desires to forsake the now 'in favor of the twilight places of dream and memory "at the *quiet* limit of the world"' (Lourie 1979, p. 27, italics mine). Where Wordsworth was 'Fostered alike by beauty and by fear' (*The Prelude*, 1.302), Tennyson sought to calm the terror and alleviate the fear. Revisioning horrific 'spots of time', such as the boat-stealing episode in Book 1 of *The Prelude*, Wordsworth gains access to 'unknown modes of being' and knowledge that 'pain and fear' are essential to an understanding of the 'grandeur in the beatings of the heart' (lines 393, 413–14). These 'spots', 'recollected in tranquility', become a means of transcendence, of insight into realms of being beyond mortality, into 'eternal Silence'. Tennyson, on the other hand, rarely recollects his emotions in tranquility. They are, as in XCV, re-experienced with a sense of bafflement, helplessness and deep sorrow. The contrast here is between a 'Romantic' poet who is able to find consolation, even an idealized awareness of immortality, by turning inward to the hallowed realms of the egotistical sublime, and his Victorian successor who is endowed with something close to what Keats called 'negative capability' in his acceptance of the inevitability of doubt, uncertainty, and even spiritual barrenness. So although Tennyson was unable to see through pain and loss to what Shelley, in *Prometheus Unbound*, called 'a diviner day' (II. v.103), he did not, like Wordsworth, ever escape his anguish and the creative conflict between the mundane present and the intensity of the past through the transformative, and perhaps illusory, powers of imagination. And in this light, D. G. James was probably wrong when he praised Wordsworth for his courage and condemned Tennyson for his self-pity (1950, p. 128). Tennyson had the courage to doubt, but Wordsworth ran away from uncertainty into a faith that perhaps only reflected his own desperate need for certainty.

But both poets knew, in faith or doubt, that we do not *see* the face of God. We *hear* God as he speaks His creation, and it is through this sound, be it the moan of the sea, the music of the spheres, or the allusive oxymoronic sound of 'eternal silence', that we achieve vision.

Notes

1.   Sections of this essay were first published in a somewhat different context in Rapf 1986. I am also indebted to two of my graduate students, Desmond Sawyer and Joseph McGrath, for giving me some new perspectives on aurality.
2.   All citations from the short poems between 1800 and 1807 are from Wordsworth 1983.

3. All citations from Tennyson are from Tennyson 1969.
4. All citations from *The Prelude* are from Owen 1985, *The Fourteen-Book Prelude*.
5. Ong discusses the interiority of sound and its relationship to the interiority of human consciousness in greater detail in *The Presence of the Word* (1967).
6. A. Dwight Culler makes a similar observation, but about the dramatic monologue, in discussing *Tithonus*. Citing Robert Langbaum (1970), he writes, 'the dramatic monologue originated when the post-Romantic poet took the lyric of experience and fathered it upon another person' (1977, p. 85).

4

Swinburne's *Tristram of Lyonesse* as Assimilationist Epic

HERBERT F. TUCKER

The trouble with *Tristram of Lyonesse* (1882) – what has kept it the most underrated major narrative in nineteenth-century English verse – is the same as the notorious trouble with Swinburne: too much rhetoric. Must he be so redundantly figurative? Critics bent on writing off freakish ingenuity used to put the question of Swinburne's rhetorical excess rhetorically and leave it that way. Lately the question has received more serious answers, but these are sometimes framed so generally that they incur the same charge of abstraction that has been levelled against the poet.[1] The following essay on Swinburne's narrative masterpiece also aims at some broad generalisations; I want to make my way, however, through a detailed consideration of the most conspicuous rhetorical convention of the genre to which *Tristram of Lyonesse* (albeit problematically) belongs: the epic simile.[2] Seeing how Swinburne's similes mingle figurative description with literal narration can provide terms in which to understand larger, correlative issues: the bearing of his rhetorical practice on his epic theme, and the stance he assumes as an epic poet transmitting traditional materials. This stance, I shall suggest in closing, exemplifies Swinburne's original Victorian position on the Romantic issue of poetic originality.

A dozen lines into the first canto Swinburne sets the scene, and introduces a principal actor, with a passage that gestures toward epic simile in such a way as to vex the distinction between scenic description and narrative action on which epic similes usually depend:

> Above the stem a gilded swallow shone,
> Wrought with straight wings and eyes of glittering stone

As flying sunward oversea, to bear
Green summer with it through the singing air.
And on the deck between the rowers at dawn,
As the bright sail with brightening wind was drawn,
Sat with full face against the strengthening light
Iseult, more fair than foam or dawn was white.

(Swinburne 1925, 1: lines 11–18)

It is among Swinburne's infamous peculiarities to distend ordinary syntax without technically breaking the rules; to obey conventions, yet in such a fashion as to make them noticed. The tiny conjunction 'as' can do so many jobs in English – comparison, temporal indication, explanation, invocation – that it normally draws attention only when syntax behaves so abnormally that we cannot tell which job to assign it. And here, I think, we cannot tell. On a first reading line 13 apparently presents a simile comparing the swallow-headed prow of a ship to a bird flying over the sea; line 16, in contrast, seems a temporal clause coordinating the moment of Iseult's appearance with the freshening of the breeze at dawn. But later in the poem Swinburne so interweaves the comparative and temporal functions of 'as' that a reader returning to this opening passage must wonder if those functions can be securely discriminated even here. There is good reason, given the commonplace comparison of sailing to flight, for taking lines 13–14 as straight narration of the ship's 'flying sunward oversea' before the west wind; especially in the vicinity of the stronger metaphors of windborne summer and singing air, what first appeared to be a simile fades back from rhetorical into literal reference. Conversely, in the ostensibly temporal lines 16–18, the striking metaphorical chiasmus of 'brightening wind' and 'strengthening light', at a moment that simultaneously fills out the sail and reveals Iseult's 'full face', lets the 'as' clause do the work of an epic simile: our heroine in her expectancy is like a taut sail.[3]

Already Swinburne's rhetoric poses a problem: the images remain vivid and distinct, but it is unclear whether they have narrative or descriptive force.[4] They seem to belong equally to the forward thrust of the storyline and to the crosswise movement of cognitive reflection, whereby epic poets traditionally repair from narration in order to embellish meaning. The purpose of Swinburne's prelusive tinkering with the epic simile emerges more clearly from a later, more complicated passage that renders Iseult's innocent predisposition to love:

yea, she felt
Through her own soul the sovereign morning melt,
And all the sacred passion of the sun;
And as the young clouds flamed and were undone
About him coming, touched and burnt away
In rosy ruin and yellow spoil of day,
The sweet veil of her body and corporal sense
Felt the dawn also cleave it, and incense
With light from inward and with effluent heat
The kindling soul through fleshly hands and feet.
And as the august great blossom of the dawn
Burst, and the full sun scarce from sea withdrawn
Seemed on the fiery water a flower afloat,
So as a fire the mighty morning smote
Throughout her, and incensed with the influent hour
Her whole soul's one great mystical red flower
Burst [. . . .]

(1: lines 449–65)

On principles of strict narrative thrift, the metaphor of dawning erotic susceptibility in the first two and a half lines says it all. But Swinburne proceeds in that troublesome supplementary way of his to add a double simile, which spreads out the constituent elements of the initial metaphor for analysis and recombination. These elements are in one sense highly rhetorical, yet in another sense they are as profoundly literal as anything in the story. Each of the two main 'as' clauses, beginning in lines 452 and 459, may be read as either a simile explaining what Iseult feels or a temporal clause telling when she feels it. The controlling introductory metaphor of lines 449–51, the repeatedly stressed 'Burst', and indeed the prevailing norms of epic narrative, all endorse the mode of simile. In the first instance, however, the odd structure of 'as' / 'also' (line 456) implies not comparison but concurrence; and in the second instance the more conventional 'as' / 'so' structure is so rhetorically embroiled – qualified first by the redundant embedded simile 'as a fire' (line 462), and then by the supervention of metaphor on simile in the trope of the bursting flower – that by sentence's end the ostensible simile feels more like a 'when' clause instead (thus Reul 1922, p. 334: 'tandis que', 'quand'). The ambiguity of such assimilative syntax in effect bursts the barriers between referential and illustrative language that traditionally organise the reading of an epic simile.

Swinburne's rhetoric contrives to have it both ways, descriptive and narrative at once. His convertible rhetoric invites the reader to take tenor and vehicle together as an instance of what our subtlest student of poetic ambiguity has called Swinburne's technique of 'mutual comparison' (Empson 1947, p. 163). There results a sense of participant reciprocation between character and environment, psyche and cosmos, which enacts rhetorically the (meta)physical copresence of 'spirit' with 'sense' on which the whole epic vision of *Tristram* is based (Vivante 1950, p. 280; Richardson 1988, p. 125). By unfolding into extended similes the metaphorical equivalence between Iseult's awakening ardour and the brilliant sunrise, Swinburne pays delicate mimetic respect to the gradual character of what his heroine is inwardly experiencing, moment by moment, within a distinctly realised external setting. Furthermore, by commingling simile and ambient narrative, he gives Iseult's experience the authority of self-evidence, within a more intricate explanatory texture than either literal or figurative language could afford on its own. The dawning eros of Iseult is like the dawning nature around her because she is a part of that nature, and because both she and it are pervaded with a single eroticised force (Harrison 1988a, p. 122).[5]

Swinburne thus assimilates simile, as it were, to narrative circumstance, and conversely approximates narrative circumstance to the condition of simile – something he does throughout the poem with various devices for reduplication, including couplet rhyme and marked episodic parallelism, as well as the kind of rhetorical redundancy confronting us here (McSweeney 1969, p. 691; McGann 1972, p. 156). If such rhetoric is 'excessive', it is so by design. And it is, we should note, the very reverse of abstract: it indeed reverses that cognitive act of abstraction from particular circumstance which originally enables the comparison of disjunct phenomena in similes. *Tristram of Lyonesse* consistently grounds simile in synecdoche – represents metaphorical correspondence as metonymic contingency – in order to enforce an epic vision of human participation in cosmic process. The 'as' of lyric resemblance ('like') is amplified through episodic casualty ('when') into epic causality ('because').[6] Swinburne's rhetorical complexity reinforces a conviction that what takes place within Iseult at sunrise here, like what passes between her and Tristram at the close of the canto, transpires as it simply must.

The poet's seemingly superfluous rhetoric is thus a means of recognising the necessity that reigns over the entire action of his poem. Swinburne expressly thematises this recognition in two adjacent passages at the end of canto 2 and the start of canto 3. The first not only repeatedly conflates descriptive and narrative rhetoric, but also introduces a textbook version of that rhetorical conflation into the actual plot:

> But ere the dusk had well the sun in sight
> He turned and kissed her eyes awake and said,
> Seeing earth and water neither quick nor dead
> And twilight hungering toward the day to be,
> 'As the dawn loves the sunlight I love thee.'
> And even as rays with cloudlets in the skies
> Confused in brief love's bright contentious wise,
> Sleep strove with sense rekindling in her eyes;
> And as the flush of birth scarce overcame
> The pale pure pearl of unborn light with flame
> Soft as may touch the rose's heart with shame
> To break not all reluctant out of bud,
> Stole up her sleeping cheek her waking blood;
> And with the lovely laugh of love that takes
> The whole soul prisoner ere the whole sense wakes,
> Her lips for love's sake bade love's will be done.
> And all the sea lay subject to the sun.

(2: lines 470–86)

The ambiguous 'as' clauses in lines 475–77 and 478–82 hover, once again, between comparative and temporal indication. To their rhetorical overdetermination Iseult's wordless surrender to 'love's will' says amen in deed; and the last line, with its implied comparison between natural elements and lovers' bodies, becomes an exquisite epic instance of Swinburnean eroticism. What is new about this powerfully physical passage is that it dramatises the origin of its power in an exemplary scene of rhetorical invention, when Tristram precedes physical with verbal love-making. '"As the dawn loves the sunlight I love thee"': this epigrammatic aubade is both less than a simile and more. Tristram's declaration of passional truth assumes the force (and the form) of a vow, sworn not as God is his witness but as nature is his inspiration. Moreover, Tristram's gentle poem seems less made than found; for it comes to him unbidden from the scene that fills his mind, as it fills the two lines between his intention to speak and his actual utterance. The way Tristram's simultaneously literal and figurative declaration originates in his 'seeing' of natural circumstances exemplifies the rhetorical practice of the poem that contains it. The courtly poet Tristram finds love's language where the epic poet Swinburne finds love's ultimate warrant: in the dynamic processes of the ambient world.

The charm of this found lyric lies in the unconsidered rightness with which it catches the lovers' happy absorption: absorption in one another, and within the privacy of an embowered space, 'The Queen's Pleasance', where time means nothing but blissful recurrence. In an epic narrative dedicated to dynamic process, however, time must come to mean more. Canto 3 accordingly opens, after a lapse of three years, with Tristram's stricken recognition of the meaning that his thoughtless words disclose in retrospect:

> '"As the dawn loves the sunlight I love thee";
> As men that shall be swallowed of the sea
> Love the sea's lovely beauty; as the night
> That wanes before it loves the young sweet light,
> And dies of loving; as the worn-out noon
> Loves twilight, and as twilight loves the moon
> That on its grave a silver seal shall set –
> We have loved and slain each other, and love yet.'

> (3: lines 1–8)

For the next fifty lines Tristram hammers out the stern meaning of his own unpremeditated art, in a self-critical meditation whose primary instruments are similes relentlessly expressive of the mortal destructiveness of time. New similes of night, noon, and twilight build up a context of cyclical transiency within which the earlier simile of dawn's love for sunlight acquires a fuller, tragic meaning. Even now in Tristram's darkest mood, that meaning acknowledges the pain of love, but only in order to affirm love the more deeply:

> 'Yea, surely as the day-star loves the sun
> And when he hath risen is utterly undone,
> So is my love of her and hers of me –
> And its most sweetness bitter as the sea.'

> (3: lines 49–52)

Love's 'most sweetness' abides 'surely' – and only – in the bitter knowledge that the deprivations of time must try love and prove it, even as loss and absence have validated Tristram's fateful simile far beyond his initial intent. That lyrically love-blinded simile, in its reference to the natural processes that inspired it, portended passional and metaphysical consequences of an epic extent. These consequences only time and narrative duration can empirically unfold, and only love's endurance amid change can bear them out (McGann 1972, p. 164). So this most overtly philosophical canto of the poem brings Tristram to understand; but the epic acceptance that he expresses as philosophy here, and that his and Iseult's passion will confirm as lived wisdom across the rest of the poem, has governed their intuitive impulse from the start.

What Tristram's thoughtless simile has come to mean between cantos 2 and 3 is what all the rhetoric of *Tristram* means within the tragically inflected curve of its epic action: the course of true love traces the lines of destiny, which constitutes the final form and object of desire, and which may be known only as it is embraced in suffering joy (Reed 1966, pp. 111–12; McSweeney 1969, p. 693; Buckler 1980, p. 256). In other words – the words to which the poem grants largest privilege – Love belongs irresistibly, originally and ultimately, to Fate. The poem both advocates and enacts a rapprochement between love and fate: between the psychic and physical drive that impels Tristram, Iseult and, by extension, all human agents; and the circumstantial, cosmic gravity that draws all agents and actions, all desires and objects, to their common end in dissolution and rest. A structural *tour de force* gives this theme unmistakable prominence: the Prologue and final canto each begin with 44 lines of identically-rhymed theses on 'Love' and 'Fate' respectively (lines 39–40 being exceptions that prove the rule). As this structure gives fate the last word, so does the long narrative it frames. The love between Tristram and Iseult commences by accident, with their unwitting draught of a love potion; and their *Liebestod* finale occurs under circumstances beyond their control. Such good hap or bad luck is the cheapest aspect of fate and possesses at best a minimal narrative dignity. What ennobles Swinburne's heroes is their gradually deepening acceptance, across the intervening narrative, of their desire's entanglement with necessity. Learning the hard way the lore that Swinburne's early similes rehearse, Tristram and Iseult come to apprehend love *as* fate in its dearest, most exigent and heroic aspect. *Tristram of Lyonesse* thus makes a tale of high romance into an epic expression of the human condition, by teaching that subjective desire faithfully pursued finds its ultimate object nowhere but in fate itself. *Liebestod* and *Todestriebe* become one.

This assimilation of love to fate in heroic *amor fati* accords closely with Swinburne's stance as a traditionary epic poet. For such a poet, tradition is the narrative equivalent of fate. In receiving the oft-told tale of Tristram and Iseult, Swinburne falls heir to a gift with many strings attached: the transmission of a foreknown plot binds him with great stringency to a corpus of legend that he loves, in part, for just this severity of demand.[7] The epic catalogue of celebrated lovers in the Prelude, for example, is an exercise in *amor fati*: the tragic doom of Swinburne's twelve Heroides, their astrological associations, the very circularity of the calendrical structure that contains them, all draw grandeur from the sense of predestination. And this same sense motivates the traditionary poet of Tristram and Iseult: 'the twain I take, and give / Out of my life to let their dead life live / Some days of mine' (*Prelude*, lines 235–7). In exchange for the gift of legend, the poet gives up the 'life' of free invention – large Romantic prerogative though it be – and chooses instead to retrace a given story along ways well-trodden: 'yet I too, / I have the heart to follow, many or few / Be the feet gone before me' (*Prelude*, lines 243–5).

The 'heart to follow', the courage of epic commitment, expresses Swinburne's willingness to assimilate his poem to a predestined itinerary. This is a version of the same choice his protagonists will make as love teaches them to embrace the inevitable: 'Let that which is be' (3: line 147). This choice is made freely yet not without reluctance: some of the most plangent passages in *Tristram of Lyonesse* express resistance to the inevitable, as when the poet opens Canto 6 by petitioning Love on his lovers' behalf for 'A little time', a period of grace before the foreknown end (6: lines 1–10). Yet such plangency can be but a minor virtue in a major verse narrative authorised by fate.[8] Swinburne makes this clear when he opens Canto 8 with a parallel passage that is built on the same rhymes but forsakes petition for command, dictating to Love from a position of fatal strength: 'O Love, thy day sets darkling: hope and fear / Fall from thee standing stern as death stands here' (8: lines 9–10). As an epic sternness overshadows the tenderness of lyric and romance, Swinburne's formally parallel passages correlate poetic authority with the poet's 'heart to follow', to conform his creative will to his legacy. The same rhythm of reluctance and acceptance that heroises Tristram and Iseult fits the poet to manage and transmit – to *conduct* – a heroic poem.[9]

The assimilation of Swinburne's individual talent to a storied tradition has a local, textural analogue in his handling of poetic allusion. Despite a reputation for rhetorical violence, Swinburne proves a curiously non-combative author when it comes to the figure of allusion. He tends to allude intertextually rather than interpoetically, citing images or passages rather than poets. He thus works in a more impersonal spirit than moves contemporaries like Tennyson and Browning or forerunners like Wordsworth and Shelley, who set the dominant mode of Romantic allusiveness to which, as I shall try to show, he takes exception. An impersonally allusive manner prevails throughout Swinburne's oeuvre, but it is especially pertinent in *Tristram*, which in keeping with its traditionary framework and fatalist ethos typically recycles turns of phrase so as to reinforce the effect of predestination. In the early episode of the love potion, for example, Swinburne echoes a famous line from the episode of Paolo and Francesca in Dante's *Inferno*: 'Their Galahault was the cup, and she that mixed' (1: line 792; *Inferno* 5: line 137). Dante's lovers were undone, to be sure, by a written book and not a mixed drink – although a pun submerged in the word 'draught' (1: line 783) may approximate Swinburne's image to Dante's – yet, all told, the allusive resemblance between lines outweighs their difference. Here, as also with the Miltonic trope 'they quaffed / Death' (1: lines 784–85; *Paradise Lost* 9: line 792), Swinburne is primarily concerned to establish traditional epic determinants for his action.

Swinburne writes to honour antecedence, not to change it. Yet this very posture of allusive acceptance discloses a higher-level paradox. For to allude in so neutrally welcoming a way to these among all narratives of sin and fall, by these among all poetic moralists, is to render a species of homage that Dante and Milton would have spurned. Swinburne's stance of traditionary responsiveness is one that the admittedly distinct Christian orthodoxies of *The Divine Comedy* and *Paradise Lost* would denounce with one voice as moral irresponsibility. To hear these echoes within Swinburne's fatalist universe, then, is to detect a certain intertextual polemic. Swinburne readily admits that the legacy of Christian epic forms part of the context in which he writes; but he admits Dante and Milton into *Tristram of Lyonesse* only after stripping away their individualist cogency and voluntarist morality. His intertextual good manners set off to disadvantage what is strident or insistent in theirs. Like the poem's major ethical antagonist, that Christian avenger Iseult of the White Hands, the Dantesque and Miltonic ethos of moral responsibility must submit to be judged by a manner that suspends judgement within a larger epic ethos of impassivity (Vivante 1950, p. 267; McGann 1972, p. 140; McSweeney 1969, p. 694).[10]

Swinburne not only represents his lovers' fatal 'draught' in images drawn from Dante and Milton, but he appropriates those images in the assimilationist spirit of one who has drunk so deep in poetic tradition that he can convert the draught to impersonalist, involuntarist ends of his own. Such passive-aggressive assimilation of tradition is a nearly constant habit of *Tristram*: an unobtrusively figured allusive continuo grounds the whole poem in a homogeneous literary antecedence, which becomes one of the poem's most typically Swinburnean, originally Victorian features. For Swinburne's intertextual serenity constitutes a firm break with the sharper allusiveness of Romanticism. Allusion, the figure of echo, is a rhetorical trope; the point of Romantic allusion – and of high Romantic rhetoric in general – is to claim independence through difference, by troping difference *as* independence. In the deep context of cultural history, Romantic allusion underscores the distinction between orthodox Christian humanism and modern secular psychology; at closer quarters, within the developing tradition of Romanticism itself, it refines distinctions among rival versions of the modern. But the generalised allusiveness of Swinburne shows how decidedly the Romantic *will to differ* affiliates Romantic humanism with the Christian humanism out of which it developed. This individualist, normatively lyrical affiliation is thrown into relief by the counter-example of the Victorian epic fatalist's *will to assimilate*. The intertextual neutrality of Swinburne thus expresses two aspects of his Victorian Romanticism: on one hand a belated poet's need to revise a fatigued originalism; on the other, a culturally estranged Victorian's call to gather up and reknit historical articulations that three wilful Romantic generations have subjected to compound fracture.[11]

An instance of Swinburne's assimilationist allusion to Romantic texts lies before us already, in Tristram's simile 'As the dawn loves the sunlight I love thee'. We have seen how the trope of dawn and day comes to Tristram from a natural context, but it arguably comes to Swinburne from a literary one. For it forms the governing trope of Shelley's *The Triumph of Life* (1824), a poem that repeatedly figures in images of dawn's absorption by harsh daylight the obliteration of personal vision by involuntary, ideologically irresistible forces of collective entropy. Shelley never completed this experimental lyrical narrative; but even from the imperfect edition available to Victorian readers it is clear that Shelley was systematically turning the dawn/day trope against his own source in Wordsworth's *Intimations* ode (1807), where 'our life's Star' shines bright in the dawn of unconditioned youth, but 'At length the Man perceives it die away,/ And fade into the light of common day' (Wordsworth 1936, lines 59, 75–6; see Harrison 1990). Wordsworth's proposal to compensate for this fadeout by merely commemorating its early gleam inspires Shelley in *The Triumph of Life* to reiterate the dawn/day image *ad nauseam* in unsparing parody of its cold comfort.[12] Within this interpoetic confrontation, nevertheless, both Romantic poets remain committed to defending the individual imagination against an impersonal threat that wears the aura of necessity as surely as dawn heralds the sun.

It is just this aura of necessity with which the Swinburne of *Tristram* is in love, whether he finds it embodied in his own epic cosmos or enacted in the rhetoric of earlier poets. Wordsworth writes an ode that whets, on Miltonic images of orthodox celestial light (*Lycidas*, lines 168–71, *Paradise Lost* 3: lines 21–55), a definitively Romantic animus against contingency; Shelley composes, on terms appropriated from Wordsworth with undisguised scorn, a lyrical nightmare that stares aghast at the way life enchains the free Romantic spirit. But the epic design of *Tristram* subsumes such lyrical, individualist urgencies within the art of its necessity. Swinburne equably regards the contingency of life and the belatedness of art as kindred and ultimately welcome imperatives; and from this vantage he can take the Romantic individualism of Wordsworth and Shelley, like the Christian humanism of Dante and Milton, in allusive stride. He accommodates the rhetorical acerbities of his predecessors, and neutralises their personal insistences, by embracing a fate so large and impassive that it absorbs into its own texture their very protests against fate.

Swinburne thus dispels Victorian anxieties of influence by epically assimilating the Romantic rhetoric of lyrical autonomy. The fatalist thesis of *Tristram* is one from which the antithetical, idealising tropes of Christian spiritualism and Romantic individualism alike seek to swerve in vain. For the predestinating power behind Swinburne's epic is unswerving – or, to use a term that the hellenising poet might prefer, atropic. Fate resists all troping: it may be neither turned *aside* (witness the poet's fidelity to legend) nor turned *from* (witness the heroic plot of tragic acceptance). Nor may fate be turned *into* anything else by rhetorical magic. Because, as Tristram puts it, fate is 'the one thing that hath being', it defies representation by 'any shadow or shape', any 'likeness', any figurative attempt to 'Clothe it with other names': 'How should it turn from its great way to give / Man that must die a clearer space to live?' (3: lines 171–80). At the same time, the very incontrovertibility of Swinburne's trope-proof fate issues a standing challenge that the poetic imagination cannot fail to take up. If the atropic necessity grounding *Tristram* is to be celebrated, deplored, or indeed conceptualised at all, then rhetoric in its turn becomes a counter-necessity. The inaccessibility of fate makes tropes for fate discursively inevitable; and it is this circumstance that lets Swinburne allusively harmonise the discordance of a chorus of precursors who wrote, after all, as they must.

How should fate turn from its great way? Being so great, how should it *not* be turned into tropes? These complementary questions frame a reply to the not quite rhetorical question about Swinburne's rhetorical excess that I posed at first. Must he be so redundantly figurative? Yes: he must be figurative, because for his vision of fate rhetoric is not an ornamental extra but a poetic prerequisite; and he must be redundantly so, for the sake of the authentic, if limited, freedom that his vision of fate maintains. The fertility with which Swinburne's epic similes cross-multiply figurative description and literal narration, and the hospitality with which his allusions house inherited tropes within a traditionary tale, together affirm the necessity of rhetorical figuration. No rhetoric, however excessive, may exceed the enormity of fate:

> nor may man's darkening breath,
> Albeit it stain, disfigure or destroy
> The glass wherein the soul sees life and joy
> Only, with strength renewed and spirit of youth,
> And brighter than the sun's the body of Truth
> Eternal, unimaginable of man [. . . .]
>
> (9: lines 78–83)

Swinburne's recognition that the ultimate truth of things is both inexorable and 'unimaginable' opens out the condition of human freedom, which subsists under the aspect of 'Fate, that of all things save the soul of man / Is lord and God' (9: lines 11–12). What excepts the soul from fate's immense rule is the agnosticism that immensity inspires, even as it incites the perennial desire to give fate an imaginative form. The vast necessity played out in this belated epic both requires human shaping and repudiates it, at once enlarging the mortal soul into creativity and emancipating it – by constant reference to 'the larger, cosmic death' (Rosenberg 1967, p. 147) – from the petty death of subjugation to its own creations.[13] As Tristram and Iseult bear their love out to the edge of doom where passion and destiny meet, so the poet's rhetorical desire finds in its extremity a fatal wisdom that waits wherever the road of excess leads.

Notes

1. Hyder (1970) reprints contemporary complaints about Swinburne's redundancy (pp. xl, 115, 117), which persist in first-generation Swinburne scholarship mainly concerned with musical effects (Gosse 1917, Reul 1922, Chew 1929). Later critics follow Eliot (1920) and Welby (1926) in referring the poet's rhetorical excess less to figures of sound than to figures of thought habitually grounded in analytic abstraction: see Rosenberg (1967), Buckler (1980) and Peters (1982). Brisman (1978 and 1984) presents the most fully theorised and illustrated account of such figures of thought.

2. Epic features of the poem are discussed by McSweeney (1969, pp. 690–1) and Harrison (1988a, pp. 98–101). See also Riede (1978, pp. 9–10, 190). Generic classification of *Tristram* more commonly proceeds by sheer assertion: for every critic who grants it epic status (Cassidy 1964, Fuller 1968, Staines 1978), another pronounces it lyrical instead (Nicolson 1926, Vivante 1950, Rosenberg 1967). Questions of genre and rhetoric converge on the epic simile, which is addressed by Peters (1982, p. 149), Tredell (1982, pp. 106–7), and Harrison (1988a, pp. 102–6).

3. These English ambiguities pose a special problem for Swinburne's translator: Reul (1922, p. 331), for example, in presenting *Tristram* to French readers translates 'as' in line 13 as 'semblait', in line 16 as 'tandis que'.

4. Swinburne's 'Dedicatory Epistle' (1904) suggests that he regarded description itself as a means of narrative presentation: *Tristram* was written 'not in the epic or romantic form of sustained or continuous narrative, but mainly through a succession of dramatic scenes or pictures with descriptive settings' (Swinburne 1966, p. 99).

5. As early as 1893 F. W. H. Myers recognised Swinburne's Victorian epic ambition to embody post-Darwinian values in a traditionary

tale: *Tristram* offers 'the most striking extant record of an important phase of thought. We have the strict materialistic synthesis clad in its most splendid colouring' (Hyder 1970, p. 194; see also Beach 1936, pp. 455–9).

6. Vivante (1950, p. 283) specifies 'the main source of Swinburne's poetry' as 'the idea of fate': 'a *core of causality* which lies either above or below, anyhow beyond personality'. The plot of *Tristram* wraps this causal core within a narrative circumstantiality extending well beyond the limits of lyric within which Vivante would confine it (p. 265). At least in this poem of epic causality, Swinburne cleaves (*pace* Brisman 1984) more to the elegiac, metonymic mode of Shakespeare than to the apocalyptic, metaphoric mode of Shelley – although in its similes, I submit, the two modes join.

7. For Swinburne's declarations of fidelity to his sources see *Letters* (1960, 4: 260, 287), and Swinburne (1966, p. 99). Sources and composition are discussed by Fisher (1972), Davis (1976), Staines (1978), and Cochran (1990). Riede (1978, p. 220) summarises Swinburne's modernist insistence 'on the creative continuation of tradition itself as the one certain bulwark against meaninglessness'.

8. The parallel passages that begin the Prelude and last canto are conspicuously not epic invocations (*contra* Harrison 1988a, p. 108) but declarations allying the poet's authority with fate. On Swinburne's poetic indifference to pathos see Wratislaw (1900, p. 102), and Brisman (1984, pp. 253–5).

9. Harrison (1988a, p. 107) asserts that such 'visionary fatalism' comes with the Arthurian corpus. Tennyson's *Idylls of the King*, which assumed epic proportions just before Swinburne went seriously to work on *Tristram*, bears out this assertion. But the parallel instances of Morris's contemporaneous *Earthly Paradise* (1870–71) and *Sigurd* (1876) – perhaps too the counter instance of Browning's *The Ring and the Book* (1868–69) – reveal a more general Victorian association between traditionary telling and the burden of tragic fatality.

10. In a letter of 1869 to W. M. Rossetti, Swinburne dubs his work-in-progress 'the moral history of Tristram' (*Letters* 1959, 2: 78): a jest, but one that forecasts the moral leverage of fatalism whereby the finished poem subverts voluntarist morality of both Christian and Romantic kinds. See Louis (1990, p. 5) on the waning of Swinburne's individualist faith by the 1880s.

11. Bloom (1973) and Hollander (1981) have brilliantly analysed within British poetic tradition the double-jointed, allusive trope of metalepsis (transumption). Swinburne's poem suggests a further speculation that metalepsis may be the constitutive trope of literary history itself, as we make and remake it by a double movement of simile and synecdoche. In constructing a literary history we begin by noting between texts, at any level from the verbal to the generic, a relation of similarity and difference; we then read that relation as historically significant by refiguring it in terms of continuity and change, positing a tradition to which both texts synecdochally belong. To see how the narrative–descriptive practice of *Tristram*

rehearses just this metaleptic, two-trope manoeuvre is to see how Swinburne's rhetorical configurations involve the reader in versions of the fundamental act of historical construction. In this way *Tristram*, notwithstanding the ostensible privacy of its 'lyrical' subject, discharges a task central to the definition of epic from Blake to Hardy.

12.   See Shelley (1977, lines 23, 79, 102, 292, 337, 389, 412, 429). The very multiplicity of Shelley's variations on the Wordsworthian image suggests that Swinburne is alluding to the image rather than to any one passage containing it. Indeed, even to single out *The Triumph of Life* seems arbitrary; *To a Skylark* or *Epipsychidion* might serve nearly as well. Swinburne's allusiveness is, characteristically, as unspecific as it is unmistakable. See his comment on Shelley's 'incalculable obligations' to Wordsworth in *Letters* (1962, 5: 63). On the literariness of Swinburne's inspiration see Morris's comment in Hyder (1970, p. 123), Welby (1926, p. 237), and Buckler (1980, p. 228). McGann (1972, pp. 310–11) ascribes to the 'analogical' habit of Swinburne's mind the fact that 'so much of his poetry is thickly allusive'.

13.   To read *Tristram* as an epic is to engage the cultural politics of its fatalism, which become explicit in the proem to Canto 9 but are rhetorically implicit throughout. Tillyard (1948) finds Swinburne's poetry protofascist because collectivist and *zeitgeistlich*, while for Harrison (1990) it is reactionary because unreconstructedly libertarian; conversely, Vivante (1950), Buckler (1980), and Richardson (1988) interpret Swinburne's tragic or elegiac fatalism as a vindication of freedom. Adjudicating between these opposite political judgements will entail a reassessment of the dialectical relation, which structures Swinburne's greatest writing, between a determinist myth and a poetics of indeterminacy (Tredell 1982, Brisman 1984).

5

Hardy's Poetic Antecedents

KERRY McSWEENEY

I

Since the great majority of his more than 900 poems were written in the first three decades of this century, Thomas Hardy can qualify as a twentieth-century poet. But he may equally well be considered the last major English poet of the nineteenth century. Born in 1840, three years after Victoria became queen, Hardy had begun his seventh decade when her long reign ended in 1901. The thematic content of his verse was largely determined by the intellectual and spiritual crises of the Victorian period; his conception of poetry and the poet's role was shaped both positively and negatively by his Romantic and Victorian predecessors; and a number of his poems come fully into focus only when their interrelationships with earlier nineteenth-century poems are recognised.

Hardy began to acquire his considerable knowledge of nineteenth-century poetry in the mid-1860s, when his interest in architecture began to wane as a 'sense of the truth of poetry, of its supreme place in literature...awakened itself in me'. He consciously set out to equip himself for a poetic career by reading nothing but verse because this seemed 'the shortest way to the fountain-head...for one who had not a great deal of spare time' (Millgate 1984, pp. 15, 51). Hardy kept to this metrical diet for almost two years. Later, during the 1870s and 1880s, he continued to read poetry, though at a more intermittent pace; and by the 1890s, when after a quarter-century of writing prose fiction he determined to return to poetry, Hardy had a longstanding familiarity with English verse, particularly that of his own century.

When literary history according to 'Mr Eliot' and the New Criticism was in the ascendent, and the study of influence was principally a matter of tracing stylistic and formal indebtedness, it was possible for even so fine a scholar–critic as Samuel Hynes to speak of Hardy's 'radical isolation from poetic tradition' and to identify the Dorset dialect poet William Barnes as 'the only poet, with the obvious exception of Shakespeare, whose influence [on Hardy] is demonstrable' (Hynes 1961, p. 31). One of the major reorientations of the past three decades in English studies has involved the recognition of an essential continuity between nineteenth- and twentieth-century poetry in English; and it is now patent that Wordsworth, Shelley, Tennyson, Browning and Swinburne were all important influences on Hardy. Thus, a consideration of the joint presence of *both* Romantic and Victorian forebears in Hardy's poetry should be of much interest to students of Romantic/Victorian continuities and discontinuities.

I want to highlight some of the salient points of interest by filling in some of the literary-historical detail, which is not as well-known as it might be; by examining the relationships between three of Hardy's poems and one poem by each of Wordsworth, Tennyson and Browning; and by suggesting some implications of my examination for the study of influence/resistance in nineteenth-century poetry. One of my conclusions, however, needs to be stated at the outset. Shelley and Swinburne are the two antecedent nineteenth-century poets whom Hardy most unequivocally admired and to whom he was ideologically and (in the case of Swinburne) temperamentally closest. But it is not their poetry with which in his own poetry Hardy was most deeply engaged. This is because there is lacking the crucial element of resistance and/or of what I shall call resistance overcome.

No poet was more highly regarded by Hardy than Shelley – 'the greatest of our lyrists' and the 'highest-soaring' among them (Purdy and Millgate 1978–88, VI, p. 101; Orel 1967, p. 81).[1] It is now widely recognised that Shelley's impact on Hardy's thought and basic outlook, which began in 1866 when he purchased a small volume entitled *Queen Mab and Other Poems*, was enormous (see Bartlett 1955; Duerksen 1966, pp. 160–5; and Pinion 1977, pp. 148–57). In the novels, Shelley is not infrequently alluded to or quoted from.[2] He is much less of a presence in the poetry, however, and when Shelleyean themes or motifs are present, there are few if any intertextual dynamics. The most conspicuous example is *Shelley's Skylark*, which Hardy wrote following a visit to the neighbourhood of Leghorn during his Italian tour of 1887. The poem is a flimsy, sentimental *éloge* which turns on the speaker's fanciful musing concerning where in the vicinity are to be found the remains of the little bird that 'inspired a bard to win/ Ecstatic heights in thought and rhyme.' In the last two of the poem's six stanzas, 'faeries' are charged to go and find that 'tiny pinch of priceless dust' so that it can be laid in a silver-lined casket framed with gems and gold and be consecrated to 'endless time'. James Richardson calls these lines 'uncharacteristically precious' and rightly finds them 'embarrassed and embarrassing' (Richardson 1977, p. 3). Shelley's *To a Skylark*, one may say, soars beyond Hardy's poetic reach; unable to engage himself imaginatively with the antecedent text, he is forced to fall back on idealising whimsy.

The difference in altitude between Swinburne's and Hardy's poetry is much less great. While the latter's senior by only three years, Swinburne was 'so early with his flotilla' and Hardy 'so late in getting my poetical barge under way' that the first series of *Poems and Ballads*, which appeared in the mid-1860s at precisely the time Hardy was considering a poetic career, had a tremendous impact on him. In a letter to Swinburne, he later recalled 'walking along the crowded London streets' reading the newly-published volume 'to my imminent risk of being knocked down' (Millgate 1984, p. 372; Purdy and Millgate 1978–88, II, p. 158). One facet of Hardy's intense admiration was Swinburne's metrical assault on the conventional morality and conventional religious beliefs of Victorian Britain. ('It was', he later recalled in *A Singer Asleep*, 'as though a garland of red roses/ Had fallen about the hood of some smug nun.') Hardy also found in the first *Poems and Ballads* the phrase 'loving-kindness' which he appropriated as the name for the mitigating and possibly saving human value that is mentioned over and over again in his work.

But perhaps the most important aspect of Hardy's wholly positive reception of Swinburne's poetry was not ideological or thematic, but temperamental. Hardy described a line in Swinburne's first *Poems and Ballads* poem 'Anactoria' ('Thee too the years shall cover') as presenting 'the finest *drama* of Death & Oblivion, so to speak, in our tongue' (Purdy and Millgate 1978–88, II, p. 158). The speaker of 'Anactoria' is Sappho, who also figures both in *Ave atque Vale*, the elegy on Baudelaire that is one of Swinburne's greatest poems, and in *A Singer Asleep*, Hardy's elegy on Swinburne. In 1961, Hynes could describe Hardy's poem as 'a weak, conventional elegy' (Hynes 1961, p. 22).[3] *A Singer Asleep* is undoubtedly conventional, but strongly and deliberately so. This can begin to be appreciated once the poem's relationship to *Ave atque Vale* is recognised. The relationship has been finely described by Peter

Sacks, who shows how Hardy's elegy 'offers an intriguing continuation of the earlier poet's style and ideology':

> By the title alone, Hardy has offered Swinburne the kind of death
> as repose that the latter had accorded Baudelaire. And the form
> of the stanzas, with their intricate rhyme schemes and nicely
> abbreviated 'musical closes', provides another initial effect of
> homage and imitation.... The poem is indeed marked by
> Swinburne's style of writing, by his almost impersonal, hieratic
> gestures, and by his ideological view of the immortal continuity
> between such poets as Sappho and himself...even those of the
> poem's moments that Hardy has made most his own yield a level
> of meaning that might escape notice if not read in the light of
> Swinburne and the [elegiac] tradition. (Sacks 1985, pp. 228, 230)

Both Swinburne's and Hardy's elegies are unflinchingly post-
Christian in their acceptance of the premise that there is no afterlife
and therefore no possibility of survival for their subjects. But
certain differences can be identified. The turn or reversal in *Ave
atque Vale*, for example, comes when the 'shut scroll' of Baudelaire's
poems is identified as a continuing presence ('Not thee, O never
thee, in all time's changes, / Not thee, but this...'). Hardy does not
reproduce this substitution in *A Singer Asleep*: his consolatory
formula is grounded in what he elsewhere calls 'an Idealism of
Fancy; that is...an imaginative solace in the lack of any substantial
solace to be found in life' (Millgate 1984, p. 333):

> And one can hold in thought that nightly here
> His phantom may draw down to the water's brim,
> And hers [Sappho's] come up to meet it, as a dim
> Lone shine upon the heaving hydrosphere,
> And mariners wonder as they traverse near,
>   Unknowing of her and him.
>
> One dreams him sighing to her spectral form:
> 'O teacher, where lies hid thy burning line;
> Where are thy songs, O poetess divine
> Whose very orts are love incarnadine?'
> And her smile back: 'Disciple true and warm,
>   Sufficient now are thine.'

But Hardy's compensatory manoeuvre supplements rather than contests or qualifies that of Swinburne. Indeed, the flow of the later poet's Fancy is channelled by the Swinburnean belief in a kind of apostolic succession of lyric poets descending from Sappho, who is identified as 'the supreme head of song' in *Ave atque Vale* and similarly designated in Hardy's elegy as 'the music-mother/ Of all the tribe that feel in melodies.'

Thus, in the relationship between *Ave atque Vale* and *A Singer Asleep* there is no tension and no resistance to be overcome. As a result, the poem lacks the added dimension that is found in the three intertextual relationships I now want to examine. The pairings are Wordsworth's *Intimations Ode* and *The Self-Unseeing*, Tennyson's *In Memoriam* and *He Prefers Her Earthly*, Browning's *By the Fireside* and *At Castle Boterel*. Each Hardy poem has a deeply personal subject, and each antecedent poem was an important point of personal reference for him over a long period of time. Each is the crucial presupposition of the Hardy poem with which it interacts; and in each case the intertextual dynamic involves an extraordinary instance of temperamental self-transcendence on Hardy's part.

II

Wordsworth's poetry meant a great deal to Hardy from first to last (see Casagrande 1977; Pinion 1977, pp. 167–74; Taylor 1986). *Domicilium*, his first poem, written before he was twenty, is Wordsworthian in both its blank verse and its familiar-with-forgotten-years subject (the Hardy family-home at Higher Bockhampton). *The Widow Betrothed*, a poem conceived in 1867 and published in 1903, is an obvious imitation of the Matthew poems in particular and the *Lyrical Ballads* in general, the 'famous preface' to which, Hardy later told Edmund Gosse, 'influenced me much, & influences the style of the poem' (Purdy and Millgate 1978–88, V, p. 253). And in the 'Apology' to *Late Lyrics and Earlier* (1922), written more than sixty years later, Wordsworth is quoted no fewer than four times in seven pages.

Elsewhere in Hardy's canon, there are numerous allusions to Wordsworth's poems. The text most frequently cited – the Wordsworthian poem most deeply imprinted on Hardy's con- sciousness – is the *Intimations Ode*.[4] In *A Pair of Blue Eyes* (1873), for example, which is based in part on Hardy's courtship of his first wife, Emma Gifford, in Cornwall in the early 1870s, there are three allusions to the *Ode*. In *The Return of the Native* (1878), references to the fading of 'the glory and the dream' are twice used to gloss Eustacia Vye's loss of romantic interest in a man. And in Hardy's autobiography the same passage from the *Ode* is used in noting the onset – less than five years after their marriage – of his and Emma's marital troubles. These and other allusions make it clear that what mattered most to Hardy in Wordsworth's poem was not the recompense of its closing sections but its memorable expression of loss and diminution. There are no references in Hardy's novels to the sustaining positives, the 'something' living in the embers, the 'first affections' and 'shadowy recollections', the 'primal sympathy', or the 'philosophic mind' that are affirmed in the closing stanzas of the *Ode*. And in Chapter 51 of *Tess of the D'Urbervilles* (1892) another feature of the *Ode* – the postulate of pre-existence – is savaged by the narrator: 'to Tess, as to not a few millions of others, there was ghastly satire in the poet's lines – "Not in utter nakedness/ But trailing clouds of glory do we come." To her and her like, birth itself was an ordeal of degrading personal compulsion, whose gratuitousness nothing in the result seemed to justify, and at best could only palliate' (Elledge 1979, pp. 296–7).

Wordsworthian compensation is similarly unavailable in Hardy's first collection of verse, the *Wessex Poems* of 1898. The dominant themes and moods in this volume concern loss and diminution, the lack of visionary power, the baffled quest for intimations of the transcendent, and the inability to hold Christian beliefs, particularly the belief in a life after death. The subject of *To Outer Nature*, for example, is precisely that of the *Intimations Ode* – the loss of the radiance and splendour that once invested external nature. In the first half of the poem, the speaker beseeches the natural world, even 'for but a moment', to show forth 'that old endowment', that 'iris-hued embowment' that he could see daily in the past. But in the second half of the poem the speaker recognises the impossibility of even a momentary 'readorning' of outer nature. Natural objects can never again be seen to be as they were 'in my morning'; the natural world is 'glow-forsaken' and nature's 'first sweetness,/ Radiance, meetness' will never come again. At the end of the poem, there is no hint of recompense, only a limp interrogative sigh: 'Why not sempiternal/ Thou and I?'

There is, however, one striking exception to the rule of Hardy's writing minuses in place of the Wordsworthian pluses. It is

The Self-Unseeing, one of his few poems containing a memory of childhood:

> Here is the ancient floor,
> Footworn and hollowed and thin,
> Here was the former door
> Where the dead feet walked in.
>
> She sat here in her chair,
> Smiling into the fire;
> He who played stood there,
> Bowing it higher and higher.
>
> Childlike, I danced in a dream;
> Blessings emblazoned that day;
> Everything glowed with a gleam;
> Yet we were looking away!

The occasion of the poem was a visit by Hardy to his childhood home. The scene recalled is a domestic one in which the child Thomas danced for his parents to a tune played by the father. The recollected moment is of great emotional intensity. The poem's abrupt opening, the repetition of the emphatic 'here', the spare, condensed quality of the notations ('Smiling into the fire'), and the metaphorical fusing of 'ancient floor' and 'former door', in which physical objects in space are described in temporal terms, all help to convey the sense of the enhanced, transporting quality of the recovery in memory and recreation in words of a scene from the childhood past.

The third stanza speaks of the 'blessings' of the remembered scene as being 'emblazoned', which suggests an heraldic brilliance and emblematic power. Given such brightness and beneficence, it is hardly surprising that the stanza alludes to one of Hardy's habitual points of reference: the rhyming words 'dream' and 'gleam' inevitably recall the end of the fourth section of the *Intimations Ode* ('Whither is fled the visionary gleam?/ Where is it now, the glory and the dream?'). In so doing, they partially prepare one for the abrupt transition to the last line of the poem in which the adult poet suddenly distances himself from his memory and comments on it, as he also does in the title given the poem. The meaning of the final line and of the title are of crucial importance in considering what presents itself as the key critical question raised by *The Self-Unseeing*: is the poem about an experience of loss or an experience of gain?

There have been sharp differences of opinion on this question. For I. A. Richards in *Science and Poetry* (1926), the answer was that the poem was about diminution and loss. In Richards' influential opinion, Hardy's poetry was important evidence for the decline of the magical view of nature and the world and its supersedence by a scientific view in which nature was neutralised and valueless. For Richards, Hardy's greatness as a poet was intimately connected with his refusal to seek comfort where it could no longer be found. This refusal, says Richards, is most impressively set out, not in Hardy's doctrinal poems, but in personal poems like *The Self-Unseeing* (Richards 1970, pp. 50–2, 67–9). Samuel Hynes, on the other hand, while agreeing with Richards that in Hardy's poem 'the aura of a past event is acknowledged to be past, and the passage of time and the finality of change and death...affirmed', insists that the tone of the poem is celebratory, that 'the remembered event has a kind of present existence' and that the blessings, even if only realised retrospectively, 'are true blessings' (Hynes 1980, pp. 46–7).

In the fullest reading of the poem to date, Peter Simpson also accentuates the positive: 'There is no disillusionment in Hardy's poem, no sense that the child's visionary ecstasy is illusory.' Two distinct interpretations of the meaning of the last stanza are possible, Simpson argues, depending on how its first and last lines are read. In one reading, the stanza expresses 'regret at the passing of a fleeting moment of joy and fulfillment without its having been fully grasped.' In 'a dream', the child is oblivious of the blessings of the gleam, which are realised only in retrospect by the adult speaker. Read another way, the last stanza can be seen to celebrate the child's ignorance: 'he does not *know* he is happy because he is wholly possessed by the ecstasy of the occasion'. The *sine qua non* of the ecstasy is the child's unconsciousness of it. 'It is *because* "we were looking away" that the blessedness was experienced.' The poem's title, says Simpson, cryptically restates these alternative possibilities: 'self-unseeing' can mean both 'self-ignorant' and 'unselfconscious' (Simpson 1979, pp. 50, 48–9).

But these alternative readings are less mutually exclusive than Simpson allows. The child's unselfconsciousness is indeed a necessary condition of the transporting intensity of the experience. This is emphasised by the emphatic 'Childlike' at the beginning of the last stanza. The word would be redundant if it referred only to the fact that the 'I' in the memory was a child. What it refers to is the child's unreflective spontaneous capacity to experience something without being aware of, or reflecting on, the fact that it is being experienced. Either of these reflexive mental activities would inevitably introduce a qualifying and complicating element, and (most damagingly) a temporal element, into an experience the intensity of which is essentially bound up with its being free from the shadow of duration. At the same time, the full significance, the emblazoned and blessed quality, of the earlier experience can only be seen retrospectively, when it is recovered in memory and recreated in language by the adult poet, whose title and whose closing line frame an icon from the past which retains its power – its magic – long after the fire has gone out, the music stopped, and the dreamlike dance ended.

It is, therefore, very hard to see how I. A. Richards could have cited *The Self-Unseeing* as an example of the neutralisation of nature that was the result of the supersedence of the magical view by the modern scientific view. The Wordsworthian analogy that the poem itself intimates should have been helpful to him: the source of the magic (the glow, the gleam, the blessings) in the *Intimations Ode* and *The Self-Unseeing* lies not in external objects *per se*, but in the eye of the childhood beholder. It is a quality of perceptual and affective experience that is within, not without. This is why it does not matter that the Wordsworthian gleam is seen in the natural world and Hardy's gleam in an interior domestic setting. Richards could also have been helped by recalling a crucial distinction made by Hardy: 'I hold that the mission of poetry is to record impressions, not convictions. Wordsworth in his later writings fell into the error of recording the latter. So also did Tennyson, and so do many other poets when they grow old' (Millgate 1984, p. 409). In *Tess of the D'Urbervilles*, the narrator took strong exception to perceived Wordsworthian convictions. But convictions are not at issue in *The Self-Unseeing*. The poem is a powerfully rendered impression of an intense childhood experience, the adult articulation of which is mediated by Wordsworth's antecedent text; and the pull of that text is strong enough to make the poem more than another item in Hardy's poetic catalogue of losses.

III

Resistance is a more conspicuous feature of Hardy's engagement with Tennyson and Browning. A number of the former's poems are quoted from or alluded to in his works; but from first to last the most important text is *In Memoriam*, which Hardy regarded as Tennyson's 'finest poem' (Purdy and Millgate 1978–88, I, p. 282). It was as deeply imprinted on his consciousness as the *Intimations Ode* and as important a point of reference. Tennyson's elegy was one of the chief sources of the quotations and word lists in the poetic notebook headed 'Studies, Specimens &c' that Hardy began keeping in 1865. In 1870 he was reading Tennyson in Cornwall with Emma Gifford during the first year of their romance; and *A Pair of Blue Eyes* contains no fewer than seven quotations from Tennyson, of which five are from *In Memoriam*. (This perhaps helps to explain why the novel was Tennyson's favourite among Hardy's works.) Hardy's copy of an 1875 edition of *In Memoriam* has pencilled markings suggesting that he came to associate the elegy with the loss of his intimate friend Horace Moule, who had taken his own life in 1873. And later references make it clear that Hardy continued to have Tennyson's poem at his fingertips at least until 1922, when two lines from it were quoted in the 'Apology' to *Late Lyrics and Earlier* – and followed by a disarming parenthesis ('if one may quote Tennyson in this century').

Hardy's familiarity with *In Memoriam* and the close personal associations it had for him, however, did not mean that he was an uncritical reader: 'I did my duty in adoring it in years past', he remarked in 1909; but while 'the details of its expression are perfect, the form as a whole is defective, & much of the content has grown commonplace nowadays. As to the form, why Tennyson, who knew so much, should not have seen the awful anticlimax of finishing off such a poem with a highly respectable middle-class wedding, is a mystery, when it ought to have ended with something like an earthquake.' And while it was Hallam Tennyson's life of his father that prompted Hardy's 1897 comment that Tennyson was 'a great artist, but a mere Philistine of a thinker', there is no reason to think he thought differently about *In Memoriam* (Purdy and Millgate 1978–88, IV, p. 5; II, p. 183).

Consider, for example, two of the reflective pieces in *Wessex Poems*. In *The Impercipient*, the subject of which is the speaker's inability to share the beliefs of Christians, there is a negative allusion (the 'All's Well' of the third stanza) to two late sections of Tennyson's elegy that are part of the rhetorical reverberations of his recovered supernatural faith. And *In Memoriam* is the key point of anterior reference in *A Sign-Seeker*, one of the central poems in

Hardy's first collection. The stanza form of the poem is the *abba* quatrain of the elegy with a lengthened last line that in some stanzas is used to emphasise the abiding quotidian realities that the speaker vainly longs to transcend ('And hear the monotonous hours clang negligently by'; 'And Nescience mutely muses: When a man falls he lies'). The speaker of *A Sign-Seeker* is impelled by the Tennysonian imperative: to find emotionally satisfying and spirit-calming evidences in the experiential world of the existence of a life after death. The speaker describes how he has scanned the perceptual limits of the natural world – 'the evening bonfires of the sun', 'the lightning-blade, the leaping star' – for 'tokens' of transcendence and 'radiant hints of times to be'. For the same reason, he has aspired to a scientific understanding of celestial events. He has even been led to the unscientific extreme of lying in dead men's beds and walking in graveyards in the hope of glimpsing a phantom loved-one smiling and whispering 'Not the end'. But for someone of the speaker's temperament, none of these strategies can succeed. He is not like those 'rapt to heights of trancelike trust' – an excellent description of the rhapsodic Tennyson of some of the closing poems of *In Memoriam* – who 'claim to feel and see' transcendent tokens. Hardy's speaker has not mistaken the wish for the deed; for him 'No warnings loom, nor whisperings/ To open out my limitings.'

The pre-eminent Tennysonian token of radiant hints of time to be was love: his love for the dead Hallam became the terrestrial sign of a transcendent Love. Several poems in Hardy's first three volumes of verse have as their point of negative reference such Victorian idealisations of love as Tennyson's. *Her Immortality*, for example, makes a shrewd psychological point concerning the ghost of a loved woman, whose continued apparitional existence is said to depend upon the memory of the grieving man, with whose death her immortality will die. *The To-Be-Forgotten* makes the same point. The spirits of the dead have a 'loved continuance/Of shape and voice and glance' in the memories of their loved ones. But when they die, the spirits must undergo a second death: 'First memory, then oblivion's swallowing sea.'

But something different from simply denying the positives of *In Memoriam* is found in two later poems of Hardy's, both of which came out of his complex emotional response to the death of Emma in 1912. One of them is his principal poetic achievement, the *Poems of 1912–13*. The relationship between this elegiac sequence and

Tennyson's is too big a subject to be considered here. Fortunately, much of it is adumbrated in the relationship between Tennyson's elegy and Hardy's fifteen-line lyric *He Prefers Her Earthly*:

> This after-sunset is a sight for seeing,
> Cliff-heads of craggy cloud surrounding it.
>   – And dwell you in that glory-show?
> You may; for there are strange strange things in being,
>   Stranger than I know.
>
> Yet if that chasm of splendour claim your presence
> Which glows between the ash cloud and the dun,
>   How changed must be your mortal mould!
> Changed to a firmament-riding earthless essence
>   From what you were of old:
>
> All too unlike the fond and fragile creature
> Then known to me ... Well, shall I say it plain?
>   I would not have you thus and there,
> But still would grieve on, missing you, still feature
>   You as the one you were.

The subject of Hardy's poem is contrasting impressions or preferences concerning a lost loved one. After-sunset is the principal time of day in Tennyson's poetry for intimations of the transcendent. Section lxxxvi of *In Memoriam*, for example, describes a similarly ravishing 'glory-show' featuring ranks of crimson-coloured clouds beyond which is the rising star of evening where a hundred spirits whisper 'Peace'. These radiant hints of times to be are confirmed in section cxxxi:

> Thy voice is on the rolling air;
>   I hear thee where the waters run;
>   Thou standest in the rising sun,
> And in the setting thou art fair.

In his poem, Hardy does not deny, but allows for, the possibility of Emma's continued existence as an 'earthless essence' in the other-worldly realm of the 'chasm of splendour' above him. Since his poem is not concerned with the inferior *materia poetica* of convictions, there is no ideological resistance between it and its crucial presupposition. There is rather the indication of a temperamental preference which is made in intimate and loving tones to the absent loved one, the 'fond and fragile creature' whose terrestrial image survives in the speaker's memory. Since it is Tennyson's text that raises the question of preference, *In Memoriam* may be said to be the enabling condition of Hardy's realisation that there is a positive value in the very fact of Emma's mortality and non-transcendence. It is this realisation that allows his poem to end, not with the chasmal image of oblivion's swallowing sea, but with the speaker's continuing to feature 'You as the one you were'.

IV

Hardy's resistance to Browning's optimism is well-known. As he remarked in a letter of 1899, the longer he lived the more Browning's character seemed, '*the* literary puzzle of the 19th century. How could smug Christian optimism worthy of a dissenting grocer find a place inside a man who was so vast a seer & feeler when on neutral ground?' And he later found a striking image to distinguish his vision of life from that of the older poet: 'Imagine you have to walk [a] chalk line drawn across an open down. Browning walked it, knowing no more. But a yard to the left of the same line the down is cut by a vertical cliff five hundred feet deep. I know it is there, but walk the line just the same' (Purdy and Millgate 1978–88, II, p. 216; Millgate 1982, p. 409). Another of Hardy's comments is of particular intertextual interest. Its subject is one of Browning's last poems, the 'Prologue' to *Asolando*. The crucial presupposition of this lyric is Wordsworth's *Intimations Ode*. The old poet is sad, Browning's poem begins, because of the perceptual diminution that comes with age. In youth the poet's eye imparted to every common object 'an alien glow/ His own soul's iris-bow'. But

> now a flower is just a flower:
> Man, bird, beast are but beast, bird, man –
> Simply themselves, uncinct by dower
> Of dyes which, when life's day began,
> Round each in glory ran.

> (lines 2–6)

It is not surprising that Hardy copied these lines into a notebook; as we have seen, he himself makes exactly the same lament in

To Outer Nature concerning the 'iris-hued embowment' that once adorned natural objects but has now gone for good. In that poem, Hardy was unable to avail himself of the Wordsworthian compensation for the loss of 'the radiance which was once so bright': the 'something' that lives on in the embers and the 'philosophic mind' brought by advancing years. Such compensation is similarly unavailable in Browning's poem, but it proves to be irrelevant. At the end of the 'Prologue', the dialectic of loss between early presence and late absence is superseded by the revelation of a transcendent future: the diminished Romantic eye is displaced by the Victorian ear that apprehends a Voice bringing supernatural reassurance: 'At Nature dost thou shrink amazed?/ God is it who transcends.' Hardy was unimpressed by this asserted substitution of supernatural gain for human loss. In his notebook he tersely remarked that the ending was simply 'a conventional piece of optimism' and that he preferred Coleridge's *Youth and Age* which was 'true throughout' in its registration of the irremediable perceptual diminution through which the 'dew-drops' that were 'the gems of morning' become in time 'the tears of mournful eve' (Björk 1985, II, p. 22).[5]

Hardy's resistance to Browning's optimism, however, did not keep him from reading and rereading Browning's poetry and valuing it highly. On the night before he died in 1928 at the age of 87, he asked his second wife Florence to read *Rabbi Ben Ezra* aloud to him; as she recited the 32 stanzas of Browning's characteristically upbeat poem, Florence was struck by 'the look of wistful intentness' with which the dying pessimist was listening (Millgate 1984, p. 480). Hardy had begun reading Browning's poetry sixty years earlier. During the 1880s the two poets not infrequently met on Sunday afternoons in the home of a London hostess; and during his Italian tour of 1887 Hardy seems to have had Browning in his thoughts as much as he did Shelley. And in 1894, as numerous pencilled markings attest, his interest in Browning's poetry was intensified when Mrs Henniker gave him a volume of *Selections from the Poetical Works of Robert Browning*.

F. B. Pinion suggests that his reading of this volume may have had an influence on Hardy's decision to abandon the writing of novels and return to poetry (Pinion 1977, p. 192). It seemed apparent to the reviewers of Hardy's volumes of poetry, and to other early commentators, that his verse had been strongly influenced by Browning's. The unpoetical diction and rough rhythms, the elaborate stanza forms and forced rhymes, the dramatic character of many of the poems: all these features suggested the example of Browning. So did the younger poet's interest in what one commentator called the 'meetings and partings of fate, its conjunctions and mistimings' (Gerber and Davis 1973, p. 179). It is not surprising that *The Statue and the Bust*, which turns on the lost chances of two lovers who never come together because the timing is never right, was Hardy's favourite among Browning's poems (Felkin 1962, p. 30). Richardson describes the work as 'the Browning poem he could most easily have written' (Richardson 1977, p. 36). But any of the several Browning poems that Hardy imitated equally deserves this designation: *Love among the Ruins*, for example, which is rescored in *Ditty*; *Youth and Art*, from which *The Opportunity* derives; or any of the love poems that understrut *Under the Waterfall*, a wholly artificial exercise in the fulsome, worldly manner of much of Browning's amatory verse.

The love poem that had the most personal importance for Hardy, however, is one that he could never have written himself. *By the Fireside*, which celebrates the opposite of a lost chance, is one of Browning's most optimistic and idealising poems. An older speaker, in the late autumn of his years, looks far back in time to the crucial moment, the turning point, in his relationship with the woman who has been his beloved wife for many years. They had been walking in the Italian countryside one autumn day when something totally unanticipated and unlooked for had happened. They had 'caught for a moment the powers at play' in the forests around them: the sights and sounds, the lights and the shades had 'made up a spell' during which a quantum leap in the intensity of their mutual feeling had occurred. The 'bar' between them was broken and two became one: 'we were mixed at last/ In spite of the mortal screen.' Until then, their relationship had been quotidian: a drawing together 'Just for the obvious human bliss, / To satisfy life's daily thirst' with 'a thing men seldom fail' to attain. But in a 'moment, one and infinite', their love had become transcendent. Two souls had mixed 'as mists do'; the lovers had felt themselves to be part of a beneficent 'general plan'; the gain of earth had become 'heaven's gain too'.

That *By the Fireside* could figure as anything but an anti-text in Hardy's work seems extraordinary. Indeed, when the poem is cited in *Tess of the D'Urbervilles* and *Jude the Obscure*, Hardy's resistance is manifest: Browning's positive becomes an ironic intensification of the novelist's negative.[6] But in two of Hardy's personal poems, in both of which he looks back over decades to special moments in the early days of his and Emma's love, resistance is overcome. *By the Fireside* becomes a lens which helps Hardy to bring into focus and to recreate two crucial moments in the most important emotional relationship of his life. Tom Paulin has noted the echo of lines from *By the Fireside* ('Oh, the little more, and how much it is! / And the little less and what worlds away!') in *At the Word 'Farewell'*, which describes the pair's crucial moment of leavetaking in Cornwall in March 1870 when 'the scale might have been turned/ Against love by a feather' (Paulin 1975, pp. 51, 67, 76). The other poem is *At Castle Boterel*, one of the climactic lyrics in the *Poems of 1912–13*. In it Hardy recalls another key moment in March 1870, the night he and Emma walked beside a chaise from which they had just alighted 'To ease the sturdy pony's load/ When he sighed and slowed' during the long uphill climb from Boscastle. The crucial stanzas of the poem are as follows:

> What we did as we climbed, and what we talked of
>   Matters not much, nor to what it led, –
> Something that life will not be balked of
>   Without rude reason till hope is dead,
>   And feeling fled.
>
> It filled but a minute. But was there ever
>   A time of such quality, since or before,
> In that hill's story? To one mind never,
>   Though it has been climbed, foot-swift, foot-sore,
>   By thousands more.
>
> Primaeval rocks form the road's steep border,
>   And much have they faced there, first and last,
> Of the transitory in Earth's long order;
>   But what they record in colour and cast
>   Is – that we two passed.
>
> And to me, though Time's unflinching rigour,
>   In mindless rote, has ruled from sight
> The substance now, one phantom figure
>   Remains on the slope, as when that night
>   Saw us alight.

The dash at the end of the second line of the first quoted stanza functions as an ellipsis for which a phrase must be silently supplied. What specifically Hardy and Emma spoke of during their climb is unimportant; what does matter is something of great value, something that life cannot well do without. The second quoted stanza attempts to describe this 'something'. Intangible and transitory, the 'it' cannot be concretely named; but the 'something' can be identified as a time of unparalleled 'quality'. It 'filled but a minute' (like the 'moment, one and infinite' of Browning's poem); but in this sudden intensification of the lovers' apprehension of each other, this mutual expansion of consciousness, duration is dissolved in presentness and quantity is replaced by quality. Against the background of geological time (the primeval rocks of the road's border), many transitory human moments have come and gone; but his and Emma's brief moment was of such intense non-spatial and non-temporal quality that the millennia-old rocks – the granite face of 'Time's unflinching rigour' – seem by comparison to shrink to the status of mere chroniclers.

In the last stanza of *At Castle Boterel*, the physical setting recedes as the backward-looking widower of the 1913 present drives away; and the poem's tone changes from the passionate affirmation of its centre:

> I look and see it there, shrinking, shrinking,
>   I look back at it amid the rain
> For the very last time; for my sand is sinking,
>   And I shall traverse old love's domain
>   Never again.

The 'it' in the first and second lines of this stanza refers less to the 'phantom figure' of Emma than to the receding slope that is part of the terrain of 'old love's domain'. The ageing speaker, who is at the point in the life-cycle for which sand in an hourglass is the appropriate geological emblem, will 'never again' return to Cornwall. But as the following lyrics in the *Poems of 1912–13* sequence show, he need not leave behind the recovered memory-image of the Emma of early days and the recovered sense of the quality of their early love.

There is no suggestion in *At Castle Boterel* of two souls becoming one or of there being any metaphysical or spiritual reality existing in some timeless realm or 'heaven' apart from the visionary memory of the poet. Hillis Miller is surely right in saying that the quality celebrated in *At Castle Boterel* has only a psychological reality, which is wholly contingent upon the continued existence of the ageing poet whose sands are fast running out and who will one day be ruled from sight by Time's unflinching rigour. (This is, of course, the point that Hardy had made years before in *Her Immortality*.) But Miller is just as surely wrong to say that this transience and inevitable extinction are what *At Castle Boterel* recognises and records (Miller 1970, pp. 247–52). The poem does no such thing; it rather affirms the psychological truth that an experience of transporting quality in the past is recoverable through memory, and that this quality is a token of the value of human love and its enhancement of human life.

At Castle Boterel may also be said implicitly to affirm that intense moments of 'obvious human bliss' are exceptional and are far from being of no lasting value and not worth recording. The infinite moment of *By the Fireside*, that is to say, is de-idealised and humanised in Hardy's poem. But this is not done through inscribing a minus for the antecedent poet's plus. Both poems record experiences of gain. In any event, convictions are not at issue in *At Castle Boterel*; an impression of extraordinary quality is. And it is partially through the mediation of Browning's antecedent text that the impression is imprinted – both in colour and cast on the primeval rocks and in the words of the poem on the page.

V

The three intertextual relationships I have examined are all exceptions to the conventional wisdom concerning Hardy's sense of belatedness and diminution *vis-à-vis* earlier nineteenth-century poets and his inability to share their more positive sense of the possibilities of human existence. But while these poems are quantitatively in the minority, they are qualitatively among Hardy's finest poems. As such, they are as appropriate bases for generalisations about Hardy and his poetic antecedents as are poems in which minuses are written – for example, the often-anthologised *The Darkling Thrush* (which has intertextual connections with Keats's *Ode to a Nightingale*).[7] The tracking of intertextual connections between earlier and later nineteenth-century poems need not always be a *via dolorosa*. One might similarly observe that in his otherwise excellent reading of *Wessex Heights*, Hillis Miller goes too far in using the poem as a basis for generalisations about Hardy's poetry. While it is true to say that 'the impossibility of freeing oneself wholly from the past is the fundamental theme of *Wessex Heights*', it is misleading to add 'and without exaggeration it may be said to be the central theme of all his work'. Another sentence reads: 'The reaching-out of the present toward the past inevitably opens up within the self as it exists in any given moment a hollow, a distance, a wound which can never be healed' (Miller 1968, pp. 345, 351). While this observation may be true of *Wessex Heights*, it is false as a generalisation about a body of poetry that includes, *inter alia*, *The Self-Unseeing* and *At Castle Boterel*.

There are more general areas of suggestiveness as well. One is that in his thinking about poetry and in his poetic practice Hardy makes no distinction between Romantic and Victorian. Wordsworth and Tennyson are equally valued for their impressions and equally criticised for their convictions; Shelley and Swinburne are equally inspiriting. For this reason, except as a chronological shorthand, the terms 'Romantic' and 'Victorian' are not particularly helpful in studying the relationship of Hardy's poems to those of his predecessors. On the other hand, a sense of the continuity of English poetry during the nineteenth century is essential.

Another example concerns Antony H. Harrison's recent study, *Victorian Poets and Romantic Poems: Intertextuality and Ideology*, in which Hardy and his poetry are unmentioned. Harrison's subject is 'the ways in which self-consciously intertextual uses of precursors by Victorian poets serve to reveal ideology, that is, to expose a system of sociopolitical – as well as moral and aesthetic – values embedded in the work of each writer and deployed to influence readers in specific ways' (Harrison 1990, p. 1). If Harrison were to trawl the waters of Hardy's *Collected Poems* with this net he would catch a certain number of fish (for example, discursive, nay-saying texts like *To Outer Nature* or *A Sign-Seeker*). But some big fish, qualitatively speaking, would get away. Like most of Hardy's finest poetry, *The Self-Unseeing*, *He Prefers Her Earthly*, and *At Castle Boterel* are concerned with impressions, not convictions. In them, ideology is not revealed through the use of intertextuality; it is overcome or put aside before the intertextual dynamic begins.

The relationships I have examined are also of interest in relation to theories of influence-anxiety and overdetermination by precursors. In Harold Bloom's model of poetic influence, a strong poet cannot escape the shadow of a precursor, with whom he is doomed to struggle; nor can he 'choose his precursor, any more than any person can choose his father'. As this last phrase suggests, the Bloomian model of influence-anxiety is Freudian and allows for only a single father-figure with whom the intertextual struggle is waged. Thus, in *A Map of Misreading*, Bloom asserts *en passant* that Hardy had a 'prime precursor' and that it was Shelley, whose *Hellas* is said to be 'hovering everywhere' in *Winter Words*, Hardy's last volume of poems, and to whom Hardy is said to owe 'so many of his ecstatic breakthroughs' (Bloom 1975, pp. 12, 19, 23, 11). It is difficult to imagine what Bloom could have meant by this last, wholly unsubstantiated, claim. Even if one agrees for the sake of argument that poems like those I have examined may be designated 'ecstatic breakthroughs', there are by no means many of them in Hardy's canon. And it is not apparent that they can be said to owe anything to Shelley. To put it bluntly, Bloom would appear to be talking through his hat; his influence model simply does not fit the facts of Hardy's case. A better model would be a pluralistic one that allowed for significant engagements with several antecedent poets – engagements that involve assimilation and adaptation as well as resistance.

Such a model could provide a helpful analogy in thinking about the relationship between poems of Hardy and the unwritten life-experiences of readers like myself who return to them again and again. *The Intimations Ode, In Memoriam* and *By the Fireside*: Hardy was deeply attached to these poems and knew them intimately over many years. They were part of his vocabulary of feeling and helped him to understand, to articulate, and to value some of his most intimate life-experiences. In the same way, *The Self-Unseeing*, *He Prefers Her Earthly*, and *At Castle Boterel* can come to have a similar power for readers whose experiences include vividly-remembered childhood incidents, bereavement, and the intensities of early love. And for the readers who are aware of the poetic presuppositions of these poems, there can be the added sense of being part of a continuity of human feeling that authenticates the value of these experiences at the same time as it clarifies and enhances them.

Notes

All quotations from Hardy's poems are from Samuel Hynes's three-volume edition of the *Complete Poetical Works* (Oxford: Clarendon Press,

1982–85). The following editions have been used for the other verse quoted in the text: Shelley 1905; Swinburne 1925; Wordsworth 1984; Tennyson 1969; Browning 1962; Coleridge 1962.

1. And in an 1897 letter Hardy told Mrs Henniker that 'of all men dead whom I should like to meet in the Elysian fields I would choose Shelley, not only for his unearthly, weird, wild appearance & genius, but for his genuineness, earnestness, & enthusiasms on behalf of the oppressed' (Purdy and Millgate 1978–88, II, p. 144).

2. A large number of these references relate to the pursuit of an equivocal and subjectively grounded ideal female love. In *The Woodlanders*, for example, Fitzpiers' rhapsodising over Mrs Charmond includes the recital of a whole stanza from *The Revolt of Islam* concerning an ideal female 'shape of brightness' (ch. 16); and later he murmurs lines from *Epipsychidion* as he rides towards 'the load-star of my one desire' (ch. 28). The same poem is invoked during a key discussion between Sue Bridehead and Jude in *Jude the Obscure* (IV, 5). And the theme of the *The Well-Beloved*, on the title page of which is a phrase from *The Revolt of Islam* ('one shape of many names'), is the pursuit of a Shelleyan ideal woman. See Bartlett 1955a and Miller 1985, pp. 115–19.

3. Hynes made this remark in a paragraph which attempted to downplay Swinburne's influence of Hardy. For a corrective to this view see Murfin 1978, pp. 78–114.

4. This is not surprising, given the importance of Wordsworth's poem as a point of reference for Victorian poets. See Kramer 1980.

5. On the relationship of Browning's poem to Wordsworth's, see Shaw 1978.

6. In chapter 35 of *Tess of the D'Urbervilles*, the narrator makes the following comment on Angel Clare's reaction to learning of Tess's past: 'He was simply regarding the harrowing contingencies of human experience, the unexpectedness of things. Nothing so pure, so sweet, so virginal as Tess had seemed possible all the long while that he had adored her, up to an hour ago; but "The little less, and what worlds away!"' (Elledge 1979, p. 197). In *Jude the Obscure*, the poet who is 'the last of the optimists' is one of the 'shades' or 'spectres' who appear to Jude as he is falling asleep one night. This shade speaks three lines from *By the Fireside* before giving way to the shades of Newman and Keble (Page 1978, p. 67).

7. See May 1973, pp. 62–5.

6

The Return of a Native Singer: Keats in Hardy's Dorset

U. C. KNOEPFLMACHER

In June of 1921, Thomas Hardy received from a group of 'younger comrades in the craft of letters' a copy of the first edition of Keats's *Lamia, Isabella, The Eve of St Agnes and Other Poems*. The occasion was Hardy's eighty-first birthday. As Michael Millgate wryly notes in his biography of Hardy, the gift seemed 'more obviously appropriate' than the model of a full-rigged ship which John Masefield, another younger 'comrade,' presented to an octogenarian no longer interested in the vessel he had coveted as a romantic young boy (Millgate 1982, p. 537).

The gift of Keats's 1820 volume was indeed appropriate. After all, 1921 not only was the year in which Hardy celebrated entering the eighth decade of his long life, but also happened to be the centenary year of Keats's death. As the donors of the book well knew, Hardy had only recently joined a national committee to purchase Wentworth Place, the Hampstead house in which Keats composed his 1819 odes and narratives. To help raise money, Hardy had sent a memorial poem, *At A House in Hampstead*, as his personal contribution to *The John Keats Memorial Volume*, which appeared on 23 February, 1921, exactly one hundred years after Keats's death in Rome. What is more, Hardy's 'younger comrades' may also have known that the poet had returned to Keats in two other recent poems, *The Selfsame Song* and *At Lulworth Cove A Century Back*, both of which he would place together with *At A House in Hampstead* into his 1922 volume, *Late Lyrics and Earlier*.

Much has been written on the bearing of both Wordsworth's and Shelley's work on the fiction and poetry of Thomas Hardy.[1] But beyond the generally accepted sense that *Ode to a Nightingale* somehow lurks behind *The Darkling Thrush*, little has been done to flesh out more fully the imaginative relation between Hardy and Keats.[2] Hardy's 1887 visit to the graves of Shelley and Keats, commemorated in the poem *Rome: At the Pyramid of Cestius Near the Graves of Shelley and Keats*, may suggest that the two younger Romantics were equally 'pre-eminent in Hardy's poetic pantheon' (Millgate 1982, p. 281). Yet it is Shelley and not Keats with whose ideas and poetic precedent Hardy always seems more eager to engage. Thus, whereas the 1887 poems of pilgrimage also include *Shelley's Skylark*, there seems to be no matching involvement with a Keatsian antecedent.

I intend to show that it was Keats, however, whom Hardy eventually came to perceive as his prime Romantic partner or 'comrade'. If echoes and citations from Wordsworth and Shelley are far more abundant in Hardy's *oeuvre*, it is because their ideology and poetic practice furnished him with foils against which he could redefine his own romanticism. Keats, on the other hand, eventually was perceived as an *alter ego*, as self-educated and self-obscuring as Hardy, yet similarly tough-minded in his mixture of idealism and scepticism. Hardy's eventual attribution of Dorset origins to Keats – his belated recollection of 'a family named Keats' who had lived a few miles from his home in Max Gate[3] – represents a deliberate attempt to implant the poet's shade in his own immediate environs. Wordsworth's 'Nature' or Shelley's 'Intellectual Beauty' were, for Hardy, ultimately less trustworthy than the formulations of the ordinary man who could fashion extraordinary verses by entering into an imaginative partnership with dead poets such as Shakespeare and Milton. The sequence of poems in which Hardy engages, surreptitiously at first and then more openly, with the ghost of Keats – a sequence which itself spans a time period of greater duration than Keats's life – culminates when Hardy wrests an English poet away from his tomb in Rome and returns him to a native soil. Like the spectre of Emma Hardy, Keats becomes a returning native whose shade can be embraced by a survivor as fragile, common, tiny, and yet also as defiant in flinging his own sound and soul against a 'darkling' world.

I

Hardy's 1887 *Poems of Pilgrimage* – first printed as a group in the 1901 *Poems of the Past and Present* – included *Shelley's Skylark* and

Rome: At the Pyramid of Cestius Near the Graves of Shelley and Keats,
but, as noted above, lacked any poem exclusively devoted to Keats.
The Shelleyan coordinates are quite overt. Ostensibly, the first of
these two poems involves an 'idealizing' engagement[4] with Shelley's
own *To a Skylark* (1820), while the second can be construed as a
looser revision of Shelley's *Ozymandias* (1818). Yet, as I shall try to
argue in this section, even these two poems anticipate – through
their sub-texts – an identification with Keats that would become
more pronounced in the poems considered in the next section.

If *Shelley's Skylark* is placed, not just against Shelley's *To a
Skylark,* but also against Wordsworth's two poems by the same title,
the notion, entertained by both Kerry McSweeney and by James
Richardson, that Hardy's poem is a 'flimsy, sentimental', and
'uncharacteristically precious' construct (McSweeney, pp. 92–3
above; Richardson 1977, p. 3) seems rather questionable. For Hardy,
characteristically self-conscious about his poetic antecedents, seems
to enter quite knowingly into a much earlier debate that had
involved Wordsworth and Shelley, as well as, indirectly, Keats.

In his original *To a Sky-Lark* (composed in 1805 and printed in
1807), Wordsworth set up a dialectic that would be adopted in
Shelley's 1820 poem, reworked in Wordsworth's 1825 *To a Skylark,*
and recast once more in Hardy's own 1887 *Shelley's Skylark.* By
contrasting the planes occupied by the vaulting skylark and a plodding human 'traveller' bound to a horizontal realm, Wordsworth
distinguishes between two kinds of song, and hence also between
two types of poets. In the poem's opening line, 'Up with me! up
with me into the clouds!', skylark and poet are so indistinguishable
from each other that it almost seems as if it were the poet's 'me'
who exhorts his air-bound fellow-singer to rise with him. Soon,
however, it becomes apparent that the 'strong' singer who repeats
this command (line 3) cannot be the poet. The conclusion of the first
stanza (which Shelley would echo in *Ode to the West Wind,* when he
implored an airy force to 'lift me as a wave, a leaf, a cloud!') clearly
establishes the inferiority of the human 'me':

> Lift me, guide me, till I find
> That spot which seems so to thy mind.

> (lines 6–7)

The ecstatic erasure of self and not-self of Wordsworth's exclamatory opening gives way to a gradual splintering in the increasingly

reflective remainder of the poem. The spot which *'seems so'* to an alien, non-verbal 'mind' cannot be reached by a poetic mind bound to words and ideas; it is a 'banqueting place in the sky' (line 15) in which an earth-bound imagination cannot aspire to feast. In a phrasing that both Hardy and Keats would surely remember, Wordsworth's speaker utters a wishful impossibility:

> Had I now the wings of a Faery,
> Up to thee would I fly.

(lines 10–11)

The separation between skylark and the speaker is completed when the bird is perceived as 'scorning' his human antitype: 'thou wouldst be loth / To be such a traveller as I' (lines 17, 20–21). The final stanza of the poem accentuates the human wanderer's inferiority by stressing the horizontal plane to which he is bound: 'Alas! my journey, rugged and uneven, / Through prickly moors or dusty ways must wind' (lines 26–7). The embers of joy that Wordsworth can rekindle at the end of 'Poems of the Imagination' that similarly mediate between an atemporal ecstasy and a tempered self-consciousness (*Resolution and Independence*, for example, or *Nutting*) are dimmed as he closes this 'Poem of Fancy' on a deliberately flat and stoic note: 'But hearing thee, or others of thy kind, / As full of gladness and as free of heaven, / I, with my fate contented, will plod on, / And hope for higher raptures, when life's day is done' (lines 28–31).

As both Wordsworth and Hardy seemed to understand, the 21 five-line stanzas of Shelley's *To a Skylark* constitute a sequel or reply to the 31 lines of Wordsworth's 1805 poem.[5] Shelley keeps Wordsworth's exclamatory opening, stresses the same 'joy' Wordsworth had imputed to the bird, retains the contrast between vertical and horizontal planes, and, even more overtly than Wordsworth, likens an air-borne singer to a higher type of poet. The 'scorning' for those who 'must wind' their earthly journeys through 'prickly moors or dusty ways' (W, lines 17, 26–7) is retained when Shelley, too, characterizes his skylark as a 'scorner of the ground' (S, line 100). But the differences underlying even these similarities nonetheless remain profound, for, unlike Wordsworth's overly self-conscious traveller, Shelley's speaker ends on a deliberate note of 'creative suspension' (Blank, 1988, p. 190). The skylark's unselfconsciousness may not be attained by humans, yet its scornful obliviousness to all forms of meditation can nonetheless be held out as a worthy model for earth-bound singers.

Shelley wants to narrow the gap between skylark and speaker that Wordsworth opened. He therefore dispenses with Wordsworth's highly individualised self-characterisation. Whereas Wordsworth's omnipresent 'me' or 'I' increasingly distances us from an alien 'mind' whose ecstasy remains untranslatable, Shelley uses the first-person sparingly throughout his much longer poem. Indeed, even when Shelley's 'I' makes its first appearance in line 20, he acts as a mere vessel for 'strains of unpremeditated art' (line 5),[6] the 'unbodied' joy he tries to reproduce through language that is itself anti-meditative: 'Thou art unseen, but yet I hear thy shrill delight' (lines 14, 20). Whereas Wordsworth conceded that his dependence on 'rugged and uneven' contours made his own measures decidedly weaker than the bird's 'strong song', Shelley tries to devise a form of expression that will allow him to emulate the lark's vocal fluidities.

Wordsworth's effort to retain his skylark as a source of inspiration is impaired by his representation of the bird as superior rival to a plodding 'I'; Shelley's similar goal, however, is aided by his avoidance of a contest between a 'Thou' and an 'I'. He achieves his end in two ways: by depersonalizing his speaker and subsuming him to a 'we' who comes to stand for a universal human awareness of time and space; and by treating the bird-who-never-was as an ineffable presence that can only be represented through the limited human constructions of simile and analogy. Shelley's insistence on such verbal and conceptual limits allows him to stress the intensity of his desire. It matters little whether the creature that inflames his imagination is 'Sprite or Bird'. Minds who must strain to grasp 'What is most like thee?' (lines 31–2) may never shed their painful self-consciousness. Nonetheless, unlike Wordsworth's stoical 'I, with my fate contented', such minds can become energized by their very discontent:

> Yet if we could scorn
>   Hate, and pride, and fear;
> If we were things born
>   Not to shed a tear,
> I know not how thy joy we ever should come near.

(lines 91–5)

The 'I' that returns here after a 70-line absence now converts the lark's unpremeditated joy into a potential model for poetic intoxication:

> Better than all measures
>   Of delightful sound,
> Better than all treasures
>   That in books are found,
> Thy skill to poet were, thou scorner of the ground.
>
> Teach me half the gladness
>   That thy brain must know,
> Such harmonious madness
>   From my lips would flow
> The world should listen then – as I am listening now.

(lines 96–105)

If Shelley had come across the *Ode to a Nightingale*, composed exactly a year earlier, before he finished his own poem, then it would seem likely that he not only conceived *To a Skylark* as a rejoinder to Wordsworth's guarded 1805 verses but also to Keats's more powerful alternation between the contrary moods of escape and self-imprisonment. That Keats himself recalled Wordsworth's *To a Sky-lark* in his ode among other antecedents (Milton's *Penseroso*, say, and Coleridge's *The Nightingale*) is borne out by several unmistakable echoes. The 'wings of a Faery' which Wordsworth's speaker had vainly hoped to sprout in order to fly 'Up to thee,' for example, are evoked when the Ode's speaker determines 'I will fly to thee' and reach the moon and all her 'starry Fays' (K, lines 31, 37). But it is through his sharpening of the painful separation between thoughtless ecstasy and a thought-burdened solipsism that Keats most poignantly reworks his predecessor's poem.[7] Keats's 'I', though as prominent as Wordsworth's, no longer traverses prickly moors or dusty ways. Instead, his speaker has become immobilised, passively grounded in his plot of 'embalmed darkness'. He cannot venture into 'near meadows', let alone travel into imaginary landscapes, 'faery lands forlorn' – in the phrase that tolls him back to his immured 'sole self' (lines 43, 70, 72).

Written after the deaths of both Keats and Shelley, Wordsworth's second *To a Skylark* (1825), a mere twelve lines long, is best read as a quasi-allegorical tribute to younger 'comrades'. Here again there is a contrast between two kinds of poetry, two types of poet. But Wordsworth has removed the self-conscious speaker of his 1805 poem and of Keats's *Ode to A Nightingale*. The opening exaltation of the skylark, now addressed as an 'Ethereal minstrel! pilgrim of the sky!' (line 1), therefore is maintained in the rest of the poem. Wordsworth even accepts Shelley's notion of a fiery mentor when he chooses to convert the bird into a 'Type of the wise who soar, but never roam' (line 11). Yet, at the same time, by humanising Shelley's 'blithe Spirit', Wordsworth also seems eager to inject a certain distancing from a pilgrim–minstrel whose very intensity, like Shelley's own, might prove alienating.

Wordsworth clearly has the younger poet in mind when, picking up Shelley's characterisation of the lark as a 'scorner of the ground' (S, line 100), he asks the bird whether it does 'despise the earth where cares abound?' (W, line 2). Can the aloof skylark stay faithful to its kind by maintaining a watch over its 'nest upon the dewy ground?' (line 4). The speaker eventually decides that the bird can be true to both 'Heaven and Home', to private ecstasy and domesticity. But the reconciliation is undermined when Wordsworth suggests that nesting may require a stilling of the music he celebrates. Shelley's skylark – and Shelley himself – seek a 'privacy of glorious light'; singers confined to their worldly nests, however, can admire but not emulate such self-abandon. Deliberately invoking the night-bird Keats found 'pouring forth' in 'such an ecstasy' (K, line 58), Wordsworth reactivates the dialectic he had initiated in his earlier poem:

> Leave to the nightingale her shady wood;
> A privacy of glorious light is thine;
> When thou dost pour upon the world a flood
> Of harmony, with instinct more divine.

> (lines 7–10)

Playing his two successors against each other, Wordsworth purports to give primacy to the soaring singer who defies boundaries and enclosures. And yet, for all his homage to such aspiration, his sympathy still rests with the 'heart and eye' that stay affixed to nesting-places on the dewy ground. By 1825, Victoria's future Laureate has moved away from the radicalism of his youthful poetry. Fifty-five years old, Wordsworth treats Shelley with the same mixture of sympathy and detachment that also characterises the attitude that Hardy will adopt when, also in his fifties, he must confront Shelley and Keats (and Wordsworth himself) as a late-born Romantic poet.

A consideration of the four poems I have examined is necessary, I think, if we are not to misread Hardy's poem of pilgrimage, *Shelley's Skylark*. Hardy goes out of his way to ground a singer on whom his three predecessors had conferred such unearthly powers. Shelley lifted his skylark far above the 'earth' from which it sprang (S, line 7); Wordsworth wondered if an aerial pilgrim deigned to return to its nest on the ground; Keats contrasted the 'immortal Bird' not born for death to his own mortal 'sod' (K, line 60). Despite their differences in emphasis, however, all three speakers were equally animated by the music they overhear. Not so Hardy. His speaker is deaf to the harmonies that so thrilled his predecessors. What is more, the bird 'unseen'-yet-heard by Shelley has decayed into a 'pinch of unseen, unguarded dust' (H, line 4). The vertical and horizontal planes that Hardy's predecessors contrasted have completely collapsed. There remains only the horizontal plane through which a speaker turned archeologist now rummages with microscopic zeal: 'Somewhere afield here something lies' (line 1). The irony is grim. The material order the Romantics tried to pierce has become an ash-heap, a repository of vestigial wastes.

Shelley's Skylark is hardly shaped by 'idealising whimsy', as Kerry McSweeney holds; nor can it be said that Hardy finds himself 'unable to engage himself' with antecedent texts (McSweeney, p. 93 above). Quite to the contrary, Hardy dramatises his engagement by creating a Shelleyan speaker who finds himself ironically compelled to reverse Shelley's emphasis. Whereas Shelley, in his concluding stanzas, upheld the bird's lyrical power above 'all treasures / That in books are found' (S, lines 98–9), Hardy's speaker – unable to hear the sounds that so stirred his Romantic predecessors – can find such treasures only through the printed record of another's words. Hardy's speaker thus is forced to side with Keats, the poet who allowed that an immortal Bird not born for death may have been nothing more than a product of his own feverish desire (K, line 61). The Keatsian nightingale which Wordsworth introduced as a foil to a Shelleyan skylark is even more prominent in Hardy's poem. When his pseudo-Shelleyan speaker acknowledges that only a poet's brain could make 'immortal through times to be' a bird that 'lived [and

died] like any other bird', he goes to Keats to undermine the
climactic credo of the poem he ostensibly sets out to celebrate (H,
line 6, 7). The very effort to find some remnant of a 'little ball of
feather and bone' (line 10) after more than six decades of decompo-
sition is as grimly comical as Jude Fawley's attempts to animate the
impassive stones of Christminster with the voices of dead idealists.

But Hardy goes further in his ironic relic-hunt. The fourth stanza
of *Shelley's Skylark*, in which the speaker vainly evokes the ideas of
transmutation expressed in Shelley's *The Cloud*, undercuts even
more radically the attempt to find on a horizontal plane some
vestige of the airy energies tapped by an earlier 'pilgrim' two-thirds
of a century before. The animated 'Thou' whom the Romantics had
apostrophised has wizened into an inert 'it':

> Maybe it rests in the loam I view,
> Maybe it throbs in a myrtle's green,
> Maybe it sleeps in the coming hue
> Of a grape on the slopes of yon inland scene.

(lines 13–16)

Shelley, whom Hardy's speaker describes as a poet moved 'to
prophecies' when engaging the material world (line 3), could
fashion the 'trumpet of a prophecy' from unextinguished ashes and
sparks. But the speaker who hopes to extract from the 'coming hue'
of an unripe grape some semblance of a Shelleyan energy, must
cling to the dubious notion that the vines of Leghorn are still being
fertilised by a speck of ashes dispersed sixty years earlier. With a
litany of 'maybes' that accentuate his doubt, the speaker merely
manages to dramatise his own plight. By trying to locate a long-
decayed body in the 'coming hue' of unripe grapes this modern
votary of Shelley demands an act of faith which he is incapable of
sustaining. His own verses, therefore, cannot ripen. Indeed, the
grapevines of Leghorn cannot even furnish him with that 'draught
of vintage' which Keats had hoped to drink in order to leave the
world unseen (K, line 11).

Keats and Wordsworth nonetheless can come to the aid of a
latter-day Shelleyan. If cheating Fancy rather than pure Imagination
is to be this earth-bound speaker's lot, then he can at least avail
himself of those 'wings of a Faery' and 'faery lands forlorn' that
Wordsworth and Keats had invoked as a compensation for their

inability to be transported into realms of thoughtless ecstasy. The speaker's abrupt construction of a fairy tale to encase unobtainable wishes stems from limits also acknowledged by his more sceptical Romantic predecessors:

> Go find it, faeries, go and find
> That tiny pinch of priceless dust,
> And bring a casket silver-lined,
> And framed of gold that gems encrust;
>
> And we will lay it safe therein,
> And consecrate it to endless time;
> For it inspired a bard to win
> Ecstatic heights in thought and rhyme.

(lines 17–24)

Unable to find traces of the 'it' which Shelley still hailed as a 'Thou', the impotent 'I' of this poem can hardly presume to address directly either Shelley or his skylark. Instead, the speaker anachronistically resorts to an outmoded machinery when he asks 'faeries' to help him find what he could not unearth on his own. His request is a mark of his desperation. The elves to whom he is forced to appeal are as much the product of a cheating Fancy as Keats's 'deceiving elf' was in *Ode to a Nightingale*. Unable to reproduce the vital partnership that animated Shelley's poem, the speaker must align himself with an imaginary host of grave-diggers. Joined as 'we', he and they will try to rebury a lost pinch of dust in a jewelled casket. Yet even if such dust could be found, the symbolic action would remain futile. Just as the dead 'it' does not require to be preserved in a new container, so does Shelley's feat in making a lark 'immortal through times to be' (line 6) hardly require another's second effort to reconsecrate it 'to endless time' (line 22). The poem's closure thus is heavily ironic. By dwelling on the dust-filled casket he wants to seal, Hardy's speaker only accentuates his inability to scale the 'Ecstatic heights in thought and rhyme' he celebrates in the very last line.

Yet it would be a mistake to read *Shelley's Skylark* as a total negation of its Romantic original. Hardy's tribute takes the shape of a deliberate deformation that is intended to signify his inability to follow a precedent he genuinely admires. Closer to Wordsworth's first skylark poem than to Shelley's text and closer to Keats's Ode than to either Wordsworth or Shelley, Hardy's negations here take Keats's negative capability one step further. The questions entertained at the end of *Ode to a Nightingale* ('Was it a vision, or a waking dream? / Fled is that music: – Do I wake or sleep') are no longer operative. The frenzied music still heard by Wordsworth, Shelley and Keats altogether eludes Hardy's deafened late-nineteenth-century speaker. He can at best admire their own surviving music and try to preserve its impact in tiny caskets silver-lined. His role is that of a witness, a guide to ecstasies not his own.

A similar irony operates in *Rome: At the Pyramid of Cestius Near the Graves of Shelley and Keats.* Like *Shelley's Skylark*, this pendant poem (which also consists of six quatrains) relies on an act of deflection. It is the unknown Roman Cestius, whose funeral pyramid stands near the resting places of two 'countrymen of mine', who ostensibly preoccupies the speaker far more than those two 'matchless singers' (lines 12, 20): 'Who, then, was Cestius, / And what is he to me?' (lines 1, 2). The sculptor of Shelley's Ozymandias had at least stamped a boastful inscription on the pedestal of the statue that desert sands converted into a 'colossal wreck'. But the record of Cestius's identity has been obliterated. His actions are as irrecoverable as the stirring sound of Shelley's skylark. Hence, once again, the speaker resorts to constructions that are purely hypothetical. If he hoped 'maybe' to sift the skylark's ashes from the loam, he can only conjecture that Cestius owed his eminence because 'in life, maybe, [he] / Slew, breathed out threatening; / I know not' (lines 13–15).

Yet the speaker finds a purpose after all in the life of Cestius the Obscure. And that purpose also underscores the speaker's sense of his own precarious position. Although Cestius's pretensions are mocked by his unvisited tomb, his mausoleum can at least direct 'pilgrim feet' to the graves of the two English Romantic poets (lines 22, 17). Reduced to a sign-post, pointing with 'marble finger high' to the resting place of worthier dead, Cestius fulfils a 'finer' design as a marker of achievements not his own (line 18, 16). The poem's concluding stanza suggests that the speaker recognises that his own function is not unlike that of Cestius:

> – Say, then, he lived and died
>   That stones which bear his name

Should mark, through Time, where two immortal Shades abide;
  It is an ample fame.

(lines 21–4)

The poet whose name is affixed to *Shelley's Skylark* and *Rome: At the Pyramid of Cestius* accepts his subsidiary role in a Romantic canon. The verbal structures he has erected in these two poems can at best point to the higher achievement of visionary predecessors. He remains an observer of, not an active participant in, their imaginative achievement. Yet as an outsider, he accepts his subordination with something of the resigned satisfaction that Matthew Arnold tried to express at the end of his essay on *The Function of Criticism at the Present Time* : to point to the preeminence of others, to salute them from afar, is to partake in their distinction. It is an ample fame for late-born Romantics.

II

The Darkling Thrush, which Hardy deliberately dated '31 December 1900', partakes of the elegiac mode of *Shelley's Skylark* and *Rome: At the Pyramid of Cestius* in marking the passage of a century that began with youthful hymns of hope and transcendence. Yet by his tentative engagement – in the waning hours of a bitter winter day – with the aged thrush's 'full-hearted evensong/ Of joy illimited', Hardy now is more willing than before to emulate the experience of the Romantic forerunner who guardedly reacted to another such dusky voice singing 'of summer in full-throated ease' (H, lines 19–20; K, line 10). *The Darkling Thrush* thus anticipates the reanimations of Keats that Hardy will eventually produce, two decades later, in the three poems he printed in his 1922 collection: *The Selfsame Song, At a House in Hampstead*, and *At Lulworth Cove a Century Back*.

The first two stanzas of *The Darkling Thrush* are taken up with the speaker's response to a grey landscape that pointedly differs from the lush and perfumed darkness in which Keats placed his melodious nightbird. Music seems impossible amidst the 'Winter's dregs' that shroud a land likened to a giant 'corpse' (H, lines 3, 10). The tangled 'bine-stems' that score the sky 'Like strings of broken lyres' (lines 5–6) would seem to strangle any lyrical outburst.

Whereas the surfeits of a vernal nightscape jointly enveloped Keats's 'darkling' listener and singer (K, line 51), Hardy's speaker assumes that all other creatures on this dry and frozen tundra must share his own 'fervourless' response (line 16).

The speaker's assumption, however, is undercut by the sudden eruption, at the poem's exact midpoint, of a 'voice' (line 17) that defies such dire projections of universal gloom. The 'happy goodnight air' (line 30) of the thrush may seem far less justified than the 'happy lot' Keats had imputed to his joyous nightingale (K, line 5). Unlike the unseen nightingale (and unlike Shelley's unseen skylark), the thrush can be vividly seen in all its crepuscular puniness: 'frail, gaunt, and small, / In blast-beruffled plume' (lines 21–2). Nonetheless, the insistent cheerfulness of this latter-day singer poses a challenge Hardy's meditative speaker cannot ignore. For the thrush not only may act a potential corrective for his own gloom but also may call into question the despondency of predecessors equally convinced that 'to think is to be full of sorrow/ And leaden-eyed despairs' (K, lines 27–8). The mid-Victorian pessimism that led Arnold to convert a 'various' and 'beautiful' nightscape into a 'darkling plain' endowed with 'neither joy, nor love, nor light, / Nor certitude, nor peace, nor help for pain' (*Dover Beach*, lines 30–2) had eradicated that capacity to entertain contrary states still possible for Keats's darkling listener. By allowing his speaker to overhear a song of 'joy illimited' amidst a landscape he has already equated with the dying century, Hardy introduces the possibility of a perspective antithetical to such joyless Arnoldian gloom.

In *The Darkling Thrush*, therefore, Hardy can be said to reinstate – very tentatively, to be sure – something approaching a Keatsian negative capability. His speaker still finds 'such ecstatic sound' more difficult to partake than the Romantic predecessor who yearned to participate in 'such an ecstasy!' (H, line 26; K, line 58). As a creature of the later nineteenth century, Hardy's sober analyst demands empirical proofs he can hardly expect to obtain from a bird known to oppose 'rough or gloomy weather' by heightening its song of instinctual delight.[8] Yet the speaker's very predicament, his inability to detect any 'cause for carolings' in the bleak landscape he has allegorised as a giant corpse, also makes him receptive to an attitude contrary to his own. Might not, he ponders, instinctual joy be as justified as his own mental projections of a cosmic despondency? The speaker thus admits, half-grudgingly, that the frail bird could be a vessel for a tremor of 'Some blessed

Hope, whereof he knew / And I was unaware' (H, lines 31–2). The possibility raises doubts about his earlier representation. The century he has pronounced to be dead might, in fact, be undergoing a cycle of renovation. If so, 'The ancient pulse of germ and birth', far from being 'shrunken hard and dry' (lines 13, 14), may throb again with something of its old vitality. Though winter is here, spring may not be far behind. Like the 'soft-dying day' Keats animated in *To Autumn*, this winter day turns out to have its music too – a music that may well restore some of the hope that stirred idealists when the century was still in its youth.

This possibility of cyclical continuity is even more strongly embraced in the three Keatsian poems that Hardy composed two decades after *The Darkling Thrush*. Indeed, the first of these, *The Selfsame Song*, significantly revises both *The Darkling Thrush* and *Shelley's Skylark*. Returning one more time to *Ode to a Nightingale*, Hardy now offers an elaboration of Keats's conjecture that a song heard 'this passing night' might perhaps be 'the self-same song that found a path / Through the sad heart' of much earlier exiles (K, lines 63, 65–6). Hardy simultaneously asserts and denies the notion of an immortal bird not born for death. The song is identical – 'Unchanged in a note!' – to that heard by the speaker and his former companions, on the same spot, 'Long years ago' (lines 8, 4). But although the speaker rejoices in the 'pleasing marvel' of finding a nightingale⁹ still capable of warbling 'the selfsame song, / With never a fault in its flow' (lines 5, 1–2), he also must acknowledge that past and present have not really coalesced:

> – But it's not the selfsame bird. –
> No: perished to dust is he....
> As also are those who heard
> That song with me.

> (lines 9–12)

In *Shelley's Skylark*, a seeker of mute vestiges failed to find the material 'dust' of the selfsame bird who had stimulated an immortal lyric. Now, however, a thrilled listener can at least assert the perpetuity of disembodied song in a physical world of severance and death. And what holds true in nature may, in fact, also hold true in art. Just as the 'rapturous rote' of one long-dead nightingale is automatically repeated by any one of its successors, so does it seem natural now to find the words of a long-dead poet repeated by one who has come to consider himself as Keats's heir. By wresting the title and opening line of his poem from *Ode to a Nightingale* Hardy can attempt an identification that seems more plausible to him than it had been in the past. Having become a live relic of the nineteenth century, Hardy now feels closer than ever before to the generation before him. The gap has diminished.

Hardy's speaker ends by memorialising 'those who heard/ That song with me'. The final personal pronoun tolls the speaker back to his own sole self. A past 'we' exists no more. And yet by hearing once again the familiar cadences of the selfsame song, a lonely 'me' has been able to indulge in a reverie that briefly blended past and present. The suspension of disbelief has allowed him to animate fellow-listeners who once moved in his own circle – his dead parents, perhaps, or dead friends, or a dead Emma Hardy. Similarly, by building his own lyric around a single Keatsian phrase, Hardy can reanimate that earlier listener/fashioner of songs.

Hardy's own song, however, must go beyond mere replication. Though indebted to its original, his text is hardly the 'selfsame song' Keats had fashioned. Nor, for all his kinship, can Hardy presume to adopt Keats's identity, to become the selfsame poet. Nonetheless, by skilfully borrowing one 'strain' from the text of an arch-appropriator of the words and images of others, Hardy displays capacities that distinctly resemble Keats's own. His sympathetic identification owes much to the poet who could assert his ability to enter into the existence of a sparrow and 'pick about the Gravel'.

At a House in Hampstead, Sometime the Dwelling of John Keats, the poem which Hardy contributed to help with the purchase of Wentworth Place, extends that sense of kinship by boldly transporting to England a ghost roused from a 'drowse' more permanent than the 'drowsy numbness' that had enveloped the torpid speaker of *Ode to a Nightingale* (H, line 5; K, line 1). Keats's Ode had ended with the speaker's self-questioning. Hardy now adopts that interrogative mode by devoting the first five quatrains of his eight-stanza poem to questions he directly asks of the shade he has disinterred and relocated. Did this spectre think he might 'find all just the same' in a place in which 'streets have stolen up all around, / And never a nightingale pours one / Full-throated sound?' (H, lines 6, 2–4). How will he react to such drastic changes? Will he show resentment by blowing 'wind-wafts' on the stairs of Wentworth, by slamming doors, or even by materialising as 'an umbraged ghost' next to the 'ancient tree' under which he had composed his famous ode (lines 13, 15)? Hardy rejects that possibility by striking a more conciliatory note in his last question:

> Or will you, softening, the while
> You further and yet further look,
> Learn that a laggard few would fain
> Preserve your nook? ...

(lines 17–20)

The reference here is not only to twentieth-century Keatsians eager to maintain Wentworth Place as a memorial site. The octogenarian author, a 'laggard' creature of the nineteenth century, clearly regards his own verses as a 'nook' in which he might preserve the spirit of his Romantic *alter ego*.

Hardy therefore rehearses his previous relation to Keats in the remaining three stanzas. He is no longer as tied as he was in his 1887 poems of pilgrimage to material remains and resting places. He remembers having stood at 'eventide' at the slope of Piazza steps, 'and thought," 'Twas here he died"' (lines 22, 24). And he again recalls the 'white hand' of the pyramid of Cestius that led him to exclaim ' " 'Tis there he sleeps" ' (line 28). But the speaker of this poem remembers these earlier utterances only to discredit the literalness of his attachment to a physical order. He is no longer the awed tourist of the Poems of Pilgrimage, a necrophiliac disturber of ashes. If Keats could build a 'fane' to Psyche in some untrodden region of his mind, so is Hardy now 'fain' to create a nook to let Keats in. His poem's subtitle is poignant: 'Sometime the Dwelling of John Keats' refers to Wentworth Place, the location which the speaker and Keats's ghost are professedly revisiting. But like the Roman house near the Piazza or the grave near the pyramid of Cestius, the Hampstead house and garden were but a 'sometime' dwelling for one who can make his habitat in the imagination of a fellow-poet:

> Pleasanter now it is to hold
> That here, where sang he, more of him
> Remains than where he, tuneless, cold,
> Passed to the dim.

(lines 29–32)

It is no longer enough to pluck and reimplant isolated Keatsian phrases. Keats himself – or 'more of him' – can be plucked away from his Roman tomb. Hardy has at last effected the return of a native singer.

If *At a House in Hampstead* hauls into the present a sleeper who died a hundred years ago, *At Lulworth Cove a Century Back*, dated 'September 1920', retreats in exactly the opposite direction. To be near Keats, Hardy's 'I' now becomes a time-traveller. Had he 'but lived a hundred years ago', he conjectures, he might well have gone, 'as I have gone this year', to the spot on the Dorset coast at which Joseph Severn and Keats presumably stopped in September of 1820 before sailing to Italy (lines 1, 2). Addressed by a personification of the hindsight denied to him, the transported visitor is emphatically thrice asked, ' "*You see that man?* " ' (lines 5, 9, 13). But the 'commonplace' youth who has just stepped off a boat strikes his observer as unworthy of notice (line 8). He considers him an 'idling town-sort; thin; hair brown in hue', a loiterer gaping in the 'evening light' at some 'star, as many do' (lines 10, 11, 12). The speaker is annoyed by his questioner's reiteration of an *ecce homo*. He has more pressing business than to take note of some obscure idler: 'I have fifteen miles to vamp across the lea, / And it grows dark, and I am weary-kneed: / I have said the third time; yes, that man I see!' (lines 14–16).

Once again, as in *The Selfsame Song* and *At a House in Hampstead*, Hardy subverts the literalism that had once led him to scour the 'loam' of Livorno and the Roman tombs of his countrymen. Stripped of hindsight, Hardy's time-traveller also becomes dispossessed of an imagination that might have profited from a better acquaintance with the 'commonplace' youth who took his last farewell from England by showing his friend Severn a part of Dorset 'he already knew'.[10] Back on board the ship bound for Italy, this idle star-gazer will present Severn with a fair copy of his famous sonnet *Bright Star*.

In his last stanza, Hardy allows foreseeing 'Time'[11] to correct the speaker who has thrice refused to recognise a sublime sufferer much as Peter thrice denied Christ. Foresight and hindsight recombine to allow a fuller grasp of the significance of the life of the obscure young visitor of Lulworth Cove:

> 'Good. That man goes to Rome – to death, despair;
> And no one notes him now but you and I:

A hundred years, and the world will follow him there,
And bend with reverence where his ashes lie.'

(lines 17–20)

Though martyred by obscurity, the man to be buried in Rome is bound to gain more worldly acclaim than Jude Fawley. Nonetheless, a reverence towards his ashes now has become a ritual of less consequence than Hardy's own animation of a Dorset compatriot. The 'weary-kneed' speaker whom Hardy ironises fails to recognise that the young city-spark he has dismissed has local ties. He is related to the Keatses 'living in the direction of Lulworth', farmers and stablemen like Hardy's own father.[12]

In 1820, the poet who opted not to go on board of an Indiaman re-embarked on the ship that would ferry him to an early death. In 1920, however, Hardy could look back on the seven decades that had passed since he had given up his early infatuation with Romantic seafaring and the four decades that had transpired since he resettled in Dorchester after his own sojourn in Keats's London. Having long ago ceased to define himself against Wordsworth's and Shelley's versions of the egotistical sublime, he had come to recognise the kinship between Keats's capacities for projection and his own. Hardy was ready to welcome a country cousin too long exiled from his vicinity. It was not enough to have brought Keats's ghost back to Hampstead. Lulworth Cove provided a better 'nook' for one who had become, not just a neighbour, but another self.

Notes

All quotations from Hardy's poems are from Hardy 1982–85. Quotations from Wordsworth, Shelley and Keats are taken from David Perkins, 1967. I have used the abbreviations 'H', 'W', 'S' and 'K' (Hardy, Wordsworth, Shelley and Keats) whenever such clarification seems desirable.

1. For recent discussions of the links between Hardy's and Wordsworth's poetry see Chapter 5, as well as my own (Knoepflmacher 1990). Despite the usefulness of the overviews furnished by Harrison 1990, the surveys offered by Bartlett 1955 and Duerksen 1966, respectively, of the textual and ideological relations between Hardy and Shelley are still worth consulting.
2. See, however, Harris 1978, May 1973, and Perkins 1959.

3.   Florence Hardy's recollection is more fully quoted in 'Hardys and Keatses' in the 1928 *Dorset Year-Book* (see Bailey 1970, p. 442).

4.   See Kerry McSweeney on p. 93 in this collection.

5.   As Kim Blank reminds us in his discussion of the many verbal echoes that demonstrate Shelley's playful 'poetic mastery of the master', the younger poet supposedly was 'fond of repeating' Wordsworth's first skylark poem (Blank 1988, p. 189).

6.   In his remarks on the 'instinct and intuition of the poetic faculty' in *A Defence of Poetry*, Shelley reminds his audience that Milton claimed to have automatically produced his 'unpremeditated song' in *Paradise Lost* (Perkins 1967, p. 1084). It is this same intuitiveness he celebrates in the skylark's 'unpremeditated art'.

7.   Keats's entire third stanza, with its protracted account of the 'weariness, the fever, and the fret' (K, line 23), reads like a painful elaboration of Wordsworth's two lines: 'I have walked through wilderness dreary,/ And to-day my heart is weary' (W, lines 8–9).

8.   Bailey quotes Hudson's *Nature in Downland* (1900), which Hardy may have read, on the song-thrush's 'fine temper' in dire weather; the bird's lyrical assertion of 'his pleasure in life', Hudson speculates, 'must greatly exceed in degree the contentment and bliss that is ours' (Bailey 1970, p. 167).

9.   Although the nature of the 'bird' remains as unspecified as the identity of the speaker's former companions, the suggestion that it is a nightingale, 'perhaps in the copse near Hardy's birthplace or in the grove at Max Gate' seems persuasive (Bailey 1970, p. 453).

10. Severn, quoted by Bailey 1970, p. 454.

11. Bailey 1970 identifies Severn as the time-traveller's interlocutor (p. 455). Since the speaker claims that it was 'Time' who 'placed his finger on me' (line 4), I prefer my own emphasis. Still, the distinction is ultimately irrelevant.

12. See note 3, above.

7

Christina Rossetti and the Romantics: Influence and Ideology

ANTONY H. HARRISON

Christina Rossetti was not a voracious, but rather a focused, reader. Apart from the Bible, Thomas à Kempis, St Augustine, Plato, Homer and the classics in Italian, her adult reading was largely in the religious literature of her day (W. Rossetti 1904, pp. lxix–lxx).[1] She appears uninfluenced by a number of authors and works we would expect her to have appropriated. References to Shakespeare and Milton are, for instance, extremely unusual in her writing, and in 1870 she acknowledged to a close friend that she was still 'the rare Englishwoman not to have read the Holy Grail'.[2] Yet her copy of Keble's *The Christian Year* was dog-eared by the time of her death in 1894. She read widely in Tractarian literature, as this fact, her sonnet on Newman, and the theological content of her books of devotional prose make clear (Chapman 1970, pp. 170–97; Tennyson 1981, pp. 197–203; Cantalupo 1988; Schofield 1988).

Christina Rossetti also read the Romantics. Unlike poetry by the other Pre-Raphaelites, however, her work reveals almost no ideological debt to Romantic precursors. Instead, her poetry most often stands as a powerful corrective to what she saw as the misguided amatory, spiritual and political values – the secular ideologies – of those Romantics most important to her: Blake, Coleridge, Wordsworth and Keats. Throughout Rossetti's poetry we find stylistic and thematic echoes, as well as structural resonances of work by these writers, whom she often deliberately parodies. Rossetti's genius is partly visible in her ability to rework a variety of Romantic styles and *topoi* in order to empower orthodox Christian values in a world where dangerously secular ideologies were increasingly parading themselves in attractive poetic garments.[3] Over forty years ago Maurice Bowra observed in her 'a truly

Romantic temperament, trained to look for beauty in mysterious realms of experience, and able to find it without any strain or forcing of herself. She might have been a purely secular poet, so great were her gifts for the interpretation of strange corners of life and fancy. But her taste for this world was countered by a belief in God' (Bowra 1949, p. 246). For Bowra, Rossetti 'presents in a remarkable manner the case of a poet whose naturally Romantic tendencies were turned into a different channel by the intensity of her religious faith' so that she 'passed beyond the Romantic spirit' (Bowra 1949, p. 269). Thus, echoes of Blake and Coleridge in her work reveal appropriation and a limited acceptance of their religious values, while other poems by Rossetti seek to undercut, overturn, and expose as false or inadequate the secular ideologies propagated in the poetry of Wordsworth and Keats. Keats was, nonetheless, the Romantic whose attraction Rossetti felt most powerfully. Her deeply conflicted responses to his poetry are visible both in the strength of his stylistic influence over her work, and in Rossetti's unrelenting attempts, in her mature years, to disavow a youthful commitment to Keatsian idealisations of erotic love. These threatened her adherence to a narrow system of High Anglican religious values that she relied upon for emotional and psychological strength throughout her adult life.

To understand Rossetti's complex assimilation of Romantic poetry, we must grasp the nature of her stark religiosity. The passion of her commitment is apparent not only in the six books of devotional commentary for which she was best known during her lifetime, but also in her approximately 1000 poems. Rossetti's poetry is homiletic and prophetic. That is, her treatment of erotic love consistently demonstrates its illusory nature, its transitoriness, or its inability to fulfil the needs of the 'craving heart'. Her obsession with death results from her impassioned anticipation of the afterlife. Her interest in the objects of nature is typological: they symbolise a host of religious truths and teach lessons in piety or virtue. Dozens of Rossetti's poems reiterate her central theme of *contemptus mundi*:

> This Life is full of numbness and of balk,
>   Of haltingness and baffled short-coming,
>   Of promise unfulfilled, of everything
> That is puffed vanity and empty talk...
> This Life we live is dead for all its breath [.]

(Rossetti 1979–90, 2.149)

The conceptual framework and the metaphors in this sonnet from *Later Life* (1881) are typical. Images of betrayal, failure, inadequacy, illusion and disappointment are the commonplaces of Rossetti's work, and they are usually borrowed either from nature or from the Bible. Belief in the truths these images serve to formulate allows Rossetti to appropriate motifs, language, structural patterns, and metaphors from Romantic poetry exclusively to reject any hope of happiness or fulfilment in this world.

BLAKE: INFANTS, SHEPHERDS, AND LITTLE LAMBS

On 12 November 1848 – in her eighteenth year – Christina Rossetti wrote a parody of Blake's *A Cradle Song* that remained unpublished for 142 years. The lyric enacts a strategy of revisionism which she frequently uses when alluding to Romantic pre-texts. Her title quotes two lines from Blake's poem: 'Sleep, sleep, happy child; / All creation slept and smiled.' *A Cradle Song* (from *Songs of Innocence*, 1789) celebrates innocent infants as types of Christ:

> Sweet babe in thy face,
> Holy image I can trace.
> Sweet babe once like thee,
> Thy maker lay and wept for me.
>
> .   .   .   .   .   .
>
> Infant smiles are his own smiles.
> Heaven & earth to peace beguiles.

> (Blake 1965, p. 12)

Blake's song was written in a year of political revolution, and it obliquely acknowledges its own historicity in its turn to Christ's birth as the ultimate solution, *in the world*, to social turmoil and war. Blake's infant slumbers, moans and sighs 'happily' in its singing mother's arms, promising peace in mankind's future. By contrast, the infant (who is also a Christ type) in Rossetti's responsive lyric – written in another year of revolution – is dead. Describing its 'slumber', she leaps from Christ's birth to the crucifixion, then to the Last Judgement, 'another Advent dawn', when man's political history will be subsumed within the larger pattern of Christian history and thus wholly devalued.

There is no more aching now
In thy heart or in thy brow.
The red blood upon thy breast
Cannot scare away thy rest.

.   .   .   .   .

Sleep, sleep; what quietness
After the world's noise is this!

.   .   .   .   .

Sleep on until the morn
Of another Advent dawn.

(Rossetti 1979–90, 3.165)

Rossetti here, as elsewhere in poems that echo Blake, extends the religious content of his work eschatologically.

Familiar with Blake's engravings as well as his early poems, Rossetti would not have felt that she was challenging either his work or his theology. *Time Flies: A Reading Diary* (1885) reveals her sense of theological kinship with Blake:

There is a design by William Blake symbolic of the Resurrection. In it I behold the descending soul and the arising body rushing together in an indissoluble embrace: and this design, among all I recollect to have seen, stands alone in expressing the rapture of that reunion. (*Time Flies*, p. 88)

Rossetti's poetry nonetheless reflects little interest in Blake's works after 1789, including his prophetic books. The image patterns she appropriates are exclusively from the *Songs of Innocence*: mothers and infants, shepherds and lambs, roses and thorns, sunflowers. All of these appear in brief lyrics, many of them from *Sing-Song* (1872). These also replicate the simple forms of Blake's *Songs*. As William Michael Rossetti told his sister's biographer, Mackenzie Bell, 'It would...be an error to suppose that C[hristina] at any time read B[lake] much or constantly [though]... certainly she prized the little she did read' (Bell 1898, p. 308).

Rossetti's own simple songs often reply overtly to Blake's. *Rejoice with Me*, for instance, significantly problematises Blake's *The Lamb*, an ontological poem that celebrates Christ as creator and redeemer:

Little Lamb who made thee
Dost thou know who made thee

Gave thee life & bid thee feed.

. . . .

Little Lamb I'll tell thee,
Little Lamb I'll tell thee!
He is called by thy name,
For he calls himself a Lamb:
He is meek & he is mild
He became a little child:
I a child & thou a lamb,
We are called by his name.

(Blake 1965, pp. 8–9)

Echoing Blake's anaphora, Rossetti produces a sophisticated, emotionally intense lyric, whose dramatic situation reflects what Lona Packer has described as Rossetti's Coleridgean, existential religious faith (1959, p. 214). *Rejoice with Me*, in fact, reinscribes Blake's song of innocence as a personalised (rather than generalised) song of penitence, guilt, and gratitude:

Little Lamb, who lost thee? –
I myself, none other. –
Little Lamb, who found thee? –
Jesus, Shepherd, Brother.
Ah, Lord, what I cost Thee!
Canst Thou still desire? –
Still Mine arms surround thee,
Still I lift thee higher,
Draw thee nigher.

(Rossetti 1979–90, 2.196–7)

While Blake's song is benedictory, suppressing awareness of sin and man's fallen condition, Rossetti's is confessional and amatory (as is much of her religious verse). This lamb of Christ, this Everywoman, despite her betrayal of God the Shepherd, remains the object of his passion (in every sense) and becomes a bride of Christ; here their marriage approaches the 'rapture' of its consummation.

Less radically revisionist are a number of lyrics from *Sing-Song* in which Rossetti appears to take delight both in reworking Blakean figures of guardianship and in Blakean wordplay, as she does in the following poem:

> A motherless soft lambkin
>   Alone upon a hill;
> No mother's fleece to shelter him
>   And wrap him from the cold: –
> I'll run to him and comfort him,
>   I'll fetch him, that I will;
> I'll care for him and feed him
>   Until he's strong and bold.

> (Rossetti 1979–90, 2.33–4)

This poem's resonances of Blake's *The Shepherd* and *The Little Black Boy* playfully reinforce the efficacy of shepherding in this world. Rossetti appropriates Blake's images as authoritative, using simple metrical and prosodic techniques to extend the work he began. The poem's final emphasis on the assonantal rhyme-word 'bold', for instance, suggests not only the condition of the revived lamb, but also the indelible character of the Shepherd as well as that of the parodic poet.

More subtle effects emerge from Rossetti's generalised allusions to the rose-imagery pervasive in Blake's *Songs*. Echoes of *The Sick Rose*, *My Pretty Rose Tree* and *The Lily* in one quatrain from *Sing-Song* suggest that Rossetti learned important symbolist techniques from Blake.

> I have but one rose in the world,
>   And my one rose stands a-drooping:
> Oh when my single rose is dead
>   There'll be but thorns for stooping.

> (Rossetti 1979–90, 2.39)

The statement communicated symbolically here is complex, though the metaphors used are both simple and common, demonstrating how Rossetti's poetry often deliberately inhabits a space of linguistic ambiguity. By the poem's final line it is clear that the rose is at once a unique flower, a beloved and Christ. The second and third lines refigure the crucifixion, enabling the fourth to dramatise the incarnation (Christ 'stooping' to become man) and its culmination in his passion, while homiletically announcing the rewards of Christian humility. Thus, in such poems as these brief lyrics, Rossetti reveals her admiration for Blake's stylistic and prosodic accomplishments, as well as his early and innocent prophetic impulses.

COLERIDGE, WORDSWORTH AND TRACTARIAN AESTHETICS[4]

Reviewing *Goblin Market and Other Poems* (1862), Caroline Norton observed thematic and temperamental affinities between Christina Rossetti and Coleridge. These, in fact, reinforce the techniques she appropriated from the early work of Blake. Norton insists that *Goblin Market* is 'incomparably the best of [Rossetti's] compositions' and argues that it 'may vie with [sic] Coleridge's "Ancient Mariner"...for the vivid and wonderful power by which things unreal and mystic are made to blend and link themselves with the everyday images and events of common life' (Norton 1863, p. 404). Later commentators also acknowledge similarities between the symbolist techniques that operate in both poems or between the moral purposes such techniques serve. Richard LeGallienne, arguing for Rossetti's preeminence among women poets in 1891, asserts that 'she is...our one imaginative descendant of the magician of "Kubla Khan"' (LeGallienne 1891, p. 130). B. Ifor Evans, some forty years later, worries that 'the same problems are raised [by *Goblin Market*] as by *The Ancient Mariner*; a theme and movement, suggesting many things and not assignable to one source, a concluding moral acting as an anti-climax to the glamour and magic which precede it' (Evans 1933, p. 156). Rossetti's biographer, Lona Packer, goes considerably further than these critics, however, locating not only thematic echoes and temperamental affinities, but also structural resonances of Coleridgean poems in works by Rossetti as diverse as *The Convent Threshold*, *From House to Home*, and *Cobwebs* (Packer 1963, pp. 132, 135). She also insists that the theology that dominates Rossetti's work (poetry and devotional prose alike) is the same 'kind of Protestant existentialism found also in Coleridge' (Packer 1959, p. 214).

Thus, while particular stylistic or prosodic echoes of Coleridge in Rossetti's poetry are rare, structural patterns, a variety of motifs and settings, as well as religious and moral dicta, resonate between their works. For instance, sensitivity to all creatures great and small is a recurrent theme in poems such as *Brother Bruin* (Rossetti 1979–90, 2.168) and a number of lyrics from *Sing-Song*, where in one poem Rossetti admonishes, 'Hurt no living thing' and catalogues sacred creatures from ladybirds and moths to 'harmless worms that creep' (Rossetti 1979–90, 2.44). Extending the Coleridgean tradition epitomised in the moral tag that concludes *The Rime of the Ancient Mariner*, Rossetti became a passionate anti-vivisectionist.

Other echoes of *The Rime of the Ancient Mariner* emerge in poems such as *Sleep at Sea* in which 'White shapes flit to and fro / From mast to mast' shouting 'to one another / Upon the blast'. Their ship 'drives apace' while these sleeping spirits 'Bewail their case'. Like Coleridge's *Rime*, this poem displays supernatural elements and pyrotechnic effects, but only in order to resolve the complexities of its precursor with an illusion to Ecclesiastes that is a commonplace of Rossetti's devotional poetry. Coleridge's Mariner re-enters the world to instruct it; Rossetti's poem advocates repudiating the world altogether. Her mariners 'sleep to death in dreaming / Of length of days' as the poem's narrative voice concludes,

> Vanity of vanities,
>   The Preacher says:
> Vanity is the end
>   Of all their ways.
>
> (Rossetti 1979–90, 1.81–2)

The poetic kinship between Rossetti and Coleridge goes deeper than thematic, structural and situational echoes, however. Its basis is a shared aesthetic ideology, derived from Coleridge's prose rather than his poetry. This ideology had been sanctioned for Rossetti by the example of the Oxford Movement writers, especially Keble.[5] As George Tennyson has demonstrated,

> Coleridgean ideas permeate Tractarian thinking on aesthetic subjects and ... probably color Tractarian poetics more than those of any other single figure. The main point of contact between the Tractarians and Coleridge lies in their dispositions to regard religion and aesthetics as kindred fields. (Tennyson 1981, pp. 17–18)

One feature of Coleridgean aesthetics fundamental to the operations of Rossetti's poetry is his natural supernaturalism, his apparent belief in the continuity of objects in the natural world with spiritual forces. This belief is expressed in a definition of the primary imagination that employs religious terms: 'a repetition in the finite mind of the eternal act of creation in the infinite I AM' (Coleridge 1987, p. 304). George Tennyson's reading of this definition is a generally accepted one: 'the human mind in its limited sphere recapitulates, because it participates in, the divine mind in its infinite sphere'. But he further observes that it is 'is the basis for [the] religiously based aesthetic ultimately developed by the Tractarians' (Coleridge 1987, p. 304; Tennyson 1981, p. 19). This aesthetic includes the Tractarian doctrine of Analogy, which pervades Rossetti's poems and prose works. According to this concept, God veils himself behind the natural surfaces of this world, as Rossetti argues in *Seek and Find*: 'All the world over, visible things typify things invisible.... [C]ommon things continually at hand, wind or windfall or budding bough, acquire a sacred association, and cross our path under aspects at once familiar and transfigured, and preach to our spirits while they serve our bodies' (pp. 244, 203). *Consider the Lilies of the Field* formulates the doctrine poetically, asserting that 'Flowers preach to us if we will hear', and illustrating the doctrine with the examples of the rose and the lilies which say, 'Behold how we/ Preach without words of purity'. Even

> The merest grass
> Along the roadside where we pass,
> Lichen and moss and sturdy weed,
> Tell of His love who sends the dew.

> (Rossetti 1979–90, 1.76)

As this poem indicates, Rossetti, like Keble and Newman, would have had severe reservations about the philosophically idealistic and secular treatment of nature in much of Coleridge's poetry, as well as that of Wordsworth (Tennyson 1981, pp. 15–23). *Dejection: An Ode* is characteristic:

> O Lady! we receive but what we give,
> And in our life alone does Nature live:
> Ours is her wedding garment, ours her shroud!
>   And would we aught behold, of higher worth,
> Than that inanimate cold world allowed
>   Ah! from the soul itself must issue forth

A light, a glory, a fair luminous cloud
    Enveloping the Earth –
And from the soul itself must there be sent
    A sweet and potent voice, of its own birth,
Of all sweet sounds the life and element!

(Coleridge 1967, p. 365)

In such poems the speaker's alienation from nature reflects his sense of unfulfilment and joylessness and bespeaks the need for rejuvenation. In lamenting these problems *Dejection* is, of course, a response to the first four stanzas of Wordsworth's Intimations ode. The 'existential' issues central to these great poems are also at the heart of Rossetti's work, but the resolution to them is inevitably that of Tractarian theology,[6] which Rossetti implicitly presents as a corrective to the misguided secular philosophies formulated by Wordsworth and Coleridge.

For Rossetti, genuine joy, as well as amatory and spiritual fulfilment, can be found exclusively in union with Christ and the resurrected hosts in Paradise, described in the *Monna Innominata* as 'the flowering land of love': lines from an unpublished sonnet written in 1849 make the point: 'Some say that love and joy are one: and so/ They are indeed in heaven, but not on earth' (Rossetti 1979–90, 3.171). In this sonnet, as in *The Thread of Life, Three Stages*, and *An Old World Thicket*,[7] Rossetti addresses the problems of alienation, unfulfilment, and joylessness that inspired the Intimations ode and *Dejection*. The pivotal issue in all of these works is expressed in the second sonnet of *The Thread of Life*, a three-sonnet sequence (the form is significantly trinitarian) in which the speaker laments her self-imprisonment, feeling 'Everything / Around me free and sunny and at ease'. The 'gay birds sing', and all 'sounds are music', but it is cacophonous to the ears of the speaker:

Then gaze I at the merrymaking crew,
    And smile a moment and a moment sigh
Thinking: Why can I not rejoice with you?

(Rossetti 1979–90, 2.123)

This speaker's situation is precisely that of Wordsworth in the first four stanzas of the Intimations ode. His alienated persona seeks spiritual unity with the jubilant objects of nature as a defence against mortality. He is able, eventually, to participate in the Mayday festival with the birds that 'sing a joyous song', the bounding lambs, and the 'happy Shepherd boy', but for him nonetheless

> The Clouds that gather round the setting sun
> Do take a sober colouring from an eye
> That hath kept watch o'er man's mortality.

(Wordsworth 1984, p. 302)

By contrast, Rossetti's speaker rejects as a 'foolish fancy' the desire for liberation from self-imprisonment and for the contemplative unity with nature achieved by Wordsworth's speaker, who – through exercise of 'the philosophic mind – attains a 'faith that looks through death'. Such faith, expressed in ambiguous metaphors of 'celestial light', 'clouds of glory' and 'mighty waters', would have appeared suspect to Rossetti, who affirms the necessity of estrangement from 'the merrymaking crew' of this world in order eventually to attain genuine, that is, heavenly, liberation.

Rossetti's anti-Wordsworthian poems inevitably acknowledge – as do *Three Stages* and *The Thread of Life* – that 'I cannot crown my head/ With royal purple blossoms for the feast,/ Nor flush with laughter, nor exult in song' (Rossetti 1979–90, 3.234). The very inabilities Wordsworth's speaker in the Intimations ode strives to overcome constitute the basis of self-affirmation in the third sonnet of *The Thread of Life*. The alienated, solipsistic self remains 'that one only thing / I hold to use or waste, to keep or give'. It is

> My sole possession every day I live,
> .   .   .   .   .
> Ever mine own, till Death shall ply his sieve;
> And still mine own, when saints break grave and sing.
>   And this myself as king unto my King
>   I give, to Him Who gave Himself for me;
> He bids me sing: O death, where is thy sting?
> And sing: O grave, where is thy victory?

(Rossetti 1979–90, 2.123)

Death, in orthodox Christian fashion, is an event to be welcomed rather than rationalised. It is the gateway to Paradise.

Rossetti thus repudiates the possibility of a marriage between mind and nature that Wordsworth repeatedly claims will generate a secular Paradise. Her speakers devote their energies, rather, to becoming brides of Christ. Wordsworth's 'Prospectus' to *The Recluse* outlines the project of a grand epic poem that will show us exactly how to attain to *his* ideal of the 'great consummation'.

> Paradise, and groves
> Elysian, fortunate islands, fields like those of old
> In the deep ocean, wherefore should they be
> A History, or but a dream, when minds
> Once wedded to this outward frame of things
> In love, find these the growth of common day?

> (Wordsworth 1984, p. 198)

In *Paradise* Rossetti presents a monitory response to any Wordsworthian seduced by such worldly transcendentalism. For her, during life, visions of Paradise can appear only in a dream:

> Once in a dream I saw the flowers
> That bud and bloom in Paradise;
> More fair they are than waking eyes
> Have seen in all this world of ours.

> (Rossetti 1979–90, 1.221)

This poem, like many by Rossetti, transposes lush, Keatsian images of nature – 'the perfume-bearing rose', birdsongs 'like incense to the skies' and 'glassy pools' – to an afterlife distinct and separate from this one. Arguing that only in Heaven can perfection exist and the problem of alienation be overcome, *Paradise* constitutes a direct attack on Wordsworth's anti-orthodox philosophical idealism, and her assault is all the more effective for presenting the afterlife as a palpable reality:

> I hope to see these things again,
> But not as once in dreams by night;
> To see them with my very sight,

And touch and handle and attain:
To have all Heaven beneath my feet
For narrow way that once they trod;
To have my part with all the saints,
And with my God.

(Rossetti 1979–90, 1.222)

KEATS: AMATORY IDEOLOGIES

By contrast with both Wordsworth and Rossetti, Keats locates paradise in the bedroom. In *The Eve of St Agnes*, Porphyro, hiding in a closet, watches Madeline disrobe seductively, say her prayers, and go to bed, where she lies 'In a sort of wakeful swoon,' 'Blissfully havened both from joy and pain' (Keats 1970, p. 468). 'Stolen to this paradise' (p. 469), Porphyro attempts to awaken his 'seraph fair' and tells Madeline, 'Thou art my heaven, and I thine eremite' (p. 471). He utters these words immediately after 'heaping' a table in the room with 'spiced dainties' in preparation to seduce his beloved. The irresistible fruits with which he plans to tempt Madeline – 'candied apple, quince, and plum, and gourd' among them – are echoed in the early lines of *Goblin Market*. The Goblin men tempt Laura and Lizzie to 'Come buy ... Apples and quinces' and other luscious fruits (Rossetti 1979–90, 1.11).

One reader Keats clearly seduced with his sensual images of an amatory paradise was Christina Rossetti. She discovered Keats at the age of nine, and, as Lona Packer explains, 'she, and not [Dante] Gabriel or Holman Hunt, was the first "Pre-Raphaelite" to appreciate' him (Packer 1963, p. 14). On St Agnes' Eve (18 January), 1849 Rossetti wrote a sonnet to his memory:

A garden in a garden: a green spot
Where all is green: most fitting slumber-place
For the strong man grown weary of a race
Soon over. Unto him a goodly lot
Hath fallen in fertile ground; there thorns are not,
But his own daisies: silence, full of grace,
Surely hath shed a quiet on his face:
His earth is but sweet leaves that fall and rot.
What was his record of himself, ere he

Went from us? *Here lies one whose name was writ*
In water: while the chilly shadows flit
Of sweet Saint Agnes' Eve; while basil springs,
His name, in every humble heart that sings,
Shall be a fountain of love, verily.

(Rossetti 1979–90, 3.168)

The 'fountain of love' that was Keats's poetry fed the hundreds of amatory poems Rossetti wrote, most of them before her thirty-fifth year. Keats was the single Romantic writer whose influence on her style, her thematic preoccupations, her dominant metaphors, and the dramatic situations of her poems was inescapable during the most productive years of her life.[8]

Throughout the three volumes of her poetry published between 1862 and 1881, Rossetti struggled against the seductive power of Keatsian amatory ideals essential to his work from *Endymion* through the major poems of 1819, including the odes *To Psyche, On Melancholy,* and *On a Grecian Urn,* as well as *La Belle Dame Sans Merci, Lamia, Isabella,* and of course, *The Eve of St Agnes.* Keats's idealisation of love as the world's most potent spiritual force begins with the famous 'Pleasure Thermometer' passage from *Endymion.* For Keats, 'at the tip-top' of life's 'self-destroying' 'enthralments' and 'entanglements' (Keats 1970, pp. 155–56) is love:

Its influence,
Thrown in our eyes, genders a novel sense....
Nor with aught else can our souls interknit
So wingedly....[M]en, who might have towered in the van
Of all the congregated world...
Have been content to let occasion die,
Whilst they did sleep in love's elysium.
And, truly, I would rather be struck dumb
Than speak against this ardent listlessness,
For I have ever thought that it might bless
The world with benefits unknowingly.

(Keats 1970, p. 156)

In effect, Keats replaces traditional Christian notions of a beneficent deity with an ideal of 'human souls' that 'kiss and greet'. In her published poems from *Goblin Market* forward, Rossetti often adopts Keatsian techniques to grapple with his ideal of love. Like Keats's lovers, Rossetti's are often dreamers, unable to distinguish fantasy from reality (as in *Endymion* and *The Eve of St Agnes*), or they are victims, betrayed by their beloveds (as is Lycius in *Lamia* or Keats's pale knight-at-arms in *La Belle Dame Sans Merci*). But most often they perceive love as 'a foretaste of our promised heaven' (Rossetti 1979–90, 3.134). Typically, Rossetti transvalues *eros* into *agape* and sees passion in life as an experience whose inevitable disappointment prepares us for fulfilment in heaven, where 'Love [is] all in all; – no more that better part/ Purchased, but at the cost of all things here' (Rossetti 1979–90, 2.106). Thus for Rossetti, though 'Many have sung of love [as] a root of bane', to her ultimately, 'a root of balm it is',

> For love at length breeds love; sufficient bliss
> For life and death and rising up again.
> Surely when light of Heaven makes all things plain,
> Love will grow plain with all its mysteries.

> (Rossetti 1979–90, 2.105)

Like Keats, but in a greater number of poems employing more diverse dramatic situations, Rossetti explores all the mysteries of Keatsian passion (both desire and its concomitant suffering), most often exposing it as a dangerously illusory ideal in this world.[9] Her speakers, 'tired/ Of longing and desire', discover their 'Dreams not worth dreaming', their scheming 'useless' and their treasure 'unattainable'. Most turn finally to 'my Heavenly Lover' 'Beyond all clouds', who will redeem life's losses and disappointments (Rossetti 1979–90, 2.101). Thus, any promise of fulfilment in this world is a fantasy, a reason for many of the speakers in her poems who are betrayed by love or who dishonour its promise, to desire death:

> Thus only in a dream we are at one,
> > Thus only in a dream we give and take
> > > The faith that maketh rich who take or give;
> If thus to sleep is sweeter than to wake,
> > To die were surely sweeter than to live.

> (Rossetti 1979–90, 2.87–8)

Many of the presumably female voices in Rossetti's poems are –
like the Keatsian persona in the *Ode to a Nightingale* – 'half in love
with easeful death', but for markedly different reasons than that
speaker. In Keats's odes, suicidal speakers are directed to the lush
beauties of this world as a source of comfort. 'When the melancholy
fit shall fall' (p. 539), Keats commands in the *Ode on Melancholy*,

> Then glut thy sorrow on a morning rose,
>   Or on the rainbow of the salt sand-wave,
>   Or on the wealth of globed peonies[.]

> (Keats 1970–90, p. 540)

By contrast, Rossetti's desperate speakers either turn their eyes
unto the hills to seek aid from God or yield to the comfort of death.
The second speaker in *Three Nuns* (1849) is an unfulfilled lover who
expects a heavenly reward for resisting the temptations of earthly
love, and she therefore desires death: 'Oh sweet is death', she
repeats, because it 'giveth rest' and 'bindeth up/ The...bleeding
heart' (Rossetti 1979–90, 3.189). The speaker in *Two Parted* (1853?) is
one of Rossetti's rare, betrayed male lovers whose passions are
sustained by dreams he cannot distinguish from reality:

> All night I dream you love me well,
>   All day I dream that you are cold:
> Which is the dream?

Ultimately, he, too, seeks certainty: to 'Know all the gladness or the
pain' so that he might 'pass into the dreamless tomb' (Rossetti
1979–90, 3.222). *The Heart Knoweth Its Own Bitterness* (1857) powerfully explains why Rossetti repudiated Keats's infatuation with *eros*:

> How can we say 'enough' on earth;
>   'Enough' with such a craving heart:
> I have not found it since my birth
>   But still have bartered part for part.
> I have not held and hugged the whole,
>   But paid the old to gain the new;
>   Much have I paid, yet much is due,
> Till I am beggared sense and soul.

> (Rossetti 1979–90, 3.265)

Rossetti's economic metaphors here, as in *Goblin Market* and many other poems, significantly align her rejection of love's false promises with the seductions of the marketplace. Rather than blessing 'The world with benefits unknowingly' (Keats 1970, p. 156), investments in worldly passions are ruinous. Rossetti's speaker can 'bear to wait' for fulfilment in the afterlife because lovers in this world merely 'scratch my surface' or 'stroke me smooth with hushing breath.' To fill her love's capacity she needs one to 'pierce...nay dig within,/ Probe my quick core and sound my depth', as only God can do. Fulfilment comes not in 'This world of perishable stuff', but only afterwards: 'I full of Christ and Christ of me' (Rossetti 1979–90, 3.266).

Rossetti's obsessive revaluations of the Keatsian ideal of love suggest the tenacity of its attractiveness to her, reflected in her appropriation of Keatsian stylistic mannerisms, her common thematic focus on illusory images of ripeness, and her preoccupation with autumnal settings. Rossetti insists in her sonnet on Keats that 'His earth is but sweet leaves that fall and rot', a line in which postlapsarian resonances reinforce the contrast between the assonantal promise of 'sweet leaves' and the harsh reality stressed in the internal slant rhymes of the concluding verbs.

While Keats – sated with the 'mellow fruitfulness' and 'ripeness' of the declining year – abjures the songs of spring in *To Autumn*, Rossetti craves the ultimate Spring and the surpassing fruits of Paradise. Her *Autumn* (1850) responds to Keats's ode:

> Go chilly Autumn,
>   Come O Winter cold;
> Let the green things die away
>   Into common mould.
>
> Birth follows hard on death,
>   Life on withering:
> Hasten, we shall come the sooner
>   Back to pleasant spring.
>
>   (Rossetti 1979–90, 3.301)

In *The World* (1857) – with Keatsian eroticism, mellifluousness, and imagery resonant of *To Autumn* – Rossetti powerfully undercuts both Keatsian hedonism and his amatory ideology. This sonnet portrays the world as a medusan Lamia, an 'exceeding fair' temptress with 'subtle serpents gliding in her hair'. In the daytime 'she wooes me to the outer air,/ Ripe fruits, sweet flowers, and full satiety'. At night, the illusion evaporates, revealing 'all the naked horror of the truth': the world of beauty reconstituted in Keats's poetry is neither 'Truth' nor all we need to know on earth. Rossetti presents an alternate perspective. The world 'stands a lie'. It is the seductive devil, 'With pushing horns and clawed and clutching hands', inviting us to sell our souls 'Till [our] feet, cloven too, take hold on hell' (Rossetti 1979–90, 1.77).

One Keatsian truth Rossetti does embrace is that 'youth and beauty die'. But she admonishes her readers to forfeit, rather than glut themselves upon, the pleasures youth and beauty yield. As with her revisionist reworkings of the other Romantics that overturn their valorisations of worldly experience, her response to Keats in *Sweet Death* (1849) argues for 'a better resurrection':

> Better than beauty and than youth
> Are Saints and Angels, a glad company;
> And Thou, O Lord, our Rest and Ease,
> Art better far than these.

> (Rossetti 1979–90, 1.75)

The question with which Rossetti's poetry, resonant of Romantic influence, thus repeatedly confronts her precursors is, 'Why should we shrink from our full harvest?' (Rossetti 1979–90, 1.75). For her, that harvest is not attained by accepting Keats's vision of life as replete with redemptive possibilities marked by our sensitivity to beauty and our susceptibility to love. Nor is it accomplished through the Wordsworthian programme for transforming the 'light of common day' into celestial light, that is, regenerating Paradise by consummating a marriage between mind and nature. Rather, 'our full harvest' comes only with death and resurrection, for which we must wait and watch with pious devotion in this world, while exercising stern self-discipline to resist its illusory temptations. With this anti-Romantic ideology, Rossetti positioned herself, as recent critics have acknowledged, not as one of the Pre-Raphaelite last Romantics, but rather as the preeminent poet of the Tractarian movement in England.[10]

Notes

1. Christina Rossetti's letters, published and unpublished, confirm her brother's view of his sister's reading, though he by no means understood the influence of the Romantic poets upon her.
2. From an unpublished letter to her close friend Caroline Gemmer (4 February 1870).
3. For the best recent commentary on Rossetti's attempts to subvert Victorian materialist and capitalist values, see McGann 1988, passim.
4. Throughout this section of my essay I am indebted to Cantalupo 1988 which accords in most details with my own discussion in Harrison 1988b.
5. For a thorough commentary on the Tractarian grounds of Rossetti's aesthetic values, see Harrison 1988b, pp. 64–88, Cantalupo 1988, and Schofield, 1988.
6. For a detailed discussion of Rossetti's poetic appropriations of Tractarian theology, see Cantalupo 1988, passim.
7. For a thorough discussion of Rossetti's revisionist reworking of Romantic precursors in *The Thread of Life*, see Cantalupo 1988, pp. 288–93; and in *An Old-World Thicket*, see Harrison 1988b, pp. 46–51 and Cantalupo 1988, pp. 293–9.
8. For the most extensive discussion to date of Keats's influence on Rossetti, see Fass 1976.
9. For a thorough discussion of Rossetti's love poetry, see Harrison 1988b, pp. 89–141.
10. See, for instance, Chapman 1970, pp. 170–97, Tennyson 1981, pp. 197–203, McGann 1988, passim, and Schofield 1988, passim.

8

'Verses with a Good Deal about Sucking': Percy Bysshe Shelley and Christina Rossetti

BARBARA CHARLESWORTH GELPI

Several years ago I noticed a verbal echo between lines in Christina Rossetti's *Goblin Market* (C. Rossetti 1979, pp. 11–26) and verses from the Shelley fragment, *Fiordispina*. The passage in *Goblin Market* is an important one, its significance highlighted by D. G. Rossetti's design that served as title-page to the volume. The lines appear after the first turn or complication of plot in the story – that is, after Laura, refusing to follow her sister Lizzie's warning, has succumbed to the temptation of eating fruits proffered by goblin men but before the sisters learn the judgement incurred thereby – and describes the beauty of the young women's relationship as it has existed so far:

> Golden head by golden head,
> Like two pigeons in one nest
> Folded in each other's wings,
> They lay down in their curtained bed:
> Like two blossoms on one stem,
> Like two flakes of new-fall'n snow,
> Like two wands of ivory
> Tipped with gold for awful kings.

> (lines 184–91)

In *Fiordispina* (Shelley 1965, Vol. IV, pp. 71–4), the two cousins, Fiordispina and Cosimo, 'almost like to twins' (line 11), are described as growing up together 'like two flowers/Upon one stem' (lines 15–16).

Rossetti would have known *Fiordispina*, under the title *A Fragment*, as a twenty-line poem (lines 11 to 30 in its present form) first published in the 1824 *Posthumous Poems* edited by Mary Shelley.[1] Modern commentators have not remarked on this small indebtedness, perhaps because of the very division between 'Romantic' and 'Victorian' under scrutiny in this volume, but some among Rossetti's contemporary readers would surely have noted it. Karsten Engelberg's bibliography of the Shelley criticism published between 1822 and 1860 records twelve allusions to *A Fragment* (Engelberg 1988, p. 87); in every one of them lines 15 and 16 appear. But the query immediately arises: does the fact that these lines were in the literary air not call Rossetti's intentional use of them into question (if one, for the sake of argument, is willing to take such an intention seriously)? Indeed, would the devoutly religious Rossetti have wanted her readers to make an associative leap between her pair of sisters and the cousin lovers described by atheistical Shelley?

Rossetti certainly had strong personal reasons to deplore Shelley's atheism. His writings had been 'an immediate occasion of sin', in the old phrase, to her brother William, confirming him in the religious disbelief that was a source of pain and difficulty between brother and sister all the rest of her life.[2] Yet on William's own testimony, Christina made a strong distinction between Shelley's opinions and his giftedness as a poet. In the *Memoir* prefacing William Rossetti's edition of his sister's poetry, he writes: 'Among modern English poets, I should say that Shelley, or perhaps Coleridge, stood highest in her esteem....As to Shelley, she can have known little beyond his lyrics; most of the long poems, as being "impious" remained unscanned' (C. Rossetti 1904, p. lxx). As such a lyric, *A Fragment* numbers among the poems Rossetti would have permitted herself to read, and placing herself within the sphere of Shelley's *poetical* influence through this allusion was no trouble to her conscience. Far from a trouble, the echo of Shelley's phrase may have functioned as a little bow acknowledging thanks for a Shelley fantasy that served as the very 'germ' of *Goblin Market*.

We have Christina Rossetti's own testimony that *Goblin Market* was composed, at least in first draft, on 27 April 1859 (C. Rossetti 1979, Vol. I, p. 234). The previous year marks a high point of 65 published works by and about Shelley, second only to the 67 that appeared in 1847 (Engelberg 1988, pp. 369–84). Among these the most notable – and controversial – was Thomas Jefferson Hogg's *Life of Percy Bysshe Shelley*. A biography of Shelley, like his lyric poetry, came under no interdict, and we can be virtually sure that Rossetti read Hogg's work. There, among the many anecdotes through which Hogg creates the impression that Shelley was a brilliant loony, is one about a garden the two young men discovered in the course of a cross-country walk in the environs of Oxford.

During their brief time at the University, the two friends enjoyed walking straight across country as sportsmen do in shooting season. '[R]esolutely piercing through a district in this manner', Hogg writes, they often found objects of interest. For example, one winter afternoon, when they had 'penetrated somewhat farther than usual', they came upon a small copse 'guarded by an old hedge, or thicket'. Shelley, finding a 'gap' in it, suddenly darted though the hedge and disappeared. Hogg, following him, found that Shelley had 'thrown himself thus precipitately into a trim flower-garden, of a circular, or rather an oval form.' It was leafless, of course, at the time of year they came upon it, but Hogg cunningly begins his description with the flowers it *might* have had at another season to give us the sense of a mysteriously beautiful and blooming nook, suddenly discovered in the midst of barren fields. In Hogg's telling, he and his companion both stood awestruck at the vision. Hogg was about to 'walk round the magic circle, in order fully to survey the place', when Shelley, without having advanced a single step, bolted back 'through the bushes and the gap in the fence with the mysterious and whimsical agility of a kangaroo'. When Hogg, protesting, followed, Shelley explained that he had seen a house nearby and feared lest he be caught trespassing: 'hence his marvellous precipitancy in withdrawing himself from the garnished retirement he had unwittingly penetrated; and we had advanced some distance along the road before he had entirely overcome his modest confusion' (Hogg 1933, Vol. I, pp. 77–9).

As the quoted phrases show, Hogg needed no help from Freud to transform a country walk into a randy tale of appropriative male desire, with mocking recognition of its attendant guilt and fear of castration – and Shelley the butt of that defensive joke. The sexuality informing the pair's excitement in their discovery becomes explicit as they walk back. With a 'rapid career of words', Shelley sublimates sexual energy into a fantasy of 'two tutelary nymphs' in 'possession' of the garden, possessed in turn by Hogg and himself. But suddenly Shelley pauses, and here the language carries so much significance that it demands being quoted almost in full:

'No!' he exclaimed...'the seclusion is too sweet, too holy to be the theatre of ordinary love; the love of the sexes, however pure, still retains some taint of earthly grossness; we must not admit it within the sanctuary....

'The love of a mother for her child is more refined; it is more disinterested, more spiritual; but...the very existence of the child still connects it with the passion, which we have discarded....

'The love a sister bears towards a sister,' he exclaimed abruptly, and with an air of triumph, 'is unexceptionable.'

The idea pleased him, and as he strode along he assigned the trim garden to two sisters, affirming, with the confidence of an inventor, that it owed its neatness to the assidous culture of their neat hands; that it was their constant haunt; the care of it their favorite pastime, and its prosperity, next after the welfare of each other, the chief wish of both. He described their appearance, their habits, their feelings, and drew a lovely picture of their amiable and innocent attachment; of the meek and dutiful regard of the younger, which partook, in some degree, of filial reverence, but was more facile and familiar; and of the protecting, instructing, hoping fondness of the elder, that resembled maternal tenderness, but had less of reserve and more of sympathy....The occupations of all females of the same rank and age are the same, and by night sisters cherish each other in the same quiet nest. Their union wears not only the grace of delicacy, but of fragility also; for it is always liable to be suddenly destroyed by the marriage of either party, or at least to be interrupted and suspended for an indefinite period.

He depicted so eloquently the excellence of sisterly affection, and he drew so distinctly, and so minutely, the image of the two sisters....that the trifling incident has been impressed upon my memory, and has been intimately associated in my mind, through his creations, with his poetic character. (Hogg 1933, Vol. I, pp. 80–1)

The parallels between the two sisters in Shelley's purported fantasy (which could be altogether Hogg's, but that need not trouble us here) and Lizzie and Laura in *Goblin Market* are striking: in both cases the girls live in mysterious isolation, for neither the Hogg passage nor Rossetti's poem provides them with parents or relatives. The tasks performed by Rossetti's pair are not precisely the garden-tending which is Shelley's focus, but their occupations are all shared in the way that he describes: 'Laura rose with Lizzie: /Fetched in honey, milked the cows,/ Aired and set to rights the house' (lines 202–4), and so on. The neatness and assiduity stressed by Shelley characterise Rossetti's pair as well: 'Neat like bees, as sweet and busy' (line 201).

More important, the whole relationship between Laura and Lizzie is similar to that of Shelley's imagined sisters: Laura (her lesson once learned) the meek, grateful and daughterly; Lizzie, the maternally protective and instructive. Indeed, Hogg's anecdote may have caught Rossetti's attention because Shelley's quoted words could serve as an idealised version of her own relation to her older sister Maria, for whom, Rossetti writes, she inscribed the poem in its manuscript form (C. Rossetti 1979, Vol. I, p. 234).[3] Finally, the perfection of their relationship has its expression for both pairs of sisters in the image of their intertwined bodies as they sleep 'in the same quiet nest'. My guess is that, when in her own lines 'Like two pigeons in one nest/ Folded in each other's wings' (lines 185–6) Rossetti echoed this simile from her 'primary source' in Hogg, she was reminded of the lines from *A Fragment* as well, and so Shelley's 'like two flowers/ Upon one stem' became her further image: 'Like two blossoms on one stem' (line 188).

So far the length of this essay and the information it conveys make it an ideal item for *Notes and Queries*. The very title – 'An Unnoticed Source for Christina Rossetti's *Goblin Market*?' – comes instantly to mind. But what if, more ambitiously, one wanted to discuss the bearing this indebtedness has on the scholarly debate surrounding Rossetti's enigmatic poem?[4] In that controversy, opinions are so varied that I must first clear myself some ground by defining my particular sense of where the enigma lies.

The fairy-tale character of the poem puts its adult readers in the position of children – all well and good – but of children experiencing the discomfort of double messages. For instance, the very first moral injunction given in the work is Lizzie's exclamation to Laura: '"You should not peep at goblin men"' (line 49). The poem is, then, an admonishment against voyeurism; yet its original title, *A Peep at the Goblins* (C. Rossetti 1979, I, p. 234), is itself voyeuristic and incites to voyeurism. Terence Holt is of the opinion that, indeed, it places its readers in the situation of voyeurs: '[A]s audience, in answering Laura's call to come hear the story of *Goblin Market* we share the place of the goblin children [at the end of the story, who mirror the earlier goblins encircling Laura]. Our stance throughout the poem as voyeurs of sexual exchange recalls that earlier, "leering" circle of goblins' (Holt 1990, pp. 63–4). Similarly, this moral tale of temptation, sin, and redemption particularises sexuality – the 'joys brides hope to have' (1.314) – as the source of the sin being warned against, while the language of the poem is consistently and at times outrageously sexual; the very signifiers thus become media for the fantasies they are supposed to signify as unacceptable.

The language virtually throughout the poem provides examples for this puzzling contradiction between message and its medium, beginning with the catalogue of fruits cried out by the goblin hucksters, but the most arresting instances turn upon the word 'suck', as Ellen Moers remarked when calling 'suck' the 'central verb' of *Goblin Market* (Moers 1976, p. 102). It appears prominently at the moment of the fall and again at the moment of redemption. After Laura sells her soul to the goblins by paying for the fruit with the price of a golden lock of hair, line 128 notes, fairly decorously, that she 'sucked their fruit globes fair or red'. In the lines immediately following – 'Sweeter than honey from the rock./ Stronger than man-rejoicing wine' – Biblical allusions and a technique of repetition reminiscent of the Psalms lend a sense of ritual solemnity to her act. Suddenly that tone changes, as Laura's pleasure in the fruit grows more intense: 'She sucked and sucked and sucked the more/ Fruits which that unknown orchard bore;/ She sucked until her lips were sore' (lines 134–6).

Laura's punishment is an insatiable and unassuageable desire for the goblin fruit which gives her symptoms of the 'green sickness' (pallor, thinning hair, loss of appetite, melancholia) that can be given different diagnoses (Hellerstein *et al.* 1981, p. 19) but that was a real phenomenon afflicting many Victorian adolescent women, including Rossetti herself (Battiscombe 1981, pp. 33–6). To save her sister, Lizzie attempts to buy fruit but is pelted with it by the goblins because she herself refuses to eat so that juice 'syrupped all her face,/ And lodged in dimples of her chin,/ And streaked her neck which quaked like curd' (lines 434–6). Triumphant, she returns to her sister and (the lines suggest) holding wide her arms, calls out to Laura: 'Hug me, kiss me, suck my juices /.... Eat me, drink me, love me' (lines 468, 471). As Laura repeatedly kisses her, the fruit she thereby eats serves as a violent antidote; after undergoing a seizure that has the character of an orgasm or an exorcism, she is restored to her former self. A bland coda moves the plot forward to a time when both sisters are wives and mothers, and Laura tells her little ones this story to illustrate the fact that 'there is no friend like a sister' (line 562).

Space allows only a cursory review of critical responses to the problem presented by the sexuality embedded in the language of *Goblin Market*. One strong reaction is blank denial. For instance, Charlotte Spivak, aligning herself with Eleanor Thomas, reiterates Christina Rossetti's own bland characterisation of the work and scolds those critics 'who "murder to dissect and botanize where no trespassers should be admitted"' (Spivak 1989, p. 60; Thomas 1966, p. 155). Such an injunction treats curious readers as by definition overly curious, as prurient voyeurs snickering over their observation of a Victorian lady poet who is herself unaware of any sexual innuendos in her language. But as a passage from Elizabeth Gaskell's *Cranford* shows, any Victorian writer would know that the physicality connoted through the word 'suck' made any use of it, much less a reiteration like the one in *Goblin Market*, a potential trespass. The narrator of *Cranford*, describing the pleasure with which the spinster sisters, Miss Jenkyns and Miss Matty, eat oranges, observes with a mischievous twinkle that 'sucking (only I think she [Miss Jenkyns] used some more recondite word) was in fact the only way of enjoying oranges; but then there was the unpleasant association with a ceremony frequently gone through by little babies.' To obviate the mutual voyeurism of the sights and sounds involved when sucking oranges, the sisters take their dessert oranges to the privacy of their separate rooms (Gaskell 1906, Vol. II, p. 31).

Spivak's acerbity is directed primarily toward those who read *Goblin Market* through a psychoanalytic lens, for any discussion of the author's unconscious introduces voyeurism into the very methodology. Germaine Greer also notes wryly, however, that 'even the most unashamed of post-Freudian critics' actually draw back from full exposition of the poem's images, 'for fear that to unravel it would be to reveal more of the psychology of the unraveler than it would of the meaning of the poem itself' (Greer 1975, p. xxxvi).

From the great range of critical works in the psychoanalytic category, I will give only two examples of what can be seen with a Freudian eye. Applying Freudian theory on development through three stages – oral, anal, and genital – Ellen Golub considers the changeable goblins to be 'the child's disjunct perceptions of the mother' and Laura representative of an infant trapped at the oral stage, in misery at being weaned (Golub 1975, pp. 161–2). With Winston Weathers' theory that the sisters are literary portrayals of a 'divided self' (Weathers 1965, p. 85), Golub takes it that '[r]egressive Laura is aided by progressive Lizzie', who moves on to the anal stage, projecting her own obsessions as the 'foulness and dirtiness of the goblins' – i.e. the mother: 'This power struggle is latently one between mother and child....Expressing the child's stubborn defiance of the withdrawal of love, she usurps the maternal hierarchy and sends the goblins into oblivion.' At the end the poem 'moves briefly to the genital level at which both sisters have matured into wives and mothers' (Golub 1975, pp. 162–4).

Interaction between mother and infant also create Maureen Duffy's scenario of the events being allegorised in *Goblin Market*. Laura's eating of the fruit is 'a powerful masturbatory fantasy of feeding at the breast' and her resultant illness the Victorian picture of 'the habitual masturbator....Contemplating her sister's aroused eroticism (since they shared the same bed she could hardly avoid it), rouses Lizzie's sexual curiosity but she resists. Laura is able to slake hers on her sister and her affection for her, not surprisingly since Lizzie will be the image of her mother, and so fulfill her homosexual fantasy. Appropriately, Laura has the last word, telling their children of the episode and that 'there is no friend like a sister' (Duffy 1972, pp. 290–1).

A calm rationalisation which eschews such fantasies about Rossetti's fantasy is another possible response to the eroticism informing the language of *Goblin Market*. D. M. R. Bentley, envisioning something very different from Holt's goblin circle of auditors, hypothesises that the poem was originally written as an exemplary tale 'to be read aloud by Rossetti to an audience of fallen women' and the Anglican Sisters dedicated to their reclamation (Bentley 1987, p. 58). In his opinion, the sexual connotations of the imagery and language, far from being an invitation to voyeurism, function as a screen decently veiling necessary allusion to sexuality rather than as vehicle for arousing sexual fantasy: 'The sensibility that created the goblins was that of a Victorian lady, a religious poet, and a social worker; the goblins' enacted enticings combine the concealment necessary for decency and the revelation necessary for the sexual nature of the unfolding events to be perceived in the proposed hermeneutical context of the poem' – that is, among those hearing it read at the St Mary Magdalene Home for Fallen Women (Bentley 1987, p. 66).

Dorothy Mermin's interpretation of the poem's intended audience and its meaning is very different but she too adopts a 'no nonsense' stance to minimise any critical complicity in voyeurism. After quoting the lines 'Hug me, kiss me, suck my juices' and 'kissed and kissed her with a hungry mouth', she continues: 'The eroticism troubles many readers; we are more nervous about manifestations of affection between women than Victorians were, and we find it hard to allow a nineteenth-century religious poet the conflation of religious and erotic intensity that we accept without question in Crashaw or Donne' (Mermin 1983, p. 113). Her suggestion, working from feminist scholarly findings such as those of Carroll Smith-Rosenberg on the intensity of relations permitted between Victorian women, is that *Goblin Market* is an untroubled celebration of a love between women that, in Lillian Faderman's phrase, surpasses the love of men (Faderman 1981). Such permissiveness stems from the equation of sexuality with masculinity on the one hand and the gendered ascription of emotion to the feminine on the other. The result is what Smith-Rosenberg calls 'a female world of love and ritual' (Smith-Rosenberg 1975), and Mermin's description of the world of *Goblin Market* repeats that theme: 'Except for the word "wives," which legitimizes the children, there is no mention of any men but the goblins, who are explicitly male. The children are apparently all girls and are exhorted to keep the female circle closed and complete. This is a world in which men serve only the purpose of impregnation' (Mermin 1983, pp. 113–14).

Within this spectrum of critical views, Mermin's seems the one most clearly substantiated by considering the Hogg passage a source for *Goblin Market*. The love Shelley's sisters bear for each other is 'unexceptionable' in his thinking precisely because, as love between two women, it has not the sexual 'taint of earthly grossness', and Victorians, Rossetti among them, would have shared his opinion. Our ahistorical post-Freudian peeping misinterprets the scenes it sees and the language it hears. Thus one could apply to Laura and Lizzie the sentences Smith-Rosenberg uses as commentary on the impassioned letters between two pairs of Victorian women, all four of whom eventually married: 'The essential question is not whether these women had genital contact and can therefore be defined as heterosexual or homosexual. The twentieth-century tendency to view human love and sexuality within a dichotomized universe of deviance and normality, genitality and platonic love, is alien to the emotions and attitudes of the nineteenth century and fundamentally distorts the nature of these women's emotional interaction' (Smith-Rosenberg 1975, p. 8). So fundamental by now is our inscription by Freudian thinking that *Goblin Market* may well continue to be a mysterious, puzzling and teasingly erotic poem, but that is because we are reading ourselves, peeping at ourselves, not at Christina Rossetti.

As a substantiation of the kind I describe, my find has some modest interest; however, its very modesty may explain my earlier disinterest in following it up. Also, used that way, the Shelley source offers no real contribution to the thesis propounded through this volume. True, as Smith-Rosenberg herself states, the 'female world of love and ritual' is a phenomenon that extends from the mid-eighteenth through the late nineteenth centuries (Smith-Rosenberg 1975, p. 3), and, as I mentioned above, a strong focus on Rossetti as a Victorian poet looks straight past important aspects of her exceedingly deep and important Romantic roots. At the same time, William's description of the parts of the Shelley canon that Rossetti permitted herself to read suggests the possibility that 'her' Shelley was the Victorian angel cannily enshrined by Mary Shelley and her daughter-in-law, Lady Jane Shelley, and rendered ineffectual by Hogg, among others. I for one interpreted the connection between them in that way. Fairly recently, however, through reading Jerome McGann's '"My Brain is Feminine": Byron and the Poetry of Deception', I suddenly – dazzlingly – saw the true link between Shelley and Rossetti, saw it as something well worth writing about and as highly relevant here.

As part of his argument about Byron's indebtedness to the poetry of the sentimental and Gothic writer, Charlotte Dacre, McGann discusses 'sentimental poetry' in its 'technical and historical sense'. He mentions its association with women writers from the late eighteenth century and into the nineteenth but notes that 'Keats and Shelley are probably our greatest sentimental poets' (McGann 1990, p. 31). Characterising the themes of this poetry, McGann writes,

> Crucial to sentimental poetry is the centrality of love to human experience and – more significantly – the idea that true love had to involve a total intensity of the whole person – mind, heart, and (here was the sticking point) body....for the 'sentimental' soul was equally diffused through the entire sensorium. The stylistic index of sentimental poetry, therefore, is a peculiar kind of self-conscious fleshiness.

With an illustrative quotation from Shelley's *Defence of Poetry*, McGann writes that the purpose of this poetry 'is to "bring the whole soul of man [and woman] into activity," an event which, in the context of such writing, means that it is to bring along the whole person – mind and body as well' (McGann 1990, p. 31).

McGann's emphasis is on the diffusion of 'soul' through all the faculties of one person; his argument does not take him into the related sentimental idea that the purpose of this intense fusion is that the 'soul' be shared, exchanged, blended with another's similarly intense soul. Medium and metaphor for this sharing is the kiss, which is a rather flimsy – intentionally flimsy – screen for the further metaphor of sexual intercourse but is also metaphorically related to the infant's suckling of breast milk.

Let me give an egregious example. The editors of *The Poems of Shelley* date the writing of *Fragment. Supposed to be an Epithalamium of Francis Ravaillac and Charlotte Cordé* to somewhere between 10 October and 17 November 1810 (Shelley 1989, Vol. I, p. 117), very close to the time at which Shelley and Hogg came upon the garden that so impressed them. It was also within the same year that Shelley had written *Zastrozzi* (Shelley 1965, Vol. V. pp. 4–103), in which he borrowed heavily from Dacre's Gothic novel, *Zofloya* (1806), and we can be sure that Shelley, like Byron, pored over Dacre's poems, published in 1805 under the title *Hours of Solitude*. He was, then, imbued with sentimentalism when he wrote the following passage:

> 'Soft, my dearest angel, stay,
> Oh! you suck my soul away;
> Suck on, suck on, I glow, I glow!
> Tides of maddening passion roll,
> And streams of rapture drown my soul.
> Now give me one more billing kiss,
> Let your lips now repeat the bliss,
> Endless kisses steal my breath,
> No life can equal such a death.'

> (Shelley 1989, Vol. I, p. 121)

The modern association of the word 'suck' with oral sex now has such salience, particularly when the context is erotic, that the editors of *The Poems of Shelley* feel the need for a fairly long footnote explaining that the convention here is that of 'lovers exchanging souls as they kiss, generally before dying (with possible equivocation over "dying").' As examples they cite Marlowe's *Faustus*, 1.1357, 'Her lips suck forth my soul'; Dryden's *Don Sebastian* III,i, 'Sucking each other's Souls while we expire'; and (an early example of sentimentalism 'in its technical and historical sense') Pope's *Eloisa to Abelard*, 1.324: 'Suck my last breath, and catch my flying soul' (Shelley 1989, Vol. I, p. 121).

Left unexplained in their note is the relation between sucking and soul. Historically, 'suck' had breast-feeding, Elizabeth Gaskell's 'ceremony frequently gone through by little babies', as its primary signification (*OED*, Vol. XVII, p. 106). A medical opinion still prevalent through the eighteenth century and on into the nineteenth, an opinion to which Shelley himself subscribed, was that the nurse's soul was sucked in by an infant along with the breast milk.[5] So the kiss in sentimental parlance becomes a metaphor for breast-feeding which in turn is the paradigm for, first, the fusion of mind, heart and body as 'soul', and then the exchange or interchange of this totality.

My point is not that Rossetti had read Shelley's *Epithalamium*, for it had not been republished. (With other Shelley devotees, she would, however, have learned of its existence from Hogg's *Life of Percy Bysshe Shelley*, where Hogg alludes to 'some verses, I remember, with a good deal about sucking in them' [Hogg 1933, Vol. I, p. 162]). I postulate rather that both Shelley's fantasy about two sisters and Rossetti's *Goblin Market* are sentimental in the sense of the term discussed above, and that the prominence of the word 'suck' in Rossetti's poem signals her allegiance to that tradition. This places her in a literary mode which, though 'associated with women writers in particular' (McGann 1990, p. 30), turns out to be no bywater off the late eighteenth- and early-nineteenth-century mainstream but instead a mighty, many-branched current running through the whole century.

Spivak, exploring Rossetti's work within its 'historical and literary context,' writes of fantasy as a major theme both in the writings of Rossetti's predecessors, Felicia Hemans and Laetitia Landon (L. E. L., 'the female Byron'), and in contemporaries or near-contemporaries: Sara Coleridge, Adelaide Proctor and Jean Ingelow (Spivak 1989, pp. 53–7). These writers have all also been labelled sentimental in the derogatory sense of the term and need now to have their work reappraised within a context that takes seriously the philosophical and psychological, theological and social theories underlying the phenomenon of sentimentalism. Stuart Curran, in his discussion of women writers of the Romantic period, makes the point that '[t]he poetry of sensibility is at base a literature of psychological exploration, and it is the foundation on which Romanticism was reared' (Curran 1988, p. 197). That suggests, given important continuities throughout the century, that this poetry is at the base of Victorianism as well. We need, therefore, to think further (for important beginnings have already been made) about the relevance of sentimentalism not only to the work of women writers like Christina Rossetti and Elizabeth Barrett Browning but to that of spasmodic Tennyson, fleshly D. G. Rossetti, plangent Arnold, and intense Robert Browning – as well as to the whole Aesthetic movement.[6] Separation into gendered spheres was a striking feature of middle-class nineteenth-century life, but we need further thinking about the ways in which sentimental exchange of soul called the very possibility of such separation into question.

The line of connection between sentimentalism and fantasy surfaces more specifically as a link between sentimentalism and the Gothic. David Morrill considers the vampire myth as Rossetti found it in *The Vampyre* (1819) written by her uncle – and Byron's doctor – John Polidori, to be a primary source of *Goblin Market* and the reason for the centrality of biting and sucking in the story's events (Morrill 1990, pp. 1–16). His characterisation of *Goblin Market* as a Gothic poem dovetails with my placing it within the sentimental tradition. The two readings (and the two literary modes) are linked in presenting in the one case a negative and in the other case a positive exchange of 'soul'.[7]

Shelley's fantasy of the two sisters' totally shared life conceptualises the imbibing of soul as an activity that provides the basis for intense, productive, loving and peaceful human interaction. Hogg was right in seeing it as central to Shelley's 'poetic character'; it does indeed surface again and again in such works as the prose fragment *On Love* and in *Epipsychidion*, and Victorians found it the most deeply congenial aspect of his work (Shelley 1862, p. 29). But as Shelley's own difficulties in setting up the fantasy show, the human capacity to exchange soul has as its flip side a horrible vulnerability and openness to invasion by an Other's soul. The two passages in *Goblin Market* in which the word 'suck' appears so prominently mark the negative and positive manifestations of the same process. In the first the fruits that Laura sucks are from an 'unknown orchard' (line 135), but once their soul informs hers we know that they were rooted in desire (as the opposite of love), appropriativeness and self-concern. The soul she sucks from the fruit on Lizzie's body has the character of Lizzie's act in obtaining it: selfless and loving concern for the good of the beloved.

This sentimental psychology with its attendant physiology – 'the idea that true love had to involve a total intensity of the total person' (McGann 1990, p. 31) – is compatible with Christian doctrines such as the loving exchange and interpenetration of soul among members of the Mystical Body of Christ. One might call *Goblin Market* at once sentimental and Gothic and still see connections with Crashaw and Donne (Mermin 1983, p. 113) in its religio-literary lineage. I would further suggest that such traditional religious sources may well have been mediated, or at least reinforced, by sentimental works. When writing *Epipsychidion*, Shelley was actually in more intense communion with Crashaw's *Hymn to…Sainte Teresa* (Crashaw 1904, pp. 266–71) than he was with Teresa Viviani. At the same time, the sentimental label relieves *Goblin Market* of deliberate participation in voyeurism, for the sentimentalist's stance is the opposite of the voyeur's. Sentimentalism scorns the stooping peep. Its psychic posture is Lizzie's on her return to Laura: head thrown back, arms open to pour forth one's own and drink an Other's 'influence'.

All the same, calling *Goblin Market* sentimental does nothing to explain away its contradictions; it simply classifies them as the usual sentimental contradictions. McGann's commentary on a Dacre poem entitled *The Kiss* applies equally cogently to both Shelley's fantasy of two sisters and to *Goblin Market*: 'So the paradoxes of this poem swirl about the demand for an experience that is at once completely impassioned ("without control"), completely physical, and yet perfectly "refin'd" as well' (McGann 1990, p. 31).

They swirl also around the marketability of the sentimental. A friend of Shelley seems to have questioned him about the advisability of publishing the 'verses…with a good deal about sucking in them', in Hogg's phrase. Shelley's response was, 'But you mistake, the Epithalamium will make it [the book of poems] sell like wildfire' (Shelley 1964, Vol. I, p. 23). McGann has argued cogently that Rossetti expresses through the goblin merchants her disdain for the mercantilism and materialism of her culture (McGann 1985, pp. 220–31). Yet she, like Shelley – and more effectively than he – concerned herself with the marketing of her work. Rossetti's

Victorian readers did not verbalise their reaction to the good deal of sucking that goes on in *Goblin Market*, but the poem, placed first in her first published volume, has always caught and held attention. When her publisher, Alexander Macmillan, read *Goblin Market* aloud to a group in the Cambridge Working Men's society, 'They seemed at first to wonder whether I was making fun of them; by degrees they got still as death, and when I finished there was a tremendous burst of applause' (Packer 1963a, p. 7). Describing sentimental exchange of soul does well in a goblin market.

Notes

1. The poem as we know it, with the title *Fiordispina*, first appeared in Richard Garnett's *Relics of Shelley*, published in 1862. *Goblin Market* was composed in 1859 (Rossetti 1979, Vol. I, p. 234). Miriam Sagan quotes from an unpublished paper by Helaine Ross which gives as a partial source for *Goblin Market* the lines from *A Midsummer Night's Dream* (III.ii.208–12): 'So we grew together, / Like to a double cherry, seeming parted, / But yet an union in partition– / Two lovely berries molded on one stem. / So, with two seeming bodies, but one heart' (Sagan 1980, p. 69). The Shakespeare text is certainly echoed by Shelley and probably by Rossetti as well, but in the latter case the intertextuality includes both Shakespeare and Shelley. Indeed, Rossetti's 'blossoms' is closer to Shelley's 'flowers' than to Shakespeare's 'berries'.

2. William Rossetti writes: 'I regard the reading and re-reading of Shelley, which began in the summer of 1844, as an epoch in my life. I revelled in his glorious idealism; and got confirmed in those general tendencies of opinion, on matters of faith and polity, to which I was already drifting' (Rossetti 1906, Vol. I, pp. 57–8).

3. I say 'idealised' because among siblings as close in age and as constantly together as the four Rossetti children one would expect considerable rivalry, and Georgina Battiscombe mentions specifically the jealousy that Maria felt as a child toward the pretty and vivacious Christina, less than four years her junior (Battiscombe 1981, p. 17).

4. According to William Rossetti, Christina repeatedly insisted that the poem had no 'profound or ulterior meaning' and described it as 'just a fairy tale' (Bell 1898, p. 206). But critics, including William, have found it impossible to leave the matter there. With increasing interest in Rossetti's work, much aided by R. W. Crump's edition of the poems and soon by Antony Harrison's forthcoming edition of the letters, scholarly interchange on the meaning of *Goblin Market* is now more animated than ever (Charles 1985 passim; Holt 1990, p. 65).

5. Shelley was deeply concerned when Harriet refused to breastfeed their first child, Ianthe, because he feared that 'the [wet] nurse's soul

would enter the child' (White 1940, Vol. I, p. 236). One finds the idea also in *The Nurse's Guide* (Anon. 1729, p. 23), in George Ensor's *The Independent Man* (Ensor 1806, Vol. I, p. 6), and in Thomas Trotter's *A View of the Nervous Temperament* (Trotter 1806, p. 93). In *Shelley's Goddess* I have a more extended discussion of the significance the idea held for Shelley.

6. Relevant here is Terry Eagleton's interweaving of the aesthetic, the task of socialisation assigned to women, and the cult of sensibility when he describes 'the "aesthetic" realm of sentiments, affections and spontaneous bodily habits' (Eagleton 1990, p. 23). Eagleton has not applied his analysis to English nineteenth-century writers, but Paul Sawyer has already noted its hermeneutic usefulness for the study of Ruskin (Sawyer 1990, pp. 136–41).

7. Terry Castle's important argument about 'the spectralization of the other' that takes its rise in sentimental works of the late eighteenth century and continues right to the present bears on my description of sentimental exchange of soul. My analysis, while admitting sentimentalism's extreme vulnerability to appropriativeness and solipsism, sees positive manifestations of it as at least possible. Castle's emphasis is on its potential for alienation: 'Other people seem bizzarely amorphous – lacking in specificity. Anyone can summon up the image of another. Everyone reminds us of someone else' (Castle 1987, p. 250).

9

Robert Browning and Romantic Allegory

THERESA M. KELLEY

Readers have often charged that Robert Browning's style is so difficult as to be more than occasionally incomprehensible. As Philip
Drew (1970) has reminded modern critics, nineteenth-century
readers often complained about Browning's difficult, obscure and
grotesque style. One exasperated contemporary reviewer called
Browning's poems 'Chinese puzzles, trackless labyrinths, unap-
proachable nebulosities' (Drew 1970, pp. 70–2). These complaints
collectively register the allegorical cast of Browning's poetic difficulty. Like the *difficultas* of classical rhetoric, Browning's style is
provoking, even deliberately so, because it insists on veiling,
obscuring its referent by means of 'quaintest conceits' and
'grotesque exaggerations' (Drew 1970, p. 72) – phrases that signal
the mixed inheritance of allegory after the Renaissance. This is not
to say that allegory was a fixed mode until the late Renaissance.
Even in medieval culture, allegory was subject to frequent generic
modulations (Fowler 1982, pp. 192–5). But in Romantic and post-
Romantic culture, allegory experiences such radical modulations
that it seems to disappear altogether as realism and naturalism
begin to dominate literary and cultural practice. My present argument concerns when and how nineteenth-century poets accommo-
date the figural power of allegory to apparently antithetical realist
values. In this context, the Victorian cast of Browning's difficulty
extends the modern reinvention of allegory that begins with his
Romantic predecessors.

Briefly put, the Romantic and post-Romantic version of allegory
I have in mind grants the classical rhetorical claim that allegory, as
an 'extended metaphor', implies narrative extension (Quintilian
1921, 9.2.46–7). But unlike medieval and much of Renaissance
allegory, this much later version necessarily inhabits an unsteady
cosmological framework. By this I mean that the traditional 'other

speech' or transcendent referent of allegory is, for Browning as for Romantic writers, more than occasionally uncertain. It is also intriguingly adhesive to the visual or material vehicle for a given allegorical tenor. So understood, the reinvention of allegory after the Renaissance dramatises the resources of the figural, a term used here to designate metaphoric language of all kinds. If Browning's style is at times overly quaint, and weirdly grotesque, it is so in keeping with the logic of allegorical figuration that emerges in the poetry of his Romantic predecessors. This essay argues further that the Victorian materialism of Browning's poetics extends Romantic efforts to negotiate the figural difficulties inherent in assigning a material shape to allegorical figures.

Although Milton's allegory of Satan, Sin and Death in *Paradise Lost* is hardly the only poem that dramatises the task of finding shapes to represent allegorical ideas, it is a pivotal text in subsequent discussions of allegory. Eighteenth-century critics often decried Milton's use of allegory in an epic, hence verisimilar context.[1] In remarkable ways, Milton's presentation of Sin and Death hovers in the background of Romantic efforts to engage or repel the representational power of allegory as visual shape. I begin with Milton's description of Sin and Death, the incestuous parents of Satan, who discovers them at the Gates of Hell:

> Before the Gates there sat
> On either side a formidable *shape*;
> The one seem'd Woman to the waist, and fair,
> But ended foul in many a scaly fold
> Voluminous and vast, a Serpent arm'd
> With mortal sting: about her middle round
> A cry of Hell Hounds never ceasing bark'd
> With wide *Cerberean* mouths full loud, and rung
> A hideous Peal: yet, when they lit, would creep,
> If aught disturb'd their noise, into her womb,
> And kennel there, yet there still bark'd and howl'd
> Within unseen. ... The other *shape*,
> If *shape* it might be call'd that *shape* had none
> Distinguishable in member, joint, or limb,
> Or substance might be call'd that shadow seem'd,
> For each seem'd either; black it stood as Night.

(Milton 1935, 2:648–58 and 666–70, pp. 62–3, my emphasis)

Throughout the episode Milton is insistent that these allegorical horrors exhibit 'shapes' appropriate to their monstrous identities. Satan pointedly addresses his father Death as 'execrable shape' (680, p. 64). Death replies in kind, then suddenly balloons in size, half-undermining the realist logic of his earlier appearance as an oxymoronic shapeless shape. Says Milton's narrator, 'So spake the grisly terror, and in shape,/ So speaking and so threat'ning, grew tenfold/ More dreadful and deform' (2:704–706, p. 65).

Milton's description of Death as an allegorical shape who swells monstrously *as he speaks* indicates the rhetorical and figural logic of subsequent Romantic engagements with allegory as rhetorical figure and visual shape. The allegorical figure whose execrable shape appals Satan forecasts Browning's poetic treatment of characters like Guido Franceschini, the murderous husband of *The Ring and the Book* whose grotesque language and physical brutality make him the oppressive yet crucial figure of that poem.

Defending Milton's allegory against earlier criticism, Coleridge argued in 1811–12 that painters who depict Death as a 'skeleton' reduce him to 'the dryest and hardest image that it is possible to discover', a 'distinct form' incapable of evoking the 'strong working of the mind' that is the sign of the poetic imagination (Coleridge 1930, 2:138–9). This restatement of Burke's aesthetics of the sublime ('a clear idea is...a little idea', Burke 1958, p. 61) promotes the version of allegory that attracts Romantic and post-Romantic writers: a figural mode that is fruitfully if problematically identified with visual shapes that move. The fact that Coleridge makes this argument about Milton's allegory without ever mentioning the term indicates another side of the covert ambivalence that also permeates his more openly antagonistic accounts of allegory as a figural mode inferior to symbol (Coleridge 1930, pp. 28–38; 1972, pp. 29–31).[2]

As Milton's Death suggests, allegorical personifications who move in realistic ways to create narratives cannot be immobilised or quarantined. Instead, they grow bigger, more aggressive. Doctor Johnson makes this transgressive feature of allegorical figures the crux of his critique. As long as Sin and Death do not build bridges, as long as Death does not attack his unwelcome son, they conduct themselves appropriately, as 'figurative' instead of real characters, 'but when they stop the journey of Satan, a journey described as real, and when Death offers him battle, the allegory is broken' (Johnson 1952, pp. 465–6). For many eighteenth-century critics, this prohibition against allegorical personifications that move masks a deeper prohibition against allegorical interpretations that cannot be fixed but are analogously on the move, as readers find themselves reading texts and images with an allegorist's conviction that this activity ought to produce more than one, unchanging statement of meaning. So roused to act, readers and allegorical shapes cannot keep still. Instead, Romantic poets like Wordsworth find themselves reluctantly attracted to 'shapes, and forms, and tendencies to shape' (Wordsworth 1979, *Prelude* 8: 721, p. 304) that invite speculation.

Despite his claim in the *Preface* to *Lyrical Ballads* that personification ought to have only a limited role in poems, Wordsworth is himself captured by an underlying and deeply classical recognition that personifications which arise from strong feeling are admissible as figures of passion, however extravagant such figures seem to be. This recognition, which emerges in successive editions of the *Preface*, acknowledges the fundamental poetic logic which links ancient rhetorical arguments about passion and figure to personification and, more generally, to poetic figures whose animating presence carries so much force in Romantic poetry, including Wordsworth's (Wordsworth 1974, 1:130–1; Kelley 1988, pp. 195–7). This, I suggest, is the residual poetic effect of the speaker's phantasmagoric London narrative in Book 7 of *The Prelude*, where 'faces' and 'shop signs' that display 'allegoric shapes' are syntactically so akin that the speaker cannot successfully separate the human from the emblematic, the abstract from human, realist particulars (Wordsworth 1979, 7:172–80, p. 234; Kelley, 1991, p. 251). So understood, Wordsworth's poetics demonstrates the degree to which Romantic poets were not able to assent to eighteenth-century efforts to stabilise wandering, potentially allegorical figures.

In Keats's late poetics, questions about the fixity or mobility of quasi-allegorical figures are frequently tinged with acknowledgements of shape or form as sculptural or sensuous. Thus in *Hyperion* Keats uses the term 'shape' to describe Mnemosyne, and Saturn calls his fellow Titans 'the first-born of all shap'd and palpable Gods' (Keats, 1978, 3:61, p. 354 and 2:154, p. 345). In both Hyperion poems, the term 'shape' is one index to a broader argument about massively sculptured personifications. As the Titans experience strong feeling for the first time, and remark on this new and unwished-for resemblance to mortals (Keats 1978, *Hyperion*, 1:332–5, p. 339 and 2:97–100, p. 343), they become resonant illustrations of the Romantic effort to renegotiate the distance between abstract personification and human character. Keats may hazard a more grotesque vision of this distance in *Lamia*. To exchange her 'gordian shape' for the 'woman's shape' Lamia says was once hers, she undergoes a metamorphosis that is at once painful, fantastic, and oddly geological.

> She writh'd about, convuls'd with scarlet pain:
> A deep volcanian yellow took the place
> Of all her milder-mooned body's grace;
> And, as the lava ravishes the mead,
> Spoilt all her silver mail, and golden brede.
>
> (Keats 1978, lines 154–58, p. 456)

If this is hardly a natural or organic birth, its fantastic use of geological figures to present elemental change as volcanic eruption makes Lamia a figure both painfully real and full of artifice. As another Keatsian example of the Romantic engagement with figure and abstraction, this passage indicates the grotesque and oddly material energy of figures that pull toward and away from recognisably human forms.

In *The Triumph of Life* and *Prometheus Unbound*, Shelley repeatedly presents 'shape' as a marker of complexly imagined and emergent allegorical identities bound to the transformative speech of characters. Prometheus begins by offering the absence of 'shape' and the intrusion of 'shapeless sights' as negative signs of his self-torture. After Prometheus renounces his curse, Asia begins to identify his 'shape' where she had before been able to discern a 'shade', then declares that Panthea's 'words / Fill, pause by pause my own forgotten sleep / With shapes' (Shelley 1977, I.i.22 and 36, pp. 136–7; II.i.120 and 141–3, pp. 163–4). Once Jupiter falls, the Spirit of the Hour characterises the human and institutional signs of his tyranny as 'barbaric' or 'foul shapes' (III.iii.168 and 180, p. 193); in the last act Panthea describes the future at hand as 'Peopled with unimaginable shapes' (IV.244, p. 201). As the poem concludes, the Earth proclaims language the 'perpetual Orphic song, / Which rules with Daedal harmony a throng / Of thoughts and forms, which else senseless and shapeless were' (IV.415–17, p. 205). In Shelley's idealist drama of cosmic and spiritual renewal, meaning and representation depend on words as the arbiter of shapes that speak allegorically. In *The Triumph of Life*, the same term ironically designates individuals and cultures as the decaying forms of civilisation. The uncertain allegorical function of the 'shape all light' commands the neo-platonic imagery of heavenly visitation which Shelley deploys in *The Sensitive Plant*. For Rousseau, who narrates this section of the poem, the 'fair shape' seems at best an interim allegorical influence. Once he drinks what the shape offers, his brain becomes 'as sand' and the shape begins to fade as a new vision takes its place in Rousseau's unsteady consciousness (lines 352–405, pp. 465–6).

In the examples discussed here, romantic considerations of shapes as personified and potentially allegorical figures specify the interest and enduring perplexity of such figures. They are presented as palpable and real forms; some are drawn toward human identity and emotion; and all dramatise the romantic attraction to allegorical narratives tied to visual or quasi-visual vehicles. As a figure whose narrative extension transgresses the boundary between what is human and alive and what is abstract and thus 'dead', allegory is a troublemaker, a figure of tyranny as well as a figural power. In a return to allegory mediated by these implied Romantic assessments and Victorian historiography and realism, Browning makes the transgressive relation between allegory, shape, and reality tell and retell the role of abstraction and materiality in his poetics.

Browning's presentation of transcendence as something longed for, half-postulated, but perennially out of human reach, registers the Romantic and post-Romantic edge of his allegorical inclination. More persistently than Romantic poets, with the possible exception of Shelley in *The Triumph of Life*, Browning's sceptical, ironic narratives introduce multiple sources, informants, and narrators who offer competing surmises about the meaning or even the facts at issue. In effect, this tactic reasserts the classical rhetorical affiliation between allegory and irony as figural modes whose implications emerge in extended formats. Put another way, just as there can be no irony without a context (implied or explicit), there can be no allegory without a referent (always implied) and a narrative field against which indications of that referent or other speech can be plotted. Browning also re-imagines the role of detail in traditional allegory in ways that extend Spenser's ambivalent use of rhetorical, visual and thus emblematic details and the neoclassical reaction against this allegorical practice. For Browning, detail – especially grotesque detail – works to offend readers' sense of realism by offering exaggerations that imply a typological or mythological order of meaning. By such means, he makes the material edge of nineteenth-century realism a *figure* whose implied ground is elsewhere, abstract and general more than concrete and individual.

From this perspective, Browning's early admiration for Shelley – as much for his idealist attraction to allegorical narratives and arguments as for a subjective or quintessentially Romantic point of view – never really dissipates, despite Browning's disillusion with Shelley after the publication of the *Essay on Shelley* in 1852. Like Coleridge, Browning envisions allegory – as text or commentary – as he responds to the theological and secular implications of the German higher criticism, which attempts to save Biblical revelation from the ravages of its own realist and historical expectations by appealing to another order of truth. This truth, often mythological, displays the hermeneutic shape of allegorical narratives and reading – multiple narrators and interpreters who manage as best they can to convey the 'other speech' of Christian revelation. In characteristic fashion, Browning meets this debate head-on by dramatising its theological difficulty in *A Death in the Desert* (*Dramatic Personae*, 1864) and extending its consequences to the secular hermeneutics of poems he published in the 1860s and 1870s. In these poems Browning's fascination with realist details that are grimy, scandalous or grotesque presses material vehicles so close to figural tenors that they risk being absorbed or debased by the material grotesque. This strategy, which reverses the direction of poetic simile in Shelley, reveals the extent to which Browning was willing to chart and even redistrict the boundaries between allegory and realism.

After his wife's death, Browning offers his first poetic investigation of the fracturing of narratives and truths in *A Death in the Desert* (1864). The subject of the poem is the apostle John, whose dying words raise questions about the reliability of the Gospels, including his own, as witnesses to the life of Christ (Shaffer, 1975, pp. 191–224). The poem is explicitly concerned with re-imagining biblical scripture *as* commentary, much as the nineteenth-century higher critics began to do when they questioned the historical verifiability of the Gospels. A critical voice in the poem pointedly objects that if John has the facts wrong, how can others be expected to believe (lines 514–30, p. 800)? What John's imagined interlocutor wants is what readers of John's Gospel and the Book of Revelations never get: plain facts and a text free of figure, of parable, of allegorical presence. Browning invokes the instabilities of flesh as an intermittent guide to spiritual meaning, to the allegorical speech that John is prone to offer.

John's disciples are themselves attentive to opportunities for this kind of speech. In an interpolated (and bracketed) explanation of why John begins by seeming to confuse those before him with disciples long dead, an unidentified commentator, perhaps the outside narrator, suggests:

> This is the doctrine he was wont to teach,
> How divers persons witness in each man,
> Three souls which make up one soul...
> I give the glossa of Theotypas.

(lines 82–4 and 104, 1:789–90)

As a fictional name that means 'god-type', 'Theotypas' is a succinct instance of the typological other speech that attracts John, whose frustrated effort to '[Grasp] ... for stay at facts which snap' (line 191, 1:792) prompts him to suggest another kind and level of assurance for those who come after him, and for those who discount his eyewitness account and thus require another basis for the assurance they seek. The image John offers of this assurance is an 'optic glass' borrowed from Francis Quarles's *Emblems* (Hyde 1985, pp. 93–6):

> Ye need, – as I should use an optic glass
> I wondered at erewhile, somewhere i' the world,
> It had been given a crafty smith to make;
> A tube, he turned on objects brought too close,
> Lying confusedly insubordinate
> For the unassisted eye to master once:
> Look through his tube, at distance now they lay,
> Become succinct, distinct, so small, so clear!
> Just thus, ye needs must apprehend what truth
> I see, reduced to plain historic fact,
> Diminished into clearness, proved a point
> And far away: ye would withdraw your sense
> From out eternity, strain it upon time,
> Then stand before that fact, that Life and Death,
> Stay there at gaze, till it dispart, dispread,
> As though a star should open out, all sides,
> Grow the world on you, as it is my world.

(lines 227–43, 1:793)

The fact and truth that occupy John's vision are Christ's 'Life and Death', which John figures as a progress characterised by intermittent 'Love' and 'Power' (lines 221–2, 1:793). John's allegorical temper echoes a similar inclination among the higher critics who at times substituted allegorical interpretations for the abandoned certitudes of fact. For example, in his own marginal commentary on Johann Gottfried Eichhorn's commentary on Revelations, Coleridge declared, 'The four first Trumpets denote the Evils that preceded and prepared the way for the Outbreak of the Zelotes, Terrorists, and Septembrizers of Jerusalem' (Shaffer, 1975, p. 59).

The vision Browning's John advises for subsequent generations is similarly tilted toward the clarity of figural distance, which permits the telescoping of events into identifiable patterns, a process of abstraction whose outcome is easier to manage than the confused mass of evidence seen in close-up. In the Blakean expansion and contraction of vision which completes the optic-glass figure, John suggests that being able to identify a larger, abstract pattern prompted by the fact of Christ's life and death is itself assurance, the guide to belief in the love that remains for John the truth of that life as both abstraction and lived particular.

In subsequent poems of the 1860s and 1870s, Browning conveys a less smooth, more unhinged account of how abstraction and particulars meet in poetic figures. Here his allegorical disposition is harder-won, more permeable to fact, to material vehicles than John's, along lines suggested by Romantic reinventions of traditional figures but more resolutely interested in the textual friction between literal vehicles and figural meaning. The chief counterexample to Browning's John in *Dramatis Personae* is Caliban, whose rhetoric and theology are earthbound as the dying John's are not. As the self-styled 'rank tongue' that 'blossom[s] into speech' (line 23, 1:805), Caliban talks and thinks from the same literal ground, with a mind and eye for detail and sense largely absent from John's narrative. Deliberately monstrous and grotesque in speech and action, Caliban displays the poetic energy Browning gains in this and later poems from the uneven, alienating style and rhythm that Elizabeth Barrett had once argued he ought not to use because it put readers off (Drew 1970, p. 71). As a comic reinvention of the newly-minted deism of the Bridgewater tracts (Browning 1981, 1:1158n.) Caliban's deism summarises what remains of theology without revelation and thus without apparent inclination toward allegorical speech. The 'Quiet' whom Caliban understands only as a dimly-perceived alternative to Prospero (lines 170–8, 1:809) remains outside the aural and material specificities of Caliban's internal dialogue on the nature and temper of God.

Mr Sludge, 'The Medium' (1864) proclaims the potential fraudulence of allegorical speech, the proximity of fiction to lying, and, to put it neutrally, problems inherent in the transmission of spiritual truths into speech as well as print. In the main, Sludge is the kind of spiritual charlatan Browning learned to despise over a long, unwilling acquaintance with mediums and mesmerism (Karlin, 1989, pp. 65–77; Goslee, 1975, pp. 40–58). Yet Sludge's self-comparisons with 'your literary man' – writers of novels and poems – and his claim to provide supernatural accounts on a par with the Bible and history, work to expose the unbound and fraying edge between fact and fraud in the secular as well as religious culture of the later nineteenth century. As Isobel Armstrong (1966, p. 212) and David Goslee (1975, p. 40) have argued, the unsavoury Sludge is given the narrative task of examining arguments that recur in Browning's poetry: the nature of truth, personal revelation and art. Sludge is a deliberately grotesque medium, one who inevitably contaminates his Browningesque message about spiritual truth and its opposites.

Besides self-correction, the grotesque exaggerations of characters like Caliban, Sludge, and even more unsavoury figures like Guido Franceschini of *The Ring and the Book* offer Browning valuable poetic revenue. As speakers, they constantly enact the potential decay of figures, those rhetorical guides to speech that extend its range beyond the quotidian, the here and now. They interrupt and query, in other words, the allegorical trajectory to a spiritual referent. As Armstrong points out, the exaggerations of this grotesque style indicate 'the centrifugal movement of Browning's poems; they throw words outwards, leaving a litter of linguistic wreckage for the reader to reconstruct, a wreckage which has a curious way of demanding more attention than it seems to deserve' (Armstrong 1969, pp. 93–4). At times, Browning's excessive demand on the reader's attention marks the residue of a coherent allegorical plot gone awry in the material and figural stresses of the rhetorical grotesque, which acts as a reality check on human efforts to create or approximate the other speech of allegory.

In a more specifically textual sense, Browning's use of grotesque figures in *The Ring and the Book* mines the literal to invent the figural. In this and other late poems, allegorical speech uses the same figural path. Browning's use of the grotesque deliberately exaggerates the impact of material, literal referents on poetic figures. The story of necks, especially Guido's, tells the tale. As

Stephen C. Walker (1976) explains, Guido begins his final monologue shorn of title, shortly to lose his head at the neck, and
verbally obsessed with necks, beginning with his 'soft neck and
throat' (11:128, p. 540). He refers to 'the way a head is set on neck',
to 'those lithe live necks of ours' (lines 284, 290, p. 544). He bitterly
recalls Pompilia as the child whose neck 'writhes, cords itself
against your kiss' and finally asserts his right to 'wring her neck'
(1019, p. 564 and 1359, p. 573). When he insists that the mob, rather
than the pope and clergy, should judge him, he offers the neck as
the virtual seat of the soul:

> Born-baptized-and-bred Christian-atheists, each
> With just as much a right to judge as you, –
> As many sense in his soul, or nerves
> I' the neck of him as I, – whom, soul and sense,
> Neck and nerve, you abolish presently.

> (11:709–13, pp. 555–6)

Guido's compulsive return to his neck creates, as Walker implies in
his astute notice of these examples (Walker 1976, pp. 27–8), a figural
net that binds Guido's terror of death to its origin, his assumption
that he could wring Pompilia's neck as though she were a captive
bird (who nonetheless lives long enough to sing).

Browning refused to modify or reduce the grotesque imagery of
The Ring and the Book despite a long exchange of letters on the topic
with Julia Wedgwood, who repeatedly questioned the poem's
emphasis on Guido and other speakers and characters who provide
similar occasions for figural vulgarity (see Curle 1937, pp. 135–209).
The figural pyrotechnics of the poem, which burn innocent as well
as guilty parties, forecast his deployment of similar figures in later
poems and, more indirectly, the poetic logic of his interest in rough,
literal translation in the 1870s. In each instance, grotesque, often
violent figures, like those Guido musters to talk about his neck and
Pompilia's, make apparent the way that material, literal facts will,
under the pressure of feeling, become figures. In this regard,
Browning's grotesque style insists on a potentially damaging
contact between the resources of human rhetoric and its gesture
toward allegorical narrative and meaning.

As Walker has remarked, the contradiction and dissonance of
figuration in *The Ring and the Book* imply a 'downhill evolution' of

images (Walker 1976, p. 20). The most disturbing instances ensure unwelcome affinities between Pompilia and Caponsacchi, the characters whose testimony the Pope and Browning's narrator evidently credit, and the whole array of sordid speakers and characters who dominate the physical space of the poem, including Guido, Violante, Pietro, the Abate and the two lawyers. As a relatively minor example, all of them are at different moments in the poem compared unflatteringly to snakes and dogs (Walker 1976, p. 14). This 'shotgun blast of imagery', as Walker calls it, makes sustained demands on readers as they evaluate the applicability of such figures in each case and examine the speakers and arguments these figures serve. Images, like the gradually deteriorating situation of Pompilia herself, are frequently caught, as Walker again remarks, in the 'strong imagistic undertow' illustrated by the succession of bird figures the Abate uses to depict Guido's capture of a wife (Walker 1976, p. 20). The narrator is The Other Half-Rome, but the sentiments are ascribed to the Abate and, behind that figure of marital bliss and authority, Guido:

> Since if his simple kinsman so were bent,
> Began his rounds in Rome to catch a wife,
> Full soon would such unworldliness surprise
> The rare bird, sprinkle salt on phoenix' tail,
> And so secure the nest a sparrow-hawk.
> No lack of mothers here in Rome, – no dread
> Of daughters lured as larks by looking-glass!
> The first name-pecking credit-scratching fowl
> Would drop her unfledged cuckoo in our nest.

(Browning 1971, 3:332–40, p. 120)

The slippage from phoenix to cuckoo is a cumulative bad omen, forecasting Pompilia's capture by Guido, who elsewhere imagines her his hawk to wound or imprison as he chooses. To be sure, as she dies, Pompilia becomes phoenix-like again, rising from the disasters of her birth and marriage to God ('And I rise'). Yet the preponderance of bird-images used for Pompilia throughout the poem works hard against this figure of resurrection.

In a different vein, Browning's personifications work the figural terrain between animate and inanimate: Pompilia compares her marital predicament to that of a goat standing on a pile of sticks as its master removes them one by one, calling that goat and thus herself 'A shuddering white woman of a beast' (7:610, p. 341); Guido's household becomes, in the mill of Tertium Quid's citation of Guido, 'the two, three creeping house-dog-servant-things' (4:1077, p. 188); Browning's narrator calls the lawyer Bottinius 'The scrannel pipe that screams in heights of head' (1:1201, p. 55); as Caponsacchi listens to the 'stone lungs' of the cathedral with its 'scrannel voice' of dead passion, he sits 'stone-still' until dawn (6:1000 and 1023, pp. 292–3); and The Other Half-Rome uses synecdoche to personify the primitive violence temporarily hidden in Guido's watchful observation of his wife's exchanges with Caponsacchi, presented namelessly as 'tooth and claw of something in the dark' (3:787, p. 132). Among the more chilling examples of the way personifications can, as Stephen Knapp observes, substitute human for inanimate or animal figures (Knapp 1985, pp. 59–60; also Walker 1976, pp. 21–2) is Guido's description of the guillotine:

> There the man-mutilating engine stood
> At ease, both gay and grim, like a Swiss guard
> Off duty.

> (11:207–9, p. 542)

Finally, recurring syntactic patterns act like electronic 'snow', verbal chatter or white noise that subtly erodes the integrity and specificity of speech in the poem. All of the speakers employ prepositional contractions, often accentuated by alliteration, which the most cynical speakers and even Browning's narrator use in ways that degrade or erode meaning. The narrator introduces the basic pattern: 'arm o' the feeler', 'mouth o' the street', 'curd o' the cream', 'flower o' the wheat', 'sense o' the city' (1:855, 875, 918–19, pp. 46–7). The pattern is often used to describe Pompilia: Tertium Quid sardonically notes her 'sudden existence, dewy dear,/ O' the rose above the dungheap, the pure child/ As good as new created' (4:246–8, p. 165); Guido derisively names her 'dirt/ O' the kennel', 'Dust o' the street' (5:772–3, p. 227). Speaker after speaker uses this and similar patterns so frequently that they become a verbal tic in the poem, used by all of them but especially by those speakers who are the most cynical, the most aware of the possibilities for rhetorical sleights of speech.[3]

Readers of the poem have variously accounted for this dissonant aural and figural density, which complicates the poem's central ring figure as well as the syntax and figures I have mentioned. For some, this density supports an organic plenitude that does not contaminate or undermine the moral claims of the Pope and the narrator about the truth of the story (e.g. Walker 1976, pp. 28–9; Woolford 1988, pp. 176–204; Hiemstra 1985, pp. 47–58; McGowan 1986, pp. 158–73; Feinberg 1985, pp. 70–96; Cook 1920, p. 293; Siegchrist 1981, pp. 7–10). For others, it demonstrates the post-structuralist, deconstructive impulse at work in Browning's longest poem, corrosive to the claims regarding truth offered by the Pope and the narrator (Slinn 1989, pp. 115–33; Shaw 1989, pp. 79–88; Dillon 1990, pp. 169–71; Froula 1986, pp. 965–92; Tucker 1985, pp. 226–43).

The first view grants the moral authority to these speakers, whose convictions reflect the progressive, secular as well as spiritual, revelation Browning uses in *A Death in the Desert* to defend John's weaknesses against the deepest anti-theological scepticisms of some of the higher critics. When the Pope declares,

> Truth, nowhere, lies yet everywhere in these –
> Not absolutely in a portion, yet
> Evolvable from the whole: evolved at last
> Painfully, held tenaciously by me...

> (10:228–31, p. 483)

he indicates the role of progressive revelation in secular as well as spiritual life. Throughout the poem, Browning's narrator indicates ample grounds for assenting to the Pope's judgement of Guido, over against the excuses and justifications offered by other speakers. Implicitly, then, the poem seems to grant the spiritual and moral legitimacy of moral choice founded on progressive (speech) acts of revelation. When the narrator assesses linguistic obstacles to knowing truth in the last book ('our human speech is naught, / Our human testimony false, our fame / And human estimation words and wind', 12:834–6, p. 627), he acknowledges the difficulty of revelation without denying it as a principle of knowing.

This is not to say, however, that the poem displays the organic wholeness readers have wished on it. For the central deconstructive insight that figural language decays is apt for *The Ring and the Book* as a poem whose very prolixity gives ample evidence of such decay (Armstrong 1969, pp. 177–97). The interpretive problem is not so much figuring out what happened – the divergences among all the versions agree on the essential details of the plot even when they disagree about motive and actual speech – but figuring out figures, getting a grip on the rhetoric of the poem. This, I think, is an important dimension of the poem's argument, one that demonstrates the verbal, rhetorical 'way o' the world', the miasma of speech, chatter, deception, and self-presentation that infects and animates the only language humans have with which to articulate their sense of human and divine revelation. The path of figure in *The Ring and the Book* is for Browning the one that human thought must travel, with more obstacles than clear guides.

The complicated imagery of *The Ring and the Book* and its apparent figural verbosity project a highly modern sense of the difficulty of knowing what is truth and how it is true. Like cosmic, human 'snow', Browning's figures deliberately disturb the medium of transmission, much as the legal advocates Archengelis and Bottinius try to obscure what happened on both sides of the case. If arriving at something like the allegorical other speech of this poem requires getting through its confused medium, this is so because linguistic confusion and betrayal are endemic to language as the necessary medium of human speech and knowing. Paul de Man's understanding of allegory as the figure of deferred and constantly disfiguring meaning registers a version of Browning's exuberant and sceptical demonstration of figural decay, as does Walter Benjamin's haunting account of allegorical meaning as the outcome, almost the phosphorescence, of fragmentation and disintegration (de Man, 1983, pp. 187–227; Benjamin, 1977, pp. 162–77). Yet neither modern theorist registers Browning's Victorian optimism that the figural clutter of the poem will finally tell with a near-Dickensian plenitude the latent allegorical truth of the story.

In the early 1870s Browning risked his recent good favour in the reviews by writing poems like *Fifine at the Fair* (1872) and *Red Cotton Night-Cap Country* (1873), whose characters and situations were at least as sordid as some in *The Ring and the Book*. The result is especially lurid in *Red Cotton Night-Cap Country*, a poem based on a contemporary event which Browning pursued through legal documents, much as he had done in writing *The Ring and the Book* (see Siegchrist 1981, pp. 3–8, 150). The story concerns a middle-class French jeweller, whom Browning calls Miranda, who burned his hands off in a fire and retreated with his lover to the country, where he later leapt off a parapet to his death. In reimagining this story, Browning presents Miranda's suicide as a leap of faith in the Virgin, whom he expects to save him (she does not). Browning's poetic assessment of this final act emphasises its spiritual conviction, however superstitious and flawed.

As the poem begins, a Browningesque narrator brings a friend to the place where Miranda had jumped and died, points to the ground, and hints about the circumstances of the death. This ghoulish toying with the audience introduces the organising figure of the poem: the turf below signifies the secular, fleshly existence that preoccupied the dead protagonist for so long; the tower, the spiritual values to which he finally assents. A more marked spirit of grotesquerie and absurdity governs Browning's graphic description of Miranda's earlier self-mutilation, his beloved's character, and his 'Cousinry'. The narrator reports the outcome:

> Two horrible remains of right and left,
> 'Whereof the bones, phalanges formerly,
> Carbonized, were still crackling with the flame.'

> (lines 2600–2603, 2:142)

Browning's use of this moment in the poem is unsettling: he follows it with an account of Miranda's beatific convalescence over the next three months, quoting him extensively as he waxes rhapsodic about spiritual gain and claims to feel no pain. Without shifting narrative tone, Browning laconically reports Miranda's sudden return to his lover's arms as soon as he is strong enough to get into a carriage (lines 2717–25, 2:145–6). And throughout the poem those burned stumps are put to extensive figural use. Asserting that there was no 'recrudescence' in Miranda's character when he retreated to the country, the narrator compares this (non-recurring) 'recrudescence' to a 'wound, half-healed before, / Set freshly running – sin, repressed as such, / New loosened as necessity of life' (lines 2815–17, 2:148). Equally grotesque and unnecessary is the diction used to convey the clergy's view of Miranda:

> There was no washing hands of him (alack,
> You take me? – in the figurative sense!)
> But, somehow, gloves were drawn o'er dirt and all.

> (lines 3106–8, 2:155)

To complete the poem's absorption in grotesque imagery that is both shocking and expected, the narrator's auditor remarks at the close (two years after Miranda's death and burial) that it might be best to 'draw your very thickest, thread and thrum, / O'er such a decomposing face of things, / Once so alive, it seemed immortal too!' So that readers won't miss the ghoulish pun, Browning begins the next line: 'This happened two years since' (lines 4145–7, 2:181).

Red Cotton Night-Cap Country is a curious poetic experiment. The poem works hard, probably too hard, to yoke its bodily grotesque with the story of Miranda's soul. In the end, the spiritual and potentially allegorical frame indicated by its turf-and-towers imagery seems at least half done-in by its deliberate exploitation of Miranda's self-mutilation. For this reason, the poem articulates a limit-case in the relation Browning seeks between a compelling spiritual referent and figures whose strangely material basis can be used to evoke some sense of allegorical possibility in human speech.

The protagonist and basic plot of *Fifine at the Fair* ought to have produced a hybrid of Byron's *Don Juan*, Molière's play (which Browning excerpts for an epigraph), and Mozart's opera. The monologist is Don Juan, bent on convincing Done Elvire that his pursuit of all women, but especially Fifine, a girl they have seen at a fair, amounts to a fleshly yet allegorical pursuit of the true amid the false or human representations of love and beauty, from Fifine to Elvire to Venus to Helen, with an intriguing mythological detour to include Eidothee, the daughter of Proteus, who helps Menelaus trap her shape-changing father.

Yet Browning frames the argument of *Fifine at the Fair* in ways that lend credence to the seriousness of Don Juan's argument, without capitulating to its self-serving rationale for more seductions, more straying from the marital bed. The Prologue, subtitled 'Amphibian', is narrated by a swimmer who wishes he could survive in air as well as water. But like the butterfly flying above him which would die if its wing touched the water, he cannot survive in air. This bare figure next animates Browning's longing for Barrett Browning, figured as a woman who has slipped from an earthly chrysalis and taken to the air. The poetic vehicle for the speaker's flight, were it possible, would be 'passion and thought', which together 'substitute' poetry for heaven (2:5–7). The true amphibian would be someone who could sport between the flesh (the sea) and the spirit (the air). In rhetorical terms, the pathos of Browning's longing for Barrett animates the simple figures of the

Prologue and the poem that follows. This use of pathos also suggests the figural logic of Browning's allegorical temper: to find figures of passion that convey human speech across the distances and barriers described here and in the Epilogue, where a cranky 'householder', who suddenly finds his dead wife has returned to him, complains of the domestic tedium he has endured since her death.

In every sense of the term made available by Browning's poem, Don Juan is amphibian. He enjoys the 'play o' the body' (lines 1039, 2:36) in the sea, an apt figure for the kind of fleshly existence he prizes: constant sexual desire and conquest of all the women he observes, including Fifine, a gypsy street-girl whose beauty contrasts sharply with the pale serenity of his wife. Don Juan anticipates his wife's charge that he is incapable of remaining faithful by claiming that a metaphysical necessity drives his erotic nature – to find or approach the ideal feminine being through just this 'play o' the body'. As the daughter of Proteus, Eidothee ratifies his claim that to find the feminine 'one', he must have 'the many'. Eidothee is, as the Greek root of her name implies, one of the mythological women of the poem whose idea fixes the multiform reality of desire, even as she tells Menelaus how to capture her father before he changes his elemental form to elude capture. As such, she is the rival Done Elvire will

> never face evolved, in earth, in air,
> In wave; but, manifest i' the soul's domain, why, there
> She ravishingly moves to meet you, all through aid
> O' the soul!

> (lines 787–91, 2:30)

What checks the persuasiveness of Don Juan's claim to be the poet's amphibian creature of mortal and ideal worlds is the edge of grotesqueness that lingers undispelled by his urbane rhetoric. The 'false shows' that objectify this aspect of the poem are the freaks and transgressive identities Don Juan sees at the fair, including Fifine. As Clyde L. de Ryals notes, the attractiveness of girls like Fifine, Toinette, and Mimi is compromised by the fakes and deformities of the fair itself, including the beast exhibited one year as a 'six-legged sheep' that had been the 'Twin-headed Babe, and Human Nondescript' the previous year (lines 123–5, 2:11). To these false identities Ryals adds Fifine and her compatriots, who strip off layers of seductive female costume to 'bounce forth, squalid girls transformed to gamesome boys' (line 26, 2:8). For Ryals, the figural trickery of the opening scene at the fair signals, like Don Juan's tricky rhetorical self-defence throughout the poem, how *Fifine at the Fair* 'systematizes what is sensuous and relativistic' and 'utterly excludes what is transcendental or metaphysical' (Ryals 1975, pp. 466 and 469).

Yet the freaks and wayward girls of Browning's fair, like those at London's Bartholomew Fair which Wordsworth describes in Book 7 of *The Prelude*, may tell another story, one oddly pitched toward the recognition of what Wordsworth had called 'allegoric shapes' amid a 'parliament of monsters' (Wordsworth 1979, 7:179, lines 683–95, pp. 234, 264). All are shape-changers in a fleshly or moral medium; they adopt or shed false disguises to assume others that are also false. The same charge is justly made about poetic figures and particularly allegory, as an exaggerated, at times grotesque meta-figure for the power of figures. Changeability is the law of figure, even as it is the self-serving 'law' of Don Juan's sexual and aesthetic appetite as he loses interest in a Raphael when he decides to acquire a Doré engraving (2:22–8). Seeking to characterise a 'prodigious fair' of human beings in Venice, Don Juan argues that all the faces belong to generic 'man', but particularised in schematic terms as

> in the main
> A love, a hate, a hope, a fear, each soul a-strain
> Some one way through the flesh – the face, an evidence
> O' the soul at work inside; and, all the more intense,
> So much the more grotesque.

> (lines 1718–21, 2:55)

Because he approaches this spectacle as 'A groundling like the rest' (line 1738, p. 55, compare Wordsworth's narrator in *The Prelude* who imagines a vantage point high above Bartholomew Fair, 7:656–9, p. 262), he conveys both its abstract and its particular human features:

> – whereas so much more monstrosities deflect
> From nature and the type, as you the more approach
> Their precinct, – here, I found brutality encroach
> Less on the human, lie the lightlier as I looked

The nearlier on these faces that seemed but now so crooked
And clawed away from God's prime purpose. They diverged
A little from the type, but somehow rather urged
To pity than disgust.

(lines 1740–7, 2:55–6)

As Don Juan elaborates his complicit recognition of human limitation and striving, he argues emphatically for a figural narrative
populated by human particulars as seen through and in abstract or
ideal types. Elaborating his theme, Don Juan warns, 'one must
abate / One's scorn of the soul's casing, distinct from the soul's self'
(lines 1789–90, 2:57).

Put in these terms, Don Juan's insistence that abstract ideas and
human identities can be joined by groundlings like him questions
the separation between figural and literal so often urged to argue
the difference between the referent of an allegorical narrative and
the literal, textual details of that narrative. In *Fifine at the Fair*,
Browning makes the hardest possible case for understanding how
such a narrative is bonded to its allegorical meaning. This union is
neither expected nor easy to grant when the literal narrative is the
deft rhetoric of a Don Juan who is not a whit excused of his traditional biases and failings.

At the end of the manuscript of *Fifine*, Browning appended two
Greek passages which link the difficulty of the poem to Greek
drama. The first passage, taken from Aeschylus's' *Libation-Bearers*,
implies the stylistic affinity between Browning and Aeschylus.
Dated several months after the publication of *Fifine* in June 1872, it
reads (in translation): 'Speaking an inscrutable word at night he
brings darkness over the eyes, and by day he is no clearer'
(Browning, 1981, 2:975n.; Prins 1989, 156). The difficulty specified by
Aeschylus's lines is the kind an allegorical text presents. Browning
later added a second inscription from Aristophanes which might
refer to his reader or to Browning himself as the 'savage' householder of the Epilogue:

> What avails me? Shall I make a speech?
> His savage nature could not take it in.
> True wit and wisdom were but labour lost
> On such a rude barbarian.

(2:975n)

An uncannily similar critique reverberates in contemporary reviews of Browning's own translation of the *Agamemnon* (1877). Readers complained, with some reason, that in his effort to produce a rough, highly literal translation, Browning had invented a grotesque, perversely distorted version of spoken and written English. For example, he translates a Greek synecdoche used to characterise Clytemnestra, γυναικὸςἀνδρὸ βουλονέ λπὶζονκέ αρ (literally 'a woman's man-willed hopeful heart'), as 'The man's-way-planning hoping heart of woman' (Browning 1988, 11, p. 403; Prins 1989, p. 67). In the scene that presents Agamemnon's sacrifice of his daughter Iphigenia, Browning matches the violence of Aeschylus's language and the moment itself:

> His ministrants, vows done, the father bade –
> Kid-like, above the altar, swathed in pall,
> Take her – lift high, and have no fear at all,
> Head-downward, and the fair mouth's guard
> And frontage hold, – press hard
> From utterance a curse against the House
> By dint of bit – violence bridling speech.

(Browning 1988, lines 247–53, p. 409)

A similarly rough handling of English syntax and vocabulary throughout his translation of *Agamemnon* displays the necessary figural violence for which this scene is a material witness. Translation thus becomes a linguistic and secular allegory because, like all exchanges across such barriers, to do its work it must foreground the alien, unstable relation between the translation and its source.

Browning's contribution to this medieval as well as modern understanding of theory of allegory is to mine the allegorical possibilities of figural violence, kept at bay by English writers at least since the early eighteenth century, where neoclassical critics sought to restrain allegorical agents from acting. Romantic interest in the relationship between allegory and violence is more often covert. Thus even as Wordsworth reluctantly implies the agency of 'allegoric shapes' in *The Prelude*, he seeks to sequester those shapes as misshapen forms of life bred by London, and absent in the restorative rural life of his childhood. Browning's more open interrogation of the resources made available by figural violence is closest to Shelley's allegorical practice in *The Triumph of Life*, where the grotesque figure of Rousseau becomes a skeletal root system which handily unhinges the sentimental, quasi-romantic view of man and nature.

In his late return to the subjective poetics of Shelley, Browning grants the necessity of a subjective origin for allegorical speech, however flawed the speaking subject. The focus of his scepticism regarding this speech is not the status of its referent. Browning's theological stance is clear, less troubled by doubt or dogma than even Coleridge's. Instead, Browning is sceptically aware of how quickly figures decay or are decoyed into false speech. Hence his interest in the grotesque, both because it dramatises the earthbound energies of human speech and because it helps to incite figures of passion, precisely the figures that are likely to take action in ways that compel us to observe the unsettled border between them and the world of abstractions to which allegory refers by way of human speech.

Notes

1. For one example among many, see Dr Johnson's critique of Milton's use of allegory in *Paradise Lost* (Johnson 1952, pp. 465–66).
2. For further discussion of Coleridge's analyses of allegory and symbol, see Gatta 1977; Christensen 1978; and Kelley 1991, pp. 245–49.
3. Although all speakers use this pattern, it usually marks a sceptical or derisive assessment. See Caponsacchi's narrative, p. 273 (all derisive of ecclesiastical disregard for Pompilia's marital dilemma); or the lawyer Bottinius' use of the pattern to get quickly over the story of Guido's marriage to Pompilia, pp. 443–66.

10

The House (of Cards) that Rome Built: Shelley's *The Cenci* and Browning's *The Ring and the Book*

MARY E. FINN

'Cenciaja' – a bundle of rags: a trifle.

Robert Browning to H. Buxton Forman

A meticulous observation of details, and at the same time a political awareness of these small things, for the control and use of men, emerge through the classical age bearing with them a whole set of techniques, a whole corpus of methods and knowledge, descriptions, plans and data. And from such trifles, no doubt, the man of modern humanism was born.

Michel Foucault, *Discipline and Punish*

God's justice, tardy though it prove perchance,
Rests never on the track until it reach
Delinquency.

Cenciaja

The epigraph to Browning's *Cenciaja* is an Italian proverb which Browning translates for H. Buxton Forman as 'every poor creature will be for pressing into the company of his betters'. He affixes it to his poem to 'deprecate the notion that I intended anything of the kind' (Browning 1933, p. 174). In the poem he explains to Shelley his humble role as a 'mere familiar' in possession of historical evidence ('That lies before me'):

Shelley, may I condense verbosity
That lies before me, into some few words
Of English, and illustrate your superb
Achievement by a rescued anecdote,
No great things, only new and true beside?
As if some mere familiar of a house
Should venture to accost the group at gaze
Before its Titian, famed the wide world through,
And supplement such pictured masterpiece
By whisper 'Searching in the archives here,
I found the reason of the Lady's fate,
And how by accident it came to pass
She wears the halo and displays the palm:
Who, haply, else had never suffered – no,
Nor graced our gallery, by consequence.'

(Browning 1981, Vol. II, p. 473, lines 15–29)

The 'Titian' signifies Shelley's textual portrait of Beatrice Cenci rendered in *The Cenci*, as well as the putative painting of her by Guido Reni that originally helped inspire him to write her story. The contents of the archives that Browning 'rescues' are what Shelley omits from the source story in his play. It would be easy to call Browning disingenuous, eschewing the company of his 'better' only to seduce that better one's audience with whispered promises of good gossip in a jockeying for poetic supremacy. This essay, however, will not directly explore the 'anxiety of influence' exhibited here; rather, it will use Browning's *Cenciaja* as a means to distinguish between the agendas of the respective murder stories – *The Cenci* and *The Ring and the Book* – written by two poets generally considered as teacher and pupil, Romantic and Victorian. In spite of Browning's disclaimer, *Cenciaja* starts a paper-trail left by him that connects the two works, and the thesis here is that Browning queries the same two issues as Shelley – criminality and defence – to related but complexly different ends. *Cenciaja*, the last-written and the least of the works discussed here, leads back not only to *The Cenci*, Shelley's verbal Titian, but also to Browning's archival excavation, *The Ring and the Book*. In following *Cenciaja* back to both fictionalised Roman murders, we can identify how Browning plays Victorian historicist to Shelley's Romantic humanist.

This relationship of historicist to humanist reverses the conventional relationship between Shelley and Browning. Instead of finding

Shelley behind Browning in the exercise of identifying allusions, we find Browning rummaging backstage through the material left unrepresented by Shelley's Romantic project. From this reversal we can extrapolate speculatively to a more general Victorian aesthetic, toward which Browning contributed so large a part. Carol Christ argues that,

> [b]y the Victorian period, the sense of the particularity of experi-ence and the disintegration of belief in the reality of universals had increased to such an extent that poets were forced to develop new aesthetics to deal with this particularity and its relationship to art's universality. (Christ 1975, p. 6)

For Browning, 'particularity of experience' amounts to a bag of trifles. His paper-trail doubles as a defence of his own aesthetic decision to imitate his predecessor in content (a Roman murder story) but depart radically from him by using a form (a twelve-book poem) that can contain the bag of trifles and establish its integrity as art. We will see that by turning a historical figure into an archetypal heroine, Shelley's work exemplifies Christ's assertion that for Romantic artists, '[t]he real became the ideal' (p. 9). In sharp, pessimistic contrast, *The Ring and the Book* represents the modern artistic aesthetic that begins in the Victorian period: that the real merely remains the real, complicated, often sordid, and never explicable in any but the most relative and therefore most multitudinous terms.[1]

Browning's *Cenciaja*, the 'bag of trifles' to which he refers, bears a relationship to Shelley's *The Cenci* similar to the one Stoppard's *Rosencrantz and Guildenstern are Dead* bears to *Hamlet*. Even more marginal than *Hamlet*'s two school-friends, Paolo Santa Croce never even appears as a character in Shelley's play, because his role in the Cenci story, both real and fictional, is to be a runaway, on the lam after killing his mother. The poem, based on historical documents, tells the story of Paolo's crime, the law's pursuit of him, his scapegoat brother, and the villain–cardinal Aldobrandini.[2] Browning offers his 'bag of trifles' to Shelley apostrophically ('May I print, Shelley, how it came to pass...') to make explicit what Shelley implies, the contingent nature of the Pope's condemnation of Beatrice and her family. Possibly on the verge of clemency, Clement hears of Paolo's matricide, and punishes Beatrice to the full extent of the law. 'Thus patricide was matched with matricide' (line 108), says Browning's speaker, and the symbolic marriage allows the Pope to succeed in tracking down delinquency by punishing the already-incarcerated symbolic spouse of the escapee. 'God's justice', claimed to be exhaustively vigilant by the historical chronicler ('Rests never on the track' [line 44]), is served by proxy. Institutional justice is as convenient as it is contingent.

As a gloss on *The Cenci*, Browning's 'bag of trifles' does what the Pope cannot: it captures the delinquent Paolo. And it does what the Pope would not: it reveals the structure of what, in *The Ring and the Book*, Guido Franceschini identifies as a 'house of cards' (line 445), within which operates the system of justice that first creates and then (sometimes) punishes criminals such as himself and Paolo (and Beatrice). Beatrice dies because Paolo escapes. Cardinal Aldobrandini finds a letter written by Paolo's brother whose meaning he retroactively misconstrues as evidence to finger Onofrio Santa Croce as an accomplice. Energised by the promise of a cardinalate, Governor Taverna undertakes Onofrio's torture himself, with great success: Onofrio breaks down, giving the Pope another parricide to behead; Taverna becomes Cardinal; and Aldobrandini avenges himself against Onofrio's public humiliation of him over a woman, which turns out to be the hapless brother's real crime. For everybody but Beatrice and Onofrio (and his daughter and his estate), Paolo's escape is the catalyst for individual success. The Pope, the Cardinal and the Governor prevail; the house of cards is built higher, until by the end of the poem its collapse is prophesied as God's real justice, however tardy: 'Ay, or how otherwise it came to pass/ That Victor [the first king, 1820–78] rules, this present year, in Rome?' (lines 299–300).

In the first of two letters to Forman in which Browning promotes *Cenciaja*, he identifies a second escapee from the Shelley text. Forman was considering the inclusion of *Cenciaja* in a volume of Shelley's works containing *The Cenci*. In the first letter, possibly to strengthen Forman's inclination toward including *Cenciaja*, Browning offers evidence for why his poem might be part of 'all connected with Shelley': 'Is it any contribution to "all connected with Shelley" if I mention that my "Book" has a reference to the reason given by Farinacci, the advocate of the Cenci, of his failure in the defense of Beatrice?' (Browning 1933, p. 174). The 'Book' is *The Old Yellow Book*, and not only is Beatrice's case cited once by Archangeli, Guido Franceschini's defence attorney, but the famous lawyer Farinacci is cited over one hundred times in the course of the written proceedings as well (Gest 1927, p. 302). *The Old Yellow Book* thus is 'connected to Shelley'; obviously it is connected to *The Ring and the Book*. Syllogistically, *The Ring and the Book* belongs to 'all connected with Shelley'. The letters to Forman remind us that Beatrice had an attorney. His prominent presence in *The Old Yellow Book* teaches us that he was a formidable jurist, a man of some fame in Roman legal circles.[3] Although Shelley would not have read *The Old Yellow Book*, even the *Relation of the Death of the Family of the Cenci*, from which he takes his raw material, suggests Farinacci's eminence, as we will see. He succeeds where others fail in getting the Pope at least to consider the Cenci's defence.

Like Paolo Santa Croce's crime, the briefs Farinacci wrote and the Pope read are only mentioned in Shelley's play. If Paolo escapes, Farinacci is almost entirely exiled from *The Cenci*, and in querying why Browning insists on rounding up these two players, we must focus first on the place in *The Cenci* that marks Paolo's and Farinacci's absence as actual characters (the last act, the last scene), and second, on the place where Beatrice 'is convicted but has not confessed' (82, V.iii.90).

Cardinal Camillo, who has stopped the secular judicial proceedings to appeal to the Pope (V.ii.186–9), returns in Scene iv with grim news about the Pope's reception of the defences offered by the Cenci's advocates:

> He frowned, as if to frown had been the trick
> Of his machinery, on the advocates
> Presenting the defences, which he tore
> And threw behind, muttering with hoarse, harsh voice:
> 'Which among ye defended their old father
> 'Killed in his sleep?' Then to another: 'Thou
> 'Dost this in virtue of thy place; 'tis well.'
> He turned to me then, looking deprecation,
> And said these three words, coldly: 'They must die.'

> (Shelley 1970, pp. 84–5, V.iv.6–14)

In Camillo's narrative (the only place in the play where legal advocates are mentioned), the Pope is hostile to the advocates immediately, and has already made his decision before his interview with them: 'They must die.' Camillo gives the reason, offered by the Pope when (according to Camillo) Camillo himself tries to intercede by emphasising Francesco Cenci's 'devilish wrong' (or as

much about the abusive Cenci as he could – or dared – 'guess'
[lines 15–17]). He quotes the Pope's response:

> Paolo Santa Croce
> Murdered his mother yester evening,
> And he is fled. Parricide grows so rife
> That soon, for some just cause no doubt, the young
> Wil strangle us all, dozing in our chairs.
> Authority, and power, and hoary hair
> Are grown crimes capital.

(Shelley 1970, p. 85, V.iv.18–24)

In Shelley's play, as Camillo tells the bad news to the Cenci family,
Paolo's crime and escape appear to be the reasons for the Pope's
hostility to Farinacci and company.If we compare these two speeches
to the *Relation of the Death of the Family of the Cenci*, Shelley's source
for his play, we see how Shelley has collapsed chronology, revised
cause and effect, obscured Farinacci's role in Beatrice's trial, and
downplayed the Cenci's real misfortune according to the *Relation*,
which was the bad timing of Paolo's crime. The *Relation* documents
in careful chronological language that – upon the Pope granting a
25-day period in which a defence was permitted to be prepared –

> the most celebrated Roman advocates undertook to defend the
> criminals; and *at the end of the appointed time*, brought their
> writings to the Pope. The *first* that spoke was the advocate
> Nicolas di Angelis; but the Pope interrupted him angrily in the
> middle of his discourse, saying that he greatly wondered that
> there existed in Rome children unnatural enough to kill their
> father; and that there should be found advocates depraved
> enough to defend so horrible a crime. These words silenced all
> except the advocate Farinacci; who said 'Holy Father, we have
> not fallen at your feet to defend the atrocity of the crime, but to
> save the life of the innocent, when your Holiness will deign to
> hear us.' *The Pope listened patiently to him for four hours*, and then,
> taking the writings, dismissed them...Instead of retiring to rest,
> *he spent the whole night in studying* the cause with Cardinal di San
> Marcello – noting with great care the most exculpating passages
> of the writing of the advocate Farinacci; with which he became
> so satisfied, that he gave hope of granting a pardon to the crimi-
> nals; for the crimes of the father and children were contrasted

and balanced in this writing; and to save the sons, the greater guilt was attributed to Beatrice; and thus, by saving the mother-in-law, the daughter might the more easily escape, who was dragged, as it were, to the committing so enormous a crime by the cruelty of her father....But since, by the high dispensation of Providence, it was resolved that they should incur the just penalty of parricide, it so happened, that *at this time* Paolo Santa Croce killed his mother in the town of Subiaco, because she refused to give up her inheritance to him. And the Pope, *upon the occurrence of this second crime* of this nature, *resolved to punish those guilty of the first*; and the more so, because the matricide Santa Croce had escaped from the vengeance of the law by flight. (Shelley 1970, p. 101, my emphasis)

Shelley read a chronology that records a persuasive Farinacci and a nearly persuaded pope. He *writes* synchronically, and in doing so, thoroughly discounts the lawyer's role in the proceedings, and his near-victory. Nonetheless, Shelley is very close to Farinacci himself in his version of the real issue in Beatrice's trial.[4] Farinacci blames his unsuccessful defence on Beatrice. In his written brief he has assembled a series of reasons why a sexually-molested daughter has firm grounds for killing her father, who yields his rights as father by such acts (Gest 1927, pp. 631–42). He cites literary examples of justifiable parricide (using the word in its widest sense, killing a member of one's family), and legal precedents, both for parricide in general, and especially for the tricky problem of elapsed time between an offence and a retaliatory murder. Beatrice suffered from 'just resentment (justus dolor)', which 'mitigates the penalty even where the homicide was committed after a lapse of time since the provocation' (p. 634). He presents fear of future danger as a defence of murder equal to the fear that one acts on at the moment of attack. From this primary defence of Beatrice, he carefully extrapolates to the innocence of her family members. And none of it works, he will later write, because Beatrice would not avail herself of it, because she would not confess that she was responsible for Cenci's death. What he writes about the outcome of the trial (and what Guido Franceschini's attorney quotes in *his* defence), is the record of an uncooperative client: 'Bernardo, being a minor, was saved from death, as, indeed, it was confidently hoped would have been the case as to his sister Beatrice, if she had proved the defence which had been put forward for her, which she did not in fact prove' (p. 642). Or, as Browning interprets this same passage in his first letter to Forman, 'she [Beatrice] was expected to avow the main outrage, and did not: in conformity with her words "That which I ought to confess, that will I confess; that to which I ought to assent, to that will I assent; and that which I ought to deny, that I will deny"' (Browning 1933, pp. 174–5; Browning is quoting Beatrice's words in the *Relation* here, not in *The Cenci*. See below for Beatrice's even more ambiguous words in Shelley's play.)

Shelley and Farinacci both see Beatrice as adamant in her refusal to admit to any responsibility at all for the death of her father. But Shelley wants to celebrate what Farinacci rues. Shelley must omit the role of Farinacci because he reassigns the role of defence attorney to Beatrice, while also turning her into a vigilante prosecutor of a corrupt system by which she and her family now stand accused. By stripping the source story of its legal apparatus, Shelley portrays his heroine as an outlaw-jurist, willing to accuse even God for the 'unutterable' horror she has experienced. In answer to the judge's question that will elicit her non-confession ('Art thou not guilty of thy father's death?' [V.iii.771]), she first parries with him, going on the offence as the best defence:

> Or wilt thou rather tax high judging God
> That he permitted such an act as that
> Which I have suffered, and which he beheld;
> Made it unutterable, and took from it
> All refuge, all revenge, all consequence,
> But that which thou hast called my father's death?

(Shelley 1970, p. 82, V.iii.78–83)

Her father's death, redefined as the only available refuge from, revenge for and consequence of what she has suffered, may be in others' eyes murder – this is the extent to which she acquiesces in the charges against her. Her speech continues in this defiant acquiescence, and these are the words by which 'she is convicted, but has not confessed' (V.iii.90):

> Which is or is not what men call a crime,
> Which either I have done, or have not done;
> Say what ye will. I shall deny no more.

(Shelley 1970, p. 82, V.iii.84–6)

She begins her speech with her indictment of God; she concludes with a burlesque of his son in Gethsemane, yielding to his father's will:

> If ye desire it thus, thus let it be,
> And so an end of all. Now do your will;
> No other pains shall force another word.

> (Shelley 1970, V.iii.87–9)

And so Beatrice allies herself with the ultimate victim in the tradition she knows well, sacrificed for humankind's evil. But as Barbara Groeclose points out, she also belongs to a specific group of women in Shelley's supposed Reni-inspired portrait of her. By not speaking the defence available to her – that she defended herself against her father's sexual assault – she hangs in portraiture among those that 'fall within the larger genre of paintings devoted to heroines who prefer death to sexual violation' (Groseclose 1985, p. 235).[5]

The implications of a Lucretia-like Beatrice are grim by modern standards: her uncooperativeness with a defence system that might free her is virtual suicide, a falling on the sword as punishment for being victimised. Shelley could be accused here of telling the same old story, of the noble woman who dies for her lost virtue. With access to *Cenciaja*, however, archival material that exposes the corrosive and arbitrary legal system in which Beatrice refuses to operate, we can follow a more complex line of logic, one which Shelley himself pursues in his fragment, *An Essay on Marriage*: when is a good defence a collusion with evil? The answer implied in Shelley's prose and dramatised in his play is that there is collusion when criminality and wrong do not coincide.

In *An Essay on Marriage*, Shelley describes how criminality and wrong become collapsed into one, and why that should not happen:

> If any assemblage of men agree to command or prohibit any action with reference to their society the omission or the commission of this action is to be called criminal. If it be an action manifestly and most extensively beneficial such is nevertheless the denomination under which, by the universal function of language, it is to be ranged. To consider whether any particular action of any human being is really right or wrong we must estimate that action by a standard strictly universal. We

must consider the degree of substantial advantage which the greatest number of the worthiest beings are intended to derive from that action. I say thus much to distinguish what is really right and wrong from that which from the equivocal application of the idea of criminality has been falsely called right and wrong....The origin of law therefore was the origin of crime, although the ideas of right and wrong must have subsisted from the moment that one human being could sympathize in the pains and pleasure of another. Every law supposes the criminality of its own infraction. If it be a law which has a tendency to produce in every case the greatest good, this supposition and even the consideration of what is lawful as what is right is salutary and may be *innocent*. If it is partial and unjust the greatest evils would flow from the abolition of this distinction. (Shelley 1954, pp. 215–16, my emphasis)

A Benthamite greatest-good operates here, as does the Utilitarian definition of universal. Law itself has only a conditional value. It is supportable (innocent) only when it serves the universal concepts of right and wrong, but there is nothing intrinsic in law itself that causes this to happen; law can be the perpetrator of evil. There is nothing intrinsic because right and wrong, serving or maligning the greatest good, pre-exist, and they measure themselves against a standard that law may, but may not, observe.

All three works under discussion here document a 'partial and unjust' system, but *Cenciaja* and *The Ring and the Book* disallow any significant individual conquest of that system. *The Cenci*, on the other hand, uses the convention of self-sacrifice has the means to symbolic victory over legal sanctions that not only have nothing to do with right and wrong, but collude with wrongdoing.

Shelley never finished *An Essay on Marriage*, so his argument is heading in the direction of but ends before a defence of divorce, adultery and non-marital sexual relations – all those things proscribed in a system that imposes marriage laws. Browning takes up where Shelley leaves off, and directly challenges a 'partial and unjust' law connected with marriage from which 'the greatest evils...flow'. But *The Cenci* also continues Shelley's aborted argument, merely changing venues from the marriage bed to the family household. Or rather, in its theme of incest, the play deliberately confuses those two venues, metaphorically the characteristic confusion of incestuous relationships. Throughout the play Beatrice makes several appeals to the law and the 'lawful', both secular and religious, to free her from her father, including her plea to be married off. By the time of her trial she has learned that the house of justice builds itself with the money of men like her father, the cowardice of men like Camillo and the cupidity of men like the Pope. To avail herself of the one viable defence, that she committed a crime excusable through extenuating circumstances, would be indefensible. It would corroborate the system that allowed her father to flourish, and her victimisation to occur.

Shelley's Beatrice is Farinacci, she is Christ, she is Lucretia (Groseclose 1985, p. 235), Rome's symbolic liberator from tyranny. To fashion such a romantic (and quintessentially Romantic) portrait of the heroic individual, Shelley must strip his source story of its legal apparatus, reduce the Pope to the most cruelly capricious of jurists, and turn the other characters into weak or pernicious bit-players. It is precisely this reductive process that Browning reverses in *The Ring and the Book*, while pursuing the same question as Shelley: When is a defence collusion with evil? His answer is this: when criminality and wrong *do* coincide, and a legally appropriate defence redresses neither. *Honoris causa*, justification for murdering an adulterous wife, is both criminal and wrong. But Browning refuses to pare down his story to a heroic, unambivalently innocent victim (Pompilia) and an arch-villain (Guido). *The Ring and the Book* is a 'systems analysis', a story accoutred with all the paraphernalia that divorce criminality and wrong in the first place: the institution of marriage, prostitution, primogeniture, the Church, the class system, the legal system. A literal 'bag of trifles', his work expands where Shelley's contracts, and encompasses every base aspect of domestic and cultural strife. By examining the legal issue at stake in condemning a man for murdering his allegedly adulterous wife together with Guido's 'house of cards' speech, we can trace the movement from the Shelleyan One to the Browningesque Many, and determine the role of *The Ring and the Book* as part of 'all connected with Shelley'.

The similarities between Shelley's Beatrice and Browning's Guido are several and significant. Both try legal means to rectify their perceived wrongs, and neither receives satisfaction. Neither kills under immediate duress; rather, each of them makes elaborate plans. The difference here is that part of Beatrice's plan is to make her father's death look accidental. Both have hired help, and in so hiring exercise their prerogative as members of the upper-class in obtaining servile brawn to carry out – or, in Guido's case, help carry out – the physically demanding job of murder. Both stand trial for murder; both deny any crime. Beatrice denies that she has done anything; Guido denies that he has done anything wrong. In standing trial, both of them again exercise the rights of their class by invoking their ancient, noble names and the shame such public scandal brings to those names. Both face the threat of sanctioned torture, realised in Guido's case, though probably not in Beatrice's.[6] Both are condemned to death by the Pope. Both are executed, offstage. Both are deemed criminals, and both are punished. Browning, however, fills in the bureaucratic detail that Shelley leaves out. *The Ring and the Book*, in its voluminousness and textual busyness, rehearses the complexities of a Roman trial, and the multitudinous public responses, all based on self-interest. It allows us to see how spare Shelley's presentation of Beatrice is, and therefore how historically suspect.

Book One of *The Ring and the Book* makes it clear that public interest in the case is due in part to the precedent it will break and the precedent it will set if Guido is found guilty:

> Better translate – 'A Roman murder-case:
> Position of the entire criminal cause
> Of Guido Franceschini, nobleman,
> With certain Four the cutthroats in his pay,
> Tried, all five, and found guilty and put to death
> By heading or hanging as befitted ranks,
> At Rome on February Twenty Two,
> Since our salvation Sixteen Ninety Eight:
> Wherein it is disputed if, and when,
> Husbands may kill adulterous wives, yet 'scape
> The customary forfeit.'

(Browning 1971, 26, I.121–31)

Just as Beatrice redefines what the courts call parricide as revenge, refuge and consequence, Book One's speaker presents the two ways Guido's actions can be interpreted: 'murder, or else/ Legitimate punishment of the other crime [adultery],/ Accounted murder by mistake' (lines 133–5). Guido never denies having killed his three victims, and he never wavers in his view of his actions as '[l]egitimate punishment'. A simpler variation on Beatrice's non-

confession, from a simpler criminal, Guido's claim of innocence
stems from his total faith in the schooling he has received from his
culture. He spars with his accusers on this point, with the insight of
an idiot-savant, or a precocious but troublesome schoolboy:

> Softly, Sirs!
> Will the Court of its charity teach poor me
> Anxious to learn, of any way i' the world,
> Allowed by custom and convenience, save
> This same which, taught from my youth up, I trod?
> Take me along with you; where was the wrong step?
> If what I gave in barter, style and state
> And all that hangs to Franceschinihood,
> Were worthless, – why, society goes to ground,
> Its rules are idiot's-rambling. Honour of birth, –
> If that thing has no value, cannot buy
> Something with value of another sort,
> You've nor reward nor punishment to give
> I' the giving or the taking honour; straight
> Your social fabric, pinnacle to base,
> Comes down a-clatter like a house of cards.

(Browning 1971, p. 218, V.430–45)

Guido's use of 'Franceschinihood' connotes a structure within
which operates a certain system that trades on 'honour of birth',
and upon which depends an even larger structure, the 'social
fabric' that contains both him and his accusers. A product of and
cog in this structure, Guido nonetheless sees the pattern of interdependence. He does not underestimate its precariousness, but he
does inflate the importance of Franceschinihood to its prosperity.
The Ring and the Book, on the other hand, does not. Other micro-
structures of 'society' receive comparable textual space: the two
halves of Rome; the neither/nor–either/or Tertium Quid; another
set of two-halves, the prosecuting and defence attorneys; the
Roman Catholic Church (Caponsacchi and the Pope); and Pompilia
herself, who counter-claims her innocence of adultery.

The inclusion of all these parts ('cards') dilutes the importance of
a noble name, and demotes Guido's defence to merely one-twelfth
of the story. To achieve this effect of levelling multitudinousness,
every one of the poem's 20 000 lines is warranted, as Browning

claims in a letter negotiating American publication: 'The poem is *new* in subject, treatment and form. It is in Twelve Parts, averaging, say, 1600 lines each. The whole somewhat exceeding 20,000. (It is the shortest poem, for the stuff in it, I ever wrote)' (Browning 1933, p. 114).[7] The 'stuff', amassed from Browning's source materials, serves his aesthetic agenda, a proto- 'make-it-new' project that augurs Ezra Pound as much as it reverberates with Shelley.[8] In *The Ring and the Book*, Browning 'makes it new' by making it long, while arguing for its economy.

Browning's parenthetical assertion will amuse anyone who has read, or, especially, taught, *The Ring and the Book*. But it speaks directly to his poetical agenda, as does his claim that the work is in all ways 'new'. On the one hand, the poem's syllogistic connection to *The Cenci* via *The Old Yellow Book* challenges this claim to newness, at least in the category of 'subject', yet another Roman murder trial.[9] Furthermore, his original title – 'The Franceschini' – reinforces the allusiveness to *The Cenci* of *The Ring and the Book* in Browning's own conception of it.[10] On the other hand, his startling defence of its length – that it is in fact an uncharacteristically *short* poem for him, given its 'stuff' – doubles as an apology for the archival method in literary production. Every line, Browning implies, is needed to communicate so large and complicated a story, all details of which must be included. *Cenciaja* and *The Ring and the Book* bear a parallel relationship to *The Cenci*. In *Cenciaja* he tells Shelley that his addendum to *The Cenci* 'supplement[s] such pictured masterpiece'. Poststructuralist readers of Browning's poem will recognise the threat in the word 'supplement'. By the time Browning writes *Cenciaja*, *The Ring and the Book* has already carried out the threat by supplanting the humanist product, the 'pictured masterpiece', with the stuff of cultural archives, the bag of trifles constitutive not only of the Franceschini, but, if only one follow the paper-trail, of the Cenci as well.

Notes

1. See Christ (1975), for '"The World's Multitudinousness": Atomism and the Grotesque', pp. 65–104.

2. Korg (1983, pp. 201–2) describes *Cenciaja* in the context of Browning's last visit to Italy, and the poem's inclusion in *Pacchiarotto, and How He Worked in Distemper, with Other Poems*. The poem's date is 1878. 'Browning did not visit Italy again for

seventeen years, until...1878...' (Korg 1983, p. 197). Korg says Browning worked in the British Museum with his source before him. DeVane (1955, pp. 410–11) discusses the historical documents from which Browning drew Paolo's story.

3.   In *The Ring and the Book*, Archangeli, the defence attorney, refers to Farinacci twice. First, he follows Farinacci's rule on drafting a speech – first, notes, second, the speech, third, translation into Latin (Browning 1971, p. 383). Second, he quotes Farinacci on the efficacy of the 'Vigil', the method of torture undergone by Guido (p. 388).

4.   Shelley almost certainly did not read Farinacci's brief, or any material about the famous lawyer. The difference between Shelley's and Browning's research methodologies goes to the point of this chapter. Shelley read the *Relation*, saw the putative portrait, and wrote his play. Browning's letters suggest that he had friends always on the lookout for historical material and original documents. *The Old Yellow Book* was only his first source. His digging, as we can see, was enough for both his and Shelley's story, hence *Cenciaja*.

5.   Groseclose argues that Shelley made up Cenci's rape of his daughter, expanding upon innuendo in the *Relation*, or at least 'responsible for changing heresay [sic] (rumors still afloat in nineteenth-century Rome) to "fact"' (p. 225). The problem with this theory is that in *The Cenci* the central event, assumed by all to be rape, happens offstage, and is never described by Beatrice. The play itself operates on the principle of powerful innuendo.

6.   In *The Cenci* Beatrice is still being threatened with torture after Giacomo and Lucretia have succumbed (Shelley 1970, p. 81). In the *Relation* she appears to have been tortured, and through her youth and strength, forbears to confess where her family succumbs (p. 100).

7.   See also Browning 1933, pp. 128 and 354n. In a response to what was probably a request for a contribution to a magazine, Browning answers that neither has he written anything during the writing of his 'some twenty thousand lines', nor are any of those lines extractable for separate publication: 'I honestly don't think, and cannot but hope, as an artist, that not a paragraph is extractable as an episode or piece complete in itself.' A huge, self-confident claim for his work, but borne out today by the fact that *The Ring and the Book* is almost never represented in anthologies, because to include any section or even a whole book is to guarantee a reader's missing the whole point.

8.   See Christ (1984, pp. 15–52) for the relationship between Victorian dramatic monologue and the Modernist mask and persona.

9.   Browning did, however, use a story virtually ignored by Italian writers (Corrigan 1960, pp. 334–5). But the Cenci trial caught the imagination of both Italian and foreign writers.

10.   See Browning (1971, p. 12) for how the work received its present title.

11

In Wordsworth's Shadow: Ruskin and Neo-Romantic Ecologies

KEITH HANLEY

I

Leslie Stephen begins *The Playground of Europe* (1871), designed for fellow Alpine enthusiasts, with an anecdote about a Swiss guide with whom he had gazed 'upon the dreary expanse of chimney-pots through which the South-Western Railway escapes from this dingy metropolis'. Stephen apologised: ' "That is not so fine a view as we have seen together from the top of Mont Blanc." "Ah, sir!" was his pathetic reply, "it is far finer!" ' (Stephen 1871, p. 1). The story introduces an account of 'The Old School' of pre-Romantic views of the Alps as ugly ruins, but it effectively points to the post-Romantic gap that had opened up in a large part of the nineteenth-century mind between the Romantic relationship with nature (that had culminated typically in the Alpine sublime) and another, perverse kind of exhilaration that depended on the recognition of the rupture of that relationship.

For the Romantics, the Alps often promised to symbolise the sacred, deflecting the gaze from the world of common social experience and offering a site, free of human trace, for timeless and transcendent aspirations. In Coleridge's words in *Hymn before Sunrise, in the Vale of Chamouni*, Mont Blanc was a 'dread ambassador from Earth to Heaven' (line 82; Coleridge 1962, I, p. 380). But such inscriptions of divinity had to be read, and so were always on the point of being undone by more human meanings. From a social, specifically Rousseauean viewpoint, the Alps' inhuman aspect was a distraction from their function as a barrier that defended a pristine mountain community from the corruptions of artificial societies beyond. In England, it was Wordsworth who insisted on a particular imaginative redirection from natural theology to social discourse that proved formative.

Wordsworth's seamless passage from a transcendental nature to human culture was first effected in completing the *Ode: Intimations of Immortality* (1802–4), where the 'celestial light' and past glories of childhood are converted into what is offered as an equivalent superstructure of moral sobriety:

> And O, ye Fountains, Meadows, Hills, and Groves,
> Forebode not any severing of our loves!
> Yet in my heart of hearts I feel your might;
> I only have relinquished one delight
> To live beneath your more habitual sway.

> (lines 188–92: Wordsworth 1952–9, IV, p. 285)

This was only an avowal, but the way it operated was centrally demonstrated in the description of the crossing of the Alps via the Simplon Pass in Book Six of *The Prelude* (composed 1804–5, partially published as *The Simplon Pass* in 1845, and finally published in full in 1850), where Wordsworth started in search of the sacred, with 'hopes that pointed to the clouds', but then experienced 'sadness' in perceiving the inability of natural experience to live up to that kind of expectation (lines 587, 560; Wordsworth 1979, pp. 217, 215). The climax of the experience follows with the discovery that, after all, natural symbolisation might gain an alternative content. Rather than divine revelation, Wordsworth had come to see the discourse of British nationalism as the 'Characters of the great Apocalypse' (line 638) represented in the Alpine pass. He felt his lost sense of power restored by transforming Miltonic theolatry (the last line of his description of the Simplon is an almost verbatim echo of *Paradise Lost*, V, 165) into a successful epic voice that could repress Napoleonic triumphalism ('Under such banners militant, the soul/ Seeks for no trophies, struggles for no spoils' [lines 609–10]):[1]

> The unfettered clouds and region of the Heavens,
> Tumult and peace, the darkness and the light –
> Were all like workings of one mind, the features
> Of the same face, blossoms upon one tree;
> Characters of the great Apocalypse,

The types and symbols of Eternity,
Of first, and last, and midst, and without end.

(lines 634–40)

Inflected in this progression was the institutionalisation of nature in the name of an established national discourse that is re-vowed in the orthodoxies of state and church in *The Excursion* (1814).

Wordsworth's crossing, however, does not acknowledge the switch of a signified; rather, it celebrates the continuing representational power of natural symbols. The elision passes itself off as the point at which nature necessarily finds its 'natural' cultural expression. As a result, Wordsworth confined himself to a kind of cultural provincialism that refused to enter into a confrontation with both the British present and the European past as anything other than a reflection of his own naturalised discourse. Going over the same terrain in later years, in a poem from *Memorials of a Tour on the Continent, 1820, Stanzas Composed in the Simplon Pass*, he piously withdraws from descending into the uncontrolled cultural otherness of Italy, and contentedly resumes the familiar circumscription:

Toward the mists that hang over the land of my Sires,
From the climate of myrtles contented I go.
...
Each step hath its value while homeward we move: –
O joy when the girdle of England appears!

(lines 19–20, 29–30; Wordsworth 1952–9, III, p. 190)

Wordsworth's denial of the gap between nature and culture was on one level a representative repression of the trauma of the French Revolution, which had revealed the reality of historical discontinuities. When, however, Victorian writers appealed to this Wordsworthian paradigm to withstand further divisions within the discourse of British nationalism itself, they were typically left with the realisation of its illusoriness and ineffectiveness for their own cultural struggles. Ruskin, for example, who was deeply implicated in the Romantic discourse of national tradition, was open to other discourses that also sought expression in nature and so problematised the necessary correlation of nature and nation. His Evangelicalism, in particular, emphasising the history of human fall from timeless unity, sat uneasily with Wordsworthian naturalism. The result was, as Harold Bloom has written, that while 'Wordsworth's quest was to find a way out of all dualisms', Ruskin came to register 'a profound protest against nineteenth-century homogeneities, particularly landscape homogeneities' (Bloom 1965, p. xxvi).

By 1871, when Ruskin began the series of monthly letters to the workmen of England called *Fors Clavigera* (issued monthly until 1878, then patchily up to 1884), in which he both castigated his times and ruminated on the making of a better social order, and when he also started up his St George's Fund, dedicated to opposing British modernism, Ruskin as much as any other contemporary had felt the pain of witnessing the terminal crack-up of the Romantic discourse of nature which he had taken as the basis of a continuing social order. The extraordinary unevenness of material and style in *Fors* was symptomatic of his alienation from the prevalent national discourse:

> 'Englishman' is now merely another word for blackleg and swindler; and English honour and courtesy changed to the sneaking and the smiles of a whipped pedlar, an inarticulate Autolycus, with a steam hurdy-gurdy instead of a voice. (Ruskin 1903–12, v.28, p. 426)

Ruskin had been left in an embarrassed posture that was eventually to undermine his campaigning energy. His historicist analysis of various phases of European culture had taught him the contingency of different cosmologies, and this eventually permitted him to understand the ideological content of specifically Romantic uses of 'nature'. Yet far from sharing in the liberal contempt for an outmoded Romantic naturalism, he occupied a humanistic position which retained a hankering for its inherited structure of moral order. At the same time, however, he realised that the pretension of Romantic naturalism to cultural effectivity obscured the reality of its hopeless marginalisation by the dominant discourse of industrial capitalism.

Ruskin's thoroughly historicist vision of the world, and the radical shift from Romantic naturalism that it represents, has tended to be denied in two recent British books that are interested in creating a neo-Romantic reading of nature in the later twentieth century. Peter Fuller in *Theoria: Art and the Absence of Grace* (1988) attempted to argue against the grain of Ruskin's progressive affirmation of the 'failure of nature' (p. 16). Fuller wished to foreground rather the natural theology of the early Romantic Ruskin and the

Ruskin of the later 1870s, who sought 'to re-establish that spiritual *rapport* with nature which he believed secular, modern science had destroyed' (p. 161), playing down the upshot of the interim, from 1858, which was uncomfortably associated with Fuller's own rejected Marxism. Jonathan Bate, in his *Romantic Ecology: Wordsworth and the Environmental Tradition* (1991), has fashionably located his argument at a time when it is suggested that the failure of the Marxist (always in the broadest sense) interlude has been demonstrated in Eastern Europe. History is at its wit's end, and both these writers attempt to construct a view of nature's primacy that is in effect a resurrection of Romantic discourse, in the unbroken naturalisation of which they appeal to Ruskin as a key link.

Such neo-Romanticism tries to re-seal not only the indeterminacies within Romantic discourse itself, but also the more glaring rents that later writers opened up in reporting on its fallibility. Wordsworth's 'nature' stood for an illusory extra-discursiveness that Ruskin came to see through before he set about remaking it as a discourse, and as Ruskin did indeed come to see 'the difference to [him]' (line 12, *She dwelt among the untrodden ways*; Wordsworth 1952–9, II, p. 30), he progressively came of (his own) age – as a Victorian.

This essay discriminates Ruskin's from Wordsworth's worldview, concentrating on those less determinate earlier and later phases surrounding the central period of Ruskin's incontestably humanist social criticism. It aims to re-establish important differences and the importance of difference, and so, finally, for those of us who are in danger, in Clifford Siskin's words, of producing 'Romantic literary histories rather than literary histories of Romanticism' (Siskin 1988, p. 18), to serve as a caution against the conflation of Romantic and Victorian periodisations (or, for that matter, Romantic and Modernist, through the repression of Victorian liberalism). As the ideology of Romanticism, however resilient, became gradually exposed as a nostalgia with the rise of the more potent discourse of economic competitiveness, so it changed utterly from the untheorised spirit of one age to emerge as one precarious oppositional agenda in the next.

II

The crossing of the Alps, with its associated challenge to socialisation, is a recurrent symbol for maturation. Freud related

Livy's narrative of Hannibal's heroic (de)feat to the theme of Oedipal emulation (Freud 1976, pp. 284–7) – a theme historicised for the Romantics in Napoleon's crossing of the St Bernard during the Italian campaign of 1800. Ruskin's own passage from Romantic naturalism to a search for a compensatory discourse is reflected in his re-readings of the Alps as a crucial representation of the sacred.

In his late autobiography, *Praeterita* (1885–9), Ruskin describes the first time he saw the Alps as his 'blessed entrance into life':

> Infinitely beyond all that we had ever thought or dreamed, – the seen walls of lost Eden could not have been more beautiful to us; nor more awful, round heaven, the walls of sacred Death. (Ruskin 1903–12, v.35, p. 115)

Looking at the Aiguilles, he claimed (in an early draft of *Modern Painters* II from 1843–4) to have seen immediately 'the real meaning of the word Beautiful' in 'the cessation of all will – before, and in the Presence of, the manifested Deity' (v.4, p. 364). But Ruskin's original feelings for the Alps were more dominantly influenced by the picturesque than by an explicit awareness of natural theology. It was Turner's illustrations for the 1830 edition of Rogers's *Italy* (about which Ruskin wrote that after receiving it as a gift in 1832 it determined 'the entire direction of my life's energies' [v.28, p. 388]) that had controlled his initial response, recorded in the poetic *Account of a Tour on the Continent*, which in 1833 the fourteen-year-old Ruskin composed in evident emulation of Rogers's poem, including illustrative vignettes.

Rogers, after Byron, set human history on the border between its unforgettableness and its transience. In the preface to *Italy* he writes that he was not 'conscious of having slept over any ground' that had been '"dignified by wisdom, bravery, or virtue"' (Rogers 1830, p. iii). The picturesque complementarity of historical landscape is matched by Turner's diminutive vignettes. The balance is, for example, tested and asserted in his illustration of Hannibal's crossing evoked in Rogers's *The Alps* (Fig. 11.1) which characteristically locks man and nature together in a detached moment of permanent correspondence.

Ruskin's verses are relatively uninterested in historical associations. They reveal an eye fascinated by exact painterly details, particularly of colour. Almost the only exception is *Passing the Alps*, which concerns his own crossing over the Simplon, 'The barrier of boundless length' (v.2, p. 379), in an extended description of

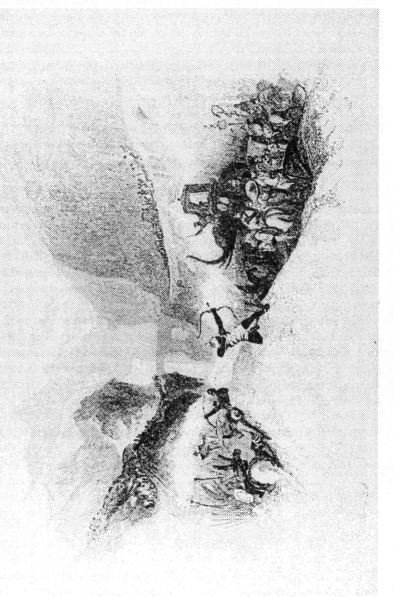

Figure 11.1 Turner, 'Hannibal Crossing the Alps', from Rogers's *Italy*, 1830

Hannibal's incursion into the 'recesses lone' of 'the yet unsullied snow' (v.2, p. 380). Ruskin's treatment has touches of the sublime indistinctness of Turner's *Snow Storm: Hannibal and his Army Crossing the Alps* (exhibited in 1812), blending men and elements in 'The armies of the sky':

> Methinks upon the mountain-side
> I see the billows of that tide, –
> Of men and horses head-long driven
> As clouds before the blast of heaven,
> That ever change their hurrying form
> In dark foreboding of the storm. (V.2, p. 380)

But rather than being arrested in the ordeal of passage, as is that painting, Ruskin follows the narrative of the vignette Turner eventually chose for the Rogers illustration, foregrounding the knowledge of battles beyond, when the army, 'bursting from the Alpine chain....meets the storm on Cannae's plain' (v.2, p. 380). For Turner, ancient Carthage was associated with his deepening pessimism. Both the original painting, which was accompanied by terrifying lines from his epic, *The Fallacies of Hope*, and earlier versions of the Rogers vignette (featuring piled dead elephants, for example), are revised in the final illustration by an attention to minute detail, and, despite the signs of approaching slaughter, the triumphalism of fiercely-won progress.[2] The neatness of composition confirms the re-emergence of the picturesque to contain the intimations of loss and despair with the heroic harmony of Alpine grandeur.

The first tour was followed by another *Journal of a Tour through France to Chamouni, 1835*, written when he was sixteen. In *Praeterita* he writes that this unfinished 'poetic diary' was modelled on the poetic 'style of *Don Juan*, artfully combined with that of *Childe Harold*' (v.35, p. 152), but a new resonance breaks into his address to Mont Blanc:

> Though then I did not have thee in my sight,
> Still wert thou like a guiding star, and all
> My hope was to be with thee once again,
> Hearing thy avalanches' fearful fall. (V.2, p. 412)

The overdeterminants of 'fearful fall' (theological and psychological as well as phenomenal) are dispelled by the echo from Wordsworth's

To the Cuckoo (published 1807): 'And thou wert still a hope, a love;/Still longed for, never seen' (lines 23–4; Wordsworth 1952–9, II, p. 208). As the bird in Wordsworth's poem is the object of an adolescent desire that may never be satisfied, but, magically, will also never be disappointed, so in Ruskin's the fearful object of desire retains its attraction by not being encountered.

III

It was at Chamonix in August 1842 that *Modern Painters* I (1843) was conceived. There Ruskin attributes to Turner's art his own vision of nature, still screened from the shock of social passage by a picturesque aesthetic and the deferments of Wordsworthian naturalism. With that art (and what it represented for Ruskin) under attack, Ruskin began to see it more explicitly as mediating a discourse of natural theology which was immanent in nature itself. By *Modern Painters* II (1846), however, despite its conscientious religious orthodoxies, Ruskin had begun to strike out on a new path of cultural analysis associated with his taste for early Italian primitives and Tintoretto.

Fuller has written persuasively about his insight that 'For many men and women, including Ruskin, the withering of natural theology in the middle of the last century resembled the Fall' (Fuller 1988, p. 102). As the discourse of natural theology became separated from the evidence of nature, the passage into an awareness of the primacy of discourse was prepared. In this way, the split between the sacred and the social constituted a fall into discursive self-consciousness. It was under pressure from scientific theorising in the 1840s that Ruskin began to espouse a more dogmatic discourse of Evangelicalism that could both acknowledge this fall from unity and offer the promise of a redemptive scheme of restoration to wholeness.

His Alpine poetry during these years demonstrates the strains of passage. *A Walk in Chamouni* (1843), for example, is distressed by the separation of opposing, but equally attractive, values. An extended evocation of the awesome self-containment of the mountains, with their 'pervading sense/ Of the deep stillness of Omnipotence', gives way to an uncomfortable recognition of human exclusion – 'no matin-bell/ Touches the delicate air with summons sweet; – / That smoke was of the avalanche' – and ends in surprised identification with the social:

Ah! why should that be comfortless – why cold,
Which is so near to heaven?...
...
And is the life that bears its fruitage best,
One neither of supremacy nor rest?

(V.2, pp. 225–6)

In 1842 and 1844 Ruskin spent a month studying the geology of Mont Blanc, but during his study-tour of Italian art in 1845 there was an important shift of interest. He wrote to his father:

Formerly I hated history, now I am always at Sismondi. I had not the slightest interest in political science, now I am studying the constitutions of Italy with great interest... (quoted by Hilton 1985, p. 93).

Following what was his first continental tour without his parents, he produced a sequence of poems, which were the last he was to write, and purposefully renounced his ambition to become a Romantic poet. They are consciously pivotal, as all his accounts of that time suggest. To his father he wrote: 'I sometimes stop...to wonder at myself, and at the realisation of all my child's ideas of felicity' (Hayman 1990, p. 3). In *Praeterita* he writes of his recognition at the time 'that I was not, as I used to suppose, born for solitude' (v.35, p. 366), and that two of the sequence 'were... extremely earnest, and express...the real temper in which I began the best work of my life' (v.35, p. 474).

Though these poems still offer the possibility of transcendent vision, they are troubled by the inability of the Alps to avoid reflecting a fallen humanity. In *Mont Blanc Revisited*, he beholds 'the twilight's sanguine stain/ Along [the] peaks expire' (v.2, p. 233), and the river in *The Arve at Cluse* is berated for its destructiveness and 'avarice', offering an 'image of my race!' (v.2, p. 236). *[Lines] Written among the Basses Alpes* is a withering tirade against the peasants of Conflans for failing to conform their lifestyle to the providential scheme available in their natural environment. It ends with an appeal for that scheme to enter human history by becoming insistently redemptive – for 'nature' to determine human society in the shape of Evangelical discourse: 'Hast Thou no blessing where Thou gav'st Thy blood?/ Wilt Thou not make Thy fair creation whole?' (V.2, p. 239)

The last of the sequence, *The Glacier*, however, is a remarkable reflection of the irrepressibility of historical process by the alleged stability of any ultimate discourse of nature:

> ... but the chain
> Of Death, upon this ghastly cliff and chasm,
> Is broken evermore to bind again,
> Nor lulls nor looses....

(v.2, p. 240)

The strikingly vulval appearance of Ruskin's chosen illustration, his pencil wash of the 'Glacier des Bossons' (1874) (Fig. 11.2), suggests an overdetermination of the repression of history by a more private one of erotic desire. Ruskin, who had been pursuing serious geological investigations since the 1844 tour, read his painful personal development in seeing the theory of catastrophism (that he had formerly accepted as reconciling traditional Christian opinion with scientific evidence), prised open by the counter-theory of Lyell's uniformitarianism (positing the continuous processes of an uncreated nature), recently given a popularising boost in Chambers's *Vestiges of the Natural History of Creation* (1844).[3] Scientific discourse had become divided from the received discourse of natural theology, which it now mastered, so that the sacred was in danger of being encroached upon by the perception of terrestrial change:

> ... Look on us,
> God! who hast given these hills their place of pride,
> If Death's captivity be sleepless thus,
> For those who sink to it unsanctified.

(V.2, p. 240)

Ruskin's sense of fall was radically discursive: from a Romantic discourse that appeared 'natural', to other discourses that problematised that naturalised relation. In his correspondence with his former tutor, Walter Brown, September–November 1847, he described the shift in his Alpine experience by echoing Wordsworth's acknowledgement of loss in *Intimations*:

> there was a time when the sight of a steep hill covered with pines, cutting against the sky, would have touched me with an emotion

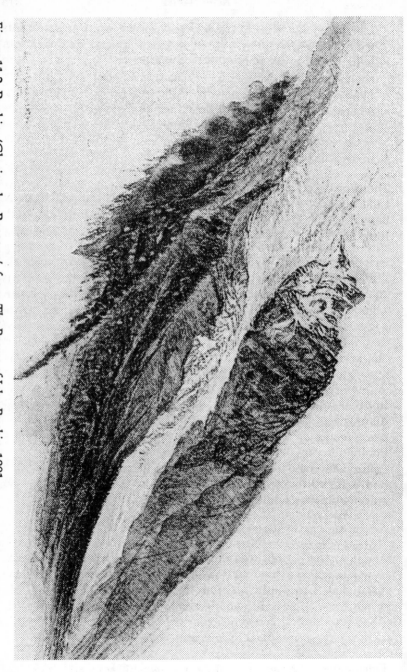

Figure 11.2 Ruskin, 'Glacier des Bossons', from *The Poems of John Ruskin*, 1891

inexpressible, which, in the endeavour to communicate in its truth and intensity, I must have sought for all kinds of far-off, wild, and dreamy images. Now I can look at such a slope with coolness, and observation of *fact*. I see that it slopes at 20° or 25°; I know the pines are spruce-fir – 'Pinus nigra' – of such and such an age; that the rocks are slate of such and such a formation; the soil, thus, and thus; the day fine and the sky blue. All this I can at once communicate in so many words, and this is all which is necessarily seen. (V.36, p. 80)

The Wordsworthian echo is overdetermined by another echo – of Coleridge's *Dejection: An Ode* (1802), which, in pointing up the gap between what Coleridge knew and what he felt, had prompted the formulation of Wordsworth's compensatory scheme in *Intimations*:

> All this long eve, so balmy and serene,
> Have I been gazing on the western sky,
> And its peculiar tint of yellow green:
>
> ...
>
> I see them all so excellently fair,
> I see, not feel, how beautiful they are!

(lines 27–9, 37–8; Coleridge 1962, I, pp. 364–5)

Implied in Ruskin's insistent Coleridgeanism is the primacy of discourse – 'I may not hope from outward forms to win/ The passion and the life, whose fountains are within' (lines 45–6) – and his inability to deny, in Wordsworth's way, the recalcitrance of cultural alienation. As Ruskin writes to Brown, the socialisation he has achieved does not necessarily entail inscription in an empowering national discourse:

> You say, in losing the delight I once had in nature I am coming down more to fellowship with others. Yes, but I feel it a fellowship of blindness. I may be able to get hold of people's hands better in the dark, but of what use is that, when I have nowhere to lead them, but into the ditch? (V.36, p. 83)

IV

During the 1840s, architecture came increasingly to rival landscape as the core of Ruskin's interest. It developed from his stress on the cultural content of forms that were indeterminately natural in origin – an indeterminacy of which the Gothic organicism was conventionally representative (see Stephen 1871, pp. 12–13).

There is an overt influence of Wordsworth's *Guide to the Lakes* (five editions between 1819 and 1835) on Ruskin's first serious aesthetic essays in *The Poetry of Architecture* (1837–8), which treats human constructs as continuous with their natural environment. But though Ruskin's descriptions of the Westmorland cottage place it firmly in a category of picturesque beauty that proceeds from a natural base, by the time he came to consider the Gothic in depth, in *The Seven Lamps of Architecture* (1849), he emphasises that architectural *power* derives rather from the human mind:

> for whatever is in architecture fair or beautiful, is imitated from natural forms; and what is not so derived, but depends for its dignity upon arrangement and government received from human mind, becomes the expression of the power of that mind, and receives a sublimity high in proportion to the power expressed. (V.8, p. 103)

He views architecture as primarily the expression of human *memory*, and the mediatory position of the Gothic as the location of the switch from nature to culture transposes the Alpine site to architectural style, within the cultural domain. Writing of *truth* in architecture, Ruskin figures the decline of the Gothic throughout Europe as the crossing of the Alps: a transition that establishes the historical narrative of a fall into the world of the Renaissance. The point of passage is a stylistic alteration in tracery – 'the substitution of the *line* for the *mass*, as the element of decoration' (v.8, p. 90):

> a pause as marked, as clear, as conspicuous to the distant view of after times, as to the distant glance of the traveller is the culminating ridge of the mountain chain over which he has passed. It was the great watershed of Gothic art. Before it, all had been ascent; after it, all was decline; both, indeed, by winding paths and varied slopes; both interrupted, like the gradual rise and fall of the passes of the Alps.... But the track of the human mind is traceable up to that glorious ridge, in a continuous line, and thence downwards. (V.8, pp. 89–90)

The historical shift *had*, of course, occurred, though Ruskin persisted in wishing the Gothic to be both culturally specific and transhistorical in a way that enabled him both to confront the shock of his own socialisation and yet possibly to evade the specific discourses that dominated in Victorian England.

The nature–human correspondence of both the Turnerian picturesque and Wordsworthian organicism had been assimilated in Ruskin's writing into the governing discourse of Burkean nationalism, in which an ideology of traditionalism grounded itself in nature. *The Lamp of Memory* is the central celebration of this cultural repression of difference:

> God has lent us the earth for our life: it is a great entail. It belongs as much to those who are to come after us, and whose names are already written in the book of creation, as to us... (v.8, p. 233).

But by the time Wordsworth died in 1850, and Turner in 1851, it had become evident that the contemporary capitalist discourse of British nationalism had effectively undermined Ruskin's own cultural edifice. The values of a booming economy were triumphantly displayed in the prefabricated Crystal Palace (1851), a secular cathedral dedicated to parading the fruits of Free Trade. In *The Stones of Venice* (1851, 1853), he further interrupted the writing of *Modern Painters* ('All that I did at Venice was bye-work' [v.35, p. 156]), to try to come to terms with this problem of identifying an acceptable contemporary discourse. As a result, he succeeded in reinventing Venetian Gothic, from the thirteenth to the fifteenth centuries, to typify an exemplary historical naturalisation of the Burkean discourse of traditionalism ('The Nature of the Gothic '). Yet his elegy for the decline of Venice was primarily a confession of the defeat of that discourse in his own day.

The Stones of Venice was in effect attempting to retrace the passage to an approved British nationalism that Wordsworth's testamentary work, *The Prelude* (published 1850), had effected at the beginning of the century. Remarkably, Ruskin does not refer to *The Prelude* throughout the whole of the Library Edition, though he possessed both the first and second editions.[4] It is as though the autobiographical peculiarity of Wordsworth's account of his cultural passage prompted Ruskin's own critical distancing from the assured dogma of *The Excursion*. Certainly by the time of its publication Ruskin's reading of the poem worked against his former assimilation of Wordsworth. In the first chapter of *The Stones of Venice*, 'The Quarry', for example, echoes of *The Prelude* amount to an intimate revision of the discourse which constituted Wordsworthian subjectivity.

In Ruskin's opening evocation, Venice is viewed from the approaching gondola as

> still left for our beholding in the final period of her decline: a ghost upon the sands of the sea, so weak – so quiet – so bereft of all her loveliness, that we might well doubt, as we watched her faint reflection in the mirage of the lagoon, which was the City, and which the Shadow. (v.9, p. 17)

The description echoes a characteristically fascinating water-reflection from Book Four of *The Prelude*, where Wordsworth writes of a newly 'pensive' awareness 'Of change, congratulation or regret', when he first returned to Hawkshead as a student (Wordsworth 1979, pp. 241, 240). Despite the interesting alterations that then struck Wordsworth, the heroic simile which represents them does not so much figure a division in time as the kind of pleasure involved in bringing past and present into correspondence:

> As one who hangs down-bending from the side
> Of a slow-moving boat, upon the breast
> Of a still water, solacing himself
> With such discoveries as his eye can make
> Beneath him in the bottom of the deep,
> Sees many beauteous sights – weeds, fishes, flowers,
> Grots, pebbles, roots of trees, and fancies more;
> Yet often is perplexed and cannot part
> The shadow from the substance, rocks and sky,
> Mountains and clouds, reflected in the depth
> Of the clear flood, from things which there abide
> In their true dwelling; now is crossed by gleam
> Of his own image, by a sun-beam now,
> And wavering motions sent he knows not whence,
> Impediments that make his task more sweet;
> Such pleasant office have we long pursued
> Incumbent o'er the surface of past time
> With like success.

(lines 256–73)

The difference between this text and Ruskin's echo turns on the ambiguity of the word 'shadow' – in Wordsworth simply a reflection, but in Ruskin also a ghostly shade, or ruined image of former glory. Ruskin's revision sees the decay in what is reflected as well as in the attenuation of the reflector, so that rather than eliding the dualism of past and present the image of the 'mirage' reduplicates the impression of fragility.

In *The Lamp of Memory*, Ruskin had gloried in the enriched agedness of buildings – 'in walls that have long been washed by the passing waves of humanity' (v.8, p. 234). He had then seen Burkean traditionalism, that 'connects forgotten and following ages with each other, and half constitutes the identity, as it concentrates the sympathy, of nations', as inscribed in a structure's enduring substance, while

> its pillars rise out of the shadows of death, that its existence, more lasting as it is than that of the natural objects of the world around it, can be gifted with even so much as these possess, of language and of life. (v.8, p. 234)

The naturalisation of nationalism depended on abrogating precisely the knowledge of destructibility that drove Ruskin's sense of mission in *The Stones of Venice*.

By then, the need to record before it would be too late haunted him: 'I must do what I can to save a little' (quoted by Unrau 1984, p. 19). He hurried, like Wordsworth's Bedouin in the dream described in Book Five of *The Prelude*, with a 'maniac's fond anxiety' (line 160), to rescue the triumphs of civilisation from 'the fleet waters of the drowning world' (line 137). In the passage which follows that quoted above from 'The Quarry', Ruskin writes:

> I would endeavour to trace the lines of this image before it be for ever lost, and to record, as far as I may, the warning which seems to me to be uttered by every one of the fast-gaining waves, that beat like passing bells, against the *Stones of Venice*. (V.9, p. 17)

The Prelude's scheme, by which 'Imagination and Taste' were first 'Impaired' and then 'Restored' (as described by the title of Books Twelve and Thirteen), was founded on the origins of Wordsworth's subjectivity laid bare in the composition of the 'spots of time' sequence (line 208: Wordsworth 1979, p. 429) in the first version of *The Prelude* (1799). In the passage above, Ruskin echoes Wordsworth's resolution in that sequence, first published in Book Twelve, to give discursive substance to a continuing structure of identity:

> ...I would give,
> While yet we may, as far as words can give,
> Substance and life to what I feel, enshrining,
> Such is my hope, the spirit of the Past
> For future restoration.

> (lines 282–6)

But whereas Wordsworth would like to record the successful repression of change, Ruskin knows that the nation is in ruins.

V

As Elizabeth Helsinger has pointed out, it is in the second half of *Modern Painters* III (1856) that Ruskin mounts 'a sustained if often indirect criticism of Wordsworth in which Ruskin distinguishes for himself a vocation and a manner of seeing different from that represented by the great romantic nature poet' (Helsinger 1982, p. 41). Wordsworth had summarised his presiding theme of nature-worship in Book Three of *The Prelude* as describing 'What passed within me...of my own heart/ Have I been speaking, and my youthful mind' (Wordsworth 1979, lines 176, 178–9), but Ruskin's similar intention, declared in his chapter, 'The Moral of Landscape', of 'stating what has passed in my own mind' (v.5, p. 364), results in his interrogating the nineteenth-century passion for landscape. His conclusion is a radical swerve from the advocacy of Turner and Wordsworth proclaimed in *Modern Painters* I.

Ruskin clarifies his knowledge of the influence of nature on human community. He argues in his chapters, 'Of Modern Landscape' and 'The Moral of Landscape', that the modern love of nature was not 'natural' but 'had been partly forced upon [his contemporaries] by mistakes in [their] social economy' (v.5, p. 354). He completely disowns natural theology – 'I never thought of nature as God's work, but as a separate fact or existence' (v.5,

p. 366); but while he realises that nature 'was never independent of associated thought' (v.5, p. 365), he acknowledges the benevolent influence of inherited associations in 'a continual perception of Sanctitity in the whole of nature' (v.5, p. 367). Though it follows that a love of nature generally shows 'goodness of heart and justness of moral *perception*', it 'by no means' guarantees goodness 'of moral *practice*' (v.5, p. 376). Rather, he had found that such susceptibility 'had not...always the power to repress what was inconsistent with it; and...might at last be crushed by what it had partly repressed' (v.5, p. 367).

His chief misgiving is that landscape may be 'a joy only to the inactive and the visionary, incompatible with the duties of life, and the accuracies of reflection' (v.5, p. 354). As with Gothic nationalism, Ruskin's discussion is embarrassed by his desire to fix the privileging of his own inherited moral perceptions, while at the same time acknowledging the discursiveness of 'nature'. But rather than positively staking the claim for an Evangelical discourse, he was preoccupied by the social inefficacy of a 'warped' (v.5, p. 330) discourse of 'nature' that had reversed the direction of cultural passage, and had 'passed from men to mountains, and from human emotion to natural phenomena' (v.5, p. 329).

Wordsworth's 'weakness' (v.5, p. 362) is representative, and Ruskin's sense of the dangers of 'the visionary' derive, in particular, from his insecurity over Wordsworth's discursive appropriation of 'nature' simply to authorise his own subjectivity: '[Wordsworth] has ... a vague notion that Nature would not be able to get on well without Wordsworth; and finds a considerable part of his pleasure in looking at himself as well as her.' (v.5, p. 343) This critique is the theme of his chapter, 'Of the Pathetic Fallacy', which examines 'a falseness in all our impressions of external things' (v.5, p. 205) that is 'entirely unconnected with any real power or character in the object, and only imputed to it by us' (v.5, p. 204), and which is enmeshed in an intimate quarrel with the compensatory scheme of *Intimations*.

Ruskin recounts the decline of his own rapturous relation with nature explicitly in terms of the sense of loss in Wordsworth's ode:

> These feelings remained in their full intensity till I was eighteen or twenty, and then, as the reflective and practical power increased, and the 'cares of this world' gained upon me, faded gradually away, in the manner described by Wordsworth in his *Intimations of Immortality*. (v.5, p. 368)

But the parallelism breaks down when it comes to weighing Wordsworth's attempt to devote the rest of his career to restoring that private relation. In a series of subdued echoes, Ruskin discriminates his own continuing alienation, which at least enables him to recognise his social responsibility for change. He takes issue, for example, with the advocacy of 'Spontaneous' wisdom (line 19; Wordsworth 1952–9, IV, p. 57) in *The Tables Turned*, and the proposition that 'Our meddling intellect/ Mis-shapes the beauteous forms of things: – / We murder to dissect' (lines 26–8):

> This was the chief narrowness of Wordsworth's mind; he could not understand that to break a rock with a hammer in search of crystal may sometimes be an act not disgraceful to human nature, and that to dissect a flower may sometimes be as proper as to dream over it. (V.5, p. 359)

He praises the dissectors if their attentiveness bespeaks a desire for 'result, effect, and progress':

> we shall find that this dreaming love of natural beauty – or at least its expression – has been more or less checked by them all, and subordinated either to hard work or watching of *human* nature. (v.5, p. 359)

Wordsworth may claim that

> The Clouds that gather round the setting sun
> Do take a sober colouring from an eye
> That hath kept watch o'er man's mortality....

(lines 196–9; Wordsworth 1952–9, IV, p. 285)

But, for Ruskin, someone who had really taken in that primary vision of human suffering would rather have been led to struggle for social reformation than find ready solace in the ability of natural objects to help him forget it through 'Thoughts that do often lie too deep for tears' (line 204).

Any discourse of 'nature' that conceals its irrepressible otherness is consequently dehumanising for Ruskin. Although Wordsworth properly belongs to the second of Ruskin's 'three orders of being' among mankind which is 'noble and sympathetic, but which sees and feels without concluding or acting', the 'lowest, sordid and selfish, which neither sees nor feels' (v.5, p. 361) perversely half-echoes the Wordsworthian sublime of Lucy's dissolution into a nature that 'She neither hears nor sees' in *A slumber did my spirit seal* (line 6; Wordsworth 1952–9, II, p. 216).

VI

'[T]he simple shepherd dynasty' (Ruskin 1903–12, v.7, p. 111) of Switzerland remained in Ruskin's mind as a living example of an organic society, enjoying an unbroken Protestant tradition uncontaminated by the Renaissance. It was, however, the growing threat to its continuity that probably caused him to turn to a close consideration of Venetian history in the early 1850s. For a time the cracks were sealed by convenient sectarian discrimination, and in the chapter on 'The Mountain Gloom' in *Modern Painters* IV (1856) he felt able to attribute the supine beastliness of Swiss peasants to the practices of Roman Catholicism, while vindicating mountain culture when not so interfered with.

Nevertheless, Ruskin's Swiss myth of 'Mountain Glory' (buoyed up by Evangelical theology) was being destroyed by the expanding utilitarian discourse of British capitalism:

> Railroads are already projected round the head of the Lake of Geneva being precisely and accurately the one spot of Europe whose character, and influence on human mind, are special; and unreplaceable if destroyed…The valley of Chamouni, another spot also unique in its way, is rapidly being turned into a kind of Cremorne Gardens. (V.6, p. 455–6)

The religious discourse on which he had relied had generally proved insufficient to meet the intellectual and socio-economic challenges of the 1840s and 1850s, and a series of personal experiences further contributed to Ruskin's Evangelical '*un*-conversion' at Turin in 1858, when copying Veronese's *Solomon and the Queen of Sheba* unleashed 'A good, stout, self-commanding, magnificent Animality' (v.7, p. xl). In particular, the re-evaluation of Turner's works as he arranged them throughout the winter months of 1857–8 had caused him to see them anew as uncanny revelations of an apparently unredeemed world-view. He came to see that Turner had always been 'appalled by the sense of the mountain pestilence and mortal war' and had been 'held in constant admiration by the physical terrors of the greater Alps'. Turner's chief subjects had, after all, been '"Snowstorm, avalanche, and inundation"' (v.13, p. 495).

While British capital and engineering was superscribing the Evangelical discourse that had seen the Alps as the great touchstone of human civilisation, the credibility of that religious discourse itself was being problematised in Ruskin's own mind. The mountains no longer bore any stable significance. Having watched the Alps at sunset, he writes: 'I don't care so much about these things as I used. I am gradually getting more interested in men and their misdoings' (Hayman 1982, p. 91). He writes of 'these nasty mountains...no bands – nothing but the moaning of the stream under its sand hills – no theatre', and complains 'I thought the top of the St Gothard very dull and stupid...I want to study goitres and drainage...' (Hayman 1982, pp. 158, 192).

VII

In part II of *Fiction Fair and Foul*, (I–IV published in the *Nineteenth Century*, 1880), reacting to Matthew Arnold's Preface to his recent *Selections of Wordsworth* (1879), Ruskin gave his most slighting assessment of Wordsworth's achievement:

> Wordsworth is simply a Westmoreland peasant...gifted (in this singly) with a vivid sense of natural beauty, and a pretty turn for reflections, not always acute, but, as far as they reach, medicinal to the fever of the restless and corrupted life around him. (V.34, p. 318)

Wordsworth's limitation, it is suggested, comes from his inability to see the disjuncture between the objects of his experience and the 'reflections' he makes on, or of, them. Wordsworth's 'studies of the graceful and happy shepherd life of our lake country' are finally, Ruskin writes, 'only...the mirror of an existent reality in many ways more beautiful than its picture' (v.34, p. 319).

Ruskin takes an image of this resistant narcissism from the poem, *So fair, so sweet, withal so sensitive,* in relation to which he comments that Wordsworth passed 'a good deal of time in wishing that daisies could see the beauty of their own shadows' (v.34, p. 319):

> Would that the little Flowers were born to live,
> Conscious of half the pleasure which they give;
>
> That to this mountain-daisy's self were known
> The beauty of its star-shaped shadow, thrown
> On the smooth surface of this naked stone!

(lines 2–6; Wordsworth 1952–9, IV, p. 125)

The pleasure of self-engrossment of which the poet is conscious and which he sees reflected in the flower's self-reflexivity (so that he wants the flower to see itself as he sees it), depends upon the Wordsworthian ambiguity of 'shadow' as reflected image. The poem tries hard to exclude what for Ruskin is the foundational polarity in earthly vision – between light and shade – which inscribes difference and the passage of time, or, as in Chapter 5 of *St Mark's Rest* (1877–84), 'The Shadow on the Dial'.

Wordsworth's 'foul fictions' are the kind of distortions to which his absolutist privacy (denying any real encounter with other discourses) gives rise. Most specifically, Ruskin takes Byron's part in rejecting Wordsworth's naturalisation of the British nationalism that had from the 1870s flowed into the 'new imperialism'. He quotes Byron's satirical refutation in *Don Juan* (Canto VIII, 1823) of Wordsworth's notorious lines in the earlier version of *Ode. 1815*:

> 'Carnage' (so Wordsworth tells you) 'is God's daughter:'
> If *he* speak truth, she is Christ's sister, and
> Just now behaved as in the Holy Land

(lines 70–2; Byron 1986, p. 644)

and agrees that 'the death of the innocent in battle carnage' is not 'His "instrument for working out a pure intent," as Mr Wordsworth puts it; but Man's instrument for working out an impure one...' (v.34, pp. 326, 328). While Byron's Calvinism made him suspicious of all pretensions to human absolutism, Wordsworth's naturalism could be used to condone absolutism, because a dominant discourse could be passed off as the voice of nature.

The way in which this manipulation works is demonstrated in Ruskin's discussion of the following lines from Wordsworth's 38th *Ecclesiastical Sonnet*, Part 1, *Scene in Venice*:

> Amazement strikes the crowd: while many turn
> Their eyes away in sorrow, others burn
> With scorn, invoking a vindictive ban
> From outraged Nature

(lines 10–14: Wordsworth 1952–9, III, p. 360).

Wordsworth is describing the effect of the change of policy from repression to clemency that found expression in Barbarossa's penitential recognition of Alexander III as pope. From what Ruskin refers to as 'the centrally momentous crisis of power in all the Middle Ages' (v.34, p. 361) resulted the truce of Venice and the peace of Constance. Ruskin points out how Wordsworth authorises the assimilation of these events to his own Protestant prejudice by representing it as the discourse of 'nature':

> the amazement, the turning, the burning, and the banning, are all alike fictitious; and foul-fictitious.... Not one of the spectators of the scene referred to was in reality amazed – not one contemptuous, not one maledictory. It is only our gentle minstrel of the meres who sits in the seat of the scornful – only the hermit of Rydal Mount who invokes the malison of Nature. (V.34, pp. 350–1)

The whole section that in 1845 Wordsworth entitled *Poems Dedicated to National Independence and Liberty* represents British nationalism in this way as the discourse of 'nature'. At bottom, Ruskin's animus was driven by his insight that Wordsworthianism was complicit in the same national false consciousness that was representatively perpetrated by *The Times*, the mouthpiece of the rising middle classes, and that was responsible for mass deaths and orphaning in the Crimean, and more recently the Second Afghan and Zulu Wars:

> neither is the Woolwich Infant a Child of God; neither does the iron-clad *Thunderer* utter thunders of God – which facts if you had had the grace or sense to learn from Byron...it had been better at this day for *you*, and for many a savage soul also, by Euxine shore, and in Zulu and Afghan lands. (V.34, p. 328)

VIII

Ruskin begins part IV of *Fiction, Fair and Foul,* before his discussion of the 38th Ecclesiastical Sonnet, with a consideration of Wordsworthianism in relation to the unsuccessful campaign to preserve Thirlmere from the Manchester waterworks in 1878. The Bishop of Manchester, a leader of 'the great Wordsworthian movement in that city for the enlargement, adornment, and sale of Thirlmere' (v.34, p. 348), had expressed a doubt if those men in London who had agitated for the preservation of the lake had ever seen it; but Ruskin, who had bitterly opposed the conversion scheme, thinks it more to the point to wonder how much of Wordsworth's poetry 'the amiable persons who call themselves "Wordsworthian"' (v.34, p. 349) actually knew. Ruskin recognised that the campaign was a struggle over discursive control as much as the land itself.

Ruskin was a member of the Wordsworth Society, and in a letter in the *Transactions* of 1883 he had explained his view that

> The grand function of the Society is to preserve, as far as possible, in England, the conditions of moral life which made Wordsworth himself possible; and which, if destroyed, would leave his verse vainer than the hymns of Orpheus. (Quoted in Austin 1990, p. 585)

In part IV, however, he concludes that Wordsworthian praxis is particularly likely to become divorced from the poet's basic moral and social teachings, and that a discriminating Wordsworthian should be especially suspicious

> when the unfinished verse, and uncorrected fancy, are advanced by the affection of his disciples into places of authority where they give countenance to the popular national prejudices from the infection of which, in most cases, they themselves sprang. (V.34, p. 353)

As a result, though Ruskin strongly advocated conservation projects, such as building the Hinksey road and founding the Guild of St George, in order effectively to promote the simple values of Wordsworthianism he was obliged to define a position only partly within it.

The pamphlet, *A Protest against the Extension of Railways in the Lake District* (1876), opposing the extension of the railway from Windermere to Ambleside and Keswick, had a preface written by Ruskin which was reprinted in *On the Old Road* (1885) as *The Extension of Railways in the Lake District: A Protest*. Ruskin's piece was consciously influenced by Wordsworth's contributions to the earlier campaign against the Kendal and Windermere railway: two letters with two sonnets, *On the Projected Kendal and Windermere Railway*, published in *The Morning Post* in October and December 1844 (revised with additions in a pamphlet the following year). He echoes Wordsworth in pointing out that building the railways was a matter of capitalisation rather than egalitarianism: to provide transport for mining industries and to make money from leisure. In arguing that the issue was one of preserving a traditional way of life from anarchic competitiveness, he even alludes to Wordsworth's own contrastive examples of Bartholomew and Grasmere Fairs, in Books Seven and Eight of *The Prelude*, by calling upon engineers and contractors to live 'in a more useful and honourable way than by keeping Old Batholomew Fair under Helvellyn, and making a steam merry-go-round of the lake country (V.34, p. 141). Furthermore, Ruskin saw that the specific rural culture of the Lake District had become something of an alternative national symbol, as Wordsworth, referring to it as 'a sort of national property' (Wordsworth 1977, p. 82), had claimed when he formulated the blueprint for the National Trust in his *Guide*.

In his second 'Railway' letter, however, Wordsworth had pathetically quoted the central lines on crossing the Alps (*The Simplon Pass* in 1845) from the unpublished *Prelude* to elegise what he himself saw was becoming an outmoded kind of cultural passage, destroyed when 'the military road had taken the place of the old muleteer track with its primitive simplicities' (Wordsworth 1977, p. 163). But by the 1870s, Wordsworthianism had not only proved an ineffectual slogan for protecting a threatened way of life, it was even in danger of becoming unconsciously assimilated by the prevalently utilitarian discourse. For example, Wordsworth's fundamental case for the preservation by isolation of the moral and social virtues of a distinctive way of life was overlooked even by his supporters. Journalists and writers of letters to the *The Times*, who, like the Bishop of Carlisle, invoked the 'Shade of Wordsworth' (Harwood 1895, p. 224), set great store by the threatened infringement of the workers' heritage, 'the narrow playground of Englishmen' and 'the...exquisite Parks which Nature has provided gratuitously for our people' (p. 230), without considering, as the chairman of the waterworks committee reminded them, that Wordsworth 'did all he could to keep visitors away from the Lakes by denouncing their only means of getting there' (p. 249). *The Daily News*, in supporting the scheme, even claimed that it responded to Wordsworth's desire to deter further population in the district! (pp. 234–5)

Ruskin's perception of the cultural inadequacy of Wordsworthianism had to do with its own presumption of its effectivity. In one of the sonnets *On the Projected Kendal and Windermere Railway, Is then no nook of English ground secure*, Wordsworth reveals how a discourse represented as 'natural', if it is not in fact the dominant national discourse, attributes to itself an illusory sense of power:

> Baffle the threat, bright Scene, from Orrest-head
> Given to the pausing traveller's rapturous glance:
> Plead for thy peace, thou beautiful romance
> Of nature; and, if human hearts be dead,
> Speak, passing winds; ye torrents, with your strong
> And constant voice, protest against the wrong

(lines 9–14; Wordsworth 1952–9, III, 62)

Here Wordsworth is effectively appealing to those who already share his own predilections, rather than conveying the values of what he is defending to the world outside. Such mirroring is primarily self-protective and refuses to enter into the kind of radical cultural engagements that affecting those who have a different and more powerful discourse requires.

The rhetoric of Wordsworth's particular national tradition employed in the second sonnet on this theme – 'Proud were ye, Mountains, when, in times of old,/ Your patriot sons, to stem invasive war,/ Intrenched your brows' (lines 1–3; Wordsworth 1952–9, III, p. 62) – was produced in answer to a different, earlier history: the planned repulse of Napoleonic invasion in the early 1800s and what Wordsworth saw as the triumph of Burkeanism at Waterloo. By the 1870s, however, the conquering discourse is that of the industrial machine, though Wordsworth still conceives it metaphorically in terms of the former military struggle. The railway is seen ambiguously as a 'long-linked Train' and 'triumphal car':

Figure 11.3 Linley Sambourne, 'Lady of the Lake Loquitur', *Punch*, 5 February 1876

Now, for your shame, Power, the Thirst of Gold,
That rules o'er Britain like a baneful star,
Wills that your peace, your beauty, shall be sold,
And clear way made for her triumphal car
Through the beloved retreats your arms enfold!

(lines 4–8)

The play on 'retreats' and enfolding 'arms' reduces his campaigning stance to the old fastness – the privately empowering submission to Burkean nationalism.

Ruskin could no longer rely on the resilience of Wordsworth's sense of injury to solve the dilemma that came from the split within national discourse. 'The Professor' was aware of the textuality of the natural environment in a way that set him apart from the organically educated peasants, among whom he classed Wordsworth. (He refers to himself as among the 'poor old quiet readers in this mountain library' [v.34, p. 139], and significantly compares the idea of admitting large numbers of day-trippers to letting 900 tourists into the Bodleian Library each day.) Nevertheless, he wanted to represent what he considered that more virtuous and socially cohesive way of life to cultural consciousness beyond it as the basis for a critical undoing of the predominant national discourse.

Since 1860, Ruskin had been explicitly waging this war over the national discourse. What the battles over the Lake District had come to signify is evident in a *Punch* cartoon with attached verses, *Lady of the Lake*, drawn by Linley Sambourne during the controversy in 1876 (Fig. 11.3). It depicts Ruskin–St George as a tube of artist's paint, wielding a palette knife, defending Scott as his own Lady of the Lake, and attacking the surveyor's level and a track-spitting dragon of a train. What is represented as being defended from 'Puffing Billy' is in effect the Burkeanism of Romantic discourse, but carnivalising the debate in this way decentres the exclusiveness of that alternative discourse. For all that *Punch* had mounted a consistent attack on railways since the 1840s it is almost equally alive in the 1870s to the excess as well as the outmodedness of Ruskin's rhetoric.[5] If Ruskin fought to re-open contemporary attitudes to nature only to re-close them with his own absolute moral discourse, Mr Punch's indeterminacy suggests more various shades of Wordsworthian conservatism.

Notes

1. For an amplification of this argument see Liu 1989, pp. 23–31, and my 'Crossings Out: The Problem of Textual Passage in *The Prelude*'. (Brinkley and Hanley 1992). I am particularly indebted to Anne Janowitz 1990, pp. 126–44, for her account of *The Prelude*'s naturalised nationalism.
2. For Turner's treatment of this subject, see the introduction to Omer n.d., and Russell and Wilton 1976, pp. 17 and 24.
3. For further explanation of these terms, see Cosslett 1984, pp. 4–7.
4. Ruskin's first edition of *The Prelude* was sold by Christie's, 18 December 1964; his second edition of 1851 is now in private hands.
5. Indeed, in its response to 'Professor Buskin's' letter on the projected new railway for Derbyshire ('On All Fours Clavigera', 23 August 1884), *Punch*'s irony takes an uncompromisingly utilitarian line.

12

Arnold and the Romantics

ROLAND A. DUERKSEN

Like virtually all the poets and essayists of high Victorianism, Matthew Arnold supports and, indeed, helps to direct the Victorian majority's anti-Romantic view. Agreeing with the Romantics that the old order has to be challenged and changed, he yet finds the Romantic means to this end – the individual's use of the identifying imagination in the discovery of truth – too uncertain and unstructured. His groping for a solution – not unlike the anguish of Tennyson and Carlyle – involves a harking back to what seems to have been effective in the past: a rebuilding of old forms, on the basis and structure of which renovation might be attempted. If religion has failed, his response is not to transcend religion but to make literature the new religion. If art has failed, artists, he insists, must not turn to their own inner resources but must find again the unifying principles and forms that made great the art of former years. In all of this he is typical of the high Victorians' turning back for reassurance to what seemed empirically corroborated generalisations of eighteenth-century rationalism.

The importance of the British Romantic poets in the formation of Arnold's Victorianism cannot easily be overestimated. Not only does he present individual essays on Wordsworth, Byron, Keats and Shelley and discuss Coleridge extensively in his essay on Joubert; he also mentions these poets frequently in various essays, echoes their poetry in his own, and refers to some of them specifically in certain of his poems. It is clear that Arnold's very typical high-Victorianism is largely a response to an overwhelming challenge that he finds in Romanticism.

To clarify our judgement of Arnold's artistic–philosophic distress and to sort out some of its likely causes, we may first of all ask to which of the Romantics Arnold responds most emphatically or spiritedly. The answer narrows quickly to a close decision between Wordsworth and Shelley. To the former he responds in a primarily positive and to the latter in a primarily negative way, but both responses are emphatic and spirited. Shelley's Romanticism, with its implications, is what ultimately he rejects or cannot bring himself to acknowledge, even though it is the Romanticism that most nearly accords with his own inclinations. However, before coming to that focus, we need to identify the two kinds of Romanticism that Arnold confronts and to distinguish among the Romantic poets as to the kind of Romanticism with which they, individually, are identified.

One kind of Romanticism evident in England in the late eighteenth and the early nineteenth century seeks assurance and vitality in the human mind's affinities with and resources in nature. Life, it maintains, receives direction and significance from contact with all that is not self-involved. Constituting a sharp break with eighteenth-century rationalism in that it recognises the importance of distinguishing individuals not in terms of their conformity to a cultural model or ideal but in terms of their unique backgrounds and responses, it is the Romanticism primarily of Wordsworth and Coleridge and also the Romanticism that challenged Byron before he reverted to the neoclassical, satirical stance.

The other kind of Romanticism is more radical, more essentially revolutionary in what it reveals about and demands of the individual human mind. Though accepting the individual as a unique product of nature, as distinguished from a being moulded by culture, this kind of Romanticism places the emphasis upon the individual mind as an unfettered power that can and must be able when necessary to override all influences and shaping pressures to arrive at a life capable of dealing creatively with modern development and flux. It is the Romanticism that Coleridge in *Dejection: An Ode* acknowledges but cannot get himself to appropriate – the consciousness that 'we receive but what we give, / And in our life alone does Nature live' (lines 47–8).[1]

Most emphatically articulating the position of the more radical Romantics is William Blake – whom Arnold does not mention in either his poetry or his prose essays, and whom he refers to in his letters only to announce that he has declined an invitation to write a 'notice of Blake the artist' for the *Daily Telegraph*.[2] Keats's agreements with Blake's kind of radical Romanticism are more subtle or subdued than are Shelley's. Thus Shelley becomes the poet who receives the brunt of Arnold's attack against an artistic mode that, because of its enormous demands along the very lines that challenge him most, Arnold seems most compelled to reject.

Wordsworth, on the other hand, is the Romantic poet whom Arnold, though not without severe criticism, ultimately rates among the truly great British poets. More than either Coleridge or Byron, Wordsworth lets Arnold find a way into the past – and into contact with what is other than self – that, without sharply contradictory twists, leads to moments of respite from modern life's contentions. Because Coleridge's ultimate retreat from Romanticism's requirements closely parallels Arnold's resort to a reliance on cultural inheritance, it may seem surprising that he does not prefer Coleridge to Wordsworth. However, not only is there the stigma of Coleridge's dependence on opium, but also Coleridge's retreat is primarily a return to religious orthodoxy – a resolution unavailable to the agnostic Arnold. Though Byron's jauntily blatant nay-saying to current systems comes close to meeting Arnold's need and inclination, it does not give him a clear sense of direction and grounding. In Wordsworth, too, he finds a certain unreliability – Wordsworth's faith in natural influence being so individualised and personal that it cannot be clearly evaluated in terms of the cultural past. The saving grace in Wordsworth, however, is that his imaginative system allows for at least moments of personal assurance from memories that mitigate the fret and fluster of modern life.

Arnold's most appreciative and direct acknowledgement of this means of retreat in Wordsworth's poetry is the elegiac poem *Memorial Verses*, which he wrote upon learning of Wordsworth's death in 1850. Although, as David Riede points out, his lack of faith in nature's benevolence is a major cause of his rejection of Wordsworth's Romanticism, especially of the concept that nature is 'a "text" that can teach the primal language' (Riede 1988, pp. 55, 53), Arnold in *Memorial Verses* places Wordsworth's ability to 'make us feel' above both Goethe's 'sage mind' and Byron's 'force'. What he finds in Wordsworth is neither the steadiness of Goethe to help the reader bear the load of modern life nor the daring of Byron that can blunt fear, but rather, an ability to 'put...by' – that is, avoid or put out of mind – 'the cloud of mortal destiny'. In other words, he values the illusory, mind-easing escape from contention that at moments he has experienced through Wordsworth's poetry.

Recognising that Wordsworth, too, had experienced 'this iron time / Of doubts, disputes, distractions, fears', Arnold gratefully acknowledges the power in Wordsworth to blot out the turmoil, to give moments of respite by transporting the consciousness to earlier, more innocent times:

> He found us when the age had bound
> Our souls in its benumbing round;
> He spoke, and loosed our heart in tears.
> He laid us as we lay at birth
> On the cool flowery lap of earth,
> Smiles broke from us and we had ease.

> (lines 41–6)

That in a letter to Clough the following month he refers to the poem in an almost bantering way – announcing that he has 'dirged W. W. in the grand style' (Allott 1979, p. 239) – need not be taken to imply insincerity in the elegy, but it does coincide with his finding in the Romantic poet's work a valued nostrum but not a cure for his troubled spirit. The use of the past tense in the above-quoted passage underscores Arnold's sense of the transience of the Wordsworthian assurances in regard to nature's nurturing involvement with the individual.

Similarly in *The Youth of Nature*, also written to commemorate Wordsworth's death, Arnold speaks of what the poet *did*, not of what he continues to do. The essence of this poem is expressed in the lines,

> But he was a priest to us all
> Of the wonder and bloom of the world,
> Which we saw with his eyes and were glad.
> He is dead, and the fruit-bearing day
> Of his race is past on the earth;
> And darkness returns to our eyes.

> (lines 53–8)

Since it has died with the poet, the vision or insight has been Wordsworth's, not Arnold's; it has been lent to the younger poet, and for that he is grateful. As Kenneth and Miriam Allott point out, this poem is a repudiation of Coleridge's assertion in *Dejection: An Ode* that 'in our life alone does Nature live' (Allott 1979, p. 259). The irony is that, once Wordsworth (who has sung nature's wonders for him) is dead, darkness returns to Arnold's eyes. His lament throughout his poetic career is that, in the darkling, grating age in which he lives, no loveliness, magic or grace can be seen.

Riede's identification of 'Arnold's lack of faith in a benevolent nature' as 'a major cause of his reaction against the romantics' (1988, p. 55) is important as we come back to the question of why Arnold, then, evaluates Wordsworth so highly as to place him among the greatest English poets. All the more clearly, after reading *Memorial Verses* and *The Youth of Nature*, we may see that the answer lies in the escape from tension that a session with Wordsworth's poetry provides for him. Though Arnold cannot break through to an appropriation of the Wordsworthian 'truth' of a benignly gratuitous influence upon the self, issuing from the best of what is not self, he can at least momentarily accept it as believable. And these moments of belief bring with them the pleasurable illusion that if we were innocent enough, such influence could be real enough to upgrade our lives.

Shortly before Wordsworth's death, Arnold had written 'Stanzas in Memory of the Author of "Obermann"'. In this poem he asserts that 'Wordsworth's eyes avert their ken/ From half of human fate' (lines 53–4) and also refers to 'Wordsworth's sweet calm' (line 79), which he differentiates from 'Goethe's wide/ And luminous view' (lines 79–80) as well as, in general, from Sénancour's grappling with the issues of his day. The implication is that Wordsworth's calm – his soothing power – results, at least in large part, from his ability to block out of his vision whatever does not accord with or foster the 'vacant...pensive mood' or the 'bliss of solitude'. That, for Arnold, is both the attraction and the flaw in Wordsworth. Unable to avert his own eyes from what he sees as the human fate of his time, Arnold wearies of the strain and, though it seems to him a neglect of duty, finds solace in moments of Wordsworth's 'sweet calm'.

Illusive though he recognises it to be, respite of this kind is for Arnold a positive value – especially since, unlike Coleridge's 'in our life alone', it does not place primary emphasis on imaginative responsibility. Thus able to appreciate and honour Wordsworth for his ability to lay us 'as we lay at birth/ On the cool flowery lap of earth', he stands in awe of the artistic magic that can so obliterate for the moment the agonies of modern life.

Arnold values Wordsworth's Romanticism more highly than that of the other Romantics, it seems, because he can use it to excuse his resting in a kind of faith, without coming to grips with the perplexity.[3] Lionel Trilling finds that, for Arnold, 'where Wordsworth eventually takes the superiority over Byron is in his power of joy and consolation – in his religious power' (1949, p. 340). As William Jamison says, 'Arnold elevated Wordsworth above his fellow poets because he believed that Wordsworth's poetry, at its best, could provide more aid and comfort to the life of the spirit in a soulless universe than could the poetry of the others' (Jamison 1958, p. 57). We need to keep in mind, though, that the solace Arnold finds in it is a matter of a comforting illusion rather than of any lasting resolution.

In Howard Fulweiler's words, 'Arnold's problem...is a basic and shattering disillusionment with the creative and formative power of human beings, especially as that power is employed in the poet's use of imaginative language' (Fulweiler 1972, p. 29). Referring to Arnold as a 'belated or postromantic poet', Riede (1988, p. 31) identifies his problem as the need of 'both an "Idea of the world" that would enable him to see life steadily and see it whole, and a justification of it that would save him from endless patching and cobbling'. This Victorian uncertainty regarding one's own voice and its uses (Johnson 1961, p. 6) – much like the disorientation of Tennyson's lotos-eating sailors or like Carlyle's desperate need for a hero–leader – moves Arnold away from Wordsworth's philosophy of a search for true self-knowledge and causes him to identify in Wordsworth's poetry an escapist element that in all likelihood Wordsworth himself would not have acknowledged. Arnold earnestly hopes that, revivified by Wordsworthian repose, he and other poets in his confused time will be able to reconstruct from the language of the past, from the cultural influence of 'the best that is known and thought in the world' (Arnold 1960–77, III, pp. 268, 270), a solid basis for meaningful life.

The essay *Byron* serves to shift our focus from Wordsworth to Shelley. It begins with a reference to the volume in which the essay *Wordsworth* first appeared and carries in its conclusion a now-famous statement about Shelley that Arnold cannot resist repeating later in his essay on Shelley. Similar to the Wordsworth essay in that it serves as an introduction to a selection of the title poet's work, the essay on Byron immediately sets Wordsworth and Byron apart from and above the other Romantic poets as the two whose works deserve the kind of selected editions that he gives them. Acknowledging that there are poems by both Coleridge and Keats that are at least equal to the best of Wordsworth's and Byron's, Arnold quickly dismisses these poets from consideration because very few of their works meet this standard. Though momentarily suggesting that Shelley's poetry may come close to deserving the kind of editorial attention that Stopford Brooke has given it, Arnold soon reminds himself that only 'by snatches and fragments' does it have 'the value of the good work of Wordsworth and Byron' (Arnold 1960–77, IX, p. 217). Despite the personal charm that Arnold claims to find in Shelley as a man, he discovers in his poetry 'the incurable fault' of insubstantiality caused by 'the incurable want, in general, of a sound subject-matter' (Arnold 1960–77, IX, p. 218).

Judging that, strong though Byron may be in his active confrontation of events, he is deficient in understanding, Arnold expresses his agreement with Goethe's estimate of him: 'The moment he reflects, he is a child' (Arnold 1960–77, IX, p. 227). Despite his exultation in Byron's energetic attacks against the Philistinism of the middle class, on which 'he shattered himself to pieces' (Arnold 1960–77, IX, p. 236), Arnold finds the deficiency in reflective understanding too large a factor to permit him to rate Byron as highly as he rates Wordsworth.

In his poetry, too, Arnold responds enthusiastically to the 'Titanic' quality in Byron but cannot praise his insight. His first poetic mention of Byron is, not surprisingly, in the poem *Courage*, in which the high praise of Byron's courage is accompanied by the modifying suggestion that such mettle is not enough for the creation of great poetry:

> And, Byron! let us dare admire,
> If not thy fierce and turbid song,
> Yet that, in anguish, doubt, desire,
> Thy fiery courage still was strong.

(lines 17–20)

In *Memorial Verses*, in which Byron is honoured for his 'Titanic strife' (line 14), the limitation is most clearly acknowledged, along with the praise:

> He taught us little; but our soul
> Had felt him like the thunder's roll.

(lines 8–9)

When, in *Haworth Churchyard*, Arnold presents Byron as an earlier exemplar of qualities laudable in Emily Brontë, he lists these qualities as 'might, / Passion, vehemence, grief, / Daring' (lines 94–6) but does not include qualities such as comprehension or insight. And in *A Picture at Newstead*, his final poetic treatment of Byron, Arnold is moved not so much by Byron's 'Titan-agony' as by the image of another man – a man who can feel, whose insights into what he has done make him capable of expressing and conveying his feelings.

The appeal of Byron's direct confrontation of life as he finds it keeps coming through to Arnold. In the essay on Byron he expresses it most emphatically in a passage contrasting Byron's method with Shelley's:

> [I]n poetry his topics were not Queen Mab, and the Witch of Atlas, and the Sensitive Plant – they were the upholders of the old order, George the Third and Lord Castlereagh and the Duke of Wellington and Southey, and they were the canters and tramplers of the great world, and they were his enemies and himself. (Arnold 1960–77, IX, p. 233)

Arnold's point is that Byron tends not to rely on myth, metaphor or allegory so much as on images directly from life. Though he neglects to note poems in which Shelley also uses this method as well as poems in which Byron does not use it, his point is in general correct. What it conveys most importantly to us is Arnold's grasping for whatever means could possibly help him and his fellow artists to get hold of their sodden, insensitive time and make it pay attention. This, perhaps ironically, is also Shelley's concern in his era, but he, though at times longing to write a great political treatise to help set things right, makes his effort through metaphorical, mythical art. Since Arnold himself on occasion writes poetry of a mythical or allegorical cast – such as *The Forsaken Merman*, *Empedocles on Etna*, *Tristram and Iseult*, and *Sohrab and Rustum* – this method alone cannot be the cause of his contempt for Shelley's poetry. That cause we shall need to explore.

The judgement on Shelley with which Arnold closes the essay on Byron and which he likes so well that he later repeats it at the end of his essay on Shelley is the well-known phrase, 'beautiful and ineffectual angel, beating in the void his luminous wings in vain' (Arnold 1960–77, IX, p. 237; XI, p. 327). In the latter version Arnold italicises *'and ineffectual'*. Evident throughout Arnold's poetic career is his yearning to hear a reassuring voice in his own time. Instead, he finds that 'humanity is left between a past authenticated by God's presence manifested in his voice and an unreachable future. But the present is a wasteland in which God's voice is not heard' (Riede 1988, p. 35). It appears that what so drastically alienates him from Shelley is the latter's open acceptance – far more deeply intellectual than Byron's bravado and more solid in its philosophical grounding than Wordsworth's faith in nature – of a personal responsibility to use imaginative creativity to correct a time gone wrong. Taking on such a responsibility seems impossible to the Victorian Arnold, who, unlike the essential Romantic Shelley, demands the guidance of a verifiably authentic voice. Shelley's recommendation of action without such validating authority seems to him reckless and ineffective.

That Arnold knew of Shelley's attempt to confront the problems of his time – an attempt which Arnold sees as parallel to Byron's and which he refers to as applying the 'modern spirit' – is clearly evidenced in the essay on Heine:

> But Byron and Shelley did not succeed in their attempt freely to apply the modern spirit in English literature; they could not succeed in it; the resistance to baffle them, the want of intelligent sympathy to guide and uphold them, were too great....The best literary creation of that time in England proceeded from men who did not make the same bold attempt as Byron and Shelley. (Arnold 1960–77, III, p. 121)

Despite what he sees as a failure on Shelley's part, Arnold seems in his early poetic career to have felt an urgency to follow the Romantic poet's example – to attempt a successful application of the modern spirit in his own time. In the poem *The Voice*, very likely written sometime between 1840 and 1845,[4] not only are the style and imagery patterned after Shelley, but also the subject matter – the evocative voice – seems most likely to be that of Shelley.[5] Opening with the generally recognised adaptation from lines 21–4 of *To a Skylark* –

> As the kindling glances
> Queen-like and clear,
> Which the bright moon lances
> From her tranquil sphere

                    At the sleepless waters
                    Of a lonely mere...

– the poem, using a variety of similes, as does Shelley's, portrays
the urgency of the voice that vainly implores him.

            O unforgotten voice, thy accents come,
            Like wanderers from the world's extremity,
                Unto their ancient home!

            In vain, all, all in vain,
            They beat upon mine ear again,
            Those melancholy tones so sweet and still,
            Those lute-like tones which in the bygone year
                Did steal into mine ear –
            Blew such a thrilling summons to my will,
                Yet could not shake it;
            Made my tossed heart its very life-blood spill,
                Yet could not break it.

                                    (lines 29–40)

In view of the numerous references in Shelley's poetry to the
supremacy of the human will, especially the declaration in *Julian and
Maddalo* that 'it is our will/ That thus constrains us to permitted ill'
(lines 170–1), the directing of the summons specifically to the will of
the poem's speaker is a strong suggestion that Arnold has Shelley's
voice in mind. That the tones of the voice are 'sweet', 'still' and 'lute-
like' correlates interestingly with Arnold's finding Shelley to be a
'beautiful... angel' with 'luminous' wings.[6] The quiet restfulness of
these terms in the poem would suggest Wordsworth's effect on
Arnold if it were not for the 'thrilling' quality of the voice's
summons to the speaker's will and heart. *The Voice* may indeed be
the poetic record of Arnold's turning against Shelleyan Romanticism.

   Whatever further echoes of Shelley there are in Arnold's poetry,
they tend to confirm his break with, or denial of, the Romantic
appeal that Shelley conveys. In *Stagirius*, written about the same
time as *The Voice*, there is, in Riede's view, also a Shelleyan voice
(1988, p. 37). With its striving to overcome 'the false dream', this
poem suggests that for Arnold 'the language of romantic aspiration
is self-indulgent, self-deceptive, and idolatrous' (Riede 1988, p. 39).

Some years later, in *Stanzas from the Grande Chartreuse*, in which the speaker directly voices Arnold's pervasive sense of his 'Wandering between two worlds, one dead,/ The other powerless to be born' (lines 85–6), there occurs Arnold's one poetic use of Shelley's name. Having asked rhetorically what help could come from Byron's scornfully satiric agony, he addresses Shelley:

> What boots it, Shelley! that the breeze
> Carried thy lovely wail away,
> Musical through Italian trees
> Which fringe thy soft blue Spezzian bay?
> Inheritors of thy distress
> Have restless hearts one throb the less?

> (lines 139–44)

Nor does he find Sénancour's ultimately hiding 'from the fierce tempest' of his age (lines 147–8) to have been the model for later times. And he ends his address to Shelley and Sénancour with a mock-applauding passage that is essentially a poetic version of the 'beautiful but ineffectual angel' judgement:

> We admire with awe
> The exulting thunder of your race;
> You gave the universe your law,
> You triumph over time and space!
> Your pride of life, your tireless powers,
> We laud them, but they are not ours.

> (lines 163–8)

Since Arnold has rhetorically discredited Sénancour for hiding his head in time of tempest, this pseudo-applause seems directed mainly at Shelley and says, as does the prose judgement of him, that since they are now obsolete, his fine efforts have been really rather foolish. What Arnold does not ask is whether his own loss of the courage demanded by Shelleyan Romanticism may be what has caused him to declare it obsolete.

As a study of the poetic qualities or achievements of Shelley, Arnold's 1888 essay *Shelley* is virtually negligible. Particularly applicable to this essay is the criticism that Jamison levels at Arnold's lack of detailed attention to Shelley's poetry:

Since Arnold found Shelley's poetry so completely inadequate, he apparently did not feel called upon to deal with it in any detail. It is unfortunate that he has not done so, for his fragmentary remarks leave many questions unanswered....[T]he influence which his view of Shelley has enjoyed was based more upon his skill with language and his reputation as a critic than upon a close examination of Shelley's poetry. (Jamison 1958, p. 124)

The essay is essentially Arnold's reaction to his having read in the new Dowden biography of Shelley some material about the poet's personal life that he finds very distasteful. As if writing a thesis sentence, Arnold expresses concisely the intent of the essay: 'I propose to mark firmly what is ridiculous and odious in the Shelley brought to our knowledge by the new materials, and then to show that our former beautiful and lovable Shelley nevertheless survives' (Arnold 1960–77, XI, p. 309). True to his word, after responding with aversion and disgust to aspects of Shelley's life and associates (at one point finding it necessary to resort to French terms when English will not suffice), and after expressing regret that Dowden has actually presented this material (Arnold 1960–77, XI, p. 320), he asserts near the conclusion that 'we have come back again, at last, to our original Shelley – to the Shelley of the lovely and well-known picture' (Arnold 1960–77, XI, p. 326). In Jamison's words, 'Arnold's treatment of Shelley's character supports Shaw's contention that the Victorians did not want to know anything about Shelley which would mar their idealized portrait of the poet' (Arnold 1960–77, XI, p. 118). So Arnold, neglecting serious attention to the poetry, can claim to see beauties in Shelley so long as he can convince himself that Shelley does not know or deal with life's realities. We may ask whether, had he discussed the great poems of Shelley, he could have maintained this illusion.

To whatever extent Arnold actually studied Shelley's work, he seems to have found in it a kind of truth that demands too much of him. Any careful examination of even so short a work as the sonnet *Ozymandias* demands that the reader come to an understanding of the traveller in the poem, who is a true Shelleyan artist in that he looks carefully at historic truth and at the artist's prophetic role and then, despite the desolation he has seen, returns to tell his story. How many who hear that story, the reader must ask, will grasp the true revolutionary implication and ironic meaning in the word 'despair' as it is used in the sonnet? Arnold is too self-consciously unsure of his own stance to look at Shelley's Romantic challenges openly and to take on the imaginative load of responsibility that they suggest. Instead, he builds his theory around the need always to evaluate called-for action in terms of the cultural background – in terms of 'the best that is known and thought in the world'.

Demanding for the poet 'a current of ideas in the highest degree animating and nourishing to the creative power', Arnold rightly asserts that, 'when this does not actually exist, books and reading may enable a man to construct a kind of semblance of it in his own mind, a world of knowledge and intelligence in which he may live and work' (Arnold 1960–77, III, p. 263). But finding the 'current of ideas' to be quite absent from his own social environment, Arnold puts his reliance almost exclusively on the best that is to be found in books. He does not trust his own will and imaginative creativity enough to let them pour a current of ideas – whether derived from life itself or from books – into the parched world about him, as Shelley has dared to do. The Romantics, he finds, have 'proceeded without having...proper data, without sufficient materials to work with. In other words, the English poetry of the first quarter of this century, with plenty of energy, plenty of creative force, did not know enough' (Arnold 1960–77, III, p. 262). With the excuse of always first needing to 'know enough', Arnold lets slip the Shelleyan urgency to 'apply the modern spirit' and thus becomes the prime example of Victorian indecision.

Wordsworth because he relies on feelings or impulses from nature, Byron because he is a mere child when reflection is required, Coleridge apparently because he cannot overcome either opium or religious dogma, and Keats because he lacks maturity – all seem to Arnold to fail in necessary knowledge. Though he sees high value and potentiality in each of them, they all fall short of his poetic standard. But it is Shelley who epitomises the Romantic inadequacy for Arnold, essentially, it appears, because he more emphatically than the other four – as emphatically, in fact, as Blake, whom Arnold avoids – insists that the best that past culture has to offer, valuable though it is, is not enough – that the responsibility of the individual's own will and insight is of ultimate importance in both life and art.

How strongly influence can manifest itself in resistance and how subtly resistance can take the form of the faint praise that damns, is emphatically demonstrated in Arnold's response to Shelley. Though not all high Victorians responded in quite the same way to Shelley, the influence of the Romantic poet upon them manifested itself in resistance of one form or another. Carlyle denounced him openly and vociferously; Tennyson fended off suggestions of Shelley's influence upon him; Browning, at first an avid admirer, ultimately used his objection to Shelley's personal life as a screen behind which to hide his retreat from the Romantic challenge; and Kingsley, after some enthusiasm for Shelley's social vision, covered his resistance with the self-excusing refrain: 'in God's good time'.

To be sure, these responses were not shared by all Victorians. Mill, Eliot, Swinburne and Hardy – to name some early, middle and late Victorians – responded to Shelley in a quite other than resisting manner. With regard, though, to the high Victorians, the resistance of Carlyle, Tennyson, Browning and Kingsley to Shelley's Romantic assertion evidences a general correlation with that of Arnold – which appears to have been essentially a loss of nerve.

Arnold, in typical high-Victorian fashion, evades the demands of Romantic responsibility and builds a system based on high culture to excuse himself from having to face the fact of this evasion. Recognising the huge weight of artistic responsibility for involvement in and betterment of life that the Romantics have laid upon their successors and longing to shoulder that weight, Arnold is, however, driven by the prospect of it to idealise the values held by the past and thus is able to avoid what the Romantics, at their best, require of him.

Notes

1. In 'The Critical Mode in British Romanticism' (Duerksen 1983) I have developed more fully my view of the distinctions between the two kinds of Romanticism.
2. Russell, I, p. 447. Until near the middle of the twentieth century Blake was not considered one of England's Romantic poets. Yet it is of interest to our study to note that Arnold does not discuss him or his work.
3. '[Wordsworth's] poetry gives us more which we may rest upon than Byron's, – more which we can rest upon now, and which men may rest upon always' (Arnold 1960–77, IX, p. 236).
4. Kenneth and Miriam Allott (1979, p. 36) note that, though the date of composition is unknown, the Shelleyan influence suggests an early date. The poem was first published in 1849.
5. Riede (1988, pp. 39–40), referring to previous biographical

conjectures that the voice is that of Newman or of Thomas Arnold, suggests that it 'represents a temptation to acquiescence (in whatever fixed belief) that has been and must continue to be sternly resisted'. The images, however, of an appeal to liveliness and action ('kindling glances', 'bright waves', 'glad music', 'thrilling summons', etc.) indicate, rather, an influence that tends to draw the speaker away from acquiescent repose.

6.   Riede (1988, pp. 41–2) finds in *The Voice* an anticipation of Arnold's later characterisation of Shelley as a 'beautiful and ineffectual angel, beating in the void his luminous wings in vain'. He effectively traces Arnold's use of the phrase 'beating the air' in reference to writers considered heretical: J. A. Froude, Francis Newman, John Wesley, and Plato.

13

Seeing Through a Glass Darkly: Perspective in Romantic and Victorian Landscape

ANN MARIE ROSS

In 'The Victorianism of Victorian Literature', Michael Timko argues that the period may largely be defined by its 'engagement' with epistemological as opposed to metaphysical issues. Timko contrasts the Romantics' 'faith in the interdependence of [self and nature]' with the Victorians' 'epistemological despair' over 'man's ability to know...at a time when it was especially urgent for him to learn more about himself and his world' (Timko 1975, p. 611). I would like to explore ways in which the shift from metaphysical to epistemological perspective transforms the landscape emblem bequeathed to the Victorians by the Romantics. The Romantics' belief in a metaphysical absolute uniting perceiver and landscape breaks down in the Victorian period; anxiety over the 'ability to know' results in a sceptical noetics that controls the presentation of landscape in Victorian poems as diverse as *Idylls of the King, In Memoriam, Empedocles on Etna*, Clough's *Amours de Voyage*, Emily Brontë's *Stars* and Hardy's *After a Journey* and *By the Runic Stone*. In Kantian terms, Romantic landscape emblematises, if not the existence, then at least the quest for the noumenon subsisting beneath perceptual transformations of phenomena in nature, while Victorian landscape emblematises the poet's quest for verification of the grounds of knowledge.

In *Biographia Literaria*, Coleridge considers the implications of a sceptical noetics for the poet's interpretation of nature. Indeed, the *Biographia* may be seen as the preeminent Romantic attempt to formulate an aesthetic theory grounded in a metaphysical principle.

Coleridge rejects both scepticism and subjective idealism because they separate the poet from the external world and provide no certain ground of knowledge. Imprisoned within the solipsism of subjectivity, the poet is condemned to see reality through a glass darkly, for 'the modern system of metaphysics...banishes us to a land of shadows, surrounds us with apparitions and distinguishes truth from illusion only by the majority of those who dream the same dream' (Coleridge 1950, p. 148). Lacking the Kantian category of freedom, the poet wanders through 'a land of darkness', 'a perfect anti-Goshen', seeing 'the mere refractions from unseen and distant truths through the distorting medium of his own unenlivened and stagnant understanding (Coleridge 1950, p. 140). By virtue of 'absolute truth...self-grounded...known by its own light', the poet is rescued from 'the land of shadows' and exalted into the 'higher ascents' of imaginative vision. Coleridge locates 'certainty of knowledge' in the 'truth...universally placed in the coincidence of the thought with the thing, of the representative with the object represented' (Coleridge 1950, p. 144). It was precisely the Coleridgian belief in the 'reciprocal concurrence' of self and nature that allowed the Romantics to avert the crisis of 'Doubt and Identity' that Andrew Cooper (1988) traces in Romantic poetry; I would argue, with Timko, that it is this crisis of doubt that most clearly distinguishes the philosophical milieu of Victorian from Romantic poetry. Unable to affirm the Coleridgian identity of subject and object or, in consequence, the correspondence of perceiver and external object, and espousing the subjective idealism Coleridge had rejected, Victorian poetics privileges Coleridge's 'land of shadows' and dream as the true habitation of the poet of nature. In so far as Victorian poetry works toward consensus or universality, it affirms 'the majority of those who dream the same dream'.

A. H. Hallam's *On Some Characteristics of Modern Poetry* is the earliest formulation of a Victorian poetics of subjectivity. Hallam divides Coleridge's 'reciprocal concurrence' into separate spheres of 'inward eye' and external world, feeling and thought, beauty and truth. Identifying 'objective amelioration' not with nature but with the 'prevalence of social activity', Hallam laments 'the decrease of subjective power' caused by the 'absorption of the higher feelings into...ordinary life' (Hallam 1973, p. 106). Whereas Coleridge had used a prose landscape to represent the movement of the poet's mind from its source in 'the furthest inaccessible falls' to the 'surrounding mountains', Hallam locates the source of poetic creativity in the 'return of the mind upon itself' (p. 105). Disjoining the Coleridgian reconciliation of 'idea with image', Hallam denigrates 'poets who *seek* for images to illustrate their conceptions', and exalts the poet who inhabits a 'world of images' divorced from universals or ethical truths. Poems take their meaning not from their correspondence with external reality but from the 'combinations' and internal arrangement of 'complex emotions' which have their source in the 'leading sentiment of the poet's mind' (p. 99). Hallam's validation of a subjective poetry which 'is a sort of magic, producing a number of impressions' is echoed in Matthew Arnold's apostrophe to 'the poet of natural magic' in *Maurice de Guérin*. And the Hallam–Arnoldian tradition of poetics, with its preference for the 'poet of sensation' over the 'poet of reflection', is continued in the 'aesthetic' criticism of Pater and Wilde. Like Hallam, Pater in *The School of Giorgione* posits an 'art...striving to be independent of the mere intelligence, to become a matter of pure perception' (Pater 1986, p. 158). Similarly, Hallam's repudiation of a poetry of reflection is echoed in Wilde's frequent disavowals of a 'low standard of imitation or resemblance' in art or art-criticism.

Victorian poetics, then, may be usefully distinguished from Romantic poetics by the former's subjectivist stance and by its resulting emphasis upon the processes of knowing and feeling rather than upon what is known or felt. Equally important in its implications for the problematic epistemology that defines the philosophical milieu of Victorian poetry, the primary documents in the formulation of a Victorian poetics promulgated a theory of interpretation that located meaning in the interrelationships among images and feelings in the poem or 'the poet's mind', rather than in the interrelationship between mind and an exterior reality, whether defined as nature or society. Like Hallam, many Victorian poets opposed the 'objective amelioration' of society to 'the return of the mind upon itself'; we may also remember in this context Keble's definition of poetry as 'the indirect expression in words...of some overpowering emotion...the direct indulgence whereof is somehow repressed' (Keble 1877, pp. 144–8).

Many long Victorian poems, most notably *Empedocles on Etna*, *Idylls of the King* and *Amours de Voyage*, dramatise the disjunction between recessed, self-reflexive forms of seeing and knowing and an alienating, rigidified social reality. Equally unable to affirm the existence of a Coleridgian 'master-current' flowing 'beneath the surface' of both human consciousness and nature, or to emblematise the cityscape as the habitation of human community, Victorian poets construct landscapes controlled by the speaker's sense of illusoriness or aporia. The 'land of shadows' which predominates in Victorian landscape description is an epiphenomenon shadowed forth by speakers who are no more than 'what our shadows seem' (Clough 1964, *Amours de Voyage*, I, iv, 84), 'Our own phantoms chanting hymns' (Tennyson 1969, *In Memoriam*, VIII, 10) even sceptics who 'make mists/ Through which to see less clear' (Arnold 1950, *Empedocles on Etna*, I, ii, 204–5).

The epistemological consequences of subjectivism are most fully and explicitly worked out in *Empedocles on Etna* and *Amours de Voyage*; indeed, the two poems comprise the *locus classicus* of a sceptical noetics for the Victorian period. In each poem the landscape emblem is contextualised within a medley of genres that in *Empedocles* includes homily, song, hymn and drama *à thèse* (the poem is subtitled 'a dramatic poem'), and in *Amours* includes or parodies the epistle or epistolary novel, the dramatic monologue and social comedy. Dominating Arnold's poem is the voice of the sceptical philosopher, Empedocles, while dominating Clough's is the sceptical perspective of the poem's principal speaker–correspondent, Claude. Embedded within the dialogical and medley-like structure of the poems, the landscape emblem is presented through the 'distorting medium' of the sceptical speakers' self-absorbed perusal of 'conscious understandings' (*Amours de Voyage* II, 259).

Letter II (Canto III) of *Amours de Voyage* dramatises Claude's explicit refusal of a metaphysical principle uniting man and nature and his espousal of an epistemological perspective dividing him from the external world. The speaker envisions 'the waters' not in the familiar Romantic terms of oceanic infinity, but as the primeval chaos from which 'we are born' (III, 51). Assailed by the 'billows that buffet and beat us' (III, 52), the speaker is thrown back upon 'one single regard of a painful victorious knowledge' (III, 53). Contextualised in the epistolary framework of the poem, Claude's self-quotation ('"This is Nature', I said") marks the difference between written and spoken, ephemeral and permanent language. Just as the passage opposes meaning and expression, so it opposes nature and knowledge. The gaze of knowledge the speaker turns toward the ocean, since it discloses no object of permanent meaning in nature, must finally turn back upon itself; in *Amours* the 'light of knowledge' resides within the recessed interiors of the self. The speaker's absorption in how rather than in what he knows partly accounts for the absence of sustained landscape descriptions within a genre that raises expectations of such description; Claude himself occasionally refers to his letters to England from Italy as 'travelogues'. The 'pictures from Italy' in the poem are notable for their brevity in proportion to the speaker's meditations upon illusion and dubiety. As is true also in *Empedocles on Etna* and *Idylls of the King*, the poem shifts constantly between brief notations of landscape and inscribed soliloquies which explore the epistemological issue in depth. What I will call the 'disappearance' of landscape in *Amours* validates the subjectivist stance of the speaker, while at the same time the speaker's scepticism undercuts, distorts and distances such landscape as is present. Again, as in *Empedocles* and *Idylls*, the speaker views land and cityscape at not one, but two removes, both as the symbol of a symbol and as a self-consciously wrought inscription whose form and meaning must undergo continual re-creation because they are continually erased by 'swallowing' chaos.

In contrast to Romantic poetry's concern with the re-creation of the self in relationship to nature, *Amours* explores the diffusion of personality that results from loss of certainty in the grounds of knowledge. Like other human creations, landscape remains fragmentary because the self (or voice) of the poem is insufficiently strong to impose order upon chaos or to fuse parts into a whole. In the famous 'fragments' letter to his sister, Jane Forster, Arnold connected the issues of poetic voice or identity with wholeness or fragmentariness of poetry structure: 'The true reason why parts suit you while others do not is that my poems are fragments – i.e., that I am fragments, while you are a whole.'[1] Christopher Ricks' strictures against the lack of 'poetic unity' in *Idylls of the King* imply an important critical crux for the Victorian long poem: did Victorian poets continue or reinvent the tradition of Romantic poetic epic, or did they discontinue it altogether? I agree with Ricks in his implicit refusal to accept a Victorian epic poetry, although I do not think that this necessitates a view of the poetry as *epic manqué* or as a 'failed attempt' to create linear unity. The dialogical, multi-vocal texture of the poems and their medley-like structures are consistent with the solipsistic, subjectivist stance of the speakers and with the underlying sceptical noetics. The polyvocal medley formally embodies Victorian poets' sense that 'the confusion of the present times is great, the multitude of voices counselling different things bewildering, the number of existing works capable of attracting a young writer's attention and of becoming his models, immense', as Arnold wrote in the 1853 *Preface*. Letters V and VI of *Amours de Voyage* present 'juxtaposition' as a way of imposing a fugitive meaning upon the multiplicity and confusion that both Arnold and Clough identify in their poetry and prose. 'Juxtaposition is great' (*Amours de Voyage* III, 151) because within the sceptical universe of the poem it provides the only way to make intelligible patterns out of multiple voices, partial views and fragments of knowledge.

If it is true 'that disparactive forms are not only intrinsic to human consciousness but receive a special emphasis in Romantic attitudes', as Thomas McFarland argues in *Romanticism and the Forms of Ruins*, then it becomes especially important to distinguish Romantic from Victorian poetic uses of the 'phenomenology of the fragment' (McFarland 1981, p. 45). McFarland explores the Romantic 'paradox' 'whereby the perception of parts and fragments implies the hypothetical wholeness of infinity, but...simultaneously...the dominance of disparactive forms' (pp. 28–9). I would argue that the shift of emphasis from wholeness to fragmentation occurs in Victorian rather than in Romantic poetry. When McFarland asserts 'that Wordsworth expresses...the sense of having been broken off...from true being,' (p. 10) he refers obliquely to the metaphysical quest which determines the value and function of fragments and ruins within *The Prelude* and *The Excursion*.

Victorian poets relinquished the quest for wholeness or transcendence, valorising the partial, the fragmentary, the contingent. For Arnold, Clough and Tennyson, wholeness itself is an illusion glimpsed fitfully through the fractured perception of multiple and self-cancelling speakers. The Victorians exhibited a greater interest than the Romantics in the illusions, velleities, and distortions of distinct percipients, whose 'juxtapositions' within the long poem determine its medley-like structure. Thus the epistemological orientation of Victorian poetry – its emphasis upon the limitations rather than upon the breadth of a speaker's knowledge – is closely connected to the 'phenomenology of the fragment' and to the medley.

Whereas in Romantic poetry the fragment image often instigates the visionary movement from incompleteness to wholeness, in Victorian poetry fragmentariness is a constituent element in human perception. We may use Book I of *The Excursion* to illustrate some Romantic uses of 'the forms of ruin'. A narrative fragment 'broken off' from the homiletic discourse of the Wanderer, which in turn is embedded within the Authorial–philosophical discourse, *The Ruined Cottage* functions as a symbol of the power of narrative to wrest 'an image of tranquility' from forms of ruin and decay. The 'creative power' of narrative rescues 'the fragment of a useless bowl' and 'a hut abandoned to decay' from oblivion, reanimating them with transcendental meaning. By virtue of his ability to read 'the forms of things' with a worthy 'eye', the Wanderer can imbue 'those weeds, and the high spear-grass on that wall' with lessons culled from the dead Margaret's life. The reanimation of dead forms catalyses the final visionary movement 'from ruin and from change' (Wordsworth 1977, *The Excursion*, I, 50) to the 'dominion of the enlightened spirit' (line 953).

If in *The Excursion* the Wanderer can 'leave behind' the passing shows of Being' (I, 951), in *Amours*, epistemological aporia seems closely connected to diffusion of self and loss of identity, the speaker's sense of being the 'shadow' of a substance whose existence he can neither affirm as an *a priori* principle nor scientifically verify. In Canto I, Letter XII, Claude envisions knowing and self-knowing as a recess or 'labyrinth' that 'closes around me,/ Path into path rounding slyly' (I, 237–8). With 'juxtaposition' the only available aesthetic and epistemological ordering principle, Claude must struggle 'to sustain the long sequences' which end in his avowal of sceptical nihilism ('and know nothing') (line 240). 'Fusing with this thing and that,/Entering into all sorts of relations' (lines 229–30), the speaker's identity shapes and reshapes itself out of a stream of impressions given an ephemeral coherence through 'juxtaposition' or 'affinity'. Disbelieving in any correspondence between internal and external reality and thus unable to objectify what he knows, Claude is caught in an infinite regress of introspection about his identity and its relationship to thought and knowledge. Although he can envision a multiplicity of other selves who create the social dialogue which partially defines individual identity, the speaker sceptically interrogates the 'gaze' turned back upon himself from the external world. This gaze of 'all one's friends and relations' (I, 29) the speaker experiences as subjection or constraint, 'all the *assujettissement* of having been what one has been,/ What one thinks one is or thinks that others suppose one' (lines 30–1).

One of the themes of *Amours de Voyage* is the evolution of consciousness conceived of as historical burden, the ever larger

accretion of experience and knowledge bequeathed to the present
by past ages. In both *Amours* and *Empedocles on Etna* scepticism is
presented as the inevitable result of the increase and division of
knowledge into separate branches during the nineteenth century.
Enclosed within their spheres of specialisation, Arnold's and
Clough's speakers perceive nature disconnectedly in broken
sequences. As the treasure-house or rubbish-heap of past civil-
isations and systems of knowledge, the cityscape of Rome in
Amours emblematises Clough's epistemological despair, akin to
Eliot's sense of shoring up fragments against the ruin of history.
Through the distorting and refracting lens of Claude's historicising
vision, Rome is reduced to a broken temporal sequence of
archeological strata strewn with indecipherable fragments and
inscriptions:

> Rome disappoints me much; I hardly
>   as yet understand, but
> *Rubbishy* seems the word that most
>   exactly would suit it.
> All the foolish destructions, and
>   all the sillier savings,
> All the incongruous things of past
>   incompatible ages,
> Seem to be treasured up here to make
>   fools of present and future.
> . . . .
> Rome, believe me, my friend, is like its own
>   Monte Testaceo,
> Merely a marvellous mass of broken and cast-
>   away wine-pots.
> Ye gods! what do I want with this rubbish of
>   ages departed,
> Things that Nature abhors, the experiments
>   that she has failed in?

> (I, 19–23, 39–42)

Like Claude's letters to England, in which he fails to 'fix her image',
'to write the old perfect inscription upon every page of remem-
brance', the ruins and fragments of Rome fail to inscribe a permanent, knowable meaning into personal or historical memory.

In *Amours* the shift from Romantic metaphysical certainty to Victorian epistemological despair is registered by Claude in the muted parody of Books I and VI of *The Prelude* that occurs in Letter XII. Whereas Wordsworth's speaker can retrospectively imbue his experience of 'the summit of a craggy ridge/ The horizon's utmost boundary' (Wordsworth 1971, *The Prelude*, I, 370–1) with the 'Wisdom and Spirit of the Universe' 'that giv'st to forms and images a breath' (I, 428; 430), Clough's speaker, shorn of memory and history, is condemned to 'sway wildly' 'from crag to crag...wide in the void' (lines 247–8). It is the transcendental power of Imagination that enables Wordsworth's speakers to 'intertwine' 'passions' and memory with 'enduring things' in nature and thus to construct a 'long sequence' of consciousness and experience. The inscription poem is the formal embodiment of the Wordsworthian belief in the association of memory and experience with natural objects. Claude's avowal of failure to inscribe meaning into historical artifacts or natural forms marks the poem's rejection of the Romantic theory of correspondences that had given unity to the 'long sequences' of Romantic epic.

The polyvocal structure of *Empedocles on Etna* results in the bifurcation of the poem's philosophy from its landscape description. The poem is organised into generic spheres of specialisation, with homily or sermon linked to ideology and lyric or song to landscape. Thus much of the poem's meaning exists in the gaps or silences between the generic boundaries. In the context of Empedocles' homily instilling a lesson of disharmony between man and nature, we may view Callicles' songs in their Apollonian harmony and lucidity as distanced both from the volcanic tempestuousness of nature on Etna and from the fragmentation of personality and intellect that prevents Empedoclean (and Arnoldian) man from seeing nature whole. Within Empedocles' homily, landscape both embodies the historical Greek philosopher's conception of ultimate reality as an eternal strife of elements and mirrors the Victorianised, Arnoldian philosopher's conception of nature as a refraction or shadow projected by a dreaming, solipsistic subject. By emphasising the conflict rather than the reconciliation of opposites in the historical Empedocles' philosophy, Arnold reinterprets his source to reflect his own epistemological rather than metaphysical concerns. At once an exteriorisation of man's fragmented and chaotic soul and an indwelling principle of nature, the Empedoclean strife of elements in the poem's landscape also accompanies and supports the speaker's jeremiad upon the unknowability of a nature he sees as inimical to human desire or need.

The perception of the fragmentariness of vision and knowledge voiced in the 'fragments letter' is inscribed at the centre of Empedocles' homily. The mirror-and-fragments image introduced in the first stanza betokens not, as it often does in Romantic poetry, the shaping power over nature of imagination or the 'correspondent breeze' between mind and nature, but rather the horrific propensity of the human observer to refract and distort what he sees. In Empedocles' depiction of 'the soul of man/...like a mirror, hung' precipitously above the contending elements, as in Clough's image of Claude twisting like a rope above the precipitous crags, there is a muted parody of Wordsworth's depiction of the crags   of Westmoreland and the Simplon Pass retrieved through the transformative powers of memory and imagination. Unlike the Wordsworthian poet shaping continuous sequences from memory and experience, the 'mirroring soul' of the Empedoclean observer 'a thousand glimpses wins/ And never sees a whole' (Arnold 1950 I, ii, 84–5). 'Wind-borne', 'hung' above 'The out-spread world to span', Empedoclean 'man', like Arnold's poet of natural interpretation in *Maurice de Guérin*, 'aspires to be a sort of human Aeolian harp, catching and rendering every rustle of nature' (Arnold 1962, III, p. 30). Callicles' songs render nature with the vividness and distinctness which Arnold ascribed to poets of Nature such as the Guérins, Sénancour, and Amiel. Indeed, it is not the human ability to perceive nature vividly that Victorian poets such as Arnold, Tennyson, Hardy, and Brontë question, but rather the ability to inscribe permanent meaning into natural forms. However, in *Amours de Voyage*, Clough's speaker's scepticism blurs the distinctness with which he perceives land and cityscape, which are rendered as shadowy projections of his 'shadow...self'. Like Hallam's poet of sensation who renders 'a sort of magic, producing several impressions' and like Arnold's poet of natural magic, Empedocles' human observer exhibits 'an extraordinary...susceptibility to impressions' which, however, he is unable to organise into meaningful sequences having reference to society or nature. Whereas the strings of Coleridge's 'Aeolian Harp' had vibrated 'with long, sequacious notes' resonating the 'rhythm in all thought', the harp with which Empedocles accompanies his homily registers the dissonance within the self or between the self and nature. The fact that 'to tunes we did not call our being must keep chime' is formally embodied in the verse form of Empedocles' homily with its alternation of short and long lines and its frequent inversions. We may speculate that the harp accompaniment, pitched in a Dorian mode of recitative, registers a dirge-like, broken harmonic pattern in contrast both to the Apollonian melodiousness of Callicles' songs and the universal 'rhythm in all things' sounded on Coleridge's 'Aeolian Harp'. Despite its initial reference to the erupting volcano of Etna, Callicles' final song implicitly refuses Empedocles' 'toil-set' life, where man must 'work as best he can/ And win what's won by strife' (I, ii, 268–70). Apollo's 'haunts' beside the Helicon represent the unavailing flight 'for refuge to past times' which Empedocles opposes to 'reality' in his speech before his plunge into the volcano. The final stanza of Callicles' song distances the Empedoclean/Victorian 'reality' of alienating toil within cities by presenting it in terms of balance and stasis. 'Juxtaposed' within the multi-vocal texture of the poem to the homily of Empedocles, the lyrics of Callicles contain no consolatory gesture for the philosopher's suicidal despair. If we identify Empedocles' homily with a poetry of 'reality', and Callicles' songs with a 'refuge to past times', then we may view the Clough–Arnold debate on Victorian poetics as entering into the representation of the various kinds of poetry juxtaposed within *Empedocles on Etna*. In 'Recent English Poetry', which appeared in the same year as Arnold's *Preface*, Clough no doubt had Arnold in mind when he asked, 'Is it...so very great an exploit to wander out into the pleasant field of Greek or Latin mythology?' In place of 'the imitations and quasi-translations which help to bring together into a single focus the scattered rays of human intelligence', Clough would substitute a poetry that treats of 'general wants, ordinary feelings, the obvious rather than the rare facts of human nature'. Such a poetry 'could console us with a sense of significance, if not of dignity, in that often dirty, or at least dingy, work which it is the lot of many of us to have to do' (Clough 1964, pp. 144–5). In the *Preface to Poems*, 1853, Arnold explains that he has suppressed *Empedocles on Etna* not because its subject 'was a Greek Sicilian born between two and three thousand years ago', but because *Empedocles* represents 'the suffering which finds no vent in action, in which a continuous state of mental distress is prolonged...in which there is everything to be endured, nothing to be done'. Just as Clough had discreetly referred to Arnold in his strictures against poetry on Greek or Latin mythology, so Arnold guardedly alludes to Clough when he notes that 'many persons would think this [the classical subject matter] 'a sufficient reason' for omitting the poem from the 1853 volume. Arnold rejects the 'painful situations' of 'ordinary life' – the life of the city and of toil – that Clough had identified as the proper objects of representation in contemporary poetry. We may read the Clough–Arnold debate about the terms of Victorian poetics and poetic practice in light of the duality between a poetry of subjective impression and a poetry of 'objective amelioration' we have already observed in Hallam's essay. Whatever their differences in theory, in practice Arnold and Clough juxtapose both kinds of poetry within their long medleys, making the various poetic genres into unalterably separate worlds of knowledge and experience. Scepticism partially consists in both *Empedocles* and *Amours* in the subject's inability to cross the boundary of his enclosed world of knowledge and memory and thus to connect knowledge with action in the external world.

In *Empedocles on Etna* scepticism also results, as in *Amours de Voyage*, from the Empedoclean/Victorian sense of belatedness, an historical, temporal sense of the sheer weight of intellectual and literary inheritance of 'each succeeding age' (II, 377). Empedocles, like Claude in *Amours*, compares the ever-accumulating 'mass' of knowledge to the ceaseless 'swell' of ocean waves. The Victorian/ Empedoclean thinker is inundated by the stream 'of volumes yet to read,/ Of secrets yet to explore' (I, ii, 334–5). The weighty volume of accumulated knowledge presses upon and overwhelms any one thinker who would take it into account in speculating upon the nature of the 'immeasurable All' (I, ii, 341). Limited to a 'measure' of knowledge and to partial or fragmentary vision, man mistakenly ascribes to the Gods 'true science' and knowledge of 'the world's immense design' (I, ii, 343). This epistemological anthropomorphism – the attribution to 'Gods' of the complete knowledge and wholeness of vision lacking in men – is roundly condemned by Empedocles: 'Fools! That in man's brief term/ He cannot all things view,/ Affords no ground to affirm/ That there are Gods who do' (I, ii, 347–50). Nowhere – except in certain passages in Clough's poetry – does the thoroughness of Victorian scepticism emerge so clearly as in Empedocles' refusal to locate a certain ground of knowledge either in nature or in a transcendental principle. Similarly, Arnold, it may be remembered, argues at length in both *Literature and Dogma* and *God and the Bible* against anthropomorphism and the use of supernaturalism to evade the implications of scepticism or the human condition of partial knowledge and limited vision. This refusal to grant even the possibility of envisioning 'the world's immense design' to 'powers' within or beyond the universe distinguishes the epistemological orientation of Victorian from Romantic poetry. Clouds of human misprision frequently obscure the sun of vision in Wordsworth's poetry, and aporia and scepticism form part of the temporal succession of moments of consciousness that constitute the historical/autobiographical texture of *The Prelude*. However, moments of doubt are sporadic and ephemeral, subsumed in the longer sequence of epistemological and imaginative affirmation.

Like Arnold's Empedocles, the 'I' or dominant elegiac voice of *In Memoriam* evokes a landscape 'darken'd' by his own subjective idealism. Two quatrains in Section LXXXV contrast the prophetic knowledge putatively vouchsafed to the subject of the elegy in the transcendental realm he now inhabits with the timebound, limited knowledge of the speaker: 'And led him thro' the blissful climes,/ And show'd him in the fountain fresh/ All knowledge that the sons of flesh/ Shall gather in the cycled times.' 'But I remain'd, whose hopes were dim,/ Whose life, whose thoughts were little worth/To wander on a darken'd earth,/ Where all things round me breathed of him.' (lines 25–32) The speaker recurrently recognises that transcendental or metaphysical reality is not only unattainable by 'mortals' but is an epiphenomenon or 'shadow' of human desire. The speaker discovers both 'in the highest place' and in nature 'mine own phantom chanting hymns' or 'the reflex of a human face' (CVIII, 10–12). The specific elegiac pattern of mourning and consolation consists in the speaker's recurrent attempts to restore absence as presence alternating with his recurrent realisation that there is no supra-sensible Presence, no Incarnation or Transfiguration. In Section XCV the speaker recalls his attempts to restore the presence of Hallam through language, as the Word made Flesh: 'So word by word, and line by line,/ The dead man touch'd me from the past/ And all at once it seem'd at last/ The living soul was flash'd on mine' (XCV, 33–6). Communion with the Real Presence of Hallam leads to the speaker's apparent receptivity to 'the deep pulsations of the world' (line 40). In the succeeding stanza, however, the speaker recognises that his momentary union with 'the empyreal heights of thought' was but a 'trance'. Section XCV dramatises the gap or disjunction between 'Matter-moulded forms of speech' and memory's retention of the past. *In Memoriam* records the failure of elegy to resurrect its subject through language, to recreate the word made flesh. The speaker's scepticism consists in his inability to grant epistemological validity, either to the trance-like moments when he fithully experiences communion with the dead and a sense of oneness with the universe or to moments of awakening when he doubts the existence of the invisible and ineffable. If we interpret the elegy as playing with, but finally abandoning the Platonic and Christological patterns bequeathed by the Miltonic–Romantic tradition of elegy, then we may well view the final invocation to 'One God, one law, one element' as a palinode sharply at variance with the pattern of scepticism which precedes it.

We may compare the ending of *In Memoriam* to stanza LII of *Adonais*, in which we find a version of the 'fragments' image so widely used by Victorian poets:

> The One remains, the many change and pass;
> Heaven's light forever shines, Earth's shadows fly:
> Life, like a dome of many-coloured glass,
> Stains the white radiance of Eternity,
> Until Death tramples it to fragments.

> (Shelley 1905, lines 450–4)

Like the speakers of *Amours de Voyage* and *Empedocles on Etna*, the speaker of *Adonais* perceives reality through a distorting lens or prism which refracts the earth into fragments of 'many-coloured glass'. But unlike the Victorian poets, Shelley is able finally to affirm the existence of the Platonic empyrean or 'Heaven's light', before which 'shadows fly'. In contrast, the 'empyreal heights of thought' in which Tennyson's speaker is 'whirl'd' are merely hallucinatory projections of his subjective longing and desire.

We may view both *In Memoriam* and *Idylls of the King* as conforming to a pattern in which trance-like states alternate with moments when trance is 'cancell'd'. The attitude of scepticism emerges from the speakers' recurrent failures to validate either a transcendental source of hallucinatory vision or to uphold an alternative, naturalistic reality that would correct the excesses of subjective vision. In the *Idylls* landscape is often presented as an embodiment of the speaker's hallucinatory or 'enchanted' vision. In keeping with the 'passing of Arthur' traced by the narrative, the landscape undergoes a gradual diminution. Just as the towers of Camelot rise and loom or recede and fade as the quester approaches or moves away from them, so the landscape shapes and reshapes itself phantasmagorically as the speakers' perspective shifts from idealism to scepticism and negation. Light and shadow transform the landscape into a 'phantom' or apparition, the fit habitation of Arthur, the 'Phantom king': 'Field after field, up to a height, the peak/ Haze-ridden, and thereon a phantom king, Now looming, and now lost' (*The Coming of Arthur*, lines 428–30). In the last idyll, *The Passing of Arthur*, 'the moonlit haze among the hills' is viewed from the perspective of a speaker who 'is blown along a wandering wind...fainter onward'. The insubstantiality of natural forms shifting and 'fading' within the mist-enshrouded landscapes is consonant with the 'fading' of Arthur into a 'phantom king' and with the deliquescence of Arthurian society. Arthur's 'dream' of Gawain's voice 'mingled' 'dim cries' with the moonlit landscape of dream, which in turn merges with 'some lonely city sacked by night' (line 43). The fragmentation of the social ideal parallels the hallucinatory or trance-like presentation of the landscape emblem. Just as the ceaseless alternation and breakup of social forms and values such as knighthood, fidelity and civility betoken the loss of a transcendent Arthurian ideal giving unity and meaning to society, so the distortion and fragmentation of landscape presented as dream, trance, or phantasmagoria betoken the loss of a transcendent ideal irradiating or interfused with nature. The predominance in the poem of 'fading' or disappearing visions of landscape, and the rapid alternation of dream and waking visions suggest as well the radical loss of epistemological certainty. Hallam's antithesis of the 'return of the mind upon itself' and 'the objective amelioration of society' applies to the Idylls as surely as it does to Arnold's and Clough's poetry. Arthur's retreat to 'the sunset bound of Lyonesse' returns him and 'his host' to the 'land of old upheaven from the abyss...where fragments of forgotten people dwelt' (lines 82, 84). The fragments-image, suggestive, as in Arnold's and Clough's poetry, both of the break-up of social order and of modern man's inability to 'shore up' the shards and fragments, the ruins of successive geological or archeological layers of time, merges with or fades into an image of wasteland, a 'land of shadows', which in turn dissolves into the image of 'the last, dim, weird' phantom battle fought between 'shadows in the mist':

> to sink into the abyss again;
> Where fragments of forgotten peoples dwelt,
> And the long mountains ended in a coast

Of ever-shifting sand, and far away
The phantom circle of a moaning sea.
. . . .
And there, that day when the great light of heaven
Burned at his lowest in the rolling year,
On the waste sand by the waste sea they closed.
. . . .
For friend and foe were shadows in the mist,
And friend slew friend not knowing whom he slew;
And some had vision out of golden youth,
And some beheld the faces of old ghosts ....

(lines 83–103)

The passage is notable for the way in which it emblematises waste-land as both the cause and the effect of the speaker's epistemo-logical despair. Tranced within the 'abyss' of the 'mind's return upon itself', imprisoned within the shadowy recesses of the self, the speaker slowly dissolves the landscape into an image of the unknowability of nature or the past. Like Arnold's 'ignorant armies [that] clash by Night,' Arthur's knights fight 'with formless fear' amid 'confusion' because, solipsistically 'not knowing whom [they] slew', they envision both other selves and natural forms as 'shadows in the mist'. The 'mist' of the solipsist likewise obscures the 'heaven' in which the knights seek 'after the Christ' (line 111). Void of meaning or knowability, neither nature nor 'heaven' can provide a context for harmonious social life. One of the triumphs achieved by Tennyson in *Idylls of the King* is the presentation of landscape as an emblem simultaneously of the 'return of the mind upon itself' and of the evisceration of a once-potent social order. More remarkably still, Tennyson builds the poem around the correspondence of the wasteland, the 'land of shadows' with the fading social order of the 'phantom king', while at the same time he insists upon gaps and dislocations between nature and society, the subject and the external world.

What is omitted from or unconfirmed in the *Idylls of the King* stands out more clearly if we gloss it with a passage from *Epipsychidion* that at first glance seems similar in its presentation of landscape. We may remember in this context that Hallam used Shelley as the preeminent exemplar in the Romantic period of the subjectivist poet, or 'the poet of sensation'. The passage opens with the speaker's evocation of the 'return of the mind upon itself':

> In many mortal forms I rashly sought
> The shadow of that idol of my thought
> . . . .
> I turned upon my thoughts and stood at bay...

> (Shelley 1905, lines 267–8; 273)

At first the speaker, having recourse to pathetic fallacy, envisions the 'cold day', which 'trembled, for pity of...strife and pain', as a projection of 'the shadow of my thought'. However, immediately with the entrance of Emilia, 'there shone Deliverance', the vision of a moon-like presence that, though changeable, is potent to pierce the clouds and to penetrate the speaker with a 'living light'. The direction and energy in the landscape emblem are vertical, moving downward from a higher sphere toward the earth:

> And from her presence life was radiated
> Through the grey earth and branches bare and dead;
> . . . .
> And music from her respiration spread
> Like light, – all other sounds were penetrated
> By the small, still, sweet spirit of that sound,
> So that the savage winds hung mute around
> . . . .
> Soft as an Incarnation of the Sun,
> When light is changed to love, this glorious One
> Floated into the cavern where I lay,
> And called my spirit, and the dreaming clay
> Was lifted by the thing that dreamed below
> . . . .
> I stood, and felt the dawn of my long night
> Was penetrating me with living light;
> I knew it was the Vision veiled from me....

> (Lines 325–6; 329–32; 335–9; 341–3)

The quasi-aubade to the incarnated vision of Emilia is immediately followed by a hymn to the 'Twin spheres of light who rule this passive Earth...and lift its billows and its mists, and guide/ By everlasting laws each wind and tide' (lines 345, 349–50). The imagery in the 'aubade' of penetration and incarnation shifts in the hymn to an imagery of 'blending' and suffusion, and the almost hectic synesthesia that betokens the speaker's desire for consummation of desire, the incarnated vision or Word Made Flesh, gives way in the hymn to a Wordsworthian wise passivity and receptivity to the 'many-mingled influence' of natural and supernatural forms. As in Coleridge's poem, the 'respiration' (or poetic inspiration) plays on the wind as an Aeolian harp that registers the music of the spheres. In contrast to Tennyson's and much other Victorian poetry, in which dreaming or sleep signifies self-enclosure, isolation from, or misprision of the external world, in Shelley's and Romantic poetry in general dream or sleep is the medium through which the poet/subject receives visionary experience or the means through which he restores and renovates his receptive and creative powers. From the abyss or 'cavern' which encloses the self the speaker is lifted by Vision or Imagination into oneness with a universe irradiated with the light that has transfigured him. In contrast to Clough's vision of the ocean as primeval Chaos that casts the subject back upon the strand of 'painful knowledge', or to Tennyson's vision of 'the phantom circle of a moaning sea' receding from the waste of sand that marks the end of the world, Shelley's version of Romantic oceanic infinity locates tide and cloud at the centre of a quasi-Newtonian universe whose elements are 'mingled' and 'married' by the forces of gravity and magnetics. In Tennyson's poetry the subject is unable to pass through the 'land of shadows' which is an emblem of his obsessive and recessive interiority; in Shelley's poetry the 'land of shadows' is continually interpenetrated by light, and transcendental vision is incarnated in the landscape.

Like part of *Epipsychidion*, Emily Brontë's *Stars* may be read as an aubade in which at dawn the speaker seeks to hold by incarnating the absent or 'departed' object of night-time dream and desire:

> I turned me to the pillow then
> To call back Night, and see
> Your worlds of solemn light, again
> Throb with my heart and me!

(Brontë 1941, lines 28–31)

The incessant play of light upon the landscape is Shelleyan, as are the lines 'While one sweet influence, near and far/ Thrilled through and proved us one'. However, its rapid alternation of the envisioned landscapes of dream and waking links 'Stars' more closely to the 'cancell'd' trances of Tennyson's poetry than to Shelley and the other Romantics. The speaker appears to acknowledge the dangers of abandoning herself exclusively to dream and reverie, identifying them with self-enclosure and sensory deprivation:

> The curtains waved, the wakened flies
> Were murmuring round my room,
> Imprisoned there, till I should rise
> And give them leave to roam.

> (lines 37–40)

In the most forceful invocation of the poem, however, she dramatically reverses herself:

> O Stars and Dreams and Gentle Night!
> O Night and Stars return!
> And hide me from the hostile light
> That does not warm, but burns –

> (lines 45–8)

The condition of being 'imprisoned' belongs equally to the speaker enclosed behind the curtains with the 'wakened flies' and the 'suffering men' burned by the 'hostile light', that 'drains the blood'. The image refers obliquely to the Victorian life of toil that Clough recommended as a subject of modern poetry and that Arnold explored in *A Summer Night* as well as *Empedocles*. Associated with waking life and 'Nature', 'suffering men' are as much a product of the speaker's transitory vision as are the 'stars' of dream and reverie. Although not explicit in the poem, epistemological uncertainty hovers in the background of the speaker's alternating belief in two distinct and self-cancelling visions.

Although I believe, on the whole, that it is more illuminating to consider differences rather than similarities between Victorian and Romantic uses of landscape, I would like to conclude by noting some of the ways in which Thomas Hardy continues the Wordsworthian tradition of landscape poetry, especially inscription poetry. Both poets depict landscapes marked by an ancient past which shapes the lives of its inhabitants, the 'folk' of Westmoreland and Wessex (Dorsetshire) whose ballads, hymns, psalm and fiddle-tunes Hardy uses as subject and verse form[2] and Wordsworth refers to in the narration of the Wanderer and Solitary in *The Excursion*. Consonant with the power of the past to shape the natural environment in their poetry, both poets also emphasise those objects in nature which endure, including human artifacts strewn over or etched into the land. Images of tombs, bones, skeletons, gnarled trees, stone benches, dials, clocks and churches occur frequently in Hardy's and Wordsworth's poetry because they epitomise the engrafting or interfusion of forms of human expression with features of nature. Hardy's *Inscriptions for a Peal of Eight Bells* and *By the Runic Stone* are in the tradition of Wordsworth's *Inscribed Upon a Rock, Inscription for a Monument in Crosthwaite Church*, and *Inscription on a Rock at Rydal Mount*. In *By the Runic Stone* human expression – 'the transport of talking' – marks a 'dent' in the landscape that, like the 'runic stone', memorialises the lovers' history by engrafting it upon nature. In Book V of *The Excursion* the Priest tells of a couple who erect a dial on the site of 'the stump of an old yew' 'their favourite resting-place' (Wordsworth 1977, line 493). The dial's 'inscriptive legend' treats of time and history, a memorial in nature to the fate of individuals who inhabit a 'particular spot'.

Hardy follows Wordsworth in his interfusion of artifacts of memory and forms of human expression with nature. However, unlike Wordsworth, Hardy emphasises the disjunction between a perceiver's immediate consciousness in the present and the patterns of experience etched into the landscape. In *After a Journey* the speaker's quest for the 'ghost' who inhabits the 'dead scenes' of the past results in the transformation of the landscape into an emblem of the speaker's desire, 'the unseen waters' ejaculations'. The ghost is 'voiceless' because the landscape which the speaker revisits cannot connect him to the past instant of near-consummation which occurred there. Rather the landscape betokens division and absence, 'the dark space wherein I have lacked you' (Hardy 1976, line 12). The frequent use of adverbs ('hazily'; 'lazily'; 'frailly') underscores misprision and uncertainty in the speakers' apperception of nature, a blurring of outline that is typical of Tennyson's poetry, less so of Hardy's. Indeed, the poem's thematisation of the quest after the unknowable we have already encountered in Tennyson's and Clough's poetry.

Focusing on the relative importance of metaphysical and epi-stemological concerns in the Romantic and Victorian periods has allowed us to make distinctions that hinge upon other critical cruxes such as the status of epic and medley in the long Victorian poem, Romantic/Victorian versions of 'the forms of ruin' and 'the phenomenology of the fragment' and changes in the presentation of the landscape emblem. The shift from metaphysical to epistemo-logical concerns cannot be considered apart from changes in the landscape, for it is the predominant vehicle for expressing either the poet/speaker's belief in a transcendental principle uniting man and nature or his disillusionment with the possibility of attaining certainty of knowledge. The Romantic tendency towards univocal utterance yields in the Victorian period to polyvocal, dialogical utterance, formally embodied in the medley. Even in Romantic poems such as *The Excursion* which contain several speakers, the Authorial–philosophical voice dominates, shaping narrative frag-ments into metaphysical wholes. This 'creative power' to shape fragments into wholes disappears in the Victorian period. In the Victorian medley fragmentation betokens gaps and disjunctions between the perspectives of multiple speakers or between the speaker and the external world. And whereas Romantic speakers read sermons on human morality and history into the forms of ruin, Victorian speakers more often see in shards and fragments the otherness of the past and their own imprisonment within a cultural and historical milieu. We should not lament the darkening of Victorian nature into a 'land of shadows' but rather celebrate the subtlety of visual effect and the richness of polyvocal texture which result from the suffusion of landscape with the poet/speaker's melancholy scepticism.

Notes

1.   Quoted in Roper 1969, p. 16. I am indebted to his illuminating analyses of both the Arnold–Clough debate and of *Empedocles on Etna*.
2.   See Potter 1979 for an excellent analysis of the influence of musical traditions and forms on Hardy's verse.

Appendix

A CHRONOLOGY OF NINETEENTH-CENTURY ENGLISH POETRY

This Chronology is by no means definitive. It does not list all the editions, though it does list many of those which demonstrate the increasing accessibility of certain poets in the nineteenth century. Neither does it list the numerous pirated editions, many of which were widely circulated and influential in promoting the popularity or reputation of the particular poet. We have also thought it useful to include some important critical works on the Romantic poets.

The true preface for studies which attempt to establish the intimate relationship between or among eras, or movements, or even poets, depends upon understanding not just the times, but the timing of publishing events. Byron, not unexpectedly, puts it well:

> I like to be particular in dates,
> Not only of the age, and year, but moon;
> They are a sort of post-house, where the Fates
> Change horses, making history change its tune,
> Then spur away o're empires and o're states,
> Leaving at last not much beside chronology....

> (*Don Juan*, I, lines 818–23)

We hope that this Chronology represents more than just a reference item, that it constitutes a critical statement, a change of tune, perhaps, about nineteenth-century English poetry.

Year	Biographical information and poetical and critical works
1757	William Blake b.
1759	William Collins d.; Robert Burns b.
1765	Edward Young d.
1770	Mark Akenside d.; Thomas Chatterton d.; William Wordsworth b.
1771	Walter Scott b.; Thomas Gray d.
1772	Samuel Taylor Coleridge b.
1774	Robert Southey b.
1777	Thomas Campbell b.
1783	Blake, *Poetical Sketches*.

1785	Thomas De Quincey b.; Thomas Love Peacock b.; Thomas Warton named Poet Laureate; Cowper, *The Task*.
1786	Burns, *Poems*.
1788	Byron b.; Blake, *There is No Natural Religion, All Religions Are One*.
1789	Blake, *Songs of Innocence, Book of Thel*.
1790	Warton d.; Henry James Pye named Poet Laureate; Blake, *Marriage of Heaven and Hell*.
1792	Percy Bysshe Shelley b.
1793	Wordsworth, *Evening Walk, Descriptive Sketches*; Blake, *Visions of the Daughters of Albion, America*.
1794	Blake, *Songs of Innocence and of Experience, Europe, Book of Urizen*; Coleridge, *The Fall of Robespierre, An Historic Drama* (Act 1 by Coleridge, remainder by Southey).
1795	Blake, *Book of Ahania, Book of Los, Song of Los*.
1796	Robert Burns d.; Coleridge, *Poems on Various Subjects*.
1797	Coleridge, *Poems*, 2nd edn.
1798	Wordsworth and Coleridge, *Lyrical Ballads*.
1800	William Cowper d.; Wordsworth and Coleridge, *Lyrical Ballads*, 2nd edn.
1801	Southey, *Thalaba*.
1802	Erasmus Darwin d.; Wordsworth and Coleridge, *Lyrical Ballads*, 3rd edn.
1803	Coleridge, *Poems*, 3rd edn.
1804	Blake, *Milton, The Four Zoas*.
1805	Wordsworth and Coleridge, *Lyrical Ballads*, 4th edn.
1806	Elizabeth Barrett (E. B. B.) b.
1807	Byron, *Hours of Idleness, Poems on Various Occasions*; Wordsworth, *Poems in Two Volumes*.
1808	Byron, *Poems Original and Translated*.
1809	Alfred Tennyson b.; Blake *Chaucer* (prospectus); Byron, *English Bards and Scotch Reviewers*.
1810	Wordsworth, *Essay on Epitaphs*; Shelley, *Original Poetry by Victor and Cazire* (co-written with Elizabeth Shelley, 'Cazire'), *Posthumous Fragments of Margaret Nicholson*.
1811	Shelley, *St Irvyne*.
1812	Robert Browning b.; Byron, *Childe Harold* I, II.
1813	Southey named Poet Laureate; Coleridge, *Remorse, a Tragedy, in Five Acts*, 1st, 2nd, and 3rd edns; Byron,

Bride of Abydos, The Giaour; Shelley, *Queen Mab*.

1814 Byron, *The Corsair, Ode to Napoleon Buonaparte, Lara*; Wordsworth, *The Excursion*.

1815 Wordsworth, *Poems, including Lyrical Ballads*, 2 vols, *The White Doe of Rylstone*; Byron, *Hebrew Melodies*.

1816 Wordsworth, *Thanksgiving Ode, A Letter to a Friend of Robert Burns*; Coleridge, *Christabel, Kubla Khan, and the Pains of Sleep*, 1st, 2nd and 3rd edns; Byron, *Prisoner of Chillon and Other Poems, Childe Harold III, The Siege of Corinth, Parisina*; Shelley, *Alastor and Other Poems*; Keats's first published poem ('Sonnet: "O Solitude"').

1817 Keats, *Poems*; Byron, *Manfred*; Coleridge, *Biographia Literaria, Sibylline Leaves, Zapolya*; Shelley, *Laon and Cythna* (published and withdrawn), *History of a Six Weeks' Tour*.

1818 Keats, *Endymion: A Poetical Romance*; Byron, *Childe Harold IV*; Shelley, *Revolt of Islam* (reissue of *Laon and Cythna*); Mary Shelley, *Frankenstein*; Hazlitt, *Lectures on the English Poets*.

1819 Byron, *Don Juan*, I and II; Wordsworth, *Peter Bell* (1st and 2nd edns), *The Waggoner*; Shelley, *Rosalind and Helen, The Cenci*.

1820 Blake, *Jerusalem*; Wordsworth, third volume added to *Poems, including Lyrical Ballads, The Miscellaneous Poems of William Wordsworth, The Excursion* (2nd edn), *The River Duddon*; Shelley, *Prometheus Unbound: with Other Poems, Œdipus Tyrannus, or, Swellfoot the Tyrant*; Keats, *Lamia, Isabella, The Eve of St Agnes and other Poems*.

1821 Keats d.; Southey, *Vision of Judgment*; Shelley, *Adonais, The Cenci* (2nd edn), *Epipsychidion*; Byron, *Don Juan* III–V, *Sardanapalus, The Two Foscari*, and *Cain*; Barrett (E. B. B.)'s first published poem: 'Stanzas, Excited by Some Reflections on the Present State of Greece'.

1822 Shelley d.; Matthew Arnold b.; Wordsworth, *Memorials of a Tour on The Continent, Ecclesiastical Sketches*; Byron, *Vision of Judgment*; Shelley, *Hellas, A Lyrical Drama*; Landor, *Apologue on Byron*.

1823 Byron, *Don Juan* VI–XIV, *Heaven and Earth, The Age of Bronze, The Island*.

1824 Byron d.; Shelley, *Julian and Maddalo, Posthumous*

Poems, ed. Mary Shelley; Byron, *The Deformed
Transformed, Don Juan* XV–XVI; R. C. Dallas,
Recollections of the Life of Lord Byron; Thomas Medwin,
Conversations of Lord Byron.

1825   Coleridge, *Aids to Reflection*; William Hazlitt, *Spirit of
the Age*; Pietro Gamba, *A Narrative of Byron's Last
Journey to Greece*; William Parry, *The Last Days of Lord
Byron*.

1826   Barrett (E. B. B.), *An Essay on Mind, with Other Poems*.

1827   Blake d.; Wordsworth, *Poetical Works*, 3rd collected
edition of 5 vols; Tennyson, *Poems by Two Brothers*.

1828   Dante Gabriel Rossetti b.; George Meredith b.;
Wordsworth, *Poetical Works* (Paris reprint of 1827
edn); Coleridge, *Poetical Works*; Leigh Hunt, *Lord Byron
and Some of His Contemporaries*.

1829   Tennyson, *Timbuctoo*; Coleridge, *Poetical Works* (2nd
edn); *The Poetical Works of Coleridge, Shelley and Keats*,
published by A. and W. Galignani, Paris, ed.
unnamed.

1830   Christina Georgina Rossetti b.; Coleridge, *The Devil's
Walk*, 1st and 2nd edns; Tennyson, *Poems Chiefly
Lyrical*.

1831   Wordsworth, *Selections From the Poems*, ed. J. Hine.

1832   Walter Scott d.; George Crabbe d.; Wordsworth, 4th
collected edn of *Poetical Works*, 4 vols; Shelley, *The
Masque of Anarchy*, ed. Leigh Hunt; *The Works of Lord
Byron, With His Letters and Journals, and His Life*, by
Thomas Moore [ed. John Wright]; Tennyson, *Poems*.

1833   Barrett (E. B. B.), *Prometheus Bound*; Browning, *Pauline*;
Tennyson, *The Lover's Tale*; *The Shelley Papers: Memoir
of Percy Bysshe Shelley*, ed. Thomas Medwin.

1834   Coleridge d.; William Morris b.; Coleridge, *Poetical
Works* (3rd edn); Lady Blessington, *Conversations of
Lord Byron with the Countess of Blessington*.

1835   Wordsworth, *Yarrow Revisited*; Browning, *Paracelsus*;
*Specimens of the Table Talk of the Late Samuel Taylor
Coleridge*, ed. H. N. Coleridge.

1836   Wordsworth, *Yarrow Revisited*, 2nd edn, *The Excursion*,
3rd edn, *Poetical Works* (5th edn, Vols I and II, reissued
with alteration in 1840, 1841, 1843); Coleridge, *Poetical
and Dramatic Works* (ed. unnamed); *Letters*,

Conversations and Recollections of S. T. Coleridge, ed. T. Allsop.

1836–39 Coleridge, *Literary Remains*, ed. H. N. Coleridge.

1837 Accession of Victoria; Algernon Charles Swinburne b.; Wordsworth, *Poetical Works* (5th edn, Vols. III–VI, reissued with alterations 1840, 1841, 1843); Browning co-writes *Strafford*; Joseph Cottle, *Early Recollections* [of/on Coleridge].

1838 *The Sonnets of William Wordsworth*; Barrett (E. B. B.), *The Seraphim*; J. Gillman, *Life of S. T. Coleridge*.

1839 *The Poetical Works of Percy Bysshe Shelley*, ed. Mary Shelley; Coleridge, *Aids to Reflection*, ed. H. N. Coleridge; Barrett (E. B. B.), *Romaunt of the Page*.

1840 Thomas Hardy b.; Browning, *Sordello*; *Essays, Letters from Abroad, Translations and Fragments, by Percy Bysshe Shelley*, ed. Mary Shelley; *The Poetical Works of John Keats*, 1st collected edn, London, ed. unnamed.

1841 Browning, *Pippa Passes*, *King Victor and King Charles* (*Bells and Pomegranates* I and II).

1842 Wordsworth, *Poems, Chiefly of Early and Late Years* (incl. 'The Borderers'); Browning, *Dramatic Lyrics* (*Bells and Pomegranates* III), 'Essay on Chatterton'; Tennyson, *Poems in Two Volumes*.

1843 Southey d.; Wordsworth named Poet Laureate; Wordsworth, *Selected Pieces*; Coleridge, *The Ancient Mariner and Other Poems* (Pocket English Classics edn); Tennyson, *Poems* (2nd edn); Browning, *The Return of the Druses*, *A Blot in the Scutcheon* (*Bells and Pomegranates* IV and V).

1844 Gerard Manley Hopkins b.; Coleridge, *Poems*, ed. Sara Coleridge; Barrett (E. B. B.), *Poems*; Browning, *Colombe's Birthday* (*Bells and Pomegranates* VI).

1845 Wordsworth, new edition of the poems, 1 vol., reissued with revisions 1847, 1849; Tennyson, *Poems* (3rd edn); Browning, *Dramatic Romances and Lyrics* (*Bells and Pomegranates* VII).

1846 Browning and Barrett (E. B. B.) marry; Browning, *Luria* and *A Soul's Tragedy* (*Bells and Pomegranates* VIII); Tennyson, *Poems* (4th edn); Wordsworth, *Poetical Works*, reissue of 1836–37, with alterations and including *Poems, Chiefly of Early and Late Years*

	(reissued 1849).
1847	Tennyson, *The Princess*.
1848	D. G. Rossetti founds P. R. B.; Tennyson, *Poems* (5th edn) and *The Princess* (2nd edn); C. G. Rossetti, first two published poems ('Death's Chill Between' and 'Heart's Chill Between'); Coleridge, *Hints towards the Formation of a Theory of Life*, ed. S. B. Watson, and *Poems* (new edn); *Life, Letters, and Literary Remains of John Keats*, ed. R. M. Milnes; Thomas Medwin, *Life of Percy Bysshe Shelley*.
1849	Wordsworth, *Poetical Works* (6 vols, publ. 1849–50); Browning, *Poems*; Arnold, *The Strayed Reveller and Other Poems*.
1850	Wordsworth d.; Tennyson named Poet Laureate; Wordsworth, *The Prelude*.
1851	Wordsworth, *The Prelude*, 2nd edn; Tennyson, *The Princess* (4th edn), *In Memoriam* (4th edn), and *Poems* (7th edn); Barrett Browning (E. B. B.), *Casa Guidi Windows*; Christopher Wordsworth, *Memoirs of William Wordsworth*.
1852	Coleridge, *Poems*, ed. Derwent and Sara Coleridge, *Dramatic Works*, ed. Derwent Coleridge; Tennyson, *Ode on the Death of the Duke of Wellington*; Arnold, *Empedocles on Etna*; Browning, 'Essay on Shelley'.
1853	Coleridge, *Complete Works*, ed. W. G. T. Shedd; Tennyson, *Poems* (8th edn), *The Princess* (5th edn) and *Ode on the Death of the Duke of Wellington* (2nd edn); Arnold, *Poems: A New Edition*.
1854	Oscar Wilde b.; Wordsworth, *Poetical Works*, ed. James Russell Lowell; *The Poetical Works of John Keats*, ed. R. M. Milnes [Lord Houghton]; *The Poetical Works of John Keats*, ed. James Russell Lowell.
1855	Tennyson, *Maud* and *Charge of the Light Brigade* first printed separately; Browning, *Men and Women*; Arnold, *Poems, Second Series*.
1856	Barrett Browning (E. B. B.), *Aurora Leigh* (dated 1857); Arnold, *Poems* (1st American edn); Tennyson, *Maud* (new and enlarged edn); *The Poetical Works of John Keats*, new edn, ed. R. M. Milnes [Lord Houghton]; Edwin Paxton Hood, *William Wordsworth*.
1857	Arnold, *Merope* (dated 1858); Wordsworth, *Poetical*

Works, new edn, 6 vols, *The Earlier Poems* (corrected edn).

1858   Morris, *Defence of Guenevere and Other Poems*; Swinburne contributes poems to John Nichol (ed.)'s *Undergraduate Papers*; Arnold, *Merope*; Thomas Jefferson Hogg, *Life of Percy Bysshe Shelley*; Edward John Trelawny, *Recollections of the Last Days of Shelley and Byron*.

1858–62   Thomas Love Peacock, *Memoirs of Shelley*.

1859   Thomas De Quincey d.; Tennyson, *Idylls of the King* (first series); Wordsworth, *Poems*, selected and ed. Robert Aris Wilmott; Lady Shelley, *Shelley Memorials from Authentic Sources*.

1860   Barrett Browning (E. B. B.), *Poems Before Congress*; Swinburne, *Queen Mother, Rosamond*.

1861   Barrett Browning (E. B. B.) d.; D. G. Rossetti, *Early Italian Poets*.

1862   Barrett Browning (E. B. B.), *Last Poems*; Tennyson, *Idylls of the King* (new edn); Meredith, *Modern Love*; C. G. Rossetti, *Goblin Market and Other Poems: Relics of Shelley*, ed. Richard Garnett.

1863   Coleridge, *Poems*, new edn, ed. Derwent and Sara Coleridge; Barrett Browning (E. B. B.), *The Greek Christian Poets and the English Poets*; Browning, *Poetical Works*; Alexander Gilchrist, *Life of William Blake* (completed after Gilchrist's death by D. G. Rossetti).

1864   Browning, *Dramatis Personae*; Tennyson, *Enoch Arden*; Swinburne, pageant in M. G. Leith's novel *The Children of the Chapel*; Arnold, 'The Function of Criticism at the Present Time'.

1865   William Butler Yeats b.; Tennyson, *A Selection from the Works of Alfred Tennyson*; Arnold, *Essays in Criticism, First Series*; Swinburne, *Chastelard, Atalanta in Calydon* (2 edns); C. G. Rossetti, *Goblin Market and Other Poems* (2nd edn); Wordsworth, selections in Moxon's *Miniature Poets*, selected Palgrave.

1866   Thomas Love Peacock d.; Swinburne, *Poems and Ballads, Atalanta in Calydon* (3rd edn), *Notes on Poems and Reviews* (2 edns); C. G. Rossetti, *The Prince's Progress and Other Poems, Elizabeth Barrett Browning's Poetical Works*, ed. unnamed; William Michael

Rossetti, *Swinburne's Poems and Ballads: A Criticism*.

1866–67   Swinburne, *Poems and Ballads* (2nd edn).

1867   Morris, *The Life and Death of Jason*; Arnold, *New Poems*;
           Swinburne, *A Song of Italy*; *William Blake: A Critical
           Essay* (dated 1868).

1868   *The Poetical Works of John Keats*, reprinted from early
           edns; Browning, *The Ring and the Book* (1868–69, in
           monthly vols), *Poetical Works*; Morris, *Earthly Paradise*
           (1868–70); Swinburne, *The Queen Mother and Rosamond*
           (2nd edn), *Atalanta in Calydon* (3rd edn), *Poems and
           Ballads* (3rd edn).

1869   Arnold, *Culture and Anarchy*; Tennyson, *The Holy Grail
           and Other Poems*.

1870   Coleridge, *Poems*, new and enlarged edn, ed. Derwent
           and Sara Coleridge; *The Poetical Works of Percy Bysshe
           Shelley*, ed. W. M. Rossetti; Byron, *Poetical Works*, ed.
           W. M. Rossetti; *The Poetical Works of William
           Wordsworth*, ed. W. M. Rossetti; Tennyson, *The Window
           and Work*, Miniature Edition, 1870–77; D. G. Rossetti,
           Poems; C. G. Rossetti, *Commonplace and other Short
           Stories*; Swinburne, *Ode on the Proclamation of the French
           Republic*.

1871   Browning, *Balaustion's Adventure*, *Prince
           Hohenstiel–Schwangau, Saviour of Society*; Arnold,
           Friendship's Garland; Swinburne, *Songs Before Sunrise*,
           Poems and Ballads (4th edn); Coleridge, *Poetical Works*,
           ed. W. M. Rossetti (Moxon Popular Poets edn).

1872   Browning, *Fifine at the Fair*; Tennyson, *Gareth and
           Lynette*; Swinburne, *Under the Microscope*; Morris, *Love
           is Enough*; C. G. Rossetti, *Sing-Song: A Nursery Rhyme
           Book*; *The Poetical Works of John Keats*, ed. W. M.
           Rossetti; Denis Florence MacCarthy, *Shelley's Early
           Life*.

1872–73   Tennyson, collected Library Edition.

1873   Coleridge, *Osorio*; Browning, *Red Cotton Night-Cap
           Country*; Arnold, *Literature and Dogma*; *The Poetical
           Works of John Keats*, ed. W. B. Scott.

1873–74   Tennyson, *Poetical Works* ('Popular Edition').

1874   Coleridge, *Poetical Works*, ed. W. B. Scott; D. G.
           Rossetti, *Dante and his Circle* (revision of 1861's *Early
           Italian Poets*); *Poetic Works of Blake, with a Memoir*, ed.

W. M. Rossetti; C. G. Rossetti, *Annus Domini, Speaking Likenesses*; Swinburne, *Bothwell; The Poetical Works of John Keats*, Lansdowne Poets, ed., reprinted from early edns.

1874–81   Tennyson, collected Cabinet Edition.

1874–81   Tennyson, *Poetical Works* (Author's Edition).

1875   Tennyson, *Queen Mary*; Browning, *Aristophanes' Apology, The Inn Album*; C. G. Rossetti, *Goblin Market, The Prince's Progress and Other Poems* (1st collected edn); Morris, *Three Northern Love Stories* and verse translation of the *Aeneid*; Swinburne, *Atalanta in Calydon* (5th edn).

1876   The Byron Club founded; *The Prose Works of William Wordsworth*, ed. Alexander B. Grosart, first collected edn; *The Poetical Works of John Keats*, ed. Richard Monckton Milnes; Tennyson, *Harold*; Browning, *Pacchiarotto*; Swinburne, *Erechtheus*; C. G. Rossetti, *Poems* ('Author's Edition', revised and enlarged).

1876–77   *The Poetical Works of Percy Bysshe Shelley*, ed. Harry Buxton Forman.

1877   Coleridge, *Poetical and Dramatic Works*, ed. Richard Herne Shepherd; Browning, *The Agamemnon of Aeschylus*; Arnold, *Poems* (2nd collected edn); Swinburne, *A Year's Letters* (in *Tatler*).

1878   Browning, *La Saisiaz: Two Poets of Croisic*; Swinburne, *Poems and Ballads* (Second Series); *Selected Poems of Matthew Arnold*; *The Poetical Works of Coleridge and Keats*, Riverside Edition, ed. unnamed; *The Poetical Works of Percy Bysshe Shelley*, ed. W. M. Rossetti, revised edn; E. J. Trelawny, *Records of Shelley, Byron, and the Author*; George Calvert, *Wordsworth*.

1879   Wordsworth, *Poems*, selected and ed. Matthew Arnold; Tennyson, *The Lover's Tale*; Browning, *Dramatic Idyls* (1st series); Arnold, *Mixed Essays*; C. G. Rossetti, *Seek and Find*.

1880   Browning, *Dramatic Idyls* (2nd series); Tennyson, *Ballads and Other Poems*; Swinburne, *Songs of the Springtides, The Heptalogia, Studies in Song*; Coleridge, *Poetical and Dramatic Works*, ed. R. H. Shepherd (2nd edn); Swinburne, *A Study of Shakespeare*; Wordsworth, *Selections*, ed. A. J. George; *The Works of Percy Bysshe*

Shelley, ed. H. B. Forman; Alexander Gilchrist, *Life of William Blake*, revised and enlarged edn.

1881   Browning Society founded; Thomas Carlyle d.; Arnold, *Poems* (reissue of 1877 edn); D. G. Rossetti, *Ballads and Sonnets, Poems* (new edn); C. G. Rossetti, *A Pageant and Other Poems, Called to be Saints*; Swinburne, *Mary Stuart; Poetry of Byron*, ed. Matthew Arnold.

1881–91   F. J. Furnivall, ed., *The Browning Society's Papers*.

1882   D. G. Rossetti d.; D. G. Rossetti, *Ballads and Sonnets*, new edn; Swinburne, *Tristram of Lyonesse*; W. Sharp, *Dante Gabriel Rossetti: A Record and a Study*; T. Hall Caine, *Recollections of Dante Gabriel Rossetti*.

1882–86   *The Poetical Works of William Wordsworth*, ed. William Knight.

1883   Browning, *Jocoseria*; C. G. Rossetti, *Letter and Spirit*; Swinburne, *A Century of Roundels; The Poetical Works and Other Writings of John Keats*, ed. H. B. Forman; Arnold, ed. *Isaiah of Jerusalem*; Wordsworth, *Selections*, ed. J. S. Fletcher.

1884   Coleridge, *Poetical Works* (Canterbury Poets Edition), *Aids to Reflection*, ed. J. Skipsey, *Table Talk and Omniana*, ed. T. Ashe; Tennyson, *Becket, The Cup and The Falcon, Poems* (1 vol.) and *Poems*; Browning, *Ferishtah's Fancies*; Swinburne, *A Midsummer Holiday, Selections*, ed. R. H. Stoddard; *The Poetical Works of John Keats*, ed. H. B. Forman; *The Poetical Works of John Keats*, ed. W. T. Arnold; *The Poetical Works of John Keats*, reprinted from original edns, ed. F. T. Palgrave; Wordsworth, *Sonnets*, ed. R. C. Trench; Henry N. Hudson, *Studies in Wordsworth*.

1884–85   Morris, *Chants for Socialists*.

1885   Tennyson, *Tiresias*; Wordsworth, *Poetical Works*, ed. Andrew James Symington; Coleridge, *Poetical Works*, ed. T. Ashe; Arnold, *Poems*; Swinburne, *Marino Faliero*; C. G. Rossetti, *Time Flies; The Poetical Works of John Keats*, ed. John Hogben; Mrs Sutherland Orr, *A Handbook to the Works of Robert Browning*.

1886   Tennyson, 3 vols added to 1872–73, Imperial Library edn and *Locksley Hall Sixty Years After*; Swinburne, *Miscellanies*; D. G. Rossetti, *Collected Works*, ed. W. M. Rossetti; Edward Dowden, *The Life of Percy Bysshe*

Shelley; H. B. Forman, *The Shelley Library*; Arthur Symons, *An Introduction to the Study of Browning*.

1887 Browning, *Parleyings*; Swinburne, *Locrine*; Morris, translation of the *Odyssey*; Shelley, *The Wandering Jew*, ed. Bertram Dobell; Joseph Knight, *Life of Dante Gabriel Rossetti*; W. M. Rossetti, *Life of John Keats*.

1888 Arnold d.; Wordsworth, *The Prelude*, ed. A. J. George, *Complete Poetical Works*, ed. John Morley, *The Recluse* and *Selections*, ed. William Knight *et al.*; Arnold, *Essays in Criticism, Second Series*; Morris, *A Dream of John Ball* and *Signs of Change*; John H. Ingram, *Elizabeth Barrett Browning*.

1888–94 Browning, *Poetical Works* (17 vols).

1889 Browning d.; Hopkins d.; Browning, *Asolando* (dated 1890); Tennyson, *Demeter and Other Poems*, *Poems* (new edn), *To Edward Lear, and Other Poems*; Barrett Browning (E. B. B.) *Poetical Works*, ed. unnamed; Swinburne, *A Study of Ben Jonson*, *Poems and Ballads (Third Series)*; Yeats, *The Wanderings of Oisin*; W. M. Rossetti, *Dante Gabriel Rossetti as Designer and Writer*.

1890 Morris, *The Roots of the Mountains*, *The Story of the Glittering Plain*; C. G. Rossetti, *Poems*, new and enlarged edition.; Tennyson, *Poems* (new edn); *Poetry and Prose by John Keats*, ed. H. B. Forman; Shelley, *Poetical Works*, ed. Edward Dowden.

1891 Shelley, *Adonais*, ed. W. M. Rossetti; Morris, *Poems by the Way*, *News from Nowhere*, *The Saga Library*, 5 vols, 1891–95 (with Eiríkr Magnússon); *The Poetical Works of Percy Bysshe Shelley*, ed. Edward Dowden; Henry Jones, *Browning as a Philosophical and Religious Teacher*.

1892 Tennyson d.; Alfred Austin named Poet Laureate; Shelley, *Complete Poetical Works*, ed. G. E. Woodberry; *Wordsworth's Prefaces*, ed. A. J. George; Tennyson, *The Foresters*, *The Death of Œnone*; Swinburne, *The Sisters*; C. G. Rossetti, *The Face of the Deep*; F. S. Ellis, *A Lexical Concordance to the Poetical Works of Percy Bysshe Shelley*.

1892–93 Wordsworth, *Poetical Works*, ed. Edward Dowden.

1893 Coleridge, *Poetical Works*, ed. James Dykes Campbell; *The Complete Poetical Works of Percy Bysshe Shelley*, ed. George Edward Woodberry; C. G. Rossetti, *Verses* (collection of reprints from *Called to Be Saints*, *Time*

Flies and *The Face of the Deep*), *The Face of the Deep: A Devotional Commentary on the Apocalypse* (2nd edn) and *Sing-Song: A Nursery Rhyme Book* (new edn); *The Poems of William Blake*, ed. W. B. Yeats; *The Works of William Blake, Poetic, Symbolic, and Critical*, ed. Edwin J. Ellis and W. B. Yeats; Alfred Thomas Story, *William Blake: His Life, Character and Genius*.

1894   C. G. Rossetti d.; Swinburne, *Astrophel, Atalanta in Calydon* (Kelmscott Press Edition) and *Studies in Prose and Poetry*; Morris, *The Wood Beyond the World*; Yeats, *Land of Heart's Desire*; J. D. Campbell, *Samuel Taylor Coleridge*.

1895   Wordsworth, *Poetical Works*, ed. Thomas Hutchinson; C. G. Rossetti, *The Face of the Deep: A Devotional Commentary on the Apocalypse* (3rd edn); *Anima Poetae, from the Unpublished Notebooks of Samuel Taylor Coleridge*, ed. Ernest Hartley Coleridge; Morris, trans., *The Tale of Beowulf*; Ellen A. Proctor, *A Brief Memoir of Christina G. Rossetti*.

1896   Morris d. Wordsworth, *Poetical Works* and *Prose Works*, ed. William Knight; Swinburne, *The Tale of Balen*; A. E. Housman, *A Shropshire Lad*; C. G. Rossetti, *New Poems*, ed. W. M. Rossetti; Morris, *The Well at the World's End*.

1897   *The Poetical Works of Elizabeth Barrett Browning*, ed. F. G. Kenyon; C. G. Rossetti, *Maude: A Story for Girls*; *Collected Works of Dante Gabriel Rossetti*, ed. W. M. Rossetti; Morris, *The Water of the Wondrous Isles* and *The Sundering Flood*; Hallam, Lord Tennyson, *Alfred, Lord Tennyson: A Memoir*; Emile Legouis, *The Early Life of William Wordsworth, 1770–1798: A Study of 'The Prelude'*, J. W. Matthews, trans. of 1896 Paris edn; T. J. Wise, *Bibliography* [for Robert Browning].

1898   Tennyson, *Collected Works*, ed. W. J. Rolfe (Cambridge Poets Edition); Browning, *Poetical Works*, ed. Charlotte Porter and Helen A. Clarke (Florentine Edition); Hardy, *Wessex Poems*; Shelley, *Original Poetry by Victor and Cazire*, new ed. Richard Garnett; Coleridge, *Poetry*, ed. Richard Garnett; Mackenzie Bell, *Christina Rossetti*.

1898–1901   Queen Victoria d.; *The Works of Lord Byron: Letters and Journals*, ed. Rowland E. Prothero.

1898–1904   *The Works of Lord Byron: Poetry*, ed. E. H. Coleridge.

1899   Swinburne, *Rosamond, Queen of the Lombards*, and *A Channel Passage; The Letters of Robert Browning and Elizabeth Barrett, 1845–1846*, ed. Robert Wiedemann Barrett–Browning; George Saintsbury, *Matthew Arnold* (critical study); *Ruskin, Rossetti, Preraphaelitism: Papers 1854–1862*, ed. W. M. Rossetti; J. W. Mackail, *The Life of William Morris*; Lilian Whiting, *A Study of Elizabeth Barrett Browning; Dante Gabriel Rossetti: An Illustrated Memorial of His Art and Life*, ed. H. C. Marrillier.

1900   Barrett Browning, *Complete Poetical Works*, ed. Harriet Waters Preston, *The Complete Works of Elizabeth Barrett Browning*, ed. Charlotte Porter and Helen A. Clarke ('Coxhoe Edition'); *Pictures and Poems of Dante Gabriel Rossetti*, arranged by FitzRoy Carrington; Elisabeth Cary, *The Rossettis: Dante Gabriel and Christina*; Theodore Wratislaw, *Algernon Charles Swinburne*.

1901   Swinburne, *Lyrical Poems*, ed. W. Sharp, *Dead Love and Other Inedited Pieces; The Complete Works of Mrs E. B. Browning* (new edn), ed. Charlotte Porter and Helen A. Clarke.

1902   Hardy, *Poems of the Past and the Present*; Hueffer, Ford Madox (Ford Madox Ford), *Rossetti*; Herbert W. Paul, *Matthew Arnold*.

1903   G. K. Chesterton, *Robert Browning; Rossetti Papers, 1862–1870*, ed. W. M. Rossetti.

1904   Swinburne, *A Channel Passage, Poems* (definitive edition); *The Poetical Works of Christina Georgina Rossetti*, ed. W. M. Rossetti; D. G. Rossetti, *Poems*, ed. W. M. Rossetti; *The Poetical Works of Elizabeth Barrett Browning*, Oxford Complete Edition; Arthur C. Benson, *Rossetti*; H. Dunn, *Recollections of Dante Gabriel Rossetti*; Edward Dowden, *Robert Browning*.

1905   Swinburne, *Love's Cross-Currents*, (reprint of *A Year's Letters*, first published in *Tatler*, 1877), *Selected Poems* (ed. W. Payne), *Tragedies*; D. G. Rossetti, *Poems*, ed. W. M. Rossetti; G. E. Woodberry, *Swinburne*; W. M. Rossetti, *A Bibliography of the Works of Dante Gabriel Rossetti*.

1906   Swinburne's *Selected Poems*, ed. Arthur Beatty; Arthur Symons, *An Introduction to the Study of Browning* (revised edn).

1907–8   *Works of Tennyson Annotated*, ed. Hallam, Lord
Tennyson (Eversley Edition); Coleridge, *Christabel*
(new edn), ed. E. H. Coleridge; *Letters of the
Wordsworth Family*, ed. William Knight.
1908   Swinburne, *The Age of Shakespeare, The Duke of Gandia;
The Poems of William Wordsworth*, ed. N. C. Smith; Mrs
S. Orr, *Life and Letters of Robert Browning* (revised edn)
by F. G. Kenyon.
1909   Swinburne d.; George Meredith d.; Swinburne,
Dramas, ed. A. Beatty, *Shakespeare, Three Plays of
Shakespeare*; Hardy, *Time's Laughing-stocks.*

Works Cited

ABRAMS, M. H. (1965) 'Structure and Style in the Greater Romantic Lyric', in *From Sensibility to Romanticism*. Ed. Frederick W. Hilles and Harold Bloom. New York: Oxford University Press, pp. 527–60.

——. (1971). *Natural Supernaturalism: Tradition and Revolution in Romantic Literature*. New York: W. W. Norton.

ALIGHIERI, Dante. (1939). *Inferno*. Tr. John D. Sinclair. New York: Oxford University Press.

ALLOTT, Kenneth, and Mariam Allott, eds. (1979). *The Poems of Matthew Arnold*. New York: Longman.

ANON. (1729). *The Nurse's Guide*: London: J. Brotherton.

ARMSTRONG, Isobel. (1966). 'Browning's *Mr. Sludge, "The Medium"*', in *Robert Browning*. Ed. Philip Drew. London: Methuen, pp. 212–22.

——. (1969). *The Major Victorian Poets: Reconsiderations*. Ed. Isobel Armstrong. Lincoln: University of Nebraska Press.

ARNOLD, Matthew. (1896). *Letters of Matthew Arnold 1848–1888*. Ed. George W. E. Russell. London: Macmillan.

——. (1932). *The Letters of Matthew Arnold to Arthur Hugh Clough*. Ed. Howard Foster Lowry. London: Oxford University Press.

——. (1950). *The Poetical Works of Matthew Arnold*. Ed. C. B. Tinker and H. F. Lowry. Oxford: Oxford University Press.

——. (1960–77). *The Complete Prose Works of Matthew Arnold*. Ed. R. H. Super. Ann Arbor: University of Michigan Press.

——. (1965). *The Poems of Matthew Arnold*. Ed. Kenneth Allott. London: Longman.

AUDEN. W. H. (1950). *The Enchafèd Flood: or The Romantic Iconography of the Sea*. New York: Random House.

AUSTIN, J. L. (1975). *How to Do Things with Words*. Cambridge: Harvard University Press.

AUSTIN, Linda M. (1990). 'Reading the Romantics: Ruskin's *"Fiction Fair and Foul"*'. *Studies in Romanticism*, XXIX, pp. 583–601.

BAILEY, J. O. (1970). *The Poetry of Thomas Hardy: A Handbook and Commentary*. Chapel Hill: University of North Carolina Press.

BARRETT, Elizabeth. (1955). *Elizabeth Barrett to Mr. Boyd*. Ed. Barbara P. McCarthy. New Haven: Yale University Press.

——. (1974). 'Two Autobiographical Essays'. *Browning Institute Studies*, II, pp. 119–34.

BARTLETT, Phyllis. (1955). 'Hardy's Shelley'. *Keats–Shelley Journal*, IV, pp. 15–29.

——. (1955a). '"Seraph of Heaven": A Shelleyan Dream in Hardy's Fiction'. *PMLA*, LXX, pp. 624–35.

BATE, Jonathan. (1991). *Romantic Ecology: Wordsworth and the Environmental Tradition*. London: Routledge.

BATTISCOMBE, Georgina. (1981). *Christina Rossetti: A Divided Life*. New York: Holt, Rinehart and Winston.

BEACH, Joseph Warren. (1936). *The Concept of Nature in Nineteenth-Century English Poetry*. New York: Macmillan.

BELL, Mackenzie. (1898). *Christina Rossetti: A Biographical and Critical Study*. London: Burleigh.

BENJAMIN, Walter. (1977). *The Origin of German Tragic Drama*. Trans. John Osborne. London: NLB.

BENTLEY, D. M. R. (1987). 'The Meretricious and the Meritorious in *Goblin Market*: A Conjecture and an Analysis'. *The Achievement of Christina Rossetti*. Ed. David A. Kent. Ithaca: Cornell University Press, pp. 58–81.

BJÖRK, Lennart A., ed. (1985). *The Literary Notebooks of Thomas Hardy*. New York: New York University Press.

BLAKE, William. (1965). *The Poetry and Prose of William Blake*. Ed. David V. Erdman. Commentary by Harold Bloom. Garden City: Doubleday.

BLANK, G. Kim. (1988). *Wordsworth's Influence on Shelley: A Study of Poetic Authority*. London: Macmillan.

BLOOM, Harold. (1969). *Shelley's Mythmaking*: Ithaca: Cornell University Press.

——. (1973). *The Anxiety of Influence: A Theory of Poetry*. New York: Oxford University Press.

——. (1975). *A Map of Misreading*. New York: Oxford University Press.

——. (1987) *The Literary Criticism of John Ruskin*. New York: Da Capo.

BOWRA, C. M. (1949). *The Romantic Imagination*. Cambridge, Mass.: Harvard University Press.

BRINKLEY, Robert J. and HANLEY, Keith, eds. (1992). *Romantic Revisions*. Cambridge: Cambridge University Press.

BRISMAN, Leslie. (1978). 'Swinburne's Semiotics'. *Georgia Review*, XXXI, pp. 578–97.

——. (1984). 'Of Lips Divine and Calm: Swinburne and the Language of Shelleyan Love', in *Romanticism and Language*. Ed. Arden Reed. Ithaca: Cornell University Press, pp. 247–62.

BRONTË, Emily Jane. (1941). *The Complete Works of Emily Jane Brontë.* Ed. C. W. Hatfield. New York: Columbia University Press.

BROWNING, Elizabeth Barrett. (1897). *Letters of Elizabeth Barrett Browning.* Ed. Frederick G. Kenyon. New York: Macmillan.

———. (1983). *The Letters of Elizabeth Barrett Browning to Mary Russell Mitford: 1836–1854.* Ed. Meredith B. Raymond and Mary Rose Sullivan. Windfield, KS: Wedgestone.

BROWNING, Robert. (1933). *Letters of Robert Browning Collected by Thomas J. Wise.* Ed. Thurman L. Hood. New Haven: Yale University Press.

———. (1962). *Poetical Works.* London: Oxford University Press.

———. (1971). *The Ring and the Book.* Ed. Richard D. Altick. New Haven and London: Yale University Press.

———. (1981). *Poems.* Ed. John Pettigrew. New Haven and London: Yale University Press.

———. (1988). *The Plays of Robert Browning.* Eds. Thomas J. Collins and Richard J. Shroyer. New York: Garland.

BUCKLER, William E. (1980). *The Victorian Imagination: Essays in Aesthetic Exploration.* New York and London: New York University Press.

BURKE, Edmund. (1958). *A Philosophical Enquiry into the Origin of Our Ideas of the Sublime and Beautiful.* Ed. J. T. Boulton. Notre Dame: University of Notre Dame Press 1968 rpt.

BYRON, G. G. N., Lord. (1986). *Byron.* Ed. Jerome J. McGann. Oxford: Oxford University Press.

CANTALUPO, Catherine. (1988). 'Christina Rossetti: The Devotional Poet and the Rejection of Romantic Nature', in *The Achievement of Christina Rossetti.* Ed. David Kent. Ithaca: Cornell University Press.

CARLYLE, Thomas. (1896–9). (1/01). *The Works of Thomas Carlyle.* Centenary Edition. London: Chapman and Hall.

CASAGRANDE, Peter J. (1977). 'Hardy's Wordsworth: A Record and a Commentary'. *English Literature in Transition: 1880–1920,* XX, pp. 210–37.

CASSIDY, John A. (1964). *Algernon C. Swinburne.* Boston: Twayne.

CASTLE, Terry. (1987). 'The Spectralization of the Other in *The Mysteries of Udolpho*', in *The New 18th Century: Theory, Politics, English Literature.* Ed. Felicity Nussbaum and Laura Brown. New York: Methuen, pp. 231–53.

CHAMBERS, Robert. (1844). *Vestiges of the Natural History of Creation.* London: John Churchill.

CHAPMAN, Raymond. (1970). *Faith and Revolt: Studies in the Literary Influence of the Oxford Movement*. London: Weidenfield and Nicolson.

CHARLES, Edna Kotin. (1985). *Christina Rossetti: Critical Perspectives. 1862–1982*. Selinsgrove: Susquehanna University Press.

CHEW, Samuel C. (1929). *Swinburne*. Boston: Little, Brown and Co.

CHRIST, Carol. (1975). *The Finer Optic: The Aesthetic of Particularity in Victorian Poetry*. New Haven: Yale University Press.

——. (1984). *Victorian and Modern Poetics*. Chicago: University of Chicago Press.

CHRISTENSEN, Jerome C. (1978). 'The Symbol's Errant Allegory: Coleridge and His Critics', *ELH*, XLV, pp. 640–59.

CLOUGH, Arthur Hugh. (1964). *Selected Prose Works of Arthur Hugh Clough*. Ed. Bruckner B. Trawick. Alabama: University of Alabama Press.

——. (1974). *The Poems of Arthur Hugh Clough*. Ed. F. L. Mulhauser. Oxford: Clarendon.

COCHRAN, Rebecca. (1990). 'An Assessment of Swinburne's Arthuriana', in *King Arthur Through the Ages*, II, New York and London: Garland, pp. 62–82.

COLERIDGE, Samuel Taylor. (1906). *Biographia Literaria,*. Ed. George Watson. London: J. M. Dent.

——. (1912). *The Complete Poetical Works of Samuel Taylor Coleridge*, Ed. Ernest Hartley Coleridge. Oxford: Clarendon.

——. (1930). *Shakespearean Criticism*. Ed. Thomas M. Raysor. Cambridge, Mass.: Harvard University Press.

——. (1950). *Biographia Literaria*. Ed. George Watson. London: Dent.

——. (1962). *The Complete Poetical Works*. Ed. E. H. Coleridge. Oxford: Clarendon.

——. (1964). *Selected Poetry and Prose*. Ed. Elizabeth Schneider. New York: Holt, Rinehart and Winston.

——. (1967). *Coleridge: Poetical Works*, Ed. Ernest Hartley Coleridge. London: Oxford University Press.

——. (1972). *The Stateman's Manual*, in *Lay Sermons*. Ed. R. J. White. *The Collected Works*, VI, ed. Kathleen Coburn. Princeton: Princeton University Press, pp. 28–31.

——. (1983). *Biographia Literaria: or Biographical Sketches of My Literary Life and Opinions*. Ed. James Engell and W. Jackson Bate. Princeton: Princeton University Press.

COOK, A. K. (1920). *A Commentary upon Browning's 'Ring and the Book'*. London.

COOPER, Andrew. (1988). *Doubt and Identity in Romantic Poetry*. New Haven: Yale University Press.

CORRIGAN, Beatrice. (1956). *Curious Annals: New Documents Relating to Browning's Roman Murder Story*. Toronto: University of Toronto Press.

———. (1960). 'Browning's Roman Murder Story'. *English Miscellany*, XI, pp. 333–400.

COSSLETT, Tess, ed. (1984). *Science and Religion in the Nineteenth Century*. Cambridge: Cambridge University Press.

CRASHAW, Richard. (1904). *Poems by Crashaw*. Cambridge: Cambridge University Press.

CULLER, A. Dwight. (1966). *Imaginative Reason: The Poetry of Matthew Arnold*. New Haven and London: Yale University Press.

———. (1977). *The Poetry of Tennyson*. New Haven: Yale University Press.

CURLE, Richard. (1937). *Robert Browning and Julia Wedgwood. A Broken Friendship as Revealed by Their Letters*. London: J. Murray and I. Cope.

CURRAN, Stuart. (1988). 'The I Altered', in *Romanticism and Feminism*. Ed. Anne K. Mellor. Bloomington: Indiana University Press, pp. 185–207.

DACRE, Charlotte. (1805). *Hours of Solitude: A Collection of Original Poems*. London: Hughes; rpt 1978.

DAVIS, Mary Bird. (1976). 'Swinburne's Use of His Sources in *Tristram of Lyonesse*'. *Philological Quarterly*, LV, pp. 96–112.

DE MAN, Paul. (1983). 'The Rhetoric of Temporality', in *Blindness and Insight*. 2nd edn. rev. Minneapolis: University of Minneapolis Press, pp. 187–227.

DEVANE, William Clyde. (1955). *A Browning Handbook*. New York: Appleton–Century Crofts.

DESCOMBES, Vincent. (1982). *Modern French Philosophy*. Berkeley: University of California Press.

DILLON, Steven C. (1990). 'Browning and the Figure of Life'. *Texas Studies in Literature and Language*, XXXII, pp. 169–86.

DREW, Philip. (1970). *The Poetry of Robert Browning: A Critical Introduction*. London: Methuen.

DUERKSEN, Roland A. (1966). *Shelleyan Ideas in Victorian Literature*. The Hague: Mouton.

———. (1983). 'The Critical Mode in British Romanticism'. *Romanticism Past and Present*, VII, pp. 1–21.

DUFFY, Maureen. (1972). *The Erotic World of Faery*. London: Hodder and Stoughton.

EAGLETON, Terry. (1990). *The Ideology of the Aesthetic*. Oxford: Basil Blackwell.

ELIOT, T. S. (1920). *The Sacred Wood: Essays on Poetry and Criticism*. London: Methuen.

——. (1950). *Selected Essays*. New York: Harcourt Brace.

ELLEDGE, Scott, ed. (1979). *Tess of the D'Urbervilles*, by Thomas Hardy. 2nd edn. New York: W. W. Norton.

EMPSON, William. (1947). *Seven Types of Ambiguity*. Rev. edn. New York: New Directions.

ENGELBERG, Karsten. (1988). *The Making of the Shelley Myth: An Annotated Bibliography of Criticism of Percy Bysshe Shelley. 1822–1860*. London: Mansell.

ENSOR, George. (1806). *The Independent Man*. London: J. Johnson.

EVANS, B. Ifor. (1933). 'Sources for Christina Rossetti's "Goblin Market"'. *Modern Language Review*, XXVIII, pp. 156–65.

FADERMAN, Lillian. (1981). *Surpassing the Love of Men*. New York: Morrow.

FASS, Barbara. (1976). 'Christina Rossetti and St. Agnes' Eve'. *Victorian Poetry*, XIV, pp. 33–46.

FEINBERG, Harvey. (1985). 'The Four-Cornered Circle: Truth and Illusion in Browning's *The Ring and the Book*'. *Studies in Browning and His Circle*, XIII, pp. 70–96.

FELKIN, Elliott. (1962). 'Days with Thomas Hardy: From a 1918–1919 Diary'. *Encounter*, XVIII, 4, pp. 27–33.

FISHER, Benjamin F., IV. (1972). 'Swinburne's *Tristram of Lyonesse* in Process'. *Texas Studies in Literature and Language*, XIV, pp. 509–28.

FORSTER, E. M. (1972). 'The Enchafèd Flood', in *Two Cheers for Democracy*. London: Edward Arnold, pp. 260–62.

FORSTER, Margaret. (1988). *Elizabeth Barrett Browning*. London: Chatto and Windus.

FOUCAULT, Michel. (1973). *The Order of Things: An Archaeology of the Human Sciences*. New York: Vintage Books.

FOWLER, Alastair. (1982). *Kinds of Literature: An Introduction to the Theory of Genres and Modes*: Cambridge, Mass.: Harvard University Press.

FREUD, Sigmund. (1976). *The Interpretation of Dreams*. The Penguin Freud Library, IV, Trans. James Strachey, ed. Angela Richards. Harmondsworth: Penguin.

FROULA, Christine. (1986). 'Browning's *Sordello* and the Parables of Modernist Poetics', *ELH*, LII, pp. 965–92.

FRYE, Northrop. (1968). *A Study of English Romanticism*. New York: Random House.

———. (1971). *The Critical Path: An Essay on the Social Context of Literary Criticism*. Bloomington: Indiana University Press.

———. (1982). *The Great Code: The Bible and Literature*. Toronto: Academic Press.

FULLER, Jean Overton. (1968). *Swinburne: A Critical Biography*. London: Chatto and Windus.

FULLER, Peter. (1988). *Theoria: Art, and the Absence of Grace*. London: Chatto and Windus.

FULWEILER, Howard. (1972). *Letters from the Darkling Plain: Language and the Grounds of Knowledge in the Poetry of Arnold and Hopkins*. Columbia: University of Missouri Press.

GARDNER, Martin. (1983). *The Whys of a Philosophical Scrivener*. New York: Quill.

GASKELL, Elizabeth. (1906). *The Works of Mrs. Gaskell*. London: Smith, Elder, & Co.; rpt 1972.

GATTA, John Jr. (1977). 'Coleridge and Allegory', *Modern Language Quarterly*, XXXVIII, pp. 62–77.

GELPI, Barbara Charlesworth. (1992). *Shelley's Goddess: Maternity, Language, Subjectivity*. New York: Oxford University Press.

GERBER, Helmut E. and W. Eugene DAVIS. (1973). *Thomas Hardy: An Annotated Bibliography of Writings about Him*. De Kalb: Northern Illinois University Press.

GEST, John Marshall. (1927). *The Old Yellow Book: Sources of Browning's The Ring and the Book*. Philadelphia: University of Pennsylvania Press.

GOLUB, Ellen. (1975). 'Untying Goblin Apron Strings: A Psychoanalytic Reading of "Goblin Market"'. *Literature & Psychology*, XXV, pp. 158–65.

GOSLEE, David F. (1975). 'Mr. Sludge The Medium – Mr. Browning The Possessed'. *Studies in Browning and His Circle*, III, pp. 40–58.

GOSSE, Edmund. (1917). *The Life of Algernon Charles Swinburne*. New York: Macmillan.

GOTTFRIED, Leon. (1963). *Matthew Arnold and the Romantics*. London: Routledge & Kegan Paul.

GREER, Germaine. (1975). 'Introduction' to *Goblin Market* by Christina Rossetti. New York: Stonehill, pp. vii–xxxvi.

GROSECLOSE, Barbara. (1985). 'The Incest Motif in Shelley's *The Cenci*'. *Comparative Drama*, XIX, pp. 222–39.

HALLAM, Arthur Henry. (1893). *The Poems of Arthur Henry Hallam Together With His Essay on the Lyrical Poems of Alfred Tennyson*.

Ed. Richard Le Gallienne. London: Elkin Matthews and John Lane, Rpt AMS Press, 1973.

HARDY, Thomas. (1976). *The Complete Poems of Thomas Hardy*. Ed. James Gibson. New York: Macmillan.

——. (1982–85). *Complete Poetical Works*. Ed. Samuel Hynes. Oxford: Clarendon.

HARRIS, Wendell V. (1978). 'Where Late the Sweet Birds Sang: Looking Back at the Victorians Looking Back at the Romantics Looking Back...'. *Victorian Poetry*, XVI, pp. 165–7.

HARRISON, Anthony H. (1988a). *Swinburne's Medievalism: A Study in Victorian Love Poetry*. Baton Rouge and London: Louisiana State University Press.

——. (1988b). *Christina Rossetti in Context*. Chapel Hill: University of North Carolina Press.

——. (1990). *Victorian Poets and Romantic Poems: Intertextuality and Ideology*. Charlottesville: University Press of Virginia.

HARWOOD, John James. (1895). *History and Description of the Thirlmere Water Scheme*. Manchester: Henry Blacklock.

HAYMAN, John, ed. (1982). *Letters from the Continent*. Toronto: Toronto University Press.

——. (1990). *John Ruskin and Switzerland*. Waterloo, Ontario: Wilfrid Laurier University Press.

HELLERSTEIN, Erna, *et al.* (1981). *Victorian Women: A Documentary Account of Women's Lives in Nineteenth-Century England, France, and the United States*. Stanford: Stanford University Press.

HELSINGER, Elizabeth. (1982). *Ruskin and the Art of the Beholder*. Cambridge, Mass., and London: Harvard University Press.

HENDERSON, Philip. (1974). *Swinburne: The Portrait of a Poet*. London: Routledge & Kegan Paul.

HIEMSTRA, Anne. (1985). 'Browning and History: Synecdoche and Symbolism in *The Ring and the Book*'. *Studies in Browning and His Circle*, XIII, pp. 47–58.

HILL, Geoffrey. (1984). *The Lords of Limit: Essays on Literature and Ideas*. London: André Deutsch.

HILTON, Tim. (1985). *John Ruskin: The Early Years*. New Haven and London: Yale University Press.

HOGG, Thomas Jefferson. (1933). *The Life of Percy Bysshe Shelley*. London: J. M. Dent.

HOLLANDER, John. (1981). *The Figure of Echo: A Mode of Allusion in Milton and After*. Berkeley and Los Angeles: University of California Press.

HOLT, Terrence. (1990). '"Men Sell Not Such in Any Town": Exchange in *Goblin Market*'. *Victorian Poetry*, XXVIII, pp. 51–67.

HYDE, Virginia. (1985). 'Robert Browning's Inverted Optic Glass in *A Death in the Desert*'. *Victorian Poetry*, XXIII, pp. 93–6.

HYDER, Clyde K., ed. (1970). *Swinburne: The Critical Heritage*. New York: Barnes and Noble.

HYNES, Samuel. (1961). *The Pattern of Hardy's Poetry*. Chapel Hill: University of North Carolina Press.

——. (1980). 'The Hardy Tradition in Modern English Poetry'. *Sewanee Review*, LXXXVIII, pp. 33–51.

JACKSON, H. J., ed. (1985). *Samuel Taylor Coleridge*: Oxford and New York: Oxford University Press.

JAMES, David Gwilym (1950). 'Wordsworth and Tennyson'. *Proceedings of the British Academy*, XXXVI, pp. 113–29.

JAMISON, William A. (1958). *Arnold and the Romantics*. Copenhagen: Rosenkilde and Bagger.

JANOWITZ, Anne. (1990). *England's Ruins: Poetic Purpose and the National Landscape*. Oxford: Basil Blackwell.

JOHNSON, Samuel. (1952). *Rasselas, Poems and Selected Prose*. Ed. Bertrand H. Bronson. New York: Holt, Rinehart and Winston.

JOHNSON, W. Stacy. (1961). *The Voices of Matthew Arnold: An Essay in Criticism*. New Haven: Yale University Press.

JUMP, John D., ed. (1967). *Tennyson: The Critical Heritage*. London: Routledge & Kegan Paul.

KARLIN, Daniel. (1989). 'Browning, Elizabeth Barrett, and "Mesmerism"'. *Victorian Poetry*, XXVII, pp. 65–77.

KEATS, John. (1970). *The Poems of John Keats*. Ed. Miriam Allott. London: Longman.

——. (1978). *The Poems of John Keats*. Ed. Jack Stillinger. Cambridge, Mass.: Harvard University Press.

——. (1982). *Complete Poems*. Ed. Jack Stillinger. Cambridge and London: The Belknap Press of Harvard University Press.

KEBLE, John. (1877). *Occasional Papers and Reviews*. Oxford.

KELLEY, Philip, and Ronald Hudson, eds. (1984). *The Brownings' Correspondence*. Windfield, KS: Wedgestone.

KELLEY, Theresa M. (1988). *Wordsworth's Revisionary Aesthetics*. Cambridge: Cambridge University Press.

——. (1991). '"Fantastic Shapes": From Classical Rhetoric to Romantic Allegory'. *Texas Studies in Literature and Language*, XXXIII, pp. 225–60.

KNAPP, Steven. (1985). *Personification and the Sublime: Milton to*

Coleridge. Cambridge, Mass.: Harvard University Press.

KNOEPFLMACHER, U. C. (1990). 'Hardy Ruins: Female Spaces and Male Designs'. *PMLA*, CV, pp. 1055–70.

KORG, Jacob. (1983). *Browning in Italy*. Athens, Ohio: Ohio University Press.

KRAMER, Lawrence. (1980). 'The "Intimations" Ode and Victorian Romanticism'. *Victorian Poetry*, XVIII, pp. 315–35.

LANDOW, George P. (1972). 'Shipwrecked and Castaway on the Journey of Life: An Essay Towards a Modern Iconography'. *Revue de Littérature Comparée*, XL, pp. 569–96.

LANGBAUM, Robert. (1970). *The Modern Spirit*. New York: Oxford University Press.

LEGALLIENNE, Richard. (1891). '*Poems* by Christina Rossetti'. *The Academy*, XXXIX, pp. 130–1.

LEIGHTON, Angela. (1986). *Elizabeth Barrett Browning*. Bloomington: Indiana University Press.

LEWIS, C. S. (1967). *The Discarded Image: An Introduction to Medieval and Renaissance Literature*. Cambridge: Cambridge University Press.

LIU, Alan. (1989). *Wordsworth: The Sense of History*. Stanford: Stanford University Press.

LOUIS, Margot K. (1990). *Swinburne and His Gods: The Roots and Growth of an Agnostic Poetry*. Montreal and Kingston: McGill–Queen's University Press.

LOURIE, Margaret. (1979). 'Below the Thunders of the Upper Deep: Tennyson as Romantic Revisionist'. *Studies in Romanticism*, XVIII, pp. 3–27.

LOVEJOY, Arthur O. (1924). 'On the Discrimination of Romanticism'. *PMLA*, XXXIX, pp. 229–53.

MARTIN, Robert Bernard. (1980). *Tennyson: The Unquiet Heart*. Oxford: Clarendon.

MAY, Charles E. (1973). 'Hardy's "Darkling Thrush": The "Nightingale" Grown Old'. *Victorian Poetry*, XI, pp. 62–5.

McFARLAND, Thomas. (1981). *Romanticism and the Forms of Ruin*. Princeton: Princeton University Press.

McGANN, Jerome J. (1972). *Swinburne: An Experiment in Criticism*. Chicago and London: University of Chicago Press.

——. (1983). *The Romantic Ideology: A Critical Investigation*. Chicago: University of Chicago Press.

——. (1985). 'Christina Rossetti's Poems: A New Edition and a Revaluation', in *The Beauty of Inflections: Literary Investigations in*

A Historical Method and Theory. Oxford: Clarendon, pp. 207–31.

——. (1988). 'Introduction', in David Kent, ed., *The Achievement of Christina Rossetti*. Ithaca: Cornell University Press.

——. (1990). '"My Brain is Feminine": Byron and the Poetry of Deception', in *Byron: Augustan and Romantic*. Ed. Andrew Rutherford. London: Macmillan, pp. 26–51.

McGOWAN, John. (1986). *Representation and Revelation: Victorian Realism from Carlyle to Yeats*. Columbia: University of Missouri Press.

McSWEENEY, Kerry. (1969). 'The Structure of Swinburne's *Tristram of Lyonesse*'. *Queen's Quarterly*, LXXV, pp. 690–702.

MEREDITH, Michael. (1985). *More Than Friend: The Letters of Robert Browning to Katharine de Kay Bronson*. Waco, TX: Baylor University Press.

MERMIN, Dorothy. (1983). 'Heroic Sisterhood in *Goblin Market*'. *Victorian Poetry*, XXI, pp. 107–18.

MILLER, J. Hillis. (1968). '"Wessex Heights:" The Persistence of the Past in Hardy's Poetry'. *Critical Quarterly*, X, pp. 339–59.

——. (1970). *Thomas Hardy: Distance and Desire*. Cambridge, Mass.: Belknap Press of Harvard University Press.

——. (1985). *The Linguistic Moment: From Wordsworth to Stevens*. Princeton: Princeton University Press.

MILLGATE, Michael. (1982). *Thomas Hardy: A Biography*. New York: Random House.

——, ed. (1984). *The Life and Work of Thomas Hardy*. London: Macmillan.

MILTON, John. (1935). *Paradise Lost*. Ed. Merritt Y. Hughes. New York: Odyssey Press.

MOERS, Ellen. (1976). *Literary Women*. Garden City: Doubleday.

MORRILL, David. (1990). '"Twilight Is Not Good for Maidens": Uncle Polidori and the Psychodynamics of Vampirism in *Goblin Market*'. *Victorian Poetry*, XXVIII, pp. 1–16.

MURFIN, Ross C. (1978). *Swinburne, Hardy, Lawrence and the Burden of Belief*. Chicago: University of Chicago Press.

NICOLSON, Harold. (1926). *Swinburne*. New York: Macmillan.

NORTON, Caroline. (1863). '"The Angel in the House", and "The Goblin Market"'. *Macmillan's Magazine*, VIII, pp. 398–404.

OMER, Mordechai. (n.d.). *Turner and the Poets: Engravings and watercolours from his later period*. Greater London Council exhibition catalogue. London: Publications Department of the Greater London Council.

ONG, Walter J. (1967). *The Presence of the Word*. New Haven: Yale University Press.

——. (1982). *Orality and Literacy: The Technologizing of the Word*. London: Methuen.

OREL, Harold, ed. (1967). *Thomas Hardy's Personal Writings: Prefaces, Literary Opinions. Reminiscences*. London: Macmillan.

OWEN, W. J. B., ed. (1985) *The Fourteen-Book Prelude*. Ithaca: Cornell University Press.

PACKER, Lona Mosk. (1959). 'The Protestant Existentialism of Christina Rossetti'. *Notes and Queries*. CCIV, pp. 213–15.

——. (1963a). The *Rossetti–Macmillan Letters*. Berkeley: University of California Press.

——. (1963b). *Christina Rossetti*. Berkeley: University of California Press.

PAGE, Norman, ed. (1978). *Jude the Obscure*. By Thomas Hardy. New York: Norton.

PATER, Walter. (1986). *Three Major Texts*. Ed. William E. Buckler. New York: New York University Press.

PAULIN, Tom. (1975) *Thomas Hardy: The Poetry of Perception*. London: Macmillan.

PEATTIE, Roger W., ed. (1990). *Selected Letters of William Michael Rossetti*. London: Pennsylvania State University Press.

PECKHAM, Morse. (1951). 'Toward a Theory of Romanticism'. *PMLA*, LXVI, pp. 5–23.

PERKINS, David. (1959). 'Hardy and the Poetry of Isolation'. *ELH*, XXVI, pp. 253–70.

——, ed. (1967). *English Romantic Writers*. New York: Harcourt.

PETERS, Robert. (1982). 'Swinburne: A Personal Essay and a Polemic', in *The Victorian Experience: The Poets*. Ed. Richard A. Levine. Athens: Ohio University Press.

PINION, F. B. (1977). *Thomas Hardy: Art and Thought*. London: Macmillan.

POLIDORI, John. (1819). *The Vampyre*. London: Sherwood, Neely and Jones.

POTTER, Vilma Raskin. (1979). 'Poetry and the Fiddler's Foot: Meters in Thomas Hardy's Work'. *The Musical Quarterly*, LXV (January), pp. 48–71.

PRINS, Yopie. (1989). '"Violence bridling speech": Browning's Translation of Aeschylus' *Agamemnon*'. *Victorian Poetry*, XXVII: pp. 151–70.

PURDY, Richard Little and Michael Millgate, eds. (1978–88).

Collected Letters of Thomas Hardy. Oxford: Clarendon.

QUINTILIAN. (1921). *Institutio oratoria.* Trans. H. E. Butler. Cambridge, Mass.: Harvard University Press.

RAPF, Joanna E. (1986). 'Visionaries of Dereliction: Wordsworth and Tennyson'. *Victorian Poetry,* XXIV, pp. 373–85.

REED, John R. (1966). 'Swinburne's *Tristram of Lyonesse*: The Poet-Lover's Song of Love'. *Victorian Poetry,* IV, pp. 99–120.

REIMAN, Donald H., and Sharon B. Powers, eds. (1977). *Shelley's Poetry and Prose.* New York: W. W. Norton.

REUL, Paul de. (1922). *L'oeuvre de Swinburne.* Bruxelles: Sand.

RICHARDS, I. A. (1970). *Poetries and Sciences: A Reissue of Science and Poetry (1926, 1935) with Commentary.* New York: Norton.

RICHARDSON, James. (1977). *Thomas Hardy: The Poetry of Necessity.* Chicago: University of Chicago Press.

———. (1988). *Vanishing Lives: Style and Self in Tennyson, D. G. Rossetti, Swinburne, and Yeats.* Charlottesville: University Press of Virginia.

RICKS, Christopher. (1972). *Tennyson.* London: Macmillan.

———. (1977). *The Poetry of Tennyson.* New Haven: Yale University Press.

———. (1987). *The Force of Poetry.* Oxford: Oxford University Press.

RIEDE, David G. (1978). *Swinburne: A Study of Romantic Mythmaking.* Charlottesville: University Press of Virginia.

———. (1988). *Matthew Arnold and the Betrayal of Language.* Charlottesville: University of Virginia Press.

ROGERS, Samuel. (1830). *Italy, a Poem.* London: T. Cadell.

ROPER, Alan. (1969). *Arnold's Poetic Landscapes.* Baltimore: Johns Hopkins University Press.

ROSENBERG, John D. (1967). 'Swinburne'. *Victorian Studies,* XI, pp. 131–52.

ROSSETTI, Christina. (1904). *The Poetical Works of Christina Georgina Rossetti.* Ed. William Michael Rossetti. London: Macmillan.

———. (1979–90). *The Complete Poems of Christina Rossetti.* Ed. R. W. Crump. Baton Rouge: Louisiana State University Press.

———. (1879). *Seek and Find: A Double Series of Short Studies of the Benedicite.* London: Society for Promoting Christian Knowledge.

———. (1885). *Time Flies: A Reading Diary.* London: Society for Promoting Christian Knowledge.

ROSSETTI, Dante Gabriel. (1965–67). *The Letters of Dante Gabriel Rossetti.* Ed. Oswald Doughty and John Robert Wahl. Oxford: Clarendon.

ROSSETTI, William Michael, ed. (1904). *The Poetical Works of Christina Georgina Rossetti*. London: Macmillan.

——. (1895). *Dante Gabriel Rossetti: His Family-Letters, with a Memoir*. London: Ellis and Elvey.

——. (1906). *Some Reminiscences of William Michael Rossetti*. London: Brown Longham.

——. (1970). *Rossetti Papers: 1862–1870* (1903). New York: AMS Press.

RUSKIN, John. (1903–12). *The Works of John Ruskin*. Ed. E. T. Cook and A. Wedderburn. London: George Allen.

RUSSELL, George W. E., ed. (1896). *Letters of Matthew Arnold 1848–1888*. New York: Macmillan.

RUSSELL, John and WILTON, Andrew. (1976). *Turner in Switzerland*. Dubendorf (Zurich): De Clivo Press.

RYALS, Claude de. (1975). *Browning's Later Poetry, 1871–1889*. Ithaca: Cornell University Press.

SACKS, Peter M. (1985). *The English Elegy: Studies in the Genre from Spenser to Yeats*. Baltimore and London: Johns Hopkins University Press.

SAGAN, Miriam. (1980). 'Christina Rossetti's "Goblin Market" and Feminist Literary Criticism'. *Pre-Raphaelite Review*, III, pp. 66–76.

SAMBROOK, James, ed. (1974). *Pre-Raphaelitism: A Collection of Critical Essays*. Chicago: University of Chicago Press.

SAWYER, Paul. (1990). 'Ruskin and the Matriarchal Logos', in *Victorian Sages and Cultural Discourse: Renegotiating Gender and Power*. Ed. Thais E. Morgan. New Brunswick: Rutgers University Press, pp. 129–41.

SCHOFIELD, Linda. (1988). 'Being and Understanding: Devotional Poetry of Christina Rossetti and the Tractarians', in *The Achievement of Christina Rossetti*. Ed. David Kent. Ithaca: Cornell University Press.

SHAFFER, Elinor S. (1975). *'Kubla Khan' and the Fall of Jerusalem: The Mythological School in Biblical Criticism and Secular Literature, 1770–1880*. Cambridge: Cambridge University Press.

SHAW, W. David. (1978). 'Browning's "Intimations" Ode: The Prologue to Asolando'. *Browning Society Notes*, VIII, 1, pp. 9–10.

——. (1987). 'Agnostic Theories of the Word: Arnold's Deconstruction', in *The Lucid Veil: Poetic Truth in the Victorian Age*. London: Athlone Press.

——. (1989). 'Browning's Murder Mystery: *The Ring and the Book* and Modern Theory'. *Victorian Poetry*, XXVII, pp. 79–98.

SHELLEY, Percy Bysshe. (1824). *Posthumous Poems*. Ed. Mary Wollstonecraft Shelley. London: J. and H. L. Hunt.

——. (1839). *The Poetical Works of Percy Bysshe Shelley*. Ed. Mary Wollstonecraft Shelley. London: E. Moxon.

——. (1862). *Relics of Shelley*. Ed. Richard Garnett. London: E. Moxon.

——. (1905). *The Complete Poetical Works by Percy Bysshe Shelley*, Ed. Thomas Hutchinson. London: Oxford University Press.

——. (1954). *Shelley's Prose: Or The Trumpet of a Prophecy*, Ed. David Lee Clark. Albuquerque: University of New Mexico Press.

——. (1964). *The Letters of Percy Bysshe Shelley*. Ed. Frederick Jones. Oxford: Clarendon.

——. (1965). *The Complete Works of Percy Bysshe Shelley*. Ed. Roger Ingpen and Walter E. Pack. New York: Gordian.

——. (1970). *The Cenci: A Tragedy in Five Acts*. New York: Phaeton.

——. (1977). *Shelley's Selected Poetry and Prose*. Eds Donald H. Reiman and Sharon B. Powers. New York: W. W. Norton.

——. (1989). *The Poems of Shelley*. Ed. Geoffrey Matthews and Kelvin Everest. London: Longman.

SIEGCHRIST, Mark. (1981). *Rough in Brutal Print: The Legal Sources of Browning's Red Cotton Night-Cap Country*. Columbus: Ohio State University Press.

SIMPSON, Peter. (1979). 'Hardy's "The Self-Unseeing" and the Romantic Problem of Consciousness'. *Victorian Poetry*, XVII, pp. 45–50.

SISKIN, Clifford. (1988). *The Historicity of Romantic Discourse*. Oxford: Oxford University Press.

SLINN, E. Warwick. (1989). 'Language and Truth in *The Ring and the Book*'. *Victorian Poetry*, XXXVII, pp. 115–33.

SMITH-ROSENBERG, Carroll. (1975). 'The Female World of Love and Ritual: Relations between Women in Nineteenth-Century America'. *Signs: Journal of Women in Culture and Society*, I, pp. 1–29.

SPIVAK, Charlotte. (1989). '"The Hidden World Below"; Victorian Women Fantasy Poets', in *The Poetic Fantastic: Studies in an Evolving Genre*. Ed. Patrick D. Murphy and Vernon Hyles. New York: Greenwood, pp. 53–64.

STAINES, David. (1978). 'Swinburne's Arthurian World: Swinburne's Arthurian Poetry and Its Medieval Sources'. *Studia Neophilologica*, L, pp. 53–70.

STEPHEN, Leslie. (1871). *The Playground of Europe*. London: Longman, Green and Co.

SWINBURNE, Algernon Charles. (1905). *The Poems of Algernon Charles Swinburne*. London: Chatto and Windus.

——. (1925). *Complete Works*. Ed. Edmund Gosse and Thomas James Wise. London: Heinemann.

——. (1927). *Swinburne's Hyperion*. Ed. Georges Lafourcade. London: Faber and Gwyer.

——. (1959–62). *The Swinburne Letters*. Ed. Cecil Y. Lang. New Haven: Yale University Press.

——. (1966). *Swinburne Replies*: Syracuse: Syracuse University Press.

SWINGLE, L. J. (1987). *The Obstinate Questionings of English Romanticism*. Baton Rouge: Louisiana State University Press.

TAYLOR, Dennis. (1986). 'Hardy and Wordsworth'. *Victorian Poetry*, XXIV, pp. 441–54.

TENNYSON, Alfred Lord. (1969). *The Poems of Tennyson*. Ed. Christopher Ricks. London: Longman.

——. (1987). *The Poems of Tennyson* (second edition incorporating the Trinity College Manuscripts). Ed. Christopher Ricks. Harlow: Longman.

——. (1990). *The Letters of Alfred Lord Tennyson*. Ed. Cecil Y. Lang and Edgar F. Shannon, Jr. Oxford: Clarendon.

TENNYSON, George (1981). *Victorian Devotional Poetry: The Tractarian Mode*. Cambridge, Mass.: Harvard University Press.

THOMAS, Eleanor Walter. (1966). *Christina Georgina Rossetti*. New York: AMS Press.

THORLBY, A. K., ed. (1966). *The Romantic Movement*. New York: Barnes & Noble.

TILLYARD, E. M. W. (1948). *Five Poems 1470–1870: An Elementary Essay on the Background of English Literature*. London: Chatto and Windus.

TIMKO, Michael. (1975). 'The Victorianism of Victorian Literature'. *New Literary History*, VI, pp. 607–27.

TREDELL, Nicholas. (1982). 'Tristram of Lyonesse: Dangerous Voyage'. *Victorian Poetry*, XX, pp. 97–111.

TRILLING, Lionel. (1949). *Matthew Arnold*. Cleveland and New York: World Publishing.

TROTTER, Thomas. (1806). *A View of the Nervous Temperament*. London: Longman.

TUCKER, Herbert F. (1985). 'Dramatic Monologue and the Overhearing of Lyric', in *Lyric Poetry: Beyond New Criticism*. Eds Chaviva Hosek and Patricia Parker. Ithaca and London: Cornell University Press, pp. 226–43.

——. (1983). 'Tennyson and the Measure of Doom'. *PMLA*, XCVIII, pp. 8–20.

——. (1988). *Tennyson and the Doom of Romanticism*. Cambridge, Mass: Harvard University Press.

UNRAU, John. (1984). *Ruskin and S. Marks*. London: Thames and Hudson.

VIVANTE, Leone. (1950). *English Poetry and Its Contribution to the Knowledge of a Creative Principle*. New York: Macmillan.

WALKER, Stephen C. (1976). 'The Dynamic Imagery of *The Ring and the Book*'. *Studies in Browning and His Circle*, IV, pp. 7–29.

WEATHERS, Winston. (1965). 'Christina Rossetti: The Sisterhood of Self'. *Victorian Poetry*, III, pp. 81–9.

WELBY, T. Earle. (1926). *A Study of Swinburne*. New York: Doran.

WHITE, Newman Ivey. (1940). *Shelley*. New York: Alfred A. Knopf.

WOLFSON, Susan J. (1986). *The Questioning Presence: Wordsworth, Keats, and the Interrogative Mode in Romantic Poetry*. Ithaca: Cornell University Press.

WOODRING, Carl. (1989). *Nature into Art: Cultural Transformations in Nineteenth Century Britain*. Cambridge, Mass.: Harvard University Press.

WOOLFORD, John. (1988). *Browning the Revisionary*. London: Macmillan.

WORDSWORTH, William. (1936). *Poetical Works*. Rev. edn, Ernest de Selincourt. London: Oxford University Press.

——. (1952–59). *The Poetical Works* Ed. E. de Selincourt, rev. H. Darbishire. Oxford: Clarendon.

——. (1965). *Selected Poems and Prefaces*. Ed. Jack Stillinger. Boston: Houghton Mifflin.

——. (1965). *The Lyrical Ballads*. Ed. R. L. Brett and A. R. Jones. London: Methuen.

——. (1971). *The Prelude: A Parallel Text*. Ed. J. C. Maxwell. Harmondsworth, Middlesex: Penguin Books.

——. (1974). Vol. 1 of *The Prose Works of William Wordsworth*. Eds W. J. B. Owen and Jane W. Smyser. Oxford: Clarendon.

——. (1977 reprint). *Guide to the Lakes*. Ed. Ernest de Selincourt. Oxford: Oxford University Press.

——. (1977). *William Wordsworth: The Poems*. Ed. John O. Hayden. New Haven and London: Yale University Press.

——. (1979). *The Prelude 1799, 1805, 1850*. Eds Jonathan Wordsworth, M. H. Abrams, Stephen Gill. New York: W. W. Norton.

——. (1983). *Poems, in Two Volumes and Other Poems, 1800–1808*. Ed. Jared Curtis. Ithaca: Cornell University Press.

——. (1984). *William Wordsworth*. Ed. Stephen Gill. Oxford: Oxford University Press.

——. (1985). *The Fourteen-Book Prelude*. Ed. W. J. B. Owen. Ithaca: Cornell University Press.

——. (1985). *The Pedlar, Tintern Abbey, The Two-Part Prelude*. Ed. Jonathan Wordsworth. London: Cambridge University Press.

WRATISLAW, Theodore. (1900). *Algernon Charles Swinburne: A Study*. London: Greening.

Index